International Conference on ICT, Society, and Human Beings 2017

Held at the Multi-Conference on Computer Science and Information Systems (MCCSIS 2017)

Lisbon, Portugal
20 – 23 July 2017

Editors:

Piet Kommers
Pedro Isaias
Luis Rodrigues

ISBN: 978-1-5108-6531-0

Printed from e-media with permission by:

Curran Associates, Inc.
57 Morehouse Lane
Red Hook, NY 12571

Some format issues inherent in the e-media version may also appear in this print version.

Printed by Curran Associates, Inc. (2018)

For permission requests, please contact International Association for Development of the Information Society (IADIS) at the address below.

International Association for Development of the Information Society (IADIS)
Rua Sao Sebastiao Da Pedreira
No. 100, 30, 1050-209
Lisbon, Portugal

Phone: 351 21 3151373
Fax: 351 21 3151244

secretariat@iadis.org

Additional copies of this publication are available from:

Curran Associates, Inc.
57 Morehouse Lane
Red Hook, NY 12571 USA
Phone: 845-758-0400
Fax: 845-758-2633
Email: curran@proceedings.com
Web: www.proceedings.com

INTERNATIONAL CONFERENCE

ICT, SOCIETY AND HUMAN BEINGS 2017

part of the

MULTI CONFERENCE ON COMPUTER SCIENCE AND INFORMATION SYSTEMS 2017

PROCEEDINGS OF THE INTERNATIONAL CONFERENCE

ICT, SOCIETY AND HUMAN BEINGS 2017

Lisbon, Portugal
JULY 20 - 22, 2017

Organised by
IADIS
International Association for Development of the Information Society

Volume Editors:
Piet Kommers

Computer Science and Information Systems Series Editors:
Piet Kommers and Pedro Isaías

Associate Editor: Luís Rodrigues

TABLE OF CONTENTS

FULL PAPERS

SHORT PAPERS

POSTERS

FOREWORD

These proceedings contain the papers of the 10th International Conference on ICT, Society and Human Beings, which was organised by the International Association for Development of the Information Society, from 21 - 23 July, 2017. This conference is part of the Multi Conference on Computer Science and Information Systems 2017, 20 - 23 July, which had a total of 652 submissions.

The Network period in the evolution of computer technology is very much based on the convergence and integration of three main technologies; computer technology, tele technology and media technology. Telecommunication technology is playing a more and more dominant role in this convergence, especially internet and web technology. Embedded (ubiquitous) computer technology is making the process invisible, and media technologies converge within itself (multimedia and cross media). The convergence process is enforced all the time by smaller, cheaper, and more powerful components.

ICT and its applications are interacting with environments, roles, and processes which can also be modelled by converging circles. The process of social and psychosocial change and ICT from a global perspective is described graphically in the convergence model in figure 1 (Bradley 2006 Routledge) with concepts and their interrelations. Both "convergence" and "interactions" are important features in the model. Read from the left hand side in the model for the titles of some main tracks of the conference:

- Globalisation and ICT:. When technology, economy, norms/values and labour market are converging on a global level, what are the hard questions? When the geographical space in the future will be both global and beyond – including virtual reality (VR) what is the state of art in research? (see the list of key words under ′globalisation′)
- Information and Communication Technology (ICT), next cluster of circles to the left in the figure, what applications contribute to desirable goals in the society?
- When Work Environment, Home Environment, and Public Environment are converging and the work and public issues tend to merge into the private sphere of our homes – what main changes in peoples Life Environment occur?.
- If the Professional Role (Work Life), Private Role (Private Life) and Citizen's Role (Public Life) converge forming a Life Role, what are the main social-psychologial changes?
- Four circles representing Virtual Reality (VR) are marked with dotted lines and are surrounding the set of converging circles. These circles reflect our participation in cyberspace on various levels. To the left part in figure we could talk about Virtual Worlds on the global level. Within the concept of ICT, the steps taken by applied Embedded and ubiquitous technology make technology more hidden to the individual and society as a whole.

  Virtual Environments are already a common concept. Finally we could talk about Virtual Human Roles, which could in more extreme forms be another personality that you play e g avatars. The converging circles are forming a Life Role and new life styles are being shaped.
- Effects on humans become more multi faceted and complex. Research focusing upon the individual is crucial i. e. research on how the use of ICT interacts with and impacts identity, social competence, creativity, integrity, trust, dependency etc. A compass rose (card) for "Effects on Humans" (to the right) is used as a metaphor reminding us of the importance to keep the direction towards desirable human and societal goals and qualities at the development and use of ICT.

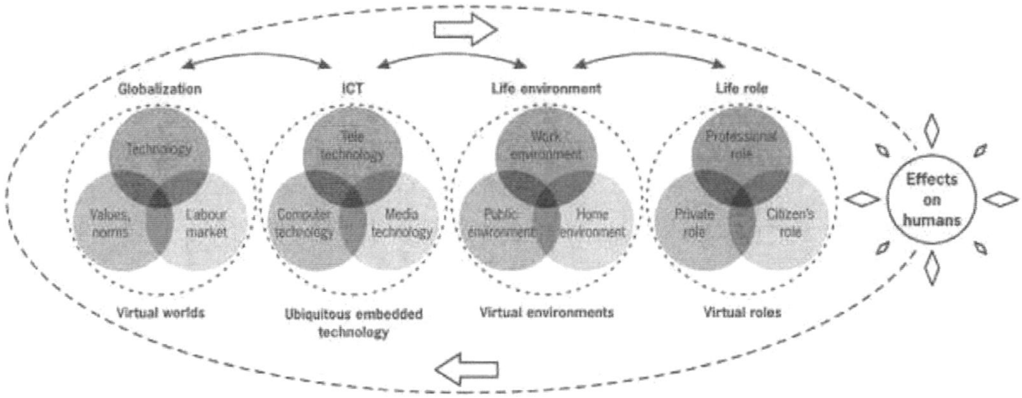

Figure 1. Convergence Model on ICT and Psychosocial Life Environment (Source: Bradley, 2005, 2006)

ICT can provide tools for promoting sustainability (environmental, economic, and social sustainability) but can also be a threat for sustainability. Sustainability as a guiding principle involves system perspective, holism, human aspects, bottom up approach, common good, and equality. A change in focus regarding research and development is taking place. Analysis and design increasingly address both the work process and management connected to the sphere of production life and people's life environment. Analysis and design of ICT and societal systems both at local level and globally become important. What research in the field exists or is needed?

Community research in a broad sense comes to the fore – both physical and virtual communities. There is also a requirement to involve new and additional actors at the deeper and broader integration of ICT in the society (children, elderly, and consumer organisations). Educational programs on Community Informatics and Social Informatics are appearing in many academic institutions. Can a new infrastructure of the society be identified?

The effects of ICT on human beings as well as the interaction between ICT, individuals, and society are all within the focus of this conference. Both analyses of interactions and effects are important. Changes in behaviour, perspectives, values, competencies, human and psychological aspects and feelings are all of interest. Reflections on past, present, and future challenges – especially planning for handling the latter – are encouraged.

Today, computer science and ICT-related disciplines are working more and more together with various behavioural and social sciences including child psychology and developmental psychology. For this reason, the conference pays attention to societal changes, global and more local organisational and institutional changes, changes in values and in lifestyles, as well as individual cognitive effects and changes, motivational and emotional changes. It also appeals to solution-building in terms of desirable goals and actions for reaching a Good Information Society.

In general all types of research strategies are encouraged, and especially cross-disciplinary and multi-disciplinary studies. Case studies, broader empirical field studies, theoretical analyses, cross-cultural studies, scenarios, ethnographic studies, epistemological analyses may all be presented.

The ICT, Society and Human Beings (ICT) conference addresses in detail seven main aspects:

- Globalization and ICT
- Life environment and ICT
- Life role and ICT
- ICT and effects on humans
- Perspectives on ICT
- Desirable goals and ICT
- Actions for reaching the Good Information Society

The ICT 2017 conference received 126 submissions from more than 30 countries. This conference includes the submissions from the Web Based Communities and Social Media conference as well as Connected Smart Cities conference that have both been integrated into ICT 2017. Their committees are listed as part of this proceedings book. Each submission has been anonymously reviewed by an average of five independent reviewers, to ensure that accepted submissions were of a high standard. Consequently only 23 full papers were approved which means an acceptance rate of 18%. A few more papers were accepted as short papers and posters. An extended version of the best papers will be published in the IADIS International Journal on WWW/Internet (ISSN: 1645-7641), and/or in the International Journal of Web Based Communities (IJWBC) (ISSN: 1477-8394), and/or in the IADIS Journal on Computer Science and Information Systems (ISSN: 1646-3692), and also in other selected journals, including journals from Inderscience.

Besides the presentation of full papers, short papers, reflection papers and posters, the conference also included two keynote presentations from internationally distinguished researchers. We would therefore like to express our gratitude to Professor Thomas C. Reeves, (Professor Emeritus of Learning Design and Technology, College of Education, The University of Georgia, USA) and Dr. Dr. Norbert Streitz (Scientific Director, Smart Future Initiative, Germany) for accepting our invitation to be keynote speakers.

This volume has taken shape as a result of the contributions from a number of individuals. We are grateful to all authors who have submitted their papers to enrich the conference proceedings. We wish to thank all members of the organizing committee, delegates, invitees and guests whose contribution and involvement are crucial for the success of the conference.

Last but not the least, we hope that everybody had a good time in Lisbon, and we invite all participants for the next edition of this conference.

Piet Kommers, University of Twente, The Netherlands
ICT, Society and Human Beings 2017 Program Chair

Piet Kommers, University of Twente, The Netherlands
Pedro Isaías, The University of Queensland, Australia
MCCSIS 2017 General Conference Co-Chairs

Lisbon, Portugal
July 2017

PROGRAM COMMITTEE

ICT, SOCIETY AND HUMAN BEINGS

PROGRAM CHAIR

Piet Kommers, University of Twente, The Netherlands

MCCSIS GENERAL CONFERENCE CO-CHAIRS

Piet Kommers, University of Twente, The Netherlands
Pedro Isaías, The University of Queensland, Australia

ICT, SOCIETY AND HUMAN BEINGS

COMMITTEE MEMBERS

Alice Robbin, Indiana University Bloomington, USA
Antonio Marturano, University of Rome Tor Vergata, Italy
Arthur Tatnall, Victoria University, Australia
Barbara Craig, Victoria University, New Zealand
Caroline Parker, Glasgow Caledonian University, United Kingdom
Cecile K. M. Crutzen, Open University of The Netherlands, The Netherlands
Daniel Pimienta, Funredes, Dominican Republic
David J. Gunkel, Northern Illinois University, USA
Dimitris Dranidis, CITY College, International Faculty of the University of Sheffield, Greece
Eila Jarvenpaa, Aalto University, Finland
Eleni Berki, University of Tampere, Finland
Elspeth Mckay, Rmit University, Australia
Elvis Mazzoni, University of Bologna, Italy
Enda Fallon, National University of Ireland Galway, Ireland
Ilkka Arminen, University of Helsinki, Finland
Ivo de Lotto, University of Pavia, Italy
Jorge Franco, Sao Paulo University, Brazil
Kai Kimppa, University of Turku, Finland
Lech Zacher, Kozminski Business School, Poland
Lynne Humphries, University of Sunderland, United Kingdom
Marco Lazzari, University of Bergamo, Italy
Margaret Tan, A*STAR IHPC, Singapore
Mikael Collan, Lappeenranta University of Technology, Finland
Miranda Kajtazi, Linnaeus University, Sweden
Monica Banzato, University of Ca' Foscari – Venice, Italy
Nestor Garay-Vitoria, Universidad del País Vasco/Euskal Herriko Unibertsitatea, Spain
Nicola Doering, Ilmenau University of Technology, Germany
Norberto Patrignani, Catholic University of Milan, Italy
Paolo Francesco Cottone, University of Padua, Italy
Patrizia Grifoni, CNR – IRPPS, Italy
Pertti Jarvinen, University of Tampere, Finland
Pirjo Elovaara, Blekinge Institute of Technology, Sweden

Reima Suomi, University of Turku, Finland
Robert Pintér, Corvinus University of Budapest, Hungary
Sangeeta Sharma, University of Rajasthan, India
Sanna Salantera, University of Turku, Finland
Sarai Lastra, Universidad del Turabo, Puerto Rico
Sebastiano Bagnara, Iuav-Università di San Marino, Italy
Seppo Vayrynen, University of Oulu, Finland
Stefania Bocconi, CNR, Istituto per le Tecnologie Didattiche, Italy
Stina Giesecke, Aalto University, Finland
Virve Siirak, Tallinn University of Technology, Estonia

WEB BASED COMMUNITIES AND SOCIAL MEDIA

COMMITTEE MEMBERS

Agisilaos Konidaris, Technological Educational Institute of Ionian Islands, Greece
Andrea Lapa, Federal University of Santa Catarina, Brazil
Andrei Semeniuta, Belarus Trade Economics University, Belarus
Anirban Kundu, Kuang-Chi Institute of Advanced Technology, Shenzhen, China
Apostolos Gkamas, University Ecclesiastical Academy of Vella of Ioannina, Greece
Arianna D'ulizia, National Research Council – IRPPS, Italy
Atila Bostan, Atilim University, Turkey
Atsuo Hazeyama, Tokyo Gakugei University, Japan
Bernhard Nett, University of Siegen, Germany
Carmen Celina Torres Arcadia, Tecnológico de Monterrey, Mexico
Charalampos Karagiannidis, University of Thessaly, Greece
Chien-sing Lee, Universiti Tunku Abdul Rahman, Malaysia
Christos Bouras, University of Patras, Greece
Cigdem Turhan, Atilim University, Turkey
Claudia Raibulet, University of Milano-Bicocca, Italy
Credine Menezes, Federal University of Rio Grande do Sul, Brazil
Cuong Nguyen, University of Nebraska at Omaha, USA
Daniela Godoy, Isistan – Conicet – Instituto de Sistemas Tandil, Argentina
Dmitry Bystrov, Tashkent State Technical University, Uzbekistan
Edison Spina, University of Sao Paulo, Brazil
Elaheh Pourabbas, National Research Council, Italy
Elisaveta Gurova, Sofia University, Bulgaria
Eliza Stefanova, St. Kl. Ohridski University of Sofia, Bulgaria
Emmanouil Stiakakis, University of Macedonia, Greece
Eugenia Kovatcheva, University of Library Studies and Information Technologies, Bulgaria
Fabio Nascimbeni, Menon Network, Belgium
Florin Popentiu-Vladicescu, The Academy of Romanian Scientists, Romania
Francesca Pozzi , Istituto Tecnologie Didattiche – CNR, Italy
Gabriela Moise, PG University of Ploiesti, Romania
Gayle Davidson Shivers, University of South Alabama, USA
Georgios Kioumourtzis, Center for Security Studies, Greece
Gert-Jan de Vreede, University of South Florida, USA
Giuliana Dettori, Istituto per le Tecnologie Didattiche, Italy
Grigorios Beligiannis, University of Patras, Greece
Guillermo Jimenez, Instituto Tecnologico de Monterrey (ITESM), Mexico

CONNECTED SMART CITIES

COMMITTEE MEMBERS

KEYNOTE LECTURES

HUMAN LEARNING, MACHINE LEARNING, AND E-LEARNING: CONFLICT OR CONFLUENCE?

Professor Thomas C. Reeves, Professor Emeritus of Learning, Design and Technology, College of Education, The University of Georgia, USA

ABSTRACT

The technologies underlying machine learning are developing so rapidly that huge swaths of career paths previously open to university graduates are being assumed by algorithms and robots. These are not just easily-automated manual labor jobs such as filling orders at online stores, but high cognitive demand professions such as those of pharmacists and journalists. Meanwhile, politicians around the world promise to bring back high-paying manufacturing jobs and voters naively believe them, seemingly unaware or unwilling to acknowledge an emerging "techno-feudalism" wherein many, perhaps most, people will have few options other than minimum wage work or government subsistence payments in the form of a "guaranteed minimum income." Amid this economic and social devolution, higher education institutions continue to offer degree programs in professions that may soon disappear or be drastically reduced in numbers. This keynote presentation will explore the implications of machine learning for human learners, and more specifically, for designers and providers of e-learning.

****

RE-DEFINING THE "SMART EVERYTHING" PARADIGM TOWARDS RECONCILING HUMANS AND TECHNOLOGY

Dr. Dr. Norbert Streitz, Scientific Director, Smart Future Initiative, Germany

KEYNOTE PAPER

RE-DEFINING THE "SMART EVERYTHING" PARADIGM: TOWARDS RECONCILING HUMANS AND TECHNOLOGY

Norbert Streitz
Smart Future Initiative, Konrad-Zuse-Str. 43, 60438 Frankfurt, Germany

ABSTRACT

My keynote presentation will address multiple issues in the intersection of the following three conferences at MCCSIS 2017: *Connected Smart Cities,* and *ICT, Society, and Human Beings,* and *Interfaces and Human-Computer Interaction.*
Starting out with the context of living in the Urban Age, I discuss different notions of "smart cities", being propagated as the blueprint for our cities in the future, and complement them with the concept of "hybrid" cities. One can currently observe a big hype about the opportunities of smart cities based on an Internet of Things (IoT) infrastructure. Due to the increasing penetration of IoT and the proliferation of smart services based on AI algorithms, one can speak of a *"smart everything" paradigm* permeating very diverse spheres of our society and determining our personal and public life in many ways. Thus, it is necessary to investigate the implications for individuals as well as for society. Exploring the challenges, but also the venues towards a *human-/citizen- centered design approach*, I take a critical look at smart services based on matching people's profiles and interests with service options available at specific locations. A major focus are the risks resulting from smart city installations, especially the serious infringements of privacy rights, i.e., usage of personal data without consent of the people concerned.
Besides the issues of privacy, designing interfaces and human-computer interaction or more general *human-technology, resp. citizen-urban environment interaction* is of major importance. A prominent challenge is the property that "traditional" affordances are often hidden in these kinds of environments. (=> invisible or disappearing computer). How can people know how to interact, when they are not aware of the options? How can people protect their privacy, when they don't "see" the sensors, the hidden devices? Another aspect is the shift from information design to experience design.
A critical reflection of different manifestations of the *"smart everything and everywhere" paradigm* is needed in order to meet the overall *goal of reconciling humans and technology*. A central aspect of this goal is to "*keep the human in the loop and in control*". Therefore, a citizen-centered design approach for future cities is needed for helping us to go "beyond smart cities" and transform them into *Humane, Sociable and Cooperative Hybrid Cities.*

KEYWORDS

Smart hybrid cities, citizen-centered design, human in the loop, reconciling humans and technology, privacy issues

1. SMART CITIES IN THE CONTEXT OF THE URBAN AGE

Already now, more than 50% of the world population is living in urban areas. Thus, cities have been and will increasingly become the central hubs of determining life in the 21th century, resulting in what has been called the 'Urban Age'. This paper is not about the Urban Age per se, but this context with its wide range of associated issues (e.g., socio-economic, ecological, sustainability aspects) has always to be kept in mind when discussing the future of our cities. While the focus of this contribution is the role of information and communication technology (ICT) for designing future cities, the goal settings should be compatible. Our overall goal is to develop *Humane, Sociable, and Cooperative Cities* motivated and inspired by a citizen-centered design approach keeping the human in the loop. The details will be presented subsequently.

Contemporary life styles become less focused and increasingly multidimensional. People's lives are taking place betwixt and between multiple offers and options. So, people's roles, intentions, motivations and behavior change within short time frames due to polyphasic activities in dynamically changing environments. Accordingly, urban environments have to accommodate different activities via appropriate spaces, e.g., transient spaces, personal and public spaces. Public spaces stand out from the rest, because they are accessible to more or less all citizens, often serving in a 'hub function' connecting different types of urban objects (buildings, streets, sidewalks, parks, bridges, etc.), often in the role of transient spaces. Transient spaces in the public context can be characterized by a certain degree of mobility when passing-through (e.g., getting from the entrance of a shopping mall to a specific shop or restaurant; entering and leaving a small city park, e.g. being placed at the intersection of several streets) or by staying in specific spaces, e.g., in a waiting area.

Streets are a specific type of space, especially in the context of cities. Streets are constituted by stationary objects, but populated by mobile objects (cars, buses, bicycles, pedestrians when crossing them, etc.). Some of them become temporary stationary objects, e.g., parking cars. Thus, the introduction of "smart mobility" concepts in cities has to address a wide range of boundary conditions when being supported by information and communication technology. I will come back to this when talking about smart parking or cars and street lights as "urban spies".

2. SMART HYBRID CITIES

The term *Smart city* has a wide range of connotations (digital city, intelligent city, ubiquitous city, green city, resilient city, sustainable city, etc.) Unfortunately, it has become a buzzword, is being exploited for many purposes and even reduced to fashionable name dropping. But, there is some common ground. Building smart cities requires establishing an ICT infrastructure that allows instrumenting all kinds of physical objects (including humans, animals, and plants). There are different types of connectivity in place and an emphasis on attached or embedded sensors and actuators. At a more advanced level, we are talking about integrated smart materials for a smart ecosystem. The relationship to the Internet of Things (IoT) or the Internet of Everything (IoE) is obvious. Urban environments are transformed into interactive spaces that are meant to be adaptive, responsive and smart by employing pervasive computing and ambient intelligence (Streitz & Privat, 2009) infrastructures.

An important aspect, especially in the context of a smart city, is that the computer disappears as a 'visible' distinctive device, either physically due to being integrated in the environment or mentally from our perception, thus providing the basis for establishing a calm technology. This is the core of the 'Disappearing Computer' approach (Streitz & Nixon, 2005; Streitz et al., 2007, Streitz, 2008). This situation has serious consequences, not only because traditional affordances for interaction are missing, but also for issues of privacy to be discussed later, because people/citizens are not aware of where sensors and with which capability are present in the urban environment.

2.1 Self-aware Cities

Beyond the general accepted notion of smart cities, I like to introduce a different interpretation of the term. This concept is based on the proposal that the '*smartness of a city*' can also be characterized by how much the city knows about itself and how this is communicated to its citizens. There are two views: 1) City officials being in charge of administering and managing the city obtain additional knowledge about the different characteristic parameters and can take more informed decisions. 2) Citizens are enabled to have a more comprehensive, even augmented view of their city. At the same, this empowers them to engage and participate in addressing open city issues. In some cases, citizens can play an active role in the data collection process. Feedback on air and sound pollution level in the city, congested traffic, broken roads, non-functioning devices, etc. are examples of this "self-awareness". There are interesting challenges how to communicate the parameters to the citizens and how to get feedback from them. The work by Konomi et al. (2013) is a very good example of how to enable and communicate self-awareness. He focused on measuring urban congestion in trains of the Tokyo subway system. He applies a clever approach of using indirect measures (the CO_2 level in the train compartments) for determining the congestion level (the more CO_2, the more passengers). At the same time, his method is an example that collecting the basic data might also involve the active and consenting participation of citizens in what is called the 'Civic Computing' approach.

2.2 Hybrid Cities

Assuming that the Internet of Things (IoT) is adopted as a pervasive and ubiquitous paradigm, it will result in very large ensembles of augmented physical objects. Physical objects in the real world will have a digital representation (also called 'digital shadow') in the virtual world. The term 'Hybrid World' denotes now the combination of real worlds and digital/virtual worlds. Depending on the level of detail of modeling the real world, there are different digital representations for different purposes. Applying this distinction to urban contexts, the term 'Hybrid City' (e.g., Streitz, 2015) is a direct consequence. I favor this conceptualization very much and have used it already for a long time (since 2008), because it reflects my understanding that we have to address the connection, balance and interaction of real worlds and virtual worlds, if we want to get the full picture of what is relevant for the design of the city of the future.

3. HUMANE, SOCIABLE AND COOPERATIVE CITIES

The basic assumption of my perspective is that technology should not be an "end in itself". Otherwise, we find ourselves in a situation which can be very well described by the statement of Cedric Price (1933-2003): "*Technology is the answer, but what was the question?*" Thus, the overall goal when designing future or refurbishing existing cities should be: *A Humane, Sociable and Cooperative Smart, Hybrid City reconciling humans and technology* (Streitz, 2017). This requires:

- Establishing a calm technology providing ambient intelligence that supports and respects individual and social life by keeping the 'human in the loop'.
- Respecting the rights of citizens, in general and especially in terms of privacy. Therefore, personal data should be – as much as possible – only collected with their consent by providing them with choices and control of the process.
- Viewing the city and its citizens as mutual cooperation partners, where the city is smart in the sense of being self-aware about itself and cooperative towards its citizens by supporting them in their activities. This requires developing mutual trust and respect for each other motives and vested interests.
- Acknowledging the capabilities of citizens to participate in the design of the urban environment (=> participatory design), especially with respect to their local expertise, and stimulating their active participation.
- Motivating citizens to get involved, to understand themselves as part of the urban community, to be actively engaged by contributing to the public good and welfare (=> collective intelligence, aspects similar to the Greek 'agora').
- Enabling citizens to exploit their individual, creative, social and economic potential and to live a self- determined life, and thus
- Meeting some of the challenges of the urban age by enabling people to experience and enjoy everyday life and work.

Figure 1 shows the merging of real and virtual representations of the city as a whole and its constituents into what we call a 'hybrid city' and the subsequent application of additional relevant features.

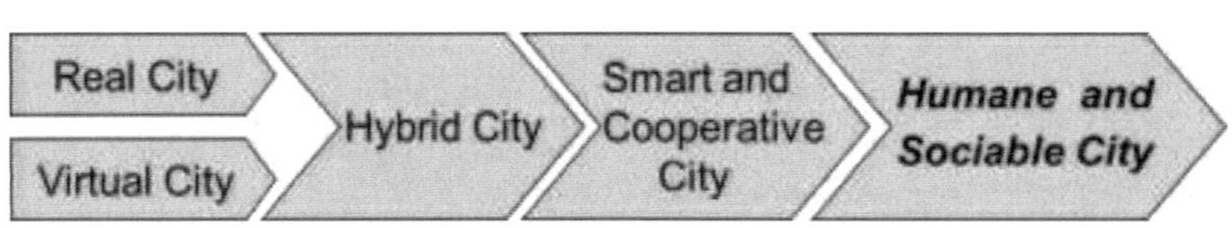

Figure 1. Relationships of smart city characteristics

The combined representations provide the basis for modeling the city in order to define how the different parts can be augmented with smart properties in order to create an urban environment with ambient intelligence. In a next step, one has to determine how this augmentation can be used for the overall benefit of the city and providing added value for each individual citizen. This is the idea of a '*Cooperative City*'.

The notion of a Cooperative City might need some explanation. It is based on our earlier work on Cooperative Buildings and Roomware (Streitz et al. 1998). In this tradition, I propose to apply human-centered design principles that have proven useful, e.g., in human-computer interaction and computer-supported cooperative work (CSCW), in this context now as 'Citizen-Centered Design'. We take such a 'co-operative/ cooperation' perspective as an overarching goal in the design process.

It allows integrating functionalities and policies from the very beginning, which account for the implications for citizens as prospective 'users' or 'customers' of the city. The city is the interface.

This somehow ideal picture of the smart city is in contrast with the increasing privatization and commercialization of many aspects of our urban life. Smart Cities are considered to be the "next big thing" by many companies, where large profits are expected.

4. REDEFINING THE '*SMART EVERYTHING*' PARADIGM

There is already a quite dramatic dependency of our urban systems on the stable and continuous availability of electricity and well-functioning "traditional" ICT components. Soon, we will be confronted with the dependency on smart systems, especially with the deployment of often non-transparent artificial intelligence components, e.g., in autonomous driving, voice-controlled smart homes.

4.1 Why redefine?

There are a number of problems which result from self-reinforcing trends in the areas of IoT and AI (Artificial Intelligence) when combined in certain application fields as, e.g., smart home, autonomous driving, smart cities, Industry 4.0. A major trend is the shift towards more or even complete automation of previously (partially) human operator controlled activities. Smart devices and underlying algorithms are gaining ground in controlling processes, services and devices as well as the interaction between devices and humans. Humans are increasingly removed from being the operator and thus from being in control. I would label this the *"Smart Everything" Paradigm* which is gaining ever more ground. The current hype about AI, amplified by abundant venture capital, forgets that progress was pretty limited when considering the history of AI since its origin in 1956. For more details see Streitz (2017). Deep learning approaches provide progress in some areas, but they are certainly not the panacea to all problems. Some of the shortcomings might be overcome, but in any case it is still a long way to go. The solutions are not just around the corner as many try to make us believe.

There are three basic problem sets of the current "Smart Everything" Paradigm. Set A: inability and error-prone behavior, set B: rigidity, and Set C: missing transparency/ traceability. Inability and error-prone behavior of AI or other algorithmic approaches can be observed today in many areas despite ubiquitous promises. For example, the expectations towards autonomous driving are disappointed by failures in recognizing simple speed-limit information signs. Moreover, wrong detection information might result in unwanted and unjustified legal implications for the driver. Rigid behavior is another problem. It can be experienced, e.g., by users and customers confronted with fully automated call centers or on-line shops without humans involved. It needs only small deviations from the standard routine or process and the system cannot handle the requests. The problem is that users and customers are and will be in the future even more completely at the mercy of companies and their algorithms and in loss of control. Recommendation systems in hotel portals repeat recommendations for hotels in cities which are not relevant anymore. In on-line shops, one is confronted with the same category of items just bought, although one does not need multiple items in this category.

While these two problem sets might be remedied (partially) by progress in the field, missing transparency/traceability and incomprehensible decisions are and will stay with us as an essential problem. Especially, when assuming further "progress", 'AI behavior' will increasingly become neither transparent nor comprehensible. Being untraceable implies in some way also that there are no reproducible outcomes and also a lack of liability. We are already now confronted with the problems and lack of transparency, as demonstrated in the financial domain with high frequency trading, not speaking of how this will develop in the future. When nobody can trace the underlying argumentation or mechanisms we have a really serious problem; an issue not too many people seem to talk about.

4.2 Keeping the Human in the Loop

Feasibility problems and transparency deficits have to be considered as warning signs, especially when looking at the planned abundance of automating everything and seeking refuge and solutions in AI environments completely operated by algorithms. While these observations sound pretty negative and disillusioned, there has to be an alternative which is summarized in our proposal of '*Keeping the human in the loop*'. I like to propose this as an alternative or at least complementary approach for redefining the ‘smart everything, everywhere and every time’ paradigm in order to reconcile the situation. It is based on earlier work we did more than 10 years ago (Streitz et al, 2005), but it is still valid and, as we observe now, becoming increasingly important. It reflects the design approach of Ambient Intelligence and its role for reconciling humans and technology (Streitz, 2017). In this context, we distinguish between ‘*System-Oriented, Importunate Smartness and People-Oriented, Empowering Smartness*’.

System-Oriented, Importunate Smartness

We consider an environment as ‘smart’ if it enables certain self-directed (re)actions of individual or an ensemble of artefacts based on previously and continuously collected information. For example, a space or a place can be ‘smart’ by having and exploiting knowledge about which people and artefacts are currently situated within its area, who and what was there before, when and how long, and what kind of activities took place. In this version of ‘smartness’, the space would be active (in many cases even proactive) and in control of the situation by making decisions on what to do next and actually take action and execute them without a human in the loop. It is more or less automated or even autonomous system behavior based on the interpretation of collected data. Some of these actions could be importunate.

People-Oriented, Empowering Smartness

We contrast the previous view with another perspective where the empowering function is in the foreground and can be summarized as ‘*smart spaces make people smarter’*. It can be achieved by keeping ‘*the human in the loop*’. It allows empowering people by making better informed decisions and take actions as mature and responsible people who are in control. The environment will also collect data about what is going on and aggregate these data but it provides and communicates the resulting information for guidance and subsequent actions determined by the people. In this case, a smart space might also make suggestions and recommendations based on the information collected but the people are in the loop and in control. Here, the place supports smart, behavior of the people present (or in remote interaction scenarios people being away ‘on the road’ but connected to the space). This approach is getting increasingly popular as work on soft actuation in pervasive computing shows. The people-oriented, empowering smartness is in line with the objectives of ‘*reconciling humans and technology*’.

The caveat of this approach: How much feedback do we want? How many data can we process? At which level of the data collection and aggregation process do we want or are we able to be involved? Obviously, the two perspectives will rarely exist in their pure and distinct manifestations. They rather represent the end points of a dimension where we can position weighted combinations of both, dependent on the specific application domain. The challenge for an appropriate system design is to find the right balance.

For me, the important points in this context are: 1) human intervention and control is possible. 2) data belong to the people, and 3) the degree of automation is configurable by humans. The design rationale should be guided and informed by the objective of keeping the ‘human in the loop and in control’ as much as possible and feasible. This perspective is reflected in what we conceptualize as the ‘cooperative building’ (Streitz et al., 1998) and now extended it to the ‘*cooperative city*’.

5. PRIVACY BY DESIGN

There is no doubt that the smart city approach provides multiple opportunities. They have been described by many authors elsewhere and are not repeated here. There are threats that have been articulated, e.g. the increase of existing dependencies on reliable and working ICT-infrastructures and the vulnerability in terms of lacking security against criminal manipulations, ransom-ware and cyber-attacks. Here, I focus on a third major risk for citizens in a smart city, i.e. the loss of privacy in terms of losing the control over personal data. Currently, the discussion on privacy addresses mainly the virtual world (e.g., misuse in social networks). The more prevalent issues will surface in the smart city context concerning personal data of citizens in the real, resp. hybrid world. The discussion of privacy issues here is based on earlier work by me (Streitz, 2016).

Obviously, a smart system will be enabled to be smarter with respect to a service offered if it has more knowledge about the person compared to a system with no or insufficient data. Thus, there is a tricky trade-off between creating smartness and providing privacy. There has to be an interaction and balance between collecting and processing data for tailoring functionality to make the system ‘smart’ and the right of citizens to be in control over which data are being collected, by whom, how they are used, i.e. the issue of privacy. In order to provide decision options to the user, the citizen, it is necessary that privacy considerations have to be first class objects of system design: not a subsequent add-on and not reflected in the system architecture.

5.1 Privacy in Smart Hybrid Cities

I am convinced and raise the warning flag, that privacy issues will become even more relevant in smart hybrid cities. In the virtual world, you can – to a certain degree – still use fake identities and anonymization services. But in the real world, it will be more difficult acting in disguise. Data that exist about you in the virtual world are now complemented by real world data and vice versa. For example, in public and transient urban spaces, there are obvious issues and implications for privacy. Beyond the almost ubiquitous and usually visible CCTV surveillance cameras, there will be many sensors hidden in the environment. Sensors and cameras are tracking you when entering a building, a shop or a public space with a known location. Face recognition identifies your personal identity. Real objects you are wearing, carrying, using, buying will be recognized by sensors in the environment because these objects are tagged.

Smart cars enhanced for autonomous driving capabilities have a wide range of sensors (cameras, ultrasonic sensors, radar, laser-based LIDAR, GPS). Are they going asleep when the cars park on the curbside of the street? Nobody knows what the sensors, e.g., cameras and microphones, are recording. Who has control over the sensors and access to these data? The car company? The fact that the engine is turned off, does not mean that the car is not active and sensing anymore. Pedestrians walking by can be monitored. Peeking into the windows of the adjacent houses and apartments is no problem either. Similar considerations apply to street lights being equipped with cameras and radar for the official and main purpose of monitoring the street looking for free parking spaces. But who knows what kinds of data are collected about the complete urban area within the view? *Smart cars and street lights can easily operate as 'urban spies'*.

The principal problem is: How can people know what is going on, when they are not aware of being tracked, when they cannot 'see' the different sensors, the manifold devices distributed in the urban environment due to the above mentioned Disappearing Computer approach?

5.2 The Shift of Perspectives on Privacy

Privacy used to be a legal and moral right, in many cases a socially negotiated feature. Now, privacy is turning into a commodity you pay for and you can trade – with the implication that privacy is becoming a privilege. In many cases, people are not really aware that the loss of their privacy is the price they pay for a seemingly free product or service, because they pay with their data.

It will become more and more difficult to avoid object and person tracking, because soon all objects and their parts will be tagged, respectively have integrated IDs (=> smart artefacts). Location-based services in a smart hybrid city exploit not only your location and preferences but can also be used to build up a complete profile by monitoring your activities (e.g., buying goods, eating food, looking at public displays/ advertisements, contacting people), when and where, including also other people present or involved in the situation.

This future predicted for 2054 in the movie "Minority Report" (created in 2002) seems to be very close now as it is becoming the subject of the commercialization promises for the smart city. Who can really predict what will happen to all the data generated in the real environment (either unobtrusively collected or voluntarily provided) and stored by numerous service providers and manufacturers, especially when these servers are based in a country that have no or very limited privacy and data security legislation?

It should also be pointed out that Mark Weiser - already at the time of his work on ubiquitous computing (Weiser, 1991) - regarded 'privacy' as a key issue for this kind of environments. Although on the mind of many researchers on and off, it was not too long ago that it actually received the attention it deserves.

We argue for so called *Privacy Enhancing Technologies (PETs)* (Streitz et al., 2007) and for '*Privacy by Design*' (Streitz, 2016), i.e. to make privacy a first-order objective of system design. This requires addressing the conflict of unobtrusive data collection vs. human control over the data at an early stage of the overall system design.

6. CONCLUSIONS

One can assume there is agreement that the smart hybrid city proposal contains many opportunities. But one should also be aware that there are several risks requiring the discussion of pros and cons. It is my opinion, that the smart city promises will only survive and be successful, if our future cities are designed as *Humane Sociable and Cooperative Smart Hybrid Cities, reconciling humans and technology*. Urban environments should be designed to enable people to exploit their creative, social and economic potential and lead a self-determined life. Ambient Intelligence can play a major role in achieving this goal by reconciling humans and technology (Streitz, 2017).

Therefore, it is necessary to redefine the "Smart Everything" Paradigm, with the implications and requirements that 1) human intervention and control is possible, 2) the data belong to the people, and 3) the degree of automation is configurable by humans. The design rationale should be guided and informed by the objective of keeping the '*human in the loop and in control*' as much as possible and feasible. This has to be complemented by the provision of so called *Privacy Enhancing Technologies (PETs)* (Streitz et al., 2007) and by '*Privacy by Design*' (Streitz, 2016), i.e. making privacy a first-order objective of system design. Taking a stand on data security, personality rights and privacy is more than a liberal rights movement as some might denigrate it. I am convinced that 'privacy by design' could even be a competitive advantage, a USP (unique selling proposition) in the global market, where Europe could take a lead by reflecting on its basic democratic and ethical values.

REFERENCES

Konomi, S., Shoji, K., Ohno, W. (2013). Rapid Development of Civic Computing Services: Opportunities and Challenges. In: Streitz, N., Stephanidis, C. (Eds.), *Distributed, Ambient, and Pervasive Interactions*. LNCS 8028, Springer-Verlag, pp. 309 – 315.

Streitz, N. (2008). The Disappearing Computer. In: Erickson, T., McDonald, D.W. (Eds.), *HCI Remixed: Reflections on Works that have Influenced the HCI Community*. MIT Press, pp.55 – 60.

Streitz, N. (2015). Citizen-Centered Design for Humane and Sociable Hybrid Cities. In: Theona, I. & Charitos, D. (Eds.), *Hybrid City 2015 - Data to the People*. University of Athens, Greece. pp. 17-20.

Streitz, N. (2016). Smart Cities Need Privacy by Design for Being Humane. In: Pop, S., Toft, T., Calvillo, N., Wright, M. (Eds.), *What Urban Media Art Can Do - Why When Where and How?* Verlag avedition. pp. 268 – 274.

Streitz, N. (2017). Reconciling Humans and Technology: The Role of Ambient Intelligence. Keynote Paper. In: A. Braun, R. Wichert, A. Mana (Eds.), *Proceedings of the 2017 European Conference on Ambient Intelligence*. Lecture Notes in Computer Science (LNCS 10217), Springer-Verlag. (pp. 1-16).

Streitz, N. Kameas, I. Mavrommati (Eds.) (2007). *The Disappearing Computer: Interaction Design, System Infrastructures and Applications for Smart Environments*. State-of-the-Art Survey, Springer LNCS 4500.

Streitz, N., Geißler, J., Holmer. T. (1998). Roomware for Cooperative Buildings: Integrated Design of Architectural Spaces and Information Spaces. In: Streitz, N., Konomi, S., Burkhardt, H.-J. (Eds.), *Cooperative Buildings – Integrating Information, Organization, and Architecture*. LNCS 1370. Springer-Verlag. pp. 4-21.

Streitz, N., Nixon, P. (2005). The Disappearing Computer. Guest Editors' Introduction to Special Issue. *Communications of the ACM*, Vol. 48, March 2005. pp. 33-35.

Streitz, N., Privat, G. (2009). Ambient Intelligence. Final section "Looking to the Future". In: Stephanidis, C. (Eds.) *The Universal Access Handbook*. CRC Press Taylor & Francis Group. Pages 60.1 - 60.17.

Streitz, N., Röcker, C., Prante, T., van Alphen, D., Stenzel, R., Magerkurth, C. (2005). Designing Smart Artifacts for Smart Environments. *IEEE Computer* (March 2005), pp. 41-49.

Weiser, M. (1991). The Computer for the 21st Century. *Scientific American* (September 1991) pp. 66-75.

Full Papers

INVESTIGATING INFORMATION SYSTEMS RESEARCH THROUGH THE LENS OF FEMINIST EPISTEMOLOGY: THE CASE OF MIS QUARTERLY

Chantal Morley
Institut Mines-Télécom, Télécom École de Management, France

ABSTRACT

Women's underrepresentation in the ICT field is an enduring issue, mainly due to persistent stereotypes that depict women as technologically incompetent. Does information system research contribute to reduce gender imbalance in the ICT field? To start answering this question, we have tried to understand how gender is pictured in the IS domain. More precisely, we have scrutinised MIS Quarterly, generally considered as a leading IS research journal, through the lens of feminist epistemology. The aim of this paper is to describe the results. Using a feminist epistemology means taking one or all of the following approaches: to view gender as a relational concept; to make women's contribution more visible; to adopt different standpoints; and to rely on emancipatory principles and contribute to reducing gender inequality and stereotypes. Our analysis shows the persistence of a narrow view on gender issues, but it also suggests hope for improvement. Taking into account social relations between men and women in socio-technical systems would provide a richer understanding of information systems implementation, adoption and use.

KEYWORDS

Gender imbalance, IS workforce, ICT adoption, ICT use, Epistemology, Diversity

1. INTRODUCTION

Women's underrepresentation in the ICT field is an enduring issue (Glass 2012) and concern (Taylor 2010). This situation is mainly due to persistent stereotypes that depict women as technologically incompetent (Clayton et al. 2012). Our broad research question is: does information system (IS) research contributes to reduce gender imbalance? To start answering this question, we have tried to understand how gender is pictured in the IS domain. More precisely, building on (Trauth et al. 2007) we have scrutinised *MIS Quarterly*, that is the first scholarly journal dedicated to IS research and that is generally considered as a leading IS research journal (Mylonopoulos&Theoharakis 2001), through the lens of feminist epistemology. We have tried to understand what, if any, impact the journal could have on gender&ICT representations and stereotypes. The aim of this paper is to present our results.

Taking a feminist epistemological stand means critically addressing processes and choices that legitimate knowledge. Feminist epistemology is diverse (Narayan 2004), but usually one or all of four approaches are involved:

- The first approach is to view gender as a relational concept, and not as a taken for granted binary category (Adam et al. 2004);
- The second approach is to make women's contribution more visible as did recent historical works (Gürer 1995; Misa 2011 ; Abbate 2012; Morley&McDonnell 2015);
- The third approach is to take into account different standpoints (Harding 1993; Haraway 1988);
- The fourth approach is to rely on emancipatory principles (Hirschheim&Klein 1994), and to contribute to reducing gender inequality and stereotypes (Peter 2003).

We first describe certain characteristics of our corpus of articles (part 1). Then we present the result of our analysis from the four viewpoints associated with a feminist epistemology (part 2 to 5). We then discuss the results.

2. CATEGORISATION OF ARTICLES INCLUDING GENDER

Our corpus of articles includes all *MIS Quarterly* research articles that include the term "gender". The search from BSC and Google Scholar (on April 16, 2016) returned 180 articles. We have sorted them according to their use of « gender ». The following categorisation has been made which includes three categories (A, B, C) and three sub-categories (B1, B2, B3) (Table 1).

- In category A, gender is a demographic characteristic, which is only used for checking gender balance in study samples.
- In category B, gender is an independent variable, usually a control variable, presumably impacting the results. We have made a distinction between three sub-categories:
  - in sub-category B1, gender has an influence on results;
  - in sub-category B2, gender has no impact on results;
  - in sub-category B3, a suggestion is made to include gender in further research.
- Category C includes papers with other usages of gender.

In Table 1, we also mentioned for each category if the authors have made comments on gender. Most papers are found in Category B, and in this category most studies do not provide evidence of gender difference.

Table 1. Categories of MIS Quarterly articles including "gender"

Category	Articles	Methodology		Comments on gender
A	**54** **30 %**	Quantitative Qualitative and quantitative Qualitative Action research Ethnography Design science	41 7 3 1 1 1	**1**
B	**101** **56%**			**34**
B1	26 14,50 %	Quantitative Qualitative and quantitative Delphi and quantitative Quantitative & MRI based experiment MRI based experiment Comparison of quantitative models	21 1 1 1 1 1	18
B2	58 **32 %**	Quantitative Qualitative and quantitative Quantitative model development Qualitative Experiment	47 7 2 1 1	15
B3	17 9,50 %	Quantitative Qualitative and quantitative Quantitative and content analyse MRI based experiment Quantitative model development Theoretical	11 2 1 1 1 1	1
C	**25** **14 %**	Theoretical Quantitative Case study Qualitative and quantitative Ethnography Design science	10 6 6 1 1 1	**25**
TOTAL	**180** **(100%)**			**60**

3. FIRST FEMINIST APPROACH: THEORIZING GENDER

The first characteristic of feminist epistemology is employing a gender theory. In the selected articles, the term "gender" has been used with four different meanings: an individual characteristic; a differentiating factor; a classification criterion; a form of social interaction.

1. In some articles, "gender" is an attribute of the participants in the study, which is merely mentioned in the sample description. All the papers in Category A articles and some articles in Category C, use "gender" with such a meaning. This demographic approach can be called "atheoretical" (Trauth 2013), and overlooks gendered relationships in organizational settings.

2. In other *MIS Quarterly* articles, men and women are explicitly associated with specific characteristics related to ICT (behaviour, emotion, attitude, skill, roles, etc.), which advocates for using a sex variable in the research. Most of the 34 articles in Category B where authors have written comments refer to gender as a differentiating factor. None of those authors discusses findings that do not bring evidence for differences between men and women, except for Sia et al. (2009) who find their results "intriguing". They suggest it comes from their sample characteristics. A few papers in Category C also use a differentialist view, one of them referring to "sexual selection" (Kock 2009).

3. Many papers use "gender" for the purposes of classification: sex is a dichotomous variable that could affect the results. Authors do not mention any difference between men and women. The 67 papers of Category B with no comment on "gender" refer to gender as a classification criterion. However, even with no differentialist discourse, using sex as a control variable implicitly suggest that there are some differences in the relation to technology.

4. Finally, a few papers, mostly in Category C, refer to a relational approach: "gender" refers to social interactions between men and women that characterise representations or social practices. For example, Carter&Grover (2015) suggest that the construction of an IT identity can be influenced by representations associated with men and women. From Liu et al. (2015)'s study, women are less likely than men to get a loan from online peers. Ahuja&Thatcher (2005) explain adding gender to their model because women are more likely than men to experience work-family conflict.

To sum up, most research in MIS Quarterly does not employ a gender theory: implicitly or explicitly they rely on common sense or on previous findings to assume the existence of gender differences in relation to ICT. The body of research invalidating gender differences in ICT is essentially ignored.

4. SECOND FEMINIST APPROCH: VISIBILITY CHALLENGES

The second aspect of a feminist epistemology is to highlight persons or knowledge usually left aside. Only a limited number amongst the selected articles increased women's visibility. On the contrary, research results showing no gender difference are underused, and power issues involving women are not an object of study in IS research.

MIS Quarterly articles that invalidate a difference between men and women concerning ICT are almost never mentioned in other articles, especially those of category B. However, such results (sub-category B2) were twice as numerous as those revealing a difference (sub-category B1), and they cover many different aspects of ICT: IS professionals' perceptions regarding working in the IS field; factors that affect users' behaviour and satisfaction in ICT adoption, whether in a professional setting or in private life; factors affecting users' performance and learning; IS security issues, etc.

The validity of studies showing an absence of gender effect seems to be questioned by many authors. Maybe they attribute this absence to some research limitation, whereas gender effects seem to consolidate an underlying belief. This contributes to reinforce the differentialist representation, where men and women deeply differ in their relation to ICT.

Power issues are not frequently encountered in *MIS Quarterly*, and female power has never been a topic. A few articles mention or deal with women's career issues in the IS field, but only two articles refer to women in a IS high level position.

5. THIRD FEMINIST APPROCH: PLURALITY OF VIEWS

Most articles provide a unique point of view; and concerning gender, feminist studies are generally overlooked.

MIS Quarterly researches involving gender are not designed to take into account several views, except (Trauth&Jessup 2000) who conducted an action-research using a group support system (GSS). Employee discussions were analysed, and two different views emerged: that of male participants, mostly in management positions, and female participants' one, mostly staff and faculty. Beyond scientific contribution, their research allowed participants to exchange on gender discrimination in the workplace.

Apart from a few exceptions, *MIS Quarterly* articles do not mention theoretical and empirical gender studies, and in particular works on the gender-technology relation from a feminist point of view. Whereas E.Trauth has been on the editorial board for many years, her numerous studies on the topic are not cited except by Carter&Grover (2015) and herself. The number of papers incorporating gender has greatly increased in the journal over the last ten years; however most of them ignore the relational dimension of gender.

6. FOURTH FEMINIST APPROCH: EMANCIPATORY OBJECTIVE

Two opposite movements can be identified in the selected *MIS Quarterly* articles. Some articles consolidates a normative social order as regards women and men, reinforcing stereotypes or failing to account for gendered social issues. Others are guided by an emancipatory rationale: they contribute to deconstruct gender-ICT stereotypes or shed light on gender related discriminations.

Concerning the effect on the persistence of stereotyping, some research maintains, purposely or not, a stereotyped view on femininity and masculinity. Most authors do not comment on strongly unbalanced study samples. This could be performative: social reality is taken as-is and left unquestioned. Some make common sense comments on behaviours or characteristics attributed to men and women. Acknowledgement of former research is sometimes ambiguous. For example, Sykes et al. (2014) quote (Igbaria& Baroudi 1995) to say that gender is associated with performance. However, these authors found no significant differences in job performance ratings, but women were perceived to have less career-advancement opportunities than men. Similarly, Ahuja&Thatcher (2005) cite (Gefen&Straub 1997)'s assumption of women using e-mail for communication and men for reporting, but they do not indicate that these authors' findings show no gender difference in the use of the e-mail.

Other *MIS Quarterly* papers contribute to deconstruct gender stereotypes. For example, Igbaria et al. (1991) found that men in IS careers reported more satisfaction than women, and women reported to be more oriented towards work-life balance. But the authors explain these differences by the unequal sharing of household chores, and they assume lifestyle career orientation could become more prevalent amongst IS employees due to changing living arrangements with men showing a growing concern for home and children. Another example can be found in Rai et al. (2009)'s study on the quality of cooperation between project managers (client and customer) in offshore ICT development projects: gender has no effect on project success, but a disparity in masculinity-femininity between client representative and project leader decreases client satisfaction. A similar finding about surface-level characteristics (such as gender) has been reported by (Kanawattanachai&Yoo 2007) in their study on virtual teams' coordination: task-oriented communications provides more opportunities to learn about others' knowledge than gender. According to (Foster&Flynn 1984)'s study at General Motors, women managers and professionals were particularly reluctant to use keyboards to avoid the age-old stigma of their being mistaken for secretaries.

In a field research involving men and women, misinterpreting results could be reduced by using a gender theory to discuss the findings. For example, in their study on GSS (Group Support System) facilitators, Niederman et al. (1996) do not point out a gender disparity in respondents: most women classified themselves as 'low experience' and they mostly focus on the group, whereas those claiming 'high experience' are mostly male and they mostly focus on technical aspects. A relational perspective of gender would have suggested the influence of gender norms in care-oriented women's roles. Another example is given by Brown&Venkatesh (2005)'s model of personal computer adoption during the phases of household life-cycle (bachelor, newlywed, married with children, etc.). Gender is not used in the model. However, many studies reveal an unbalanced distribution of domestic tasks between women and men, which could have an effect on women's intention to adopt a PC for household use.

Other authors contribute to highlight discriminations in the ICT field, whether in pay or in career opportunities (Truman&Baroudi 1994; Igbaria&Baroudi 1995; Joseph et al. 2007; Armstrong et al. 2015). Such findings can be used in further research or for questioning practices. However, *MIS Quarterly* papers tackling discrimination issues can be found at the beginning of the 1990s, but afterwards the term 'discrimination' is rarely used except in (Trauth&Jessup 2000). In their study of ICT careers, Joseph and al. (2012) describe women as having less stable careers, using the terms 'barriers' or 'job segregation'

7. DISCUSSION

Our analysis through the lens of a feminist epistemology of *MIS Quarterly* papers that explicitly use the term "gender" firstly shows that in most cases gender is under-theorized. Authors who provide reasons for including a gender variable in their research frequently appear to be influenced by a stereotyped view of the gender and information technology relation. Many of them search for differences between men and women in ICT adoption or use, but the majority of findings show no significant differences, and this is not usually considered as a result. In most cases, differentialist comments are not discussed in the light of contradicting results. As a consequence, no-difference results are much less visible than results showing a gender difference, and the former are almost never cited in further research. On the contrary findings showing gender differences are frequently cited, and their limits are generally not mentioned.

In addition, feminist research on gender and ICT is ignored except for rare exceptions, and women visibility is limited. The topic of women and power is almost completely absent in *MIS Quarterly* papers, and only a few articles contribute to a better understanding of gender imbalance in the IT field. Several researchers have proposed technology acceptance models which include a gender variable. These models rely on a narrow view of organizational reality (Terrade et al. 2009) especially concerning gender. They often do not take into account job positions, work organization or social relations between men and women at work.

Thus our analysis of IS research published in a leading journal suggests that it may contribute to reinforce gender inequality. Repeated stereotyped or scientifically flawed statements on the differences between men and women in relation to ICT can be performative. Stereotypes are reinforced, and they can lead to discrimination. Moreover, some uncritical articles using neuro-sciences techniques (Riedl et al. 2010; Dimoka 2010) or relying on the controversial evolutionary psychology theory (Kock 2009) suggest biological determinism.

Relevance of IS research has been a concern for more than twenty years (Recker and al. 2009). Taking into account a feminist epistemology could produce stronger, richer, and more qualified results in IS research. Interest in research findings could rise, especially among practitioners or researchers from other fields.

What are the methodological implications of a feminist epistemology? Firstly, a feminist epistemology does not require a specific research methodology. Obviously, gender is not considered as a concept in most quantitative research papers; however some of them (e.g. Webster&Martocchio 1992) have an emancipatory objective. Trauth (2013) calls for a diversity of methodologies. Quantitative and positivist studies can document gender relations in the IS field, interpretative approaches can provide a deeper understanding of these relations, and a critical approach can examine what enables such relations.

Secondly, in most articles where the term gender is employed, the focus is on ICT use, or employment and workforce aspects of the IS field (women underrepresentation, job selection, career choices, etc.). Researchers generally try to find differences between women and men, and sometimes they highlight discriminatory practices against women. As suggested by (Wilson 2004) a feminist epistemology could shed a new light on other research topics such as: information systems jobs competences (determination, evaluation, evolution); information systems governance (forms, decision-making process, role of the CIO); work organisation; and human interactions in an ICT project. Taking into account gender relations can lead to questioning the social norms and the power relations that structure an information system in an organisational setting (e.g. in ICT projects teams, between professionals and users, etc.).

Thirdly, a feminist epistemology requires a theoretical framework concerning gender, whatever methodology is used, and for any research topic. Researchers should break away from the premise of fundamental differences between women and men in their relation to ICT. Previous findings that are based on stereotypes and superficial observations should not be used without being discussed in the light of gender as a relational concept. Researchers taking an essentialist standpoint sometimes refer to biological factors, but more frequently they assume that gender socialisation has the same effect as if differences were innate characteristics of men and women. The differences among women or among men are often more greater than between men and women (Trauth 2006). Insufficient attention to these differences may result in unexplained contradictory findings. For example, concerning technology adoption, Venkatesh&Morris (2000) found that women were more influenced by perceptions of ease of use and organisational norms, whereas men were more strongly influenced by their perceptions of usefulness. This finding is at odds with (Gefen&Straub 1997)'s result stating that women rate the perceived usefulness of e-mail higher than men. In the past twenty years, intersectionality theory (Hancock 2007) has received a growing interest within gender studies. The intersectional approach moves beyond studying one category (gender), and draws attention to several intersecting categories of difference (gender, race, social class, sexual orientation, and ethnicity). Relations between men and women should not be studied without including other social relations of power. In the IS field, intersectionality theory was used by (Trauth and al. 2012)'s research on gender norms and stereotypes about IT professionals. Some IT skills were perceived by nearly all participants as being feminine, but they were identified by African American males as gender neutral. From a feminist epistemology viewpoint, using a gender theory may be only a part of the research theoretical framework. Gender concept can be used in data collection and/or data analysis design. Researchers will then pay closer attention to participants' characteristics (beyond sex) and/or to the relations between stakeholders in the organisational setting. Pozzebon and al. (2014)'s research that has been conducted with a pluralist theoretical framework (structuration theory, diffusion of innovations, and gender relations theory) has produced rich findings on decision support systems use including materiality and gendered roles, which shed light on the mutual shaping of institutional pressures and human agency.

Fourthly, a feminist epistemology promotes researchers' reflexivity when designing and conducting a research. They should question their own implicit assumptions regarding men and women associated with the study. They should also investigate if and how being a man or a woman could impact data collection, for example in accessing certain key persons as in (Alvesson 1993) or in interacting with actors in the field under study as in (Schultze 2000). Researchers who adopt a feminist epistemology should be sensitive to gender relations in any empirical study. They should wonder if their research will make those interactions visible, and if different stakeholders will be given a voice. Lastly, as underlined by Faulkner& Runde (2013), sex often contributes to define a social position, and many women are marginalised through horizontal and vertical segregation. Critical approaches in IS research have usually an emancipatory aim, which could encourage researchers to collect the viewpoint of those who are not in situations of authority.

8. CONCLUSION

Our analysis of *MIS Quarterly* papers in the light of feminist epistemology shows the persistence of a narrow view on gender issues, but it also suggests hope for improvement. In recent decades, many studies have shed light on gender as a social construction. Gender is a continual reconstruction, and gendered interactions take various forms depending on cultural and historical contexts, that can only be understood by considering the social and symbolic aspects in the relations between women and men. Research on gendered cultures associated with ICT has made theoretical and practical contributions to help reduce the gender gap. For example, a key success factor for women inclusion in two top technological universities (Carnegie Mellon University and Norwegian University of Science and Technology) has proved to be changing the internal culture that contributed to exclude female students (Margolis&Fisher 2003; Lagesen 2011; Frieze&Quesenberry 2013). We also suggest that the theorisation of the 'inscription' of cultural and social relations within technology developed by Allen and al. (2013) could be of use for studying gender in the ICT field: implicitly prescribed roles, associated resistances, gender inscription in design process and outcome, could be investigated. The concept of gender as a doing (Butler 1990; West&Zimmerman 1987) could also be used to study how ICT control, use or management practices are influenced by gender performances. Taking into account social relations between men and women in socio-technical systems would provide a richer understanding of information systems implementation, adoption and use.

REFERENCES

Abbate, J. (2012). Recoding gender: women's changing participation in computing. MIT Press.

Adam, A., Howcroft, D. & Richardson, H. (2004). A decade of neglect: reflecting on gender and IS. New Technology, Work and Employment, 19, 3, 222-240.

Ahuja, M. K., Thatcher, J. B. (2005). Moving beyond intentions and toward the theory of trying: effects of work environment and gender on post-adoption information technology use. MIS Quarterly, 29, 3, 427-459.

Allen, D. K., Brown, A., Karanasios, S., & Norman, A. (2013). How Should Technology-Mediated Organizational Change Be Explained? A Comparison of the Contributions of Critical Realism and Activity Theory. MIS Quarterly, 37, 3, 835-854

Alvesson, M. (1993). Organizations as rhetoric: Knowledge- intensive firms and the struggle with ambiguity. Journal of Management studies, 30, 6, 997-1015.

Brown, S. A., & Venkatesh, V. (2005). Model of adoption of technology in households: A baseline model test and extension incorporating household life cycle. MIS Quarterly, 29, 3, 399-426.

Butler, J. (1990). Gender trouble. Routledge.

Carter, M., Grover, V. (2015). Me, My Self, and I (T): Conceptualizing Information Technology Identity and its Implications. MIS Quarterly, 39, 4, 931-957.

Clayton, K., Beekhuyzen, J. & Nielsen, S. (2012). Now I know what ICT can do for me! Information Systems Journal, 22, 5, 375–390.

Dimoka, A. (2010). What does the brain tell us about trust and distrust? Evidence from a functional neuroimaging study. MIS Quarterly, 34(2), 373-396.

Faulkner, P., & Runde, J. (2013). Technological Objects, Social Positions, and the Transformational Model of Social Activity. Mis Quarterly, 37, 3, 803-818.

Foster, L. W., & Flynn, D. M. (1984). Management information technology: its effects on organizational form and function. MIS Quarterly, 8, 4, 229-236.

Frieze, C. & Quesenberry, J. (2013). From Difference to Diversity: Including Women in the Changing Face of Computing. Proceeding of the 44th ACM Technical Symposium on Computer Science Education. Denver, 6-9 Mars.

Gefen, D., & Straub, D. W. (1997). Gender differences in the perception and use of e-mail: An extension to the technology acceptance model. MIS Quarterly, 21, 4, 389-400.

Glass, R. L. (2012). The Gender Gap: Does It Include Information Systems?. Information Systems Management, 29, 1, 83-84.

Gürer D.W., (1995). Pioneering Women in Computer Science. Communications of the ACM, 58, 1, 45-54.

Hancock, A. M. (2007). When multiplication doesn't equal quick addition: Examining intersectionality as a research paradigm. Perspectives on politics, 5, 1, 63-79.

Haraway, D. (1988). Situated knowledge: the science question in feminism as a site of discourse on the privilege of partial perspective. Feminist Studies, 14, 3, 575-599.

Harding, S. (1993). Rethinking standpoint epistemology: What is “strong objectivity”? In Alcoff, L. & Potter, E. (1993) Feminist epistemologies, 49-82, Routledge.

Hirschheim, R. & Klein, H.K. (1994). Realizing Emancipatory Principles in Information Systems Development: The Case for ETHICS. MIS Quarterly, 18, 1, 83-109.

Igbaria, M., & Baroudi, J. J. (1995). The impact of job performance evaluations on career advancement prospects: An examination of gender differences in the IS workplace. MIS Quarterly, 19, 1, 107-123.

Igbaria, M., Greenhaus, J. H., & Parasuraman, S. (1991). Career Orientations of MIS Employees: An Empirical Analysis. MIS Quarterly, 15, 2, 151-169.

Joseph, D., Boh, W. F., Ang, S., & Slaughter, S. (2012). The career paths less (or more) traveled: a sequence analysis of IT career histories, mobility patterns, and career success. MIS Quarterly, 36, 2, 427-452.

Joseph, D., Ng, K. Y., Koh, C., & Ang, S. (2007). Turnover of information technology professionals: a narrative review, meta-analytic structural equation modeling, and model development. Mis Quarterly, 31, 3, 547-577.

Kanawattanachai, P., & Yoo, Y. (2007). The impact of knowledge coordination on virtual team performance over time. MIS Quarterly, 31, 4, 783-808.

Kock, N. (2009). Information systems theorizing based on evolutionary psychology: an interdisciplinary review and theory integration framework. MIS Quarterly, 33, 2, 395-418.

Lagesen, V. (2011). Getting women in computer science. In : Sorensen K., Faulkner W. & Rommes E. (Eds). Technologies of inclusion. Gender in the information society. Trondheim, Tapir.

Liu, D., Brass, D., Lu, Y., & Chen, D. (2015). Friendships in online peer-to-peer lending: Pipes, prisms, and relational herding. MIS Quarterly, 39, 3, 729-742.

Margolis, J., & Fisher, A. (2003). Unlocking the clubhouse: Women in computing. MIT press.

Misa, T. J. (Ed.). (2011). Gender codes: Why women are leaving computing. John Wiley & Sons.

Morley, C., Mc Donnell, M. (2015). The gendering of computer programming in Finland, France and the United Kingdom between 1960 and 1990. In: Schafer , V. & Thierry, B. (ed.) Women, Gender and ICT, Ch. 8, 119-135, Springer (2015).

Mylonopoulos, N. A., & Theoharakis, V. (2001). On site: global perceptions of IS journals. Communications of the ACM, 44, 9, 29-33.

Narayan, U. (2004). The project of feminist epistemology: Perspectives from a nonwestern feminist. In: The feminist standpoint theory reader: Intellectual and political controversies, Psychology Press, 213-224.

Niederman, F., Beise, C. M., & Beranek, P. M. (1996). Issues and concerns about computer-supported meetings: the facilitator's perspective. MIS Quarterly, 20, 1, 1-22.

Peter, F. (2003). Critical realism, feminist epistemology, and the emancipatory potential of science: a comment on Lawson and Harding. Feminist Economics, 9, 1, 93-101.

Pozzebon, M., Mackrell, D., & Nielsen, S. (2014). Structuration bridging diffusion of innovations and gender relations theories: a case of paradigmatic pluralism in IS research. Information Systems Journal, 24, 3, 229-248.

Rai, A., Maruping, L. M., & Venkatesh, V. (2009). Offshore information systems project success: the role of social embeddedness and cultural characteristics. MIS quarterly, 33,3, 617-641.

Recker J. C., Young, R., Darroch, F., Marshall, P., McKay, J. (2009). ACIS 2007 panel report: lack of relevance in IS research. Communications of the Association for Information Systems, vol. 24, n°18, 303-314.

Riedl, R., Hubert, M., & Kenning, P. (2010). Are there neural gender differences in online trust? An fMRI study on the perceived trustworthiness of eBay offers. MIS Quarterly, 34, 2, 397-428.

Schultze, U. (2000). A confessional account of an ethnography about knowledge work. MIS Quarterly, 24, 1, 3-41.

Sia, C. L., Lim, K. H., Leung, K., Lee, M. K., Huang, W. W., & Benbasat, I. (2009). Web strategies to promote internet shopping: is cultural-customization needed? MIS Quarterly, 33, 3, 491-512.

Sykes, T. A., Venkatesh, V., & Johnson, J. L. (2014). Enterprise system implementation and employee job performance: Understanding the role of advice networks. MIS Quarterly, 38, 1, 51-72.

Taylor, V. E. (2010). Cultivating cultural diversity in information technology. Communications of the ACM, 53, 7, 35-36.

Terrade, F., Pasquier, H., Reerinck-Boulanger, J., Guingouain, G., & Somat, A. (2010). L'acceptabilité sociale: la prise en compte des déterminants sociaux dans l'analyse de l'acceptabilité des systèmes technologiques. Le travail humain, 72, 4, 383-395.

Trauth, E. M., Jessup, L. M. (2000). Understanding computer-mediated discussions: positivist and interpretive analyses of group support system use. MIS Quarterly, 24, 1, 43-79.

Trauth, E.M. (2006). Theorizing gender and information technology research. Encyclopedia of gender and information technology, 2, 1154-1159.

Trauth, E.M. (2013). The role of theory in gender and information systems research. Information and Organization, 23, 4, 277-293.

Trauth, E.M., Cain, C.C., Joshi, K.D., Kvasny, L. & Booth, K. (2012). Understanding Underrepresentation in IT through Intersectionality. Proceedings of the 2012 iConference (Toronto, CA), 56-62.

Trauth, E.M., Kvasny, L., & Greenhill, A. (2007). Conducting Feminist Gender Research in the Information Systems Field. In Stahl, B.C. (ed.) (2007). Issues and Trends in Technology and Human Interaction. Idea Group. Chap. 1, 1-24.

Truman, G. E., & Baroudi, J. J. (1994). Gender differences in the information systems managerial ranks: an assessment of potential discriminatory practices. MIS Quarterly, 18, 2, 129-142.

Venkatesh, V., & Morris, M. G. (2000). Why don't men ever stop to ask for directions? Gender, social influence, and their role in technology acceptance and usage behavior. MIS Quarterly, 24, 1, 115-139.

Webster, J., & Martocchio, J. J. (1992). Microcomputer playfulness: Development of a measure with workplace implications. MIS Quarterly, 16, 2, 201-226.

West, C. & Zimmerman, D.H. (1987). Doing Gender. Gender and Society, 1, 2, 125-151.

Wilson, M. (2004). A conceptual framework for studying gender in information systems research. Journal of Information Technology, 19, 81–92.

TRENDS IN STUDYING IT DEGREES AT NATIONAL UNIVERSITY OF LA PLATA – ARGENTINA A GENDER ANALYSIS REVISITED

Francisco J. Díaz, María Alejandra Osorio, Ana Paola Paola Amadeo and Rogelio Biasella
Research Laboratory in New Information Technologies, Computer Science School. National University of La Plata Calle 50 y 120. La Plata (1900). Buenos Aires. Argentina

ABSTRACT

This article addresses gender in IT courses in the UNLP, taking into consideration multiple contexts:
a) The proportion of gender in STEM courses in the UNLP and specifically IT courses (these numbers are compared with a previous analysis from 2009).
b) Gender statistics in computer science courses in Argentina.
c) The international gender context globally and in the US in particular.
The paper also describes some of the actions carried out to promote the study of IT and perspective of young students about their future job prospects. Due to the fact that the women studying IT degrees in UNLP largely exceed by 60% the figures of national statistics these action are referred to as good practices for reducing gender gap.

KEYWORDS

Gender, STEM, young women, IT degree

1. INTRODUCTION

The gender dimension in science and technology became a hot topic in 2000 when it was adopted as one of the eight Millennium Development Goals [MDGs - UNESCO, 2017]. The relevance of promoting gender equality is evident, for example, in How the European Union or is Putting Gender Equality at the Heart of Horizon 2020 [EU, 2017].

In 2009, a study was carried out (Díaz et al, 2009) analyzing the situation of women in the academic units related to these disciplines at the National University of La Plata and the University of Zaragoza in Spain, with very similar results. This university currently has a Gender Observatory [University of Zaragoza, 2017], which includes publications and a monitoring of the subject at the university, including a thorough diagnosis of the problem which has resulted in the 1st Plan for Equality at the University of Zaragoza.

In the United States, the reality of gender issues is no different. Studies conducted by GirlsWhoCode [GirlsWhoCode, 2017], an NGO sponsored by IBM, Microsoft, Amazon, Accenture, among others, realized that only 4% of nationwide 1st year university students are women. In 1984, 37% of the graduates in Computer Science were women whereas at present this percentage does not reach 18%.

The World Economic Forum, in its Global Gender Gap Report of 2016, includes a chapter on STEM and gender, analyzing it from the importance of workforce and diversity and the needs of the sector to have professionals at short, medium and long term in this 4th Industrial Revolution.

The Harvard Business Review, in its article "Why Do So Many Women Who Study Engineering Leave the Field?" of April 2016 (Silvey, 2016), presents the results of a longitudinal study on the gender gap among students from MIT, UMass, Olin College of Engineering, and the Picker Engineering Program for girls at Smith College. The study, started in 2003 and then continued with the graduates, shows how socialization or learning of the "culture" of engineering affects the future employment of students.

For its part, the report published by the World Economic Forum attributes the causes of the small number of women studying and leaving STEM in general, to a lack of role models and the existence of negative stereotypes related to science and technology.

This article presents a comparative study of the UNLP, analyzing the offers that attract more women by examining the numbers of newcomers to courses taught at the Schools of Computer Science, Engineering, Exact Sciences and Computer Engineering during the year 2015, continuing with the descriptive study started in 2009, compared to the global situation in all universities of the country and comparing it with studies of the topic of gender and Computer Science in Argentina made by the Sadosky Foundation [Sadosky, 2017]. Likewise, results are presented regarding the first descriptive and exploratory studies of a qualitative and quantitative nature carried out on the subject, followed by an analysis of whether previous studies and the maximum level of study of the parents can be factors that define the choice. The paper also describes the activities carried out in the Computer Science School that mitigate the gap and allow statistics in the UNLP to be significantly better than the national and international average.

2. EVOLUTION OF THE STUDENTS BY GENDER IN COMPUTER SCIENCE, EXACT SCIENCES AND ENGINEERING

The National University of La Plata (UNLP, 2017) is 3rd in national ranking in number of students, with more than 100,000 students studying from Art to Engineering, Agricultural Sciences, Architecture, Law, Medicine, and IT, among others.

In 2009, study was conducted on the total amount of newcomers to courses given at the Schools of Exact Sciences, Engineering and Computer Science in the UNLP to identify the selection of women. This study showed that the women's preference was for the courses in the School of Exact Sciences, where women predominated in all courses except the B.Sc. in Physics.

In analyzing the new enrollees of 2015, the Secretary of University Policies of the Ministry of Education (Statistics, 2015), requested a different indicator of new enrollees for the first time, (which was not available in 2009). This new distribution for the different courses is presented in Figure 1. The first legends in bold belong to offers from the School of Exact Sciences, the following non - bold to the School of Computer Science, the following bold to the intersection between the Schools of Computer Science and Engineering and the following without bold to the School of Engineering.

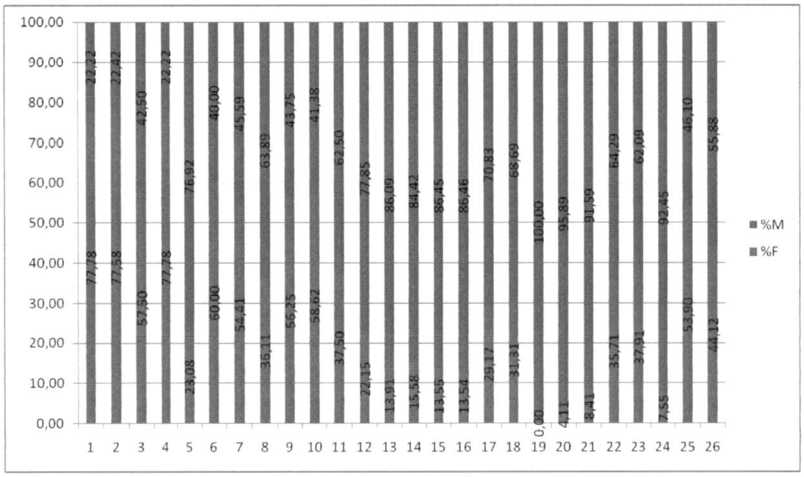

Figure 1. - 1. Pharmacology - 2. Biochemistry - 3. Biotechnology and Molecular Biology - 4. Food Science and Technology - 5. Physics - 6. Medical Physics - 7. Mathematics - 8. Chemistry - 9. Chemistry and Environmental Technology - 10. Ocular Optics and Optometry - 11. Chemistry Technology - 12. University Programming Analysis - 13. Computer Science - 14. Systems - 15. Computer Engineering - 16. Aeronautical Engineering - 17. Surveying Engineering - 18. Civil Engineering - 19. Electrical Engineering - 20. Electromechanical Engineering - 21. Electronic Engineering - 22. Hydraulic Engineering - 23. Industrial Engineering - 24. Mechanical Engineering - 25. Chemical Engineering - 26. Materials Engineering

Most new enrollees in 2015, total and for the first time, are in the School of Exact Sciences with 67.79% and 62.68% respectively, similar to the study by the authors in 2009 wherein the percentage was 65.84%. In 2009, the proportion of women was higher in almost every course.

If we analyze the choice of courses between the total first-time enrollees in the entry 2015 of the analyzed Schools, Figure 2 shows that the preference is the B.Sc. in Biochemistry (16%), followed by the B.Sc. in Biotechnology and Molecular Biology, Industrial Engineering and Chemical Engineering 9%. Less chosen were Electrical Engineering, Electromechanical Engineering and Chemistry Technology, this last course having such a low rate of enrolments due to it being an intermediate degree in a number of other courses. In the study conducted in 200 9 on the total number of new enrolments, women preferred Pharmacology first (20%) followed by the B.Sc. in Biochemistry (19.46%) and the B.Sc. in Systems (10.29%). In 2015, the new total registered for the B.Sc. in Systems represented only 2% of the female gender preference, in the same proportion as the B.Sc. in Computer Science and three points below University Programming Analysis (5%).

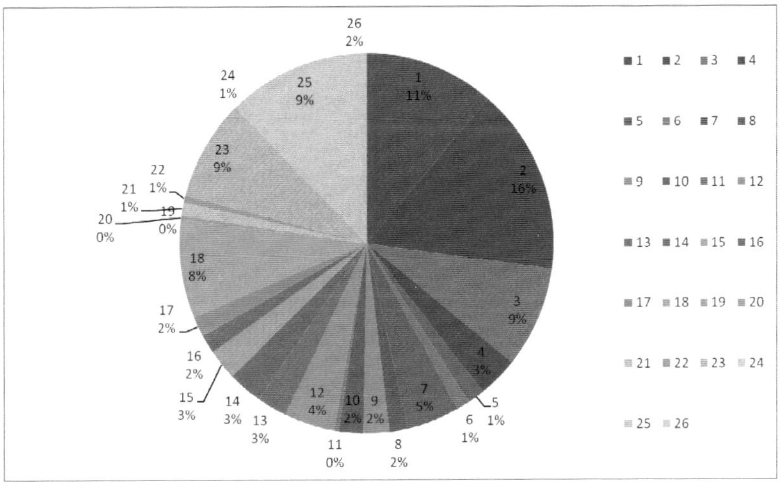

Figure 2. - Distribution of 2015 enrolments of women in UNLP courses - Pharmacology - 2. Biochemistry - 3. Biotechnology and Molecular Biology - 4. Food Science and Technology - 5. Physics - 6. Medical Physics - 7. Mathematics - 8. Chemistry - 9. Chemistry and Environmental Technology - 10. Ocular Optics and Optometry - 11. Chemistry Technology - 12. University Programming Analysis - 13. Computer Science - 14. Systems - 15. Computer Engineering - 16. Aeronautical Engineering - 17. Surveying Engineering - 18. Civil Engineering - 19. Electrical Engineering - 20. Electromechanical Engineering - 21. Electronic Engineering - 22. Hydraulic Engineering - 23. Industrial Engineering - 24. Mechanical Engineering - 25. Chemical Engineering - 26. Materials Engineering

Regarding students' graduation, in 2015, the proportion of women and men who complete their studies is similar to 2007, with more women than men in the Exact Sciences (65% vs 68% in the 2007), an improvement in Engineering (20% vs. 17.70% in 2007) similar to the United States where a gender survey at Bachelor's degree level shows women represent 20 % (NCES, 2015) and a significant decrease in Computer Science (20% vs. 32.29% in 2007). Computer Science and Engineering recorded their first graduates in the year 2013, with a significant difference, as can be observed in figure 3.

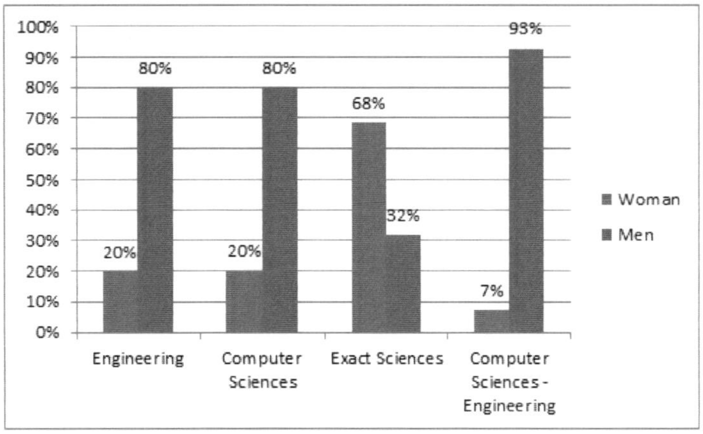

Figure 3. - 2015 graduates in the Schools of Computer Science, Engineering, Exact Sciences and Computer Science – Engineering. Relationship by gender

3. COURSES TAUGHT AT THE COMPUTER SCIENCE SCHOOL

Regarding the courses taught at the Computer Science School of the UNLP, in 2015, it was chosen by 17.28% of the total number of new students enrolled for the first time in the academic units analyzed. This percentage is higher than presented by the Sadosky Foundation (Sadosky, 2013) which made reference to the Scientific Computer (CC) course offered by the University of Buenos Aires (UBA). This university is the first in the country in number of students, but in 2013 it reported only 11% of new enrolments made by women. The study mentions that this was not always the case, as 70 to 75% of new CCs recorded were women. However, in 2000, less than 20% was recorded, with a negative tendency. These figures are lower than those of the UNLP, which show 19,53% in 2007 with a decline in new women enrolled, as shown in Table 1.

Table 1. Percentage of New Enrolments at the Computer Science School of the UNLP. 2007 vs 2015

Course	Total NE 2007	1st NE 2015	Total NE 2015
Computer Analyst / University Programming Analysis	23,53%	22,15%	17,85%
B.Sc. in Computer Science	15,98%	13,91%	13,94%
B.Sc. in Systems	21,50%	15,58%	14,42%

University Programming Analyst was launched in 2009 as an independent variation of Computing Analyst, closed in 2008. Both offers are the most chosen by females in the Computer Science sector, both in 2007 and in 2015 with 23,53% and 17,85% respectively. The course is shorter than the Bachelor's degrees and has a more professionally-oriented profile. The BS in Systems was launched in 2007, with a decrease since its inception, and some improvements in 2013 and 2014. It should be noted that the new offer from the joint School of Computer Science and Engineering was launched in 2010.

In the country there are numerous public and private universities that teach courses related to Computing, Information Technology and Technology, from the University of Tierra del Fuego in the south of the country to the University of Jujuy in the north. Analyzing the IT enrollment behavior in the country, we can observe that it is similar to the UNLP. The distribution according to gender in courses related to technology at country level is 16% for the year 2015 (SIU Araucano, 2015), with values slightly lower than the average of the Computer Science School of the UNLP (17.21%), which shows the state of gender concerns in the country.

The study of the Sadosky Foundation (Sadosky, 2015) shows that 22% of the sample (649 students in secondary public schools of the province of Buenos Aires) shows some potential for development in IT, but it is comprised of three times as many males as females. The partial study presented by these researchers reports a preference for complex games that require concentration, organization and strategic planning as a significant indicator among those that include software development as a potential course of studies (29% women vs. 35% male). In addition, analysis on primary computer use as related to information and programming yielded a 14% difference between the genders, as it was chosen by 24.5% of women vs 38.5% of males. They also claim that "The performances that keep women away from computer science are already stabilized in adolescence both among males and females. "

This difference in gender along Computer Science courses and the need in the country to train professionals in this sector is evidenced in the National plan 111mil of 2017 (11mil, 2017) or the previous project ProgramAR (Programar, 2017), requiring deep interdisciplinary analyses and activities that demystify and effect a cultural change that has a significant short- and long-term impact on teenagers and even children in primary schools.

4. ACTIONS OF THE COMPUTER SCIENCE SCHOOL TO PROMOTE STEM AMONG WOMEN

International Girls in ICT Day is an international event organized by the International Telecommunication Union (ITU) (ITU, 2017). It is a global effort to strengthen and promote the participation of girls and young women as ICT students and their future performance in this field (Girls ITU, 2017). This event has been held each year since 2011 and so far more than 177,000 young women have participated in more than 5300 meetings in 150 countries around the world. The Computer Science School, through its Gender Commission, joined this initiative in 2015, issuing the second edition of the event on April 27 of this year.

The first year of the event, in order to organize activities that are attractive for young women and to carry out an exploratory study to begin to investigate the causes of the low enrollment of women in the Computer Science School, the commission decided to conduct a survey of the students, both women and men. The questionnaire was issued to 169 students of the School: 124 men and 45 women, inquiring about the activities that they wanted to partake in before enrolling in the School, and the relationship between the genders, among other issues. Among the questions asked regarding the first aspect, "If you had had that opportunity ... do you think the activity would have helped you to adapt better to the School?" the answers show the importance that women give to become familiar with the subject, as can be seen in Figure 4.

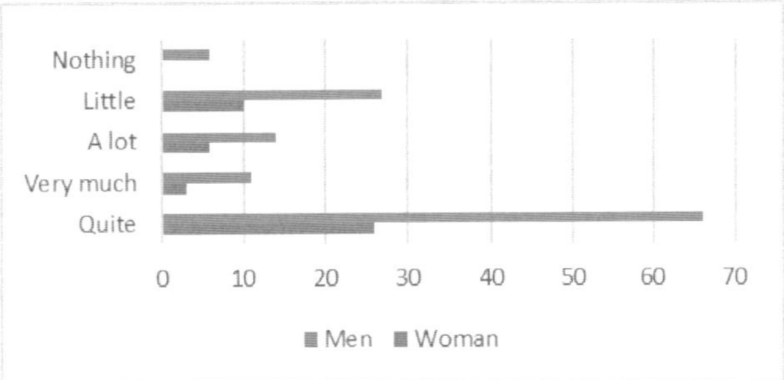

Figure 4. Evaluation of how helpful it is to carry out activities to become immersed in the School prior to enrolment, by gender

With regard to figure 4, it is worth noting that in proportion, most of the women responded Bastante (a lot) and none answered Nada (Nothing), a response selected by some men. This answer relates to the question: “Do you have any proposals to help encourage more girls to choose our courses?”. For the majority of the female students who attend the course, they refer to the lack of information not only regarding the contents of that course but also the different job opportunities. This is also confirmed by the Sadosky Foundation report where 63% of women stated not knowing what a computer program or piece of software is. In connection with the Harvard Business Review, at the beginning of the practice period they begin to wonder if engineering is really what they want. It is interesting to analyze the highest level of training of the parents of the girls who choose these types of courses and compare them with those who enroll in courses related to "Humanities" and careers related to "Individuals and Speech". Taking the new enrollees of the last 3 years, where the quality of the data allows to carry out this type of studies, we can conclude that the training of the parents is a differential factor between both groups, as can be observed in figure 5.

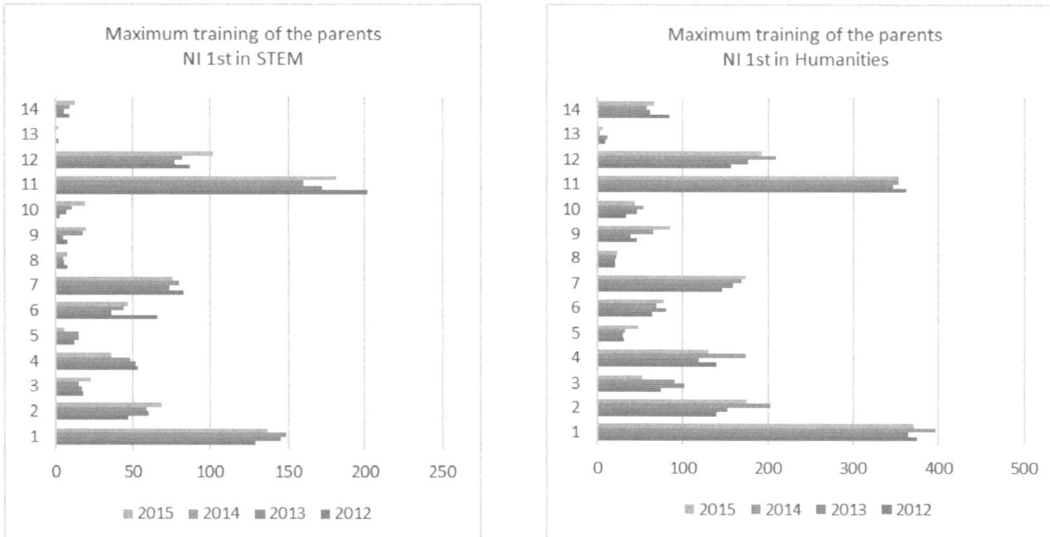

Figure 5. – Evolution of the newly-enrolled students in STEM vs the newly-enrolled students in Humanities and Social Sciences by highest level of training of the parents 1. Graduated secondary school – 2. Unfinished secondary school – 3. Unknown – 4. Finished primary school – 5. Unfinished primary school – 6. Graduate studies – 7. Higher education – 8. Unfinished higher education – 9. University or higher education – 10. Unfinished university or higher education – 11. University studies – 12. Unfinished university studies – 13. No studies – 14. Unfinished/Unknown

Knowing university life and the course offers and having passed through the classrooms could provide more information to the girls and would reduce this barrier or demystify the cultural construct in some way.

The analysis by sector of school, into the categories of public or private, also offers interesting information. While in the Humanities the trend indicates a greater influx of women from the state sector, converging in recent years, in Engineering, Computer Science, Engineering and Exact Sciences the tendency is that they come from privately-managed schools, as can be seen in figure 6.

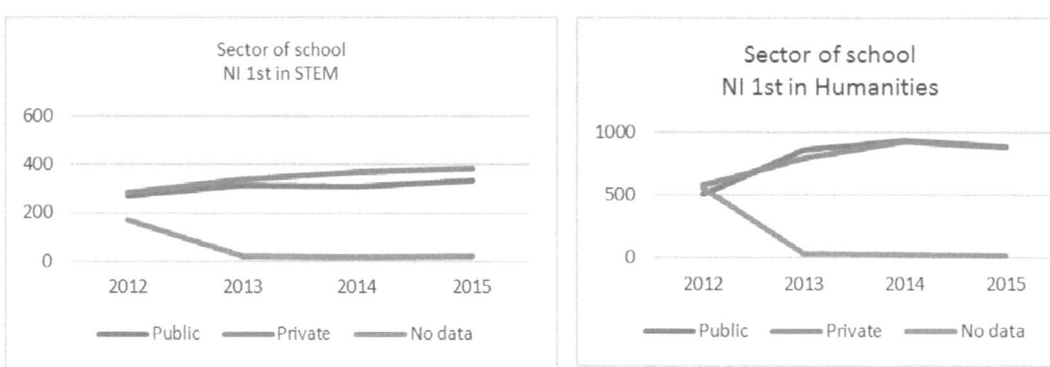

Figure 6. Evolution of newly-enrolled students in STEM vs newly-enrolled students in Humanities and Social Sciences by sector of the school of origin

They generally express that men have earlier Access to Computer Science than women, as expressed in the phrase "they can get their hands on it before we can". Examples, perspectives, expressive articulations are related to men such as Jobs, Gates, in films that are in the commercial circuit and both in popular science and academic articles. Women are not highlighted in these projects, so one of the suggestions offered by the students of the B.S. in Computer Science is to publicize those women who have excelled in projects and who have become leaders in this context. This lack of female models is also referred to in the World Economic Forum as one of the causes of the low rate of enrollment and permanence of women in STEM-related courses.

They propose to promote the different disciplines, to show society that it is not exclusive to "men" to relate to these types of careers. For them, they lack better publicity of the activities that women in the field of computer science partake in, and they propose a channel of communication that allows the professional exchange. On the other hand, they express that they are not informed of the different branches of the discipline, with many teenagers in their last years of secondary school thinking that the only possible practice is to program. It is interesting to note that it is in the basis of this reasoning where the answers lie to try to make a change in the cultural construct and in this way to establish gender equality. Girlswhocode gives a reference of this and their Summer Immersion Programs work in projects of art, storytelling, robotics, video games, apps and websites among other possibilities.

Also, the free question Did you have high school friends who would have liked to study Computer Science and could not get enough enthusiasm? Most of the women (22.22%) answered No, including interesting answers such as "I met people who believed that to excel in computing, you have to excel in the media, you have to be very intelligent. It would have to break down such myths and show that people who study computers are the same as people who study any other thing." Or "... women find it harder to keep up with studies, work and family. I think they feel more responsibility and it is very difficult to study, work and be a mother, so the first thing that gets left behind is their career." Both points are related to the previous answer, where it is necessary to give more diffusion to the scope and real possibilities of work insertion as women to demystify certain preconceptions and make a change in the socio-cultural construct that can promote actual gender equality. These same results also arise from the analysis of responses 6, 7 and 8 where the response of the female gender to the question - Why do you consider that your choice of career was a surprise to them? (Family, friends, friends) – the choice of career is related to a sociocultural construct.

5. CONCLUSIONS

The paper thoroughly describes the main issues in gender preferences in IT degrees not only in UNLP but in the national and international context.

Taking account these statistics we conclude that despite the action to promote girls into studying IT degrees the figures are low, despite the fact that UNLP are quite better than the national statistics both from the Fundacion Sadosky work and the Official Statistics from the Ministry of Education.

These low figures are global tendency that can also be observed at all argentine universities. The UNLP`s figures of gender distribution in IT degrees is better than the national and international standards. Some of the actions are also included in this article as a mean to contribute to a good practices standard for mitigating gender inequalities in TI studies. None the less we have to keep up promoting IT studying in both girls and boys overcoming the common miss concepts in IT degrees and IT labor market.

REFERENCES

Díaz et al, 2009. Díaz, Osorio, Amadeo, 2009, Trends in studying it degrees at National University of La Plata – Argentina. A gender analysis. *Northeast American Society of Engineering Education Conference. University of Bridgeport*. Bridgeport, Estados Unidos. http://catalogo.info.unlp.edu.ar/meran/opac-detail.pl?id1=6907 Last visit May 2017.

EU, 2017. *How the European Union is Putting Gender Equality at the Heart of Horizon* https://stemgenderequality.com/eu-putting-gender-equality-heart-horizon-2020/ Last visit May 2017.

Girls ITU, 2017. *Portal de Girls in ICT de ITU*, 12 http://girlsinict.org/es Last visit May 2017

GirlsWhoCode, 2017. https://girlswhocode.com/about-us/#the-problem. Last visit May 2017

Gloal Gender Gap Report, 2016. http://reports.weforum.org/global-gender-gap-report-2016/economies/#economy=ALB. World Economic Forum.

ITU, 2017. *What is Girls in ICT Day?* https://www.itu.int/en/ITU-D/Digital-Inclusion/Women-and-Girls/Girls-in-ICT-Portal/Pages/Portal.aspx Last visit May 2017

NCES, 2015. *Degrees in engineering and engineering technologies conferred by postsecondary institutions, by level of degree and sex of student: Selected years, 1949-50 through 2013-14 National Center for Education Statistics.* https://nces.ed.gov/programs/digest/d15/tables/dt15_325.45.asp Last visit May 2017

NSF, 2016. *National Science Fundation & National Center for Science and Engineering Statistics, special tabulations of U.S. Department of Education, National Center for Education Statistics, Integrated Postsecondary Education Data System Bachelor's degrees awarded, by citizenship, ethnicity, race, sex, and field: 2014* https://www.nsf.gov/statistics/2017/nsf17310/static/data/tab5-7.xlsx Last visit May 2017

Programar, 2017. http://program.ar/ Last visit May 2017

ODM – UNESCO, 2017. *Objetivos de Desarrollo del Milenio.* http://www.unesco.org/new/es/natural-sciences/environment/water/wwap/facts-and-figures/millennium-development-goals/. UNESCO. Last visit May 2017

Sadosky, 2013. *Y las mujeres.. ¿Dónde están?* http://www.fundacionsadosky.org.ar/wp-content/uploads/2015/05/resumen-mujeres-y-computacion-2013.pdf Last visit May 2017

Sadosky, 2015. Zukerfeld, Yansen & Dughera. *Género e informática. La relación de los jóvenes con la computadora. Un estudio empírico en el conurbano bonaerense.* http://sedici.unlp.edu.ar/bitstream/handle/10915/41821/Documento_completo.pdf?sequence=1 Last visit May 2017

Statistics, 2015. *Sistema de Consultas Universitarias.* http://estadisticasuniversitarias.me.gov.ar Last visit May 2017

Silvey, 2016. *Why Do So Many Women Who Study Engineering Leave the Field?* del mes de abril año 2016. *Harvard Business Review.* https://hbr.org/2016/08/why-do-so-many-women-who-study-engineering-leave-the-field

SIU Araucano, 2017 *Estadísticas Universitarias. Población de grado y pregrado.* http://estadisticasuniversitarias.me.gov.ar/#/seccion/1_Last visit May 2017.

University of Zaragoza, 2017. *Observatorio de Igualdad. Universidad de Zaragoza*, Zaragoza, España. https://observatorioigualdad.unizar.es/ Last visit May 2017.

UNLP, 2017. *Universidad Nacional de La Plata* http://unlp.edu.ar Last visit May 2017

11mil, 2017. *Proyecto 11mil.* https://www.argentina.gob.ar/111mil. Last visit May 2017

DESIGNING WORKPLACES FOR CONTROL ROOMS: A STUDY USING FOCUS GROUPS AND STAKEHOLDER INTERVIEWS

Elisabeth Weissenböck[1], Margit Pohl[1], Peter Judmaier[2], Andrea Viertelmayr[2] and Gernot Rottermanner[2]
[1]*Vienna University of Technology - Argentinierstraße 8, A-1040 Vienna, Austria*
[2]*St. Pölten University of Applied Sciences - Mathias Corvinus-Straße 15, A-3100 St. Pölten, Austria*

ABSTRACT

Control rooms for supervising traffic or emergency situations are increasingly introduced in companies and other governmental organisations. Employees of safety-critical workplaces have to deal with a large amount of problems every day: Quick decision-making, coping with an overload of information and stress are the most important. Designing appropriate workplaces for employees in such organisations is essential. The following paper provides the results of focus groups and stakeholder interviews which were conducted in two companies with control rooms regarding these issues.

KEYWORDS

Interface design, large screens, gender, evaluation

1. INTRODUCTION

Supervising complex processes in industry and governmental organisations is an increasingly important research area. Power plants, traffic control, and the organisation of emergency and rescue operations require a close control. Computer technology is typically used to achieve this. It is clear that the supervision of such processes is a challenging activity and has to be supported appropriately. In this context the design of the workplaces of control room operators plays a crucial role so that the attention of these employees is maximised and stress minimised. A specific challenge in this context is, for example, the fact that control room operators work with large screens. Therefore, information has to be presented in a way so that the necessary data can be perceived immediately. In addition, gender issues have to be taken into account. It is an open question whether the appropriate design of control room workplaces can help to make them more attractive for women.

The investigation presented in this paper addresses these issues. On the one hand, we studied, more generally, how the physical design of the workplace influences the work of the control room operators. In this context, we are especially interested in the design of the interfaces of the large screens which are used in control rooms. In addition, we also addressed more general issues of workplace organisation (choice of chairs, personalisation of workplaces,...). We did not specifically address the issue of work organisation, although we would like to point out that these issues are related to each other.

We also addressed, more specifically, the issue whether physical workplace design might be one factor which is responsible for the lack of women in control rooms. There is some indication in the literature that under some circumstances women might prefer a different interface design than men.

The research described in this paper was conducted in the context of a research project. We were lucky to be able to cooperate with two organisations which permitted us access to control room operators who were willing to participate in this study. It is well known that such access is difficult to get, therefore, our results are especially valuable.

2. DESCRIPTION OF THE PROJECT

The aim of the project GenSiSys was to analyse the work in control rooms and also to develop a set of recommendations how to evaluate gender and diversity aspects in safety-critical workplaces regarding needs and requirements of employees in ergonomics and human computer interaction..

Safety- critical workplaces are systems where decisions, actions or mistakes by operators and controllers directly affect human lives. Working at a safety-critical workplace means to make quick decisions, coping with an overload of information and stress.

We were lucky to find two very open and cooperative partners which provided the project team with comprehensive support. One of the partners was the 144 emergency call control centre of Lower Austria (144 Notruf Niederösterreich) in St. Pölten. The other partner was the operations management centre of the Austrian Federal Railways (ÖBB).

In the context of the project, we conducted an extensive review of the literature. Based on this, we developed 19 issues which have to be taken into account when investigating the physical work environment of control room operators. We also identified a set of research methods from Social Sciences and Hum an-Computer Interaction which are appropriate for the investigation of these issues. In the following, we present one of the studies we conducted during the project which is based on a subset of the issues mentioned above and two methods – focus groups and stakeholder interviews.

3. RELATED WORK

There are several features of systems deployed in control rooms which influence the quality of the work of the operators.

Size of the display: Large displays raise challenging new questions concerning interface design. One of the most important problems which may arise in this context is the fact that humans only perceive a small portion of the screen with high acuity (change blindness, inattentional blindness). Due to the size of the screen it may happen that relevant parts of the information is not perceived by the user. Mancero et al (2007) discuss empirical results concerning these issues. They argue that change blindness can have negative effects on the efficiency of users of large displays. They point out that there are several aspects which have to be taken into account. Slow changes, for example, are difficult to perceive. Changes which happen outside the focus of attention of the users are often overlooked. Saliency of important information should be aimed at. In addition, they also point out that meaning and relevance play an important role.

Complexity of the System: Providing the user with the right information and visualisation at the right time is necessary for prompt decision making. It is therefore important to support users to deal with a complex system. A complex system provides a large amount of information from heterogeneous sources and a great variability of interaction possibilities. On average, simplicity of a system is more important to women than men (Stadler, 2006). A high complexity of the system often leads to stress.

Decision making: Men and women *"... both carefully process information, retrieve the relevant decision-related data from their memories, categorize the data if they are very diverse, think logically about the alternatives, predict results, evaluate the consequences, solve the problems posed by the situation, and monitor all the decision stages"* (Sanz de Acedo Lizárraga et al. 2007, p. 387). Making fast decisions and analysing data seem to be more important for men, whereas women, on average, seem to take more time and are more worried about the consequence of their decisions (it doesn't matter if the decision has an influence on themselves or others) (Reiter, 2013).

Design of the displays: In control rooms, the usage of large displays has increased (Pohl, 2013). It is very challenging to find relevant information on large displays. Large displays with a wide field of view can support both women and men, although women benefit more (Czerwinski et al. 2002). Icons are a way to provide users with important information: it is necessary to use simple figures which are easy to recognize for the user, and they should be used when the user's interaction is required (Yu & He, 2010). Not only in control rooms, also in emergency medical situations icons have to be promptly recognized (Salman et al. 2012): to guarantee that, it is a viable option to design and implement icons together with the users. This cooperation of user and designer is necessary to achieve an reliable recognition of an icon (Gatsou et al. 2011).

Personalisation: According to (Wells, 2000) personalisation of workplaces can have a positive impact on job satisfaction and well-being. Ease of use and usefulness of software can be positively influenced by personalisation (Henriksen & Pedersen, 2009).

Stress: Stress as a factor influencing the work of operators in control rooms has been discussed extensively, e.g. in the context of nuclear power plants. Desaulniers (1997) provides a general discussion of stress in control rooms. He discusses the consequences of stress (narrowing of attention, reduced working memory capacity, …) and possibilities to reduce the number of stressful situations in control rooms (training, improved procedure design, …). Farkas et al (2011) point out the importance of reducing the operator's mental load to ensure that he or she can react efficiently in emergency situations. Mukherjee et al (2010) discuss the design of control rooms, especially the trend to reduce the amount of information which is presented to the operator. In this context, some of the tasks which were carried out manually by operators were taken over by computers, especially repetitive and monotonous tasks. This leads to a reduction in panel complexity. In this way, stress can be reduced.

4. DESCRIPTION OF THE INVESTIGATION

The goal of the investigation described in this paper is to identify how workplaces for employees in control rooms can be improved to reduce stress and increase the efficiency of their work. The work described in this paper focuses on this issue and does not address the problem of work organisation, but both issues are, of course, related to each other.

Our research goal was to identify which factors concerning the workplace influence the quality of the work of operators in control rooms. We were especially interested how the design of the system affected the decision making process. We assumed that stress is an important factor in this context. The research questions were developed as a result of an extensive literature study by experts from different fields (usability experts, ergonomics experts, cognitive psychologists, gender studies experts).

There are several possibilities how the quality of the design of the workplace could be investigated. We think that the employees' views and attitudes plays an important role in this context, therefore we chose focus groups and stakeholder interviews as research methodologies. We conducted three focus groups with control room operators of two organisations. We conducted focus groups with the operators because we were interested in the discussion among these employees and the shared sensemaking processes. In addition, we conducted interviews with stakeholders from management to clarify their view of the issues related to the work processes in control rooms. We decided to conduct interviews with the managers because we also wanted to discuss more sensitive issues with them which could not be discussed in a group.

4.1 Focus Groups

Focus groups are group discussions. They are a form of qualitative research (Kuniavsky 2003). A facilitator using guidelines asks participants questions they can and should discuss. Possible ambiguities can be removed through repeated discussion of an issue. One main advantage of focus groups is that unclear or controversial issues can be clarified in the discussion. Sometimes, problems occur when single participants in focus groups dominate the discussion. Facilitators can mitigate this phenomenon by encouraging all participants to share their thoughts with the others.

While using experiments in safety-critical systems, special conditions have to be considered: operators cannot leave their workplace for long. In many situations, tests can only be conducted after the employee's shift, which often lasts 12 hours, or during a break. Therefore we were glad to get the chance that a considerable number of employees took time to participate in the focus groups. It has been a great advantage for our work to get to know employees and to talk about their problems, issues and needs in a real setting.

Based on the literature, these were the questions we asked:

Ergonomics: Are you satisfied with your chair?

Complexity of the systems: On the one hand there are systems which provide many features and are therefore difficult to learn and master, on the other hand there are systems which have fewer features and are therefore less error-prone, easy to learn but do not provide many features. How would you describe your system?

Decision making: How do you make decisions in situations where you have to act as quickly as possible?

Displays: How do you get along with many/big displays? Do you ever have the feeling of overlooking something important? Are there any ambiguities in the software? (Icons, shortcuts,...) Do they lead to delays? Are mistakes made because of unclear icons? Are there any parts of the software where graphics should replace text or vice versa? If so, why?

Personalisation of software: Which parts of the software can be personalized? Do you use it? What do you use personalisation for? Is there a need for more? If so, why and where?

Stress: How would you describe your stress level at work? Which actions or times of day are most stressful? Do parts of the software stress you? How do you cope with stress, do you take stress home? If you think of a typical work day, when are the most stressful situations?

4.1.1 Focus Group NNÖ (Emergency Control Centre)

At "Notruf NÖ" two focus groups with a total of eight participants were conducted; four male and four female. Complexity of the used system, decision making, orientation/coping with many screens and stress seem to be the most interesting themes.

Employees are in general satisfied with the software because it is continually developed further and their feedback is taken into account. Nevertheless, there is some controversy in the group: Long-term employees have grown with the software. In contrast to that, newer employees have to get used to the system, the features and the processes fairly quickly. The common opinion concerning the complexity of the system is that it is directly linked to the main task. There are, basically, two groups of employees – call takers and dispatchers. Call takers receive emergency calls and decide which action has to be taken; dispatchers organise all activities (e.g. ambulances which are sent to a road accident). Call takers do not need as many functions as the dispatchers because they do not need all of them for their work. Most of the dispatchers are highly experienced females, whereas the call takers are younger males.

Decision making is a very important part of the participant's job; they think that the system provides the right amount of support. Participants, who have worked for a longer period of time for Notruf think they have no problem with choosing the right protocol when it comes to an emergency call (every emergency has its own protocol, so they can ask the caller the right questions and provide help), whereas less experienced employees are not always that sure. If there is a difficult decision to master, they are never left entirely on their own: asking a colleague or the shift supervisor for help is always an option.

Call takers use two displays whereas dispatchers have got four displays which provide them with different information: the first is for transportation, the second for showing ambulances, the third for the map and the fourth is for additional information. The prevailing opinion is that, due to the fixed places of the displays, it is clear which display provides which information.

Stress seems to be the most important issue of the two focus groups, due to the diversity of stress factors: medical service which starts at 7 pm, the wish for more personnel and issues regarding the building (e.g. heat) are mentioned as stress factors. In Lower Austria, it is possible to get advice from a physician after 7 p.m. via the Notruf, either on the telephone or, in emergency cases, the physician will visit the patient at home. This leads to an increased workload for the call takers after 7 p.m. and acts as an additional stress factor.

Four participants mentioned that the building, a low-energy house, is not ideal: sometimes it is too warm; high levels of noise are also a problem. The participants did not just talk about stress factors; they also were trying to find solutions during the focus group: a resting place, power napping and separated rooms were suggestions which came up in the discussion.

4.1.2 Focus Group ÖBB (Austrian Federal Railway)

At the ÖBB one focus group with six participants was conducted; three of them male and three female. Four topics were addressed: complexity of the used system, decision making, icons and stress.

Participants use many different systems; the prevailing opinion is that systems which are used often are well known. Systems are kept simple, but most systems are quite comprehensive. Employees are rather satisfied with the operation of the systems and are not overwhelmed by the features these systems provide. One participant observed that the telephone provides too many features; most of them are not used often which can lead to a tedious search.

Personalising the screens is very important for the employees to make it easier for them to find all information they need in emergency situations. One participant mentioned that he/she moved unnecessary information to the top right screen because he/she knows that this is his/her "blind spot". The disadvantage of personalisation is that employees cannot use another person's workplace easily, as they need to log out and then in with their own profile

Icons which are needed in safety-critical situations are well known; an icon catalog provides help if needed. Disturbances are shown in yellow unless they are acknowledged. A blue signal indicates a track disturbance and a textbox shows which trains are affected and which measures should be taken. A search function is a proposal of one of the participants and is approved by the others.

Stress can go from zero to hundred very quickly, it depends on the disturbance. Malfunction of the switch, construction works and conservation work are mentioned as typical disturbances. Participants think that an update of the database is stressful, because they cannot access the information system during that process. Most disturbances are handled on the phone, so a failure of the telephone system would also lead to a stressful situation.

4.1.3 Discussion

In our study the number of participants is too small to make a general statement about gender. Nevertheless, we think that we can clarify some methodological issues for research in this environment and, in addition, indicate some areas where further research is necessary. We identified four areas which are relevant for the design of workplaces: complexity of the system, decision making, navigation/personalisation, and stress.

In general, employees in the control rooms we investigated were quite happy with the systems they used. This indicates that the problem of designing large displays for control rooms is not as challenging as is discussed in the literature (Mancero et al 2007). This is to a certain degree dependent on the experience they already have. A few minor usability issues were mentioned. Personalisation is used to counteract possible negative effects of these large displays. This seems to be a possible solution for some of the problems of large displays. Decision making processes are fairly well supported by the systems. The employees also mentioned that cooperation between employees is very important for reliable decision making. Stress is mentioned as the most important problem by employees from both organizations, although it is more relevant for Notruf than for ÖBB. The participants of the focus groups not only discussed stress but also made interesting suggestions how this could be overcome.

Gender does not seem to be a factor which is highly relevant for workplace design in this context. We could not identify indications that there are different approaches based on gender as has been suggested in the literature. We would also like to point out that Notruf is a specific kind of organization because a considerable amount of operators, especially the dispatchers who have more responsibilities than the call takers, are mostly women. These women feel very comfortable with a fairly complex system. This also indicates that the situation in control rooms is not as stereotyped as can be expected from the literature.

4.2 Stakeholder Interviews

Stakeholder interviews offer, in combination with other evaluation methods, in particular with a focus group, a high gain in knowledge (Bortz & Döring 2006, Goodwin 2009). The analysis can be done in areas such as work environment, workplace design, software interaction, stress perception and problem awareness. The two perspectives (stakeholder, focus group) decrease the risk of a one-sided analysis. Furthermore, stakeholder interviews are characterized by low cost in equipment, as only sound recording (e.g. with a voice recorder or mobile phone) is necessary. The interviews can be conducted by a single person who should have experience in negotiation (clear language and skills in conversation techniques). Unlike other methods - contextual inquiry, for example - this method is not tied to the actual workplace, but rather can take place wherever the requirements for a confidential, undisturbed conversation are provided.

While there are quite some advantages, there are also a few disadvantages. For one, the organisation of appointments for the stakeholder interviews and working on an interview outline can be quite time-consuming. Evaluating the recorded interviews is also rather laborious, as they ought to be transcribed or at least summarized. The aggregation of the results and the knowledge analysis is yet another time consuming-task.

4.2.1 Stakeholder Interview NNÖ (Emergency Control Centre)

The three main topics of the three stakeholder interviews conducted at "Notruf NÖ" in Lower Austria were workplace, stress level and work atmosphere.

One of the challenges stated in these interviews was to acquire appropriate chairs to ensure that employees can sit comfortably for as long as possible. At the control rooms employees can choose between three different types of chairs by various manufacturers. Though, these chairs do not always comply with the various requirements of the employees. To reduce the quantity of information, the work environment itself is characterized by a low amount of monitors and the possibility to personalise the software environment to one's specific needs. Furthermore, usage of the colour red in the user interface was reduced, as important elements did no longer stand out enough.

The main focus concerning the topic stress level was the work load (processing emergency calls and dispatching vehicles), especially when dealing with extensive emergencies. So, the primary goal is to improve the standardized procedure (Advanced Medical Priority Dispatch Systems – AMPDS), that the semi-automated decision process can help reducing the stress level for employees. Furthermore, measures like basic & advanced training and pre- and post-care are offered, and simulated situations are being run through to increase experience and help in turning tasks into a routine more quickly.

The interviewed stakeholders put emphasis on the fact that the equal gender ratio makes for great teamwork in the individual teams. The balance is due to the fact that the percentage of women and men working as paramedics is even, and these are the people mainly applying for a job in an emergency control room.

4.2.2 Stakeholder Intervew ÖBB (Austrian Federal Railway)

In the interviews, carried out with four stakeholders of the Austrian Federal Railways, four topics seem to be relevant. These topics are ergonomic issues concerning the work places, the monitors themselves at the workplace, and coping with stress and the work atmosphere.

Almost all of the employees use the possibility to set up an individual workplace for their requirements during their shift. This encompasses the desk height which can be adapted to sitting or standing posture or the content of the monitor of the 10 monitors, and the colour of the track lines, which show the location of the trains in real time. The profile of an employee is active when they log into their account at their workplace.

As mentioned every employee has 10 monitors to interact with, although some of them only use around five of them, as the work profile of the dispatcher varies and includes diverse needs. The occupational health care and the transport inspection limited the monitors to 10 in regard to the limit of the coverage possibility of a human being.

The employee's work in an open plan office and the background noises, which naturally come with this form of work organisation, were mentioned by some interviewed stakeholders, as kind of disturbing. In general, trainings are seen as support for the employees as well as the cooperation among each other, especially from seniors to younger colleagues.

4.2.3 Discussion

Interview partners in the stakeholder interviews talked mostly about ergonomic issues and stress. They pointed out that workplaces can be arranged individually to make it easier for the employees to work in front of computer screen for several hours and to enable them to concentrate on their work. Operators can choose between different types of chairs, change the height of their tables, personalise the contents of their screens etc. Screens and interfaces are designed in a way to support human perception (e.g. reduction of the number of screens, avoidance of the colour red). Both organisations adopt measures to reduce stress (improved protocols, training). Stakeholders from Notruf especially pointed out the gender balance in their organisation in control rooms.

5. CONCLUSION

The goal of the study presented in this paper is the analysis of workplaces in control rooms. The emphasis was on the design of the computer interfaces and the physical design of the workplaces. We conducted focus groups with employees and interviews with the managers. This provides us with the possibility to look at the challenges of the design of control rooms from different perspectives. The employees tended to discuss these issues from the point of view of their personal experience. In general, they were satisfied with the interface design of the software systems they used and had no major problems with the system. Working with large screens does not pose specific problems. Based on existing literature, we had expected that working with large screens would pose more serious problems. The interview partners mentioned several possibilities how to cope with the large amount of information provided by large screens (especially personalisation and appropriate screen design). The major problem mentioned in both organisations was stress, especially in Notruf. The managers discussed these issues from a leadership perspective and mentioned various measurements taken to alleviate the problem of stress (training, collaboration among employees, improvement of protocols).

It is well-known that the employees in most control rooms are predominantly male. Therefore, we also addressed the question whether aspects of the interface design or the physical organisation of the workplace favour male employees. In our investigation, we could not find such aspects. We would like to point out, however, that one of the organisations we cooperated with had an even distribution of women and men as control room employees. On the one hand, this might have influenced our results. On the other hand, it indicates that the work of operators does not per se have a "male" character.

Conducting studies in control rooms poses specific challenges. It is one of the advantages of this investigation that, thanks to the cooperation with the two organisations, we had access to a considerable number of control room employees. Due to their workload it is, in general, not possible to conduct investigations with this type of employees during working hours. Therefore, focus groups and interviews are appropriate methods for this kind of investigation. We found, that we were able to gain interesting insights into their work processes and the specific problems they have.

One limitation of this study is the fact that we were only able to conduct focus groups and stakeholder interviews with a limited number of persons. This makes it difficult to generalise these results. Nevertheless, we would like to point out that it is extremely difficult to find interview partners in this area. Therefore, this study is still a relevant contribution to the field. Another limitation is that we did not investigate work organisation and relationship among employees. It can be assumed that gender issues are more easily visible in this area. Nevertheless, we did not want to mix up these two issues (design of workplaces and work organisation). There is less research concerning gender issues in the design of computer interfaces and more general in the layout of the workplace, therefore we wanted to investigate this issue in more detail.

Further research concerning these topics is necessary. One possibility in this context would be to conduct a study with more participants from other organisations. In addition, it would be valuable to include additional questions, as for example, organisational issues and also additional aspects from the area of ergonomics. It would also be interesting to study the workflow of the employees in more detail to get more objective data on the interaction processes of the participants with the IT systems.

ACKNOWLEDGEMENT

The project GenSiSys was funded by the Austrian Ministry for Transport, Innovation & Technology, FEMtech 2nd call.

REFERENCES

Bortz, J., Döring, N., 2006. *Forschungsmethoden und Evaluation für Human- und Sozialwissenschaftler*. 4.Auflage, Springer, Heidelberg, Deutschland.

Czerwinski M., Tan, D.S., Robertson, G.G., 2002. Women Take a Wider View. *Proceedings of the SIGCHI Conference on Human Factors in Computing Systems*, pp. 195-202.

Desaulniers, David R., 1997. Stress in the control room: effects and solutions. *Proceedings of the 1997 IEEE Sixth Conference on Human Factors and Power Plants,* pp. 14/1-14/5.

Farkas, Z., Mischinger, G., Szabó, G., 2011. Auxiliary information system applications to support control room operator activities. *Proceedings of the 2nd International Conference on Cogntive Infocommunications*, pp. 1-6.

Gatsou, C., Politis, A., Zevgolis, D., 2011. From icons perception to mobile interaction. *Proceedings of the Federated Conference on Computer Science and Information Systems*, pp. 705-710.

Goodwin, K., 2009. *Designing for the Digital Age: How to Create Human-Centered Products and Services.* Wiley, Indianapolis, USA.

Mancero, G., Wong, W., Amaldi, P., 2007. Looking but Not Seeing: Implications for HCI. *Proceedings of the ECCE 2007* Conference, pp.28-31.

Henriksen, A., Pedersen, P.E., 2009. Enterprise portal personalization: Direct and indirect end-user effects, and the moderating effects of gender. *Proceedings of the 42nd Hawaii International Conference on System Sciences*, pp. 1-10.

Kuniavsky, M., 2003. *Observing the User Experience.* Morgan Kaufmann, San Francisco, San Diego, New York.

Mukherjee, S., Gandhi, S., Koley, J., Rao, S.N., 2010. Regulatory and safety aspects of Control Room design in Indian NPPs – criteria & practices. *Proceedings of the 2nd International Conference on Reliability, Safety and Hazard (ICRESH).*

Pohl, M., 2013. Organising Information on Big Walls – Human Perception and Large Displays. In: Rester, M., et al. (eds.), *Collaborative Human-Computer Interaction with Big Wall Displays – BigWallHCI2013*. Luxembourg: Publication Office of the European Union, pp. 9-11.

Reiter, K.R., 2013. *Gender Differences in Decision Making When Faced with Multiple Options*. College of Saint Benedict and Saint John's University.

Salman, Y.B., Cheng H., Patterson P.E., 2012. Icon and user interface design for emergency medical information systems: A case study. *International Journal of Medical Informatics* 81, pp. 29-35.

Sanz de Acedo Lizárraga, M.L., Sanz de Acedo Baquedano, M.T., Cardelle-Elawar, M., 2007. Factors that affect decision making: gender and age differences. *International Journal of Psychology and Psychologial Therapy* 7/3, 381-391.

Stadler, H., 2006. Technik und Geschlecht. Wege zu einer gendersensitiven Technikausbildung. In Erharter, D. (ed.): *Gender Mainstreaming in Bildungseinrichtungen*. St. Pölten: Verlag Forum Neue Medien, pp. 73-89.

Wells, M.M., 2000. Office clutter or meaningful personal displays: the role of office personalization in employee and organizational well-being. *Journal of Environmental Psychology*, 20/3, pp. 239-255.

Yu, Y. & He, J., 2010. An Analysis of Users' Cognitive Factors Towards Icon in Interactive Interface. *Proceedings of the Second International Conference on Intelligent Human-Machine Systems and Cybernetics*, pp. 26-28.

THE EFFECT OF FLIPPED CLASSROOM WITH PEER INSTRUCTION ON ESL STUDENTS' READING COMPREHENSION AND ENGAGEMENT

Hani Alhasani, Fauzy Wan Mohd and Mona Masoof
University of Science, Malaysia

ABSTRACT

This study investigated the effects of a pioneering pedagogical approach, Flipped Learning (FL) on undergraduate students during English reading comprehension and engagement. A framework was designed to measure the students' engagement while a pre-test and post-test was administered for comprehension. The method requires the students to visit and use the Learning Management System, LMS (Moodle) in their own time and was later questioned on what they learned and how they approached the given task. During the class time, participants were grouped whereby peer instruction (PI) was conducted. Results show that FLO group showed positive results than FLPI group in both achievement test and engagement questionnaire due to its simplicity for students which keep them active with instructors' feedback. Furthermore, there was a significant interaction effect for engagement between the flipped learning modes by gender with females reporting higher engagement.

KEYWORDS

Flipped learning, Framework, Achievement, Engagement, F2F, peer instruction, Reading Comprehension

1. INTRODUCTION

Flipped Learning (FL) can be defined as a class where the homework and the lecture have been reversed; alternatively, the lecture that have traditionally taken place inside the classroom and moves to take place outside the classroom and vice versa so that students engage more deeply (Giannakos, Krogstie, & Aalberg, 2016; Holmes, Tracy, Painter, Oestreich, & Park, 2015; Szparagowski, 2014). Students are provided with online material in order to gain the necessary knowledge before class, while class time is devoted to active leaning (Berrett, Mangan, Neshyba, Talbert, & Young, 2015), and the application of content in the form of peer instruction (henceforth, PI). The course content, which is provided for self-study, may be delivered in the form of video casts, PDF, Lecture Maker, PowerPoint slides pre-class reading and exercises, while class time is mainly used for group work activities. In general, student engagement is concerned with interaction between time, energy and other resources, by the students and their institutions for the purposes of optimizing the student experience and improving learning outcomes, student development, achievement, and the reputation of the institution (Trowler, 2010).

The 2015 Gallup Student Poll defined engagement as, "the involvement in and enthusiasm for school. Engaged students are excited about what's happening at their school and what they're learning. These students contribute to the learning environment, and they are psychologically committed to their school." ("Gallup Student Poll Engaged Today — Ready For Tomorrow Fall 2015 Survey Results," 2016, p.3)

PI in this paper is a simple way to incorporate some genuine interaction and engagement in lectures. It is cheap, simple to implement, and delivers useful feedback to both students and to the lecturer. All the students in the class were grouped into 4 peers sharing with others their knowledge; then "vote" on the answer to the question either by flash cards, or by show of hands (Mazur, 1997).

1.1 Problem Statement

To address this gap, professors/instructors require to design and coordinate teaching activities that engage students and require a cultivation of interactive participation, focusing on concepts and insuring that the students understand the material (Steele, 2015).

Regarding reading comprehension in ESL Malaysian context, factors such as low level proficiency of the English language, and low interest are those often mentioned by researches as contributing towards students' English language problems (Normazidah et al., 2012). Based on the constructs of student engagement such as "student-faculty interaction" and "active learning", the same scenario of disengagement can be observed in Malaysian universities. Moreover, student engagement is a requirement for learning (Mo, Singh & Chang, 2013), so schools that want to increase achievement often focus on this foundational need. Dutton (2015) highlighted that participants often rely on ordinary tools, for instance, LMS due to its familiarity and time saving nature; hence, technology can be effectually enabled to instructive objectives as well as increasing student engagement in university-level humanities education.

The personal experience frequency increases in flipped classroom environments using certain activities such as forming groups of active learners, learning by analysis engagement, and evaluation and synthesis engagement; more than passive learners who learn by collecting information from watching and listening videos (Jensen, Kummer, & Godoy, 2015; Shimamoto, 2012). Studies on flipping learning, however, have mostly focused on general subject areas, such as mathematics (Fulton, 2012), and pharmacotherapy (Pierce & Fox, 2012), rather than language learning. Therefore, its effectiveness in the English language teaching (ELT) setting still remains scarce (Han, 2015). For this reason, the current study perhaps will give a better idea on student engagement in public higher institutions and filling the gap in the literature in this area. Limited research has been conducted on how instructors can motivate and engage students in active participation and critical discussions in-class within flipped learning environment, as well as how technology can assist in that direction (Giannakos, Krogstie & Chrisochoides, 2016). The study deals directly with students' engagement and in Malaysian public university are even scant.

2. RESEARCH MODEL

The research Model is constructed and linked based on a number of theories and models from the literature. In this study, some of the key suggested models of this research are:

2.1 Community of Inquiry Theory (CoI)

The Community of Inquiry (CoI) theoretical framework represents a process of creating a deep, experiential and meaningful engaging learning experience through the development of three interdependent elements– social, cognitive and teaching presence. Firstly, social presence is "the ability of participants to identify with the community, communicate purposefully in a trusting environment, and develop inter-personal relationships by way of projecting their individual personalities" (Garrison, 2009). Secondly, cognitive Presence is the extent to which learners are able to construct and confirm meaning through sustained reflection and discourse (Garrison, Anderson, & Archer, 2000). Thirdly, teaching presence is the design, facilitation, and direction of cognitive and social processes for the purpose of realizing personally meaningful and educationally worthwhile learning outcomes (Anderson, Rourke, Garrison, & Archer, 2000). The CoI framework addressed an apparent need to provide order and a methodology to study the growing phenomena of online and blended learning (Garrison, Anderson, & Archer, 2010); thus, as the flipped learning is a part of blended learning, it can be applicable for the framework of this paper.

2.2 Nicol and Macfarlane (2006) Feedback Model

Nicol and Macfarlane-Dick (2006) present a framework of seven principles of good feedback practice and methods and techniques, which extend beyond written comments, to support each of the principles. Nicol *et al.* (2006) suggests that students are already engaged in self-assessment when they engage with the assessment task in hand, and to further this, students could reflect on the kind of feedback they would want on the work, and providing assessment of their work. Their work is built on the idea that feedback should strengthen the student's capacity to self-regulate their own performance and contribute to the student's ability to learn for the longer term. Nicol (2010) proposes that feedback should be conceptualized as a dialogue between teacher-student and/or peer-to-peer where meaning is constructed, as dialogue is fundamental to successful learning and teaching.

The eight factors in this study, namely learner goals, tactics and strategies; personal knowledge; shared knowledge; social presence; cognitive presence; teaching presence; Web were distributed in the theoretical framework (Figure 1) based on CoI theory by (Garrison & Anderson, & Archer, 2000) and formative assessment model by Nicol and Macfarlane (2006). The framework essentially needed the trust dimension under social presence because it's important for participatory environment in the class tasks. Trust is another factor affecting knowledge sharing within groups. Based on Brown and Skinner (2007), trust was defined as the degree to which a group member believes his/her partners work well with each other.

All these dimensions were applied for the new framework for this study. These factors were divided and classified with the components of the following: a) Student Goals/Tactics and Strategies/Outcomes, b) Social Presence, c) Trust, d) LMS, e) Cognitive Presence, f) Personal Knowledge, g) Shared Knowledge, and h) Teaching presence. The conceptual framework of this study, modified from Nicol *et al.* (2006) and Garrison et al. (2000) is presented in Figure 1.

In this study, based on the conceptual framework, student engagement is divided into 3 parts:

1. Individual engagement consists of cognitive presence elements, namely, student goals, strategies, tactics, use of LMS and personal knowledge. As the instructor set a task, the students follow the instructions and ask the quizzes regularly. The individual tack occurs when the students goes through the internal processes by checking their tasks on the LMS, getting cognitive presence by: a student task, tactics, follows with outcomes to be wrapped up as a final personal knowledge.

2. Social presence engagement consists of social presence, trust, and shared knowledge. In that part, the students socialize their learning by having new tentative knowledge for sharing their answers together in peers either on LMS or in the class.

3. Teaching presence engagement occurred in the external processes which consist of instructor feedback and the setting of the overall tasks or learning goals. The final stage, the students have to listen to the instructor feedback for their answers.

Thus, after the three stages the differences can be seen in case of to what extent they engage in the peer instruction teaching strategy from the Engagement questionnaire findings.

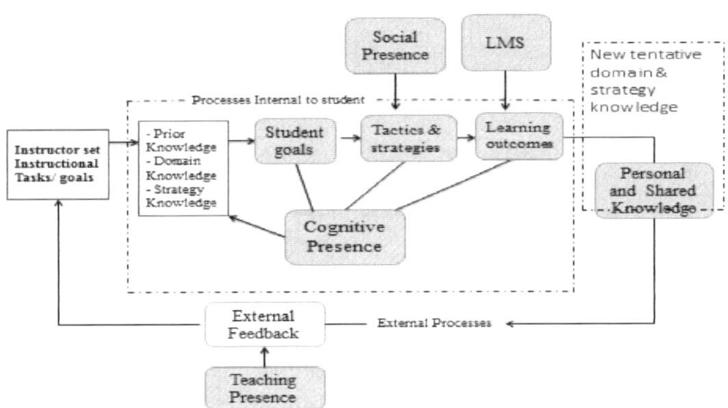

Figure 1. Conceptual Framework of the study (Modified from Nicole and Macfarlane, 2006)

3. METHODS

A quasi-experimental research design was adopted for the study. This survey research consists of measurement procedures that involve asking questions of respondents on aspects related to Flipped Learning Only (FLO) or Flipped Learning with Peer Instruction (FLPI) strategies and observing the influence on the development of students' engagement by their gender differences. Moreover, this study was carried out to determine the feasibility of using the Achievement Test and Engagement Questionnaire to answer the study hypotheses. This study employs quantitative methodology, using achievement test and engagement questionnaire to collect data. Quantitative analysis was suitable for the data analysis, and based on several statistical calculations such as the means, frequencies, and variance (Crandell, Voils, & Sandelowski, 2012). Two classes were randomly assigned as either an experimental or a control group, which involve forty (40) undergraduate Malaysian students at a Malaysian university, 20 for each group. The students' have studied an English course during the 2nd semester in their first year.

3.1 Research Instruments

Regarding the achievement test, it consisted of the pre-test and post-test which are constructed to measure the students' performance score in the two experimental and control groups; namely FLPI and FLO. Both groups were given the pre and post-test. The achievement of the students was recorded to determine the effectiveness of the treatment. The pre-test and post-test consist of three structured questions covering with a total score 20 marks

Items for the Engagement questionnaire were adapted from different studies. Forty-five items were used for measuring learning Engagement level. For example, the subscales were organized as Kim et al. (2014) (four items for students goals/strategies and five items, two items for social presence, four items for LMS, six items for cognitive presence and three items for teaching presence were adapted). The students' response to statements on a 5-point Likert scale that ranges from 1 (Strongly Agree) to 5 (Strongly Disagree).The engagement questionnaire was chosen because it is reliable and deemed a valid instrument used to measure undergraduate freshman students' engagement.

4. DATA ANALYSIS

Since the aim of this study is to find the significant differences in achievement and engagement when learning English reading comprehension task using the conventional flipped learning with peer instruction and flipped learning without peer instruction, descriptive analysis with Two-way ANCOVA and Two-way ANOVA test used for estimating the significant differences among students in both groups. The level of significance (alpha) is set at .05. Because null hypotheses are used the effective *p*-value is .025

H01: There is no significant difference in achievement between students that experienced FLO and FLPI.

Table 1 gives the Means, Std. Deviations and results of ANCOVA for achievement by the treatment groups. The FLO group reported a mean of 15.65 with SD of 1.81 while the FLPI group reported a mean of 13.95 with SD of 2.83. The ANCOVA test reported $F(1,37) = 7.048$ at $p = .012$. As $p < .025$ H01 is rejected. The FLO group performed significantly better than the FLPI group, indicating that the treatment for FLPI was not beneficial to the students.

Table 1. Means, Std. Deviations and results of ANCOVA for Achievement

Group	Mean	Std. Deviation	N	ANCOVA
FLO	15.65	1.81	20	F(1,37) = 7.048
FLPI	13.95	2.83	20	*p* = .012

H02: There is no significant difference in achievement between students that experienced FLO and FLPI by gender.

Table 2 gives the Means, Std. Deviations and results of Two-way ANCOVA for achievement by gender. For the FLO group, males reported a mean of 15.00 at SD of 2.28 and females reported a mean of 15.92 at SD of 1.59 while for the FLPI group, males reported a mean of 12.75 at SD of 2.91 and females reported a mean of 14.75 at SD of 2.59. The ANCOVA test reported $F(1,35) = 1.838$ at $p = .184$. As $p > .025$ H02 failed to rejected. There are no significant differences in achievement by gender.

Table 2. Means, Std. Deviations and results of Two-way ANCOVA for Achievement by gender

Group	GEN	Mean	Std. Deviation	N	ANCOVA	Interactionv Group* Gender
FLO	Male	15.00	2.28	6	F(1,35) = 1.838 P = .184	F(1,35) = .546 P = .465
	Female	15.92	1.59	14		
FLPI	Male	12.75	2.91	8		
	Female	14.75	2.59	12		

H03: There is no significant interaction effect between the Flipped Learning modes (FLO & FLPI) and gender by student achievement.

A further analysis was conducted to test for interaction effect between the flipped learning modes and gender. Table 3 reports the results with $F(1,35) = .546$ at $P = .465$. As $p > .025$, H03 failed to be rejected. There is no significant interaction effect for achievement between the flipped learning modes by gender.

H04: There is no significant difference in engagement between students that experienced FLO and FLPI.

Table 4 gives the Means, Std. Deviations and results of ANOVA for engagement by the treatment groups. The FLO group reported a mean of 163.95 with SD of 16.39 while the FLPI group reported a mean of 182.80 with SD of 20.27. The ANOVA test reported $F(1,38) = 10.449$ at $P = .003$. As $p < 0.025$, H04 is rejected. The FLPI group performed significantly better than the FLO group, indicating that the treatment increased student engagement.

Table 3. Means, Std. Deviations and results of ANOVA for engagement

Group	Mean	Std. Deviation	N	ANOVA
FLO	163.95	16.39	20	F(1,38) = 10.449
FLPI	182.80	20.27	20	P = .003

H05: There is no significant difference in engagement between students that experienced FLO and FLPI by gender.

Table 4 gives the Means, Std. Deviations and results of Two-way ANOVA for achievement by gender. For the FLO group, males reported a mean of 170.66 at SD of 21.34 and females reported a mean of 161.07 at SD of 13.71 while for the FLPI group, males reported a mean of 172.00 at SD of 18.47 and females reported a mean of 190.00 at SD of 18.75. The ANOVA test reported $F(1,36) = 0.519$ at $p = .476$. As $p >$ 0.025, H05 failed to be rejected. There are no significant differences in engagement by gender.

Table 4. Means, Std. Deviations and results of Two-way ANOVA for Engagement by gender

Group	GEN	Mean	Std. Deviation	N	ANOVA	Interaction
FLO	Male	170.66	21.34	6		
	Female	161.07	13.71	14	F(1,36) = .519	F(1.36) = 5.593
FLPI	Male	172.00	18.47	8	P = .476	P = .024
	Female	190.00	18.75	12		

H06: There is no significant interaction effect between the Flipped Learning modes FLO and FLPI and gender by student engagement.

A further analysis was conducted to test for interaction effect between the flipped learning modes and gender. Table 4 reports the results with $F(1,36) = 5.593$ at $p = .024$. As $p < .025$, H06 is rejected. There is a significant interaction effect for engagement between the flipped learning modes by gender with females reporting higher engagement.

4.1 Summary of Findings

Contrary to expectation, the FLO group performed significantly better than the FLPI group, but there were no significant differences in achievement in interaction effect by gender. The FLPI group showed significantly higher levels of engagement than the FLO group, but there was no significant difference by gender. However, there was a significant interaction effect for engagement between the flipped learning modes bgender with females reporting higher engagement.

5. DISCUSSION

5.1 Flipped Learning and Achievement

Previous studies have reported that students achieved more with flipped learning approach (Giannakos,Krogstie, & Aalberg, 2016; Holmes, Tracy, Painter, Oestreich, & Park, 2015; Steele, 2015). However, the findings of this study reported that contrary to expectation, the FLO group performed significantly better than the FLPI group, but there were no significant differences in achievement in interaction effect by gender. Thus, these findings contradict many previous scholars. The students in both FLO and FLPI achieved good score after general treatment by flipped learning approach as $F(1,35) = 1.838$ at $p = .184$.

Failure to change group composition on a frequent basis led to students' roles and interactions within a group being influenced more by students' sociocultural status (Malay, Chinese, and Indian) than by assigned tasks and responsibilities. Long-term assignment to any type of group worked against the positive outcomes of instructional grouping (Dumont, 2014), so the students waste their time to understand their own responsibilities as well as there is no leader for a group. In contrast, FLO significantly outperformed FLPI because of the effort they put to read carefully based on pre-class LMS lesson.

There is strong evidence for the importance of participating in class (Rocca, 2010). In contrast, Nicole and Macfarlane modified model of the FLPI group has not followed the instruction carefully for shared knowledge among each other. Then, students need more time in discussion or presentation. Instructors late feedback on students' answer also led them to lose trust in their group members. To do so, FLPI students unsystematic homogenous groups made them distrust their mates somehow.

Successful implementation of peer instruction method depends on supportive heterogeneous groups (Sapin-Shevin, Ayres, & Duncan, 1994). According to Stahl (1994), Forming of heterogeneous groups; Fair opportunities and positive dependence among each other; social interaction and positive attitude; allocation of sufficient time; and responsibility of every individual

Another result for the study that no significant difference by gender and no significant interaction effect. In fact, FLO and FLPI worked equally well by gender because the duration of the treatment is very short, or they all have good entry ability for the English course which is minimum of band 4 out of 6 of the Malaysian University English Test (MUET).

5.2 Engagement in Flipped Learning

There are numerous ways to make the classroom more conducive to participation and to make that participation more engaging (Rocca, 2010). In FLPI mood the students utilized response by cards on ConcepTests, which are index cards with a/b/c/d multiple choice answers on them that students hold up in lieu of verbal responses during a class lecture. The use of the cards was found to increase participation and they paid more attention to the lecture during the response card time period, and would encourage other professors to utilize this method (Marmolejo, Wilder, & Bradley, 2004). The challenge is to get engagement from all types of students (Kipka, Morland, Brown, Rich, & Holtham, 2014).

Unfortunately, the grouping for the FLPI was based on friendship, so the groups maybe homogenous in terms of ability or gender; therefore that lead to less achievement level for FLPI group. English is difficult, it is not intuitive, so it requires expert inputs and guidance which are missing in the homogenous group. Thus, the group work can be more effective when the following components were included: individual accountability, group goals, task specialisation, face-to-face interaction, interpersonal and small-group skills, social skills development, equal opportunities for success, team composition, adaptation to individual needs and positive interdependence (Johnson and Johnson, 1987). Thus, when assigning learners for group work, membership should be based on the expertise level and learning style of individual group members, so that individual team members can benefit from one another's strengths (Ally, 2004).

The findings exposed that Nicole and Macfarlane (2006) model did not work out well with FLPI group. The researcher notified that they need more time in discussion or presentation. (Feedback may not have been honest nor critical enough). Further, instructors may be somewhat unaware of their negative communication behaviours, and this impacts the participation rates of their students, even when they are not intending to show negativity (Rocca, 2010).

In line with Rocca's (2010) results, this study found that females have a much higher level of engagement with most forms of reading activities; they read more diverse material and online materials more often than males. Myers et al. (2002) found that females were more likely to participate for functional reasons and males for sycophantic reasons.

Eventually, Christiansen and Salm (2015) note that, "student engagement is much more complicated than just putting people into groups and having them learn together"). Students can be active but not engaged. Ultimately, engagement in the AL exercises must occur for learning to take place (Chi & Wylie, 2014).

6. CONCLUSION

This paper provides a structured framework, achievement test as well as engagement questionnaire fit to flipped learning approach for class activities fixed in good educational practice and theory to address students' university achievement and engagement. Flipped learning contributes a teaching-innovative which authorizes students to take responsibility for their learning, and creates active and engaged learning-centered classrooms through peer instruction. This study proposes future insight into student achievement and engagement by using flipped learning in a Malaysian context, specifically in reading comprehension English course and stands with the effectiveness of flipped learning as it proposes the higher educational institutions endorse this type of learning. On the one hand, the findings of this study presented negative findings achievement test; nevertheless, positive results have be shown for engagement level as it increases by a group of peer instruction intervention. On the other hand, the FLO group showed positive results in both achievement test and engagement questionnaire due to its simplicity for students which keep them active with instructors' feedback.

It can be a suggestion, that instructors should be aware of the possibility of sex differences both in the way students react and in the way they may interact with their students, but there is no real evidence to support treating males and females differently to increase their participation.

For practical purposes, this project will be limited to an investigation of on-campus small-class size delivery, hence, monitoring of students individually enable the project to be acknowledged achievement. Agreeing with the claim of Szparagowski (2014) that the flipped classroom lessons follow a small time table, the instructor might focus the use of developing student background knowledge more effectively.

ACKNOWLEDGEMENT

The work described in this paper was part of the research for a PhD study. Funding for Research grant was provided by University of Science, Malaysia (USM) to Centre for Instructional Technology and Multimedia (CITM) with no: (1001/PMEDIA/816287).

REFERENCES

Anderson, T., Rourke, L., Garrison, D. R., & Archer, W. (2001). Assessing teaching presence in a computer conferencing context. *Journal of Asynchronous Learning Networks*, *5*(2) Retrieved February 20, 2016, from http://www.aln.org/publications/jaln/v5n2/v5n2_anderson.asp

Babalhavaeji, F., & Kermani H.Z. (2011). Knowledge sharing behaviour influences: a case of Library and Information Science faculties in Iran. *Malaysian Journal of Library & Information Science*, 16(1), pp.1-14

Berrett, D., Mangan, K., Neshyba, S., Talbert, R., & Young, J., R. (2015). The Chronicle of Higher Education). A guide to the flipped classroom, http://images.results.chronicle.com/Web/TheChronicleofHigherEducation/%7B42b09a27b-42baad69-a455e627572b%7D_AD-CHE-FlippedClassroomBooklet.pdf.

Brown, D., & Skinner, D. (2007). Brown-Skinner Model for Building Trust with At-Risk Students. *National Forum of Applied Educational Research Journal*. 20(3), 1-7.

Chi, M., & Wylie, R. (2014). The ICAP framework: Linking cognitive engagement to active learning outcomes. *Educational Psychologist, 49*(4), 219–243. http://doi.org/10.1080/00461520.2014.965823

Christiansen, K., & Salm, T. (2015). Understanding engagement in grade 8 health education. *Revue phénEPS / PHEnex Journal*, *7*(1), 1–18. Retrieved from http://ojs.acadiau.ca/index.php/phenex/article/view/1563

Crandell J.L, Voils C.I, Sandelowski M. (2012). Bayesian approaches to the synthesis of qualitative and quantitative research findings. In: *Hannes K, Lockwood C, editors. Synthesizing qualitative research: Choosing the right approach.* Oxford, UK: Wiley-Blackwell.

Dutton, S. E. (2015). *Education In Rhythm and By Rhythm: Exploring Holistic Experiences in Dalcroze Pedagogy.* University of Toronto.

Fulton, K. (2012). Inside the flipped classroom. *The Journal*. Retrieved from: http://thejournal.com/articles/2012/04/11/the-flipped-classroom.aspx

Garrison, D. R. (2009). Communities of inquiry in online learning: Social, teaching and cognitive presence. In C. Howard et al. (Eds.), *Encyclopedia of distance and online learning* (2nd ed., pp. 352 355). Hershey, PA: IGI Global.

Garrison, D.R., Anderson, T., & Archer, W. (2010). The first decade of the community of inquiry framework: A retrospective. *Internet and Higher Education,* 13, pp. 5–9.

Garrison, D.R., Anderson, T., and Archer, W. (2000). Critical Inquiry in a Text-Based Environment: Computer Conferencing in Higher Education. *The Internet and Higher Education, 2*(2-3), 87±105.

Giannakos M. N. Krogstie, J., & Chrisochoides, N. (2014).Reviewing the Flipped Classroom Research: Reflections for Computer Science Education. Conference CSERC '14, 5-6, Berlin, Germany.

Giannakos, M. N., Krogstie, J., & Aalberg, T. (2016). Toward a Learning Ecosystem to Support Flipped Classroom: A Conceptual Framework and Early Results *State-of the-Art and Future Directions of Smart Learning* (pp. 105- 114): Springer.

Gormley, S. (2012). Understanding Participation in Knowledge Sharing in Virtual Communities of Practice on the HSELanD elearning Portal. *MA Thesis.* Trinity College Dublin.

Han, Y. J. (2015). Successfully Flipping The Esl Classroom For Learnerautonomy1. *Nys Tesol Journal, 2*(98), 98-109.

Holmes, M. R., Tracy, E. M., Painter, L. L., Oestreich, T., & Park, H. (2015). Moving from flipcharts to the flipped classroom: using technology driven teaching methods to promote active learning in foundation and advanced masters social work courses. *Clinical Social Work Journal, 43*(2), 215-224.

Jensen, J. L., Kummer, T. A., & Godoy, P. D. d. M. (2015). Improvements from a flipped classroom may simply be the fruits of active learning. *CBE-Life Sciences Education, 14*(1), ar5.

Johnson, R., Johnson, D. W., Stanne, M., Smizak, B., & Avon, J. (1987). *Effect of composition pairs at the word processor on quality of writing and ability to use the word processor.* Minneapolis: Cooperative Learning Center, University of Minnesota

Kahiigi, K.E. et al. 2012. Modelling a Peer Assignment Review Process for Collaborative E-learning. *Journal of Interactive Online Learning,*11(2), 67-79. Retrieved from: http://www.ncolr.org/jiol/issues/pdf/11.2.2.pdf

Kim, M. K., Kim, S. M., Khera, O., & Getman, J. (2014). The experience of three flipped classrooms in an urban university: an exploration of design principles. *The Internet and Higher Education, 22*, 37-50.

Kipka, Professor Mollie Painter Morland, C., Brown, A., Rich, M., & Holtham, C. (2014). Student engagement and learning: Case study of a new module for business undergraduates at Class business school. *Journal of Management Development, = 33*(6), 603-619.

Lee, V. and Oguntebi, J. (2012). Toward learning and knowledge creation: Operation alising the Social. *Journal of General Management..* 37(4).

Lindquist, T., & Long, H. (2011). How can educational technology facilitate student engagement with online primary sources? A user needs assessment. *Library Hi Tech, 29*(2), 224-241.

Lueg, K., Lueg, R. (2014). From teacher centered to peer tutoring in the heterogeneous international classroom: a Danish case of Instructional change. Journal of Social Science Education, 13(3), 39-62.

Mazur, E. (1997). *Peer instruction: a user's manual.* Upper Saddle River, N.J.: Prentice Hall.

Meijer, J. et al. (2013). The development of a questionnaire on metacognition for students in higher education. *Educational Research,* 55(1), 31–52, Retreived from http://www.ut.ee/BG/sts/Metacognition%20questionnaire%20AILA.pdf

Mo, Y., Singh, K. & Chang, M. (2013). Opportunity to learn and student engagement: a HLM study on eighth grade science achievement. *Educational Research for Policy & Practice*, 12(1), 3-19

Myers, S. A., Martin, M. M., & Mottet, T. P. (2002). Students' motives for communicating with their instructors: Considering instructor socio-communicative style, student socio-communicative orientation, and student gender. *Communication Education*, 51, 121133. (ES).

Nicol, D. J. & Macfarlane-Dick, D. (2006). Formative assessment and self-regulated learning: A model and seven principles of good feedback practice. *Studies in Higher Education*, 31 (2), pp.199-218.

Nicol, D. J. (2010) 'From monologue to dialogue: improving written feedback processes in mass higher education'. Assessment & Evaluation in Higher Education, Vol. 35, Noo. 5, pp. 501 517.

Nor Hashimah Jalaludin, Norsimah Mat Awal & Kesumawati Abu Bakar. (2008). The mastery of English language among lower secondary school students in Malaysia: A linguistic analysis. *European Journal of Social Sciences*, 7 (2), 106-119.

Normazidah, C. M., Koo, Y. L., & Hazita, A. (2012). Exploring English language learning and teaching in Malaysia. *GEMA Online™ Journal of Language Studies*, 12(1), 35-55.

Pierce, R., & Fox, J. (2012). Vodcasts and active-learning exercises in a "flipped classroom" model of a renal pharmacotherapy module. *American Journal of Pharmaceutical Education*, 76 (10), 1-5

Rocca, K.A. (2010). Student participation in the college classroom: an extendedmultidisciplinary literature review. *Communication Education*, 59(2), 185-213.

Shimamoto, D. (2012). *Implementing a flipped classroom: An instructional module.*

Steele, G. A. (2015). New postgraduate student experience and engagement in human communication studies. *Journal of Further and Higher Education, 39*(4), 498-533.

Szparagowski, R. (2014). The Effectiveness of the Flipped Classroom. *Honors Projects*. Paper 127.

Trowler,V. (2010). Student engagement literature review. *The Higher Education Academy*, pp.1-74.

THE PRO-ACTIVE RESOURCE MANAGEMENT FOR HOTELS' HOUSEKEEPING SERVICE

Alla G. Kravets[1], Alexandr Morozov[1] and Inna Strukova[2]
[1] *Volgograd State Technical University, 28 Lenin av., Volgograd, 400005, Russia*
[2] *"RGS-Volgograd" Ltd., 7 Balonina st., Volgograd, 400066, Russia*

ABSTRACT

Decision-making support systems are the integral tool for forming of operational management decisions at all management levels of the new entity including hotels. As an evolutionary development of interactive support decision-making systems transition to pro-active systems is proposed. The executed forecast bases excellent control in such systems. Resource (material, human, etc.) requirements are the subject of the prediction. In the article, ML –based (machine learning) approach to the automated pro-active decision-making support of a hotels' housekeeping services' management is described. The service of a housekeeping holds the central position in the hotel and approves all other business subsystems. Competent optimum control of a hotel housekeeping service resources in many respects determines prestige and the status of all hotel in general. During 1,5 years, we collected data of housekeeping service resources by the two modules: personnel management & motivation module and laundry service module. The methodology is based on the intelligent core, which consists of the ML methods set. In this article, the analysis of developed ML models is shown.

KEYWORDS

Pro-active management, Hotel, Housekeeping service, Personnel management, Polynomial regression

1. INTRODUCTION

The service of housekeeping (HK) is the largest hotels' division. It is responsible for the purity of rooms, the comfort of guests. HK is the center of coordination of resources of all other business subsystems: bookings, food, procurements, personnel management and others. At the same time, "purity" is one of the leading indicators in case of hotel assessment in all known reservations systems (booking.com, TripAdvisor, and others). Activities of HK service include some complex business processes: preparation of rooms for the settling of guests, cleaning of busy rooms, the content of free zones and the adjacent territory of the hotel in purity, provision of laundry services and others (Kuo, Chen, Chen & Liu 2015).

The hotel in present time a set of the interconnected services consists, such as:
- the function of acceptance and placement;
- service of food;
- service of booking;
- procurements management;
- personnel department;
- accounting department;
- housekeeping.

For high-quality management of all business processes, the modern hotel uses automated systems (Belov&Kravets 2013). Current automated systems have rather rich functionality on automation of business processes practically of all the hotels' services (Demeke 2014). However, there are services of the hotel which activities are automated insufficiently. To be among such services is the service of a housekeeping. But for excellent resources' control of HK service and hotels in general, it isn't enough to use the available automated systems (Romanenko, Kravets 2013). In addition to automated systems, it is reasonable to apply so-called systems of decision-making support (DMS).

DMS systems are the essential tool for forming of operational management decisions at all levels of management of the enterprise (Kravets, Gurtjakov & Kravets 2013). There is an opinion that effective management model is considered as a competitive advantage and the competition among the entities is performed at the level of the management model competition (Ukusov, Makarov, Kravets&Romanenko 2013). Therefore, the efficient DMS system can also be considered as a component of competitive advantage of the enterprise.

Traditionally two types of management are process management and project management. On that, it is also possible to assign two types of DMS systems. Within this research, the process approach is considered. It is caused by the following:

- a formalization of the main stages (operations of business processes);
- a binding of business processes operations' performance indicators to data sources for automatic calculation of measured values of efficiency;
- availability of the dataset for the machine learning models as "situation-decision" for automatic generation of the possible decisions set.

As the main idea which is the cornerstone of the solution of the problems (Zhong, Ma, Tu & Li 2016) allocated with various researchers and also as an evolutionary development of interactive systems of decision support, a transition to pro-active DMS systems is proposed (Teslya&Kontsevych 2013; Park, Yaduma, Lockwood&Williams 2016). The idea can be formulated as knowing (predicting) future change of a condition of an object and its environment with a precise accuracy, it is possible to manage and minimize more precisely empirical risk in the future (Sallam, Li, Ouyang &Li 2014; Walker 2016).

2. THE METHODOLOGY DESCRIPTION

2.1 The Problem Statement

The biggest problem at which solution the research is aimed is the lack of tools for assessment of expected need for resources, including human. Assessment of projected needs for resources is necessary for ensuring high-quality rendering of services of the hotel that, positively, affects not only efficient management of separate division – service of housekeeping, but also the hotel in general (Öğüt 2011).

The generalized scheme of the developed methodology concept includes the following steps (fig.1):

1. Providing to system information on a hotels' load and work schedule of service personnel.
2. Processing of the obtained data.
3. Creation of the short-term/long-term forecast (Yin Shulu, Yang Lixun 2008) in need of service personnel, the need for means for cleaning of rooms, and also the need for expendables for a laundry.
4. Making a decision on excellent resources for control of housekeeping services of the hotel with the maximum satisfaction for clients and the minimum expenses for hotels in general.

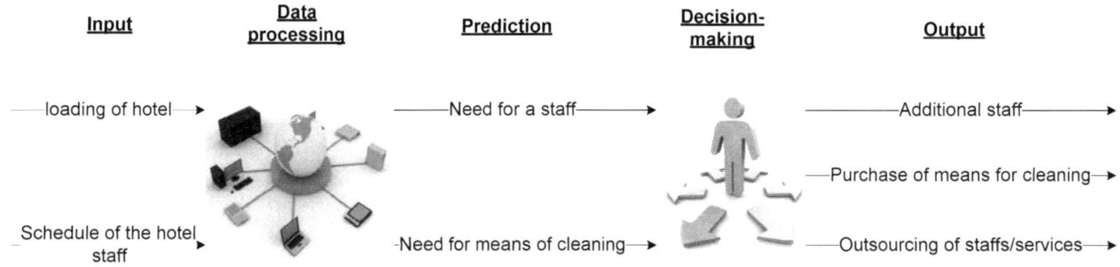

Figure 1. The generalized scheme of methodology

As a result of the research performance, the new results corresponding to world tendencies in the field of forecasting, modeling, and management will be received. The main scientific result will be the developed compound the pro-active resource management methodology for housekeeping services of the hotel, unlike existing, allowing to make the analysis and indicators' forecasting an operational condition of HK service resources by information processing about changes of the array with input parameters. Within a technique will be:

– the model of support for decision-making and pro-active resource management methods of HK service realizing it differing in a methods integration of extraction of knowledge and approaches to forecasting are for the first time created;

– the architecture of the intellectual kernel consisting of methods of forecasting and predictive modeling which, unlike known, allows to involve optimum labor both the HK service material resources and outsourcing is developed;

– algorithms of the automated pro-active resource management for housekeeping services of the hotel are developed.

Forecast human resource demand in the context of the hotel can be understood as the process of predicting the required number of employees in the near future, based on the given number of customers (Yap, Ineson, Alexieva, & Tang 2015). In the current work, we predict the number of service staffs and cleaning staffs in the period of a month. The prediction result is an effective resource to establish the working schedule of hotel staffs. Factors which strongly affect to the prediction result can be historical registration (customer's check in, checkout time, the number of customers in each room, a number of staffs, etc.

The approach used for predicting is to use big data processing framework to analyze historical customer load and employee workload of the hotel from collected data in the duration of a year. Several machine learning algorithms (Chumak, Kravets 2015; Cao Shumin, Du Qingling 2008) are used to analyze the collected data in order to see the differences between real data and data from machine learning algorithms have learned. Based on the training output (scored), the most suitable algorithms are chosen as the method to predict human resource demand in the future.

2.2 Pro-active Resource Management for the Hotels' Housekeeping Service

Development the complex automated system of pro-active resource management for the hotels' housekeeping services is based on machine learning models and methods of pro-active management. We suggest the procedure of building the pro-active resource management model of HK service (figure 2).

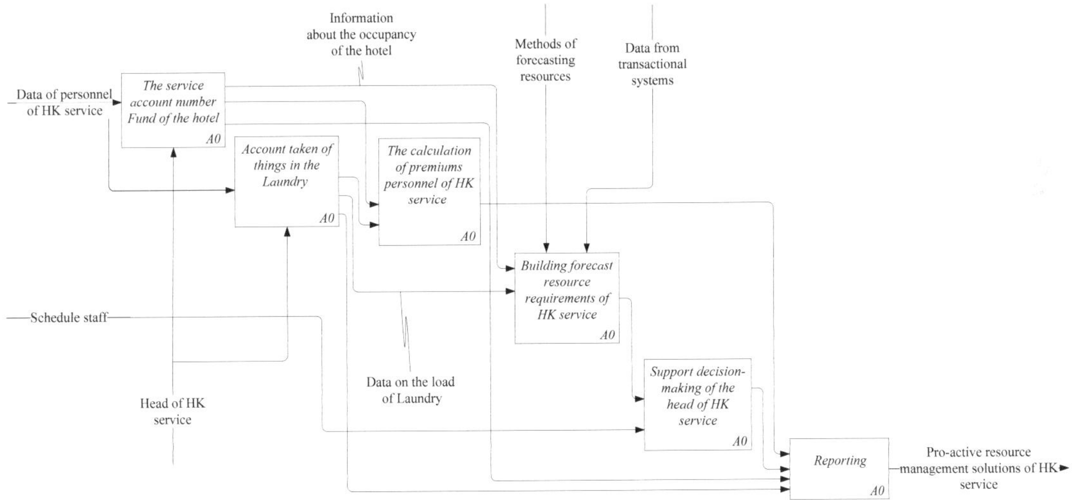

Figure 2. The scheme of building a Pro-active model

Specifications, which have to move to an entrance of the developed system, are hotels' loading and personnel schedule of a housekeeping service.

Booking systems, transaction systems of accounting and management accounting, and also, given the room service (their quantity) can be data sources. Such data collected using the developed system for automation of work of service of a housekeeping of the hotel. Let's consider it realization in more detail. The system has undergone a trial operation in network Hotel Park Inn Radisson in the city of Volgograd.

Use of system taking into account integration with already operating transaction systems has allowed increasing labor productivity of staff of service of a housekeeping of hotel.

The developed system contains six modules and has three levels (fig. 3).

The first tier is data management level. It provides functions of long-term data storage and organizes the multiuser access to them. For the realization of the level of data management MySQL 5.5 DBMS is used.

The second tier is the application server presented to web–server. It provides access to the functionality of the automated system through web–browser. For the realization of this level web–server, Apache is used.

The third level is the level of clients presented to web–browsers.

Thus, the developed system provides in the SaaS model (Software as a service).

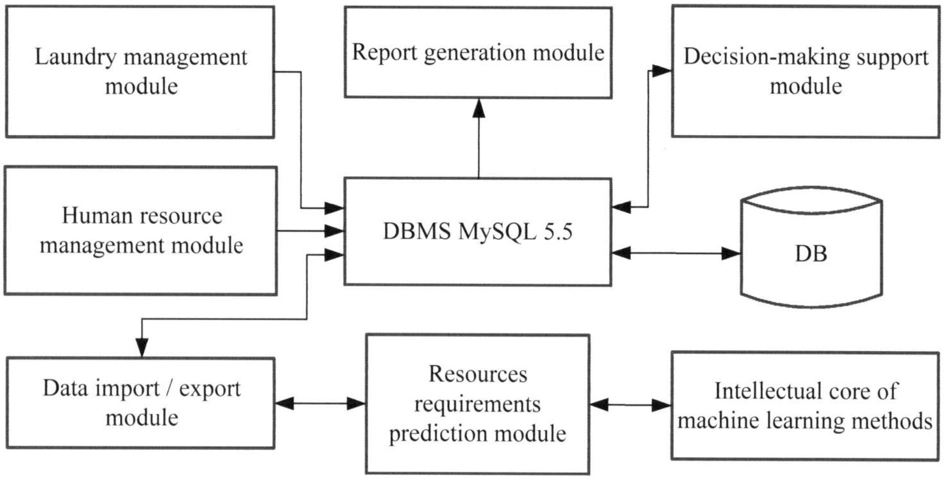

Figure 3. Scheme of system architecture

In figure 4 the interface of the Room service form is presented. In the provided table the accounting of rooms cleaning is displayed. Characteristic is existence in a system of a possibility of the personnel motivation. The motivation of staff represents the calculation of bonus payments taking into account the executed norms by the team of service of a housekeeping of the hotel. From a reduced form it is possible to obtain information on daily loading of the hotel that it is necessary for the creation of the forecast of a need for resources of service of housekeeping.

ROOM SERVICE

	Date	Full name	Post	Inhabited	Dirty	Inhabit suite	Dirty suite	Number of rooms	Norm of inhabitec	Norm of dirty	The amount for inhabited	The amount for dirty	The amount for inhabited a luxe	The amount for dirty a luxe	Total	Comment
1	30.12.2015	Seliverstc	chamber	7	5	0	0	12	10	5	-150	0	0	0	-150	
2	29.12.2015	Seliverstc	chamber	14	4	1	0	20	10	5	0	0	0	0	0	work order
3	28.12.2015	Seliverstc	chamber	14	4	1	0	20	10	5	150	0	70	0	220	
4	25.09.2015	Samoteyl	chamber	0	9	0	0	9	0	3	0	600	0	0	600	
5	25.09.2015	Bartasins	cleaner	0	0	0	0	0	0	3	0	-300	0	0	-300	
6	25.09.2015	Salova	cleaner	2	11	0	0	13	0	3	100	800	0	0	900	

Figure 4. Room service

The percent of the hotels' loading in general and the status of the rooms' number is considered on the separate form presented in figure 5. The collecting data are also necessary for the realization a forecasting model (Ostertagová, 2012) of a need for resources.

STATUS OF THE ROOMS NUMBER

	Date	Dirty in the morning	Cleaned	Dirty in the evening	Percent of loading
1	04.11.2016	120	0	0	22
2	03.11.2016	135	80	55	49
3	02.11.2016	135	124	11	89
4	01.11.2016	114	98	16	88
5	31.10.2016	89	89	0	76
6	30.10.2016	51	39	12	56
7	29.10.2016	45	44	1	33
8	17.06.2016	129	0	0	42
9	16.06.2016	128	112	16	75
10	15.06.2016	104	104	0	85

Figure 5. Status of the rooms

Necessary data for laundry pro-active resource management system realization of a housekeeping service can be obtained using the developed module of supporting a laundry management. Using this module, it is possible to have pins and needles in the current a laundry loading in the form of the accepted things from lodgers of the hotel. By loading of a laundry and loading of the hotel, in general, it is possible to construct the forecast of further loading of a laundry. By the forecast, the support system of decision-making will propose the most optimal solution: or to involve own resources, or to use the outsourcing company services, the providing service of a laundry. "Pro-activity" of the system also consists in it. That is the forecast to issue the optimal solution for resource management of service of a housekeeping of the hotel.

In figure 6, the interface of a form of the journal of reception of things is presented to a laundry. On this form cost account of the accepted things, given the price list of the prices is also kept. The price list can be edited bearing in mind hotels' requirements or outsourcing company, the providing a laundry service.

GUEST THINGS JOURNAL OF RECEPTION

	Date	Full name worker	№ room / Surname	Category	Description	Brand	Defects	Quantity (dry-cleaner)	Quantity (washing)	Quantity (ironing)	Total price (RUB)	Status	Date of issue	Discount	Comments
1	15.06.2016	Tupchiy	2340/Shein	Jeans	-	-	-	0	0	1	230	accepted	15.06.2016	0	
2	15.06.2016	Tupchiy	2340/Shein	Trousers	-	Nike	-	1	0	0	750	accepted	16.06.2016	0	
3	15.06.2016	Tupchiy	2285/Ivanov	Trousers	-	-	-	0	1	0	350	accepted	16.06.2016	0	
4	13.06.2016	Isakova	0304	Socks	-	-	hole	0	5	0	500	accepted	13.06.2016	0	
5	29.06.2016	Tupchiy	2367	Trousers	-	-	-	0	4	0	750	accepted	30.06.2016	0	
6	28.06.2016	Ort	50	Trousers	-	-	-	1	1	1	1995	urgently	30.06.2016	0	
7	03.05.2016	Volkova	35/Pavlova	Dress	-	-	hole	3	3	3	4788	accepted	05.05.2016	5	
8	02.05.2016	Ort	35/Pavlova	Dress	-	-	hole	3	3	3	4889	accepted	04.05.2016	3	
9	02.05.2016	Volkova	34/Pavlov	Jacket	-	-	hole	2	2	2	3060	urgently	04.05.2016	0	
10	02.05.2016	Volkova	34/Pavlov	Jeans	-	-	hole	2	2	2	3015	urgently	04.05.2016	0	

Figure 6. Guest things reception journal

2.3 Implementation of the Intellectual Core

For the implementation of the intellectual core (IC) from models, their training, and prediction, and also for assessment of the quality of the received decisions the Scikit-Learn library was selected. This library provides a wide set of opportunities for preliminary automated processing of basic data and representation of results, such as the experimental selection of model parameters of the qualifier and regression, the partition of the casing of data on the trained and test selection etc.

The machine learning methods used in the IC:

- Support vector regressor.
- Random forest regressor.
- Decision tree regressor.
- Ada boost regressor.
- Gradient boosting regressor.

The information received from other modules and saved in a DB are processed in the developed module of import/export and will be transformed to the file of the *.csv format. The received file contains the following specification: "index" – an index of activities of HK service and "value" – its value. In a research selection by n volume = 18 indices of activities of HK service was used. The fragment of data is shown in Table 1.

Table 1. Fragment of data in the CSV format

Year.month.day	Index1	Index2	…	Index n
2015.01.01	xx	xx	…	xx
…				
2015.02.01	xx	xx	…	xx
2015.02.02	xx	xx	…	xx
…				

The data was loaded from CSV files and split into two datasets – one for training in a random selection η first part data and one for testing, $\eta \in (0, 1)$. Recommended by the developers of the library value η=0.7.

Such parameters were as a result received: training time, the predicted values (man-hours) on loading of a staff, coefficients of the regression equation between indices and the predicted values (table 2, figure 8).

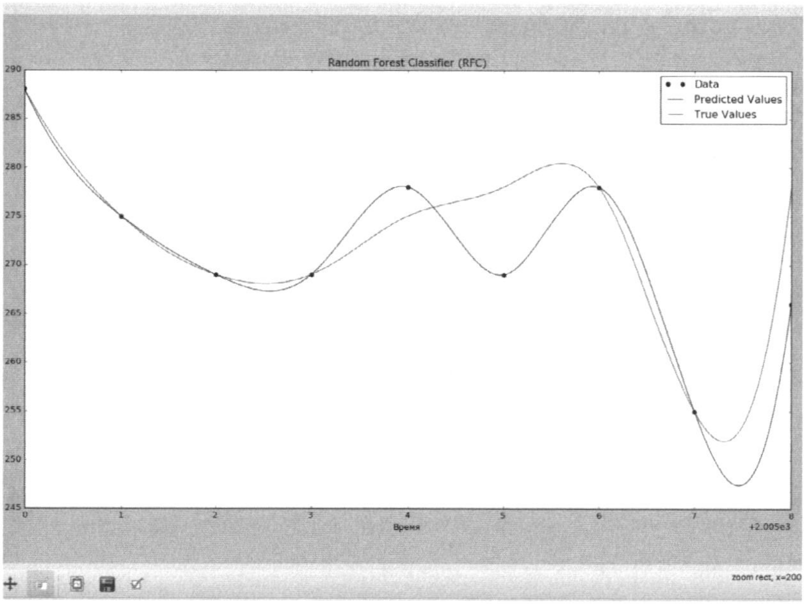

Figure 7. The experimental and predicted data on loading of a staff of HK service (staff-hours)

Table 2. Predicted and true values

Predicted	True
288	288
275	275
269	269
269	269
275	278
278	269
278	278
255	255
278	266

To assess the quality of the models, we used the following metrics supported by the library Scikit-Learn: precision, recall, and F-measure. We estimated the quality of the model (table 3, fig. 9).

Table 3. The models quality assessment

Fitting Time	Predicting Time	MSE	MAE	R-Square	F1 score	Precision score	Recall score
26.09	0.001	26.00	2.67	0.66	0.65	0.68	0.67

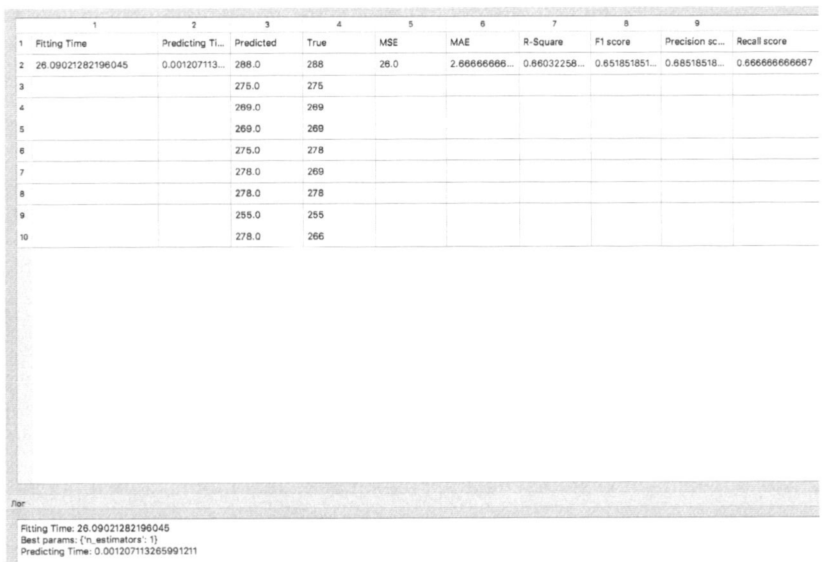

	1	2	3	4	5	6	7	8	9	
1	Fitting Time	Predicting Ti...	Predicted	True	MSE	MAE	R-Square	F1 score	Precision sc...	Recall score
2	26.09021282196045	0.001207113...	288.0	288	26.0	2.66666666...	0.66032258...	0.651851851...	0.68518518...	0.666666666667
3			275.0	275						
4			269.0	269						
5			269.0	269						
6			275.0	278						
7			278.0	269						
8			278.0	278						
9			255.0	255						
10			278.0	266						

Лог

Fitting Time: 26.09021282196045
Best params: {'n_estimators': 1}
Predicting Time: 0.001207113265991211

Figure 8. The models quality assessment

3. CONCLUSION

Due to the fact that the actual employee's demand and supply are influenced by many reasons, such as political, economic conditions and critical cultural and physical activities, the prediction result is difficult to get absolute accuracy and the modeling results still need the practical test. However, this research proposes the innovative methodology for planning hotel human resources.

In an analysis result of the selected methods, the most accurate prediction result showed RandomForestRegressor, and also it has the smallest time of the model training. This method is chosen as the basis for the further forecasts creation of staff requirements.

Advantages of the created product are entirely connected with the program functionality predictive component.

The efficiency leading indicators of the proposed solution are:

1. Operating time reduction over the analysis of expected need for personnel and material resources of the head of the hotels' housekeeping service (1 hour/day).
2. Increase in labor personnel productivity of a housekeeping service by 10%.
3. Reduction of possible losses due to the introduction and use a system pro-active technique.

As a result of system development the following results will be received:

- The sophisticated automated pro-active management methodology consisting of forecasting methods is developed.
- The service quality system of the hotels' housekeeping is designed.
- The motivation system of a hotels' housekeeping service personnel is designed.

ACKNOWLEDGEMENT

This research was partially supported by the Russian Fund of Basic Research (grant No. 15-07-06254 A).

REFERENCES

Belov, A.G., Kravets, A.G., 2013.Business performance management in small and medium businesses and functional automation *World Applied Sciences Journal*, 24 (24), pp. 7-11.

Cao Shumin, Du Qingling, 2008. The Human Resource Demand Forecast based on BP Neural Network [J].*Journal of Shandong University of Technology (Natural Science Edition),* pp.26-29.

Chumak, A.A., Kravets, A.G., 2015. The method of support vectors in the analysis of social networks user profiles () *International Journal of Soft Computing*, 10 (3), pp. 242-246.

Demeke, W., 2014. Adoption Of information and communication technologies in the hotel and associated businesses in Addis Ababa, Ethiopia *Proceedings of the 7th IADIS International Conference Information Systems 2014, IS 2014,* pp. 11-18.

Kravets, A.G., Gurtjakov, A., Kravets, A., 2013. Corporate intellectual capital management: Learning environment method. *Proceedings of the IADIS International Conference ICT, Society and Human Beings 2013, Proceedings of the IADIS International Conference e-Commerce 2013*, pp. 3-10.

Kuo, J.-Y. , Chen, Y.-C. , Chen, C.-Y. , Liu, L.-W., 2015. Study on correlation between hotel cleaners' musculoskeletal pain and cleaning pose by RULA (Upper limb assessment) and MSDS checklist: Using hot spring hotels and motels in Taiwan as examples. *Open Cybernetics and Systemics Journal*, 9 (1), pp. 1199-1206.

Li Tao, Song Guangxing. Study on Regional Human Resources Demand Forecast[J]. *Yunnan Finance & Economics University Journal of Economics &Management*, 2006(03):pp.91-95.(In Chinese).

Martin Otava, *2014.* Regression with Enriched Random Forest ,*Non-Clinical Statistics Conference Brugge, Belgium.*

Ostertagová, E., 2012. Modelling using polynomial regression, *Technical University of Košice, Faculty of Electrical Engineering and Informatics, Department of Mathematics and Theoretical Informatics, NČmcovej 32, 042 00 Košice, Slovak Republic.*

Öğüt, H. 2011. The determinants of online hotel reservation. *Proceedings of the IADIS International Conference e-Commerce 2011, Part of the IADIS Multi Conference on Computer Science and Information Systems 2011, MCCSIS 2011*, pp. 165-169.

Park, S., Yaduma, N., Lockwood, A.J., Williams, A.M., 2016. Demand fluctuations, labour flexibility and productivity. *Annals of Tourism Research*, 59, pp. 93-112.

Romanenko E. V., Kravets A. G., 2013. Development and Implementation of Multi-Agent Approach to Support the Process of Requests Execution in a Distributed Information System "TourEast: CRM AI".*World Applied SciencesJournal (WASJ)*, Vol. 24, pp.145-150.

Sallam A., Li K., Ouyang A., Li Z., 2014. Proactive workload management in dynamic virtualized environments. *Journal of Computer and System Science*, Vol. 80, No. 8, pp. 1504-1517.

Teslya Y. N., Kontsevych V. V., 2013.Improving the project quality using the introformation method of the proactive human resource management. *Project management and development of production*, Vol. 45, No. 1, pp. 1-6.

Ukusov S. S., Makarov I., Kravets A. G., Romanenko E. V., 2013. On Math Approach to Tourist Project Team Formation Problem Concerning Performance and Cooperative Effects.*World Applied Sciences Journal (WASJ)*, Vol. 24, pp. 238-242.

Walker, M., 2016. Hospitality in Jeopardy: Organizing Diverse Low-Wage Service Workers. *SAGE Open*, 6 (3), .

Yap, M.H.T. , Ineson, E.M. , Alexieva, I. , Tang, C.M.F., 2015. Bulgarian Hotel Managers' Recruitment Perceptions. *Journal of Human Resources in Hospitality and Tourism*, 14 (2), pp. 133-152.

Yin Shulu, Yang Lixun, 2008. Review of Tourism Demand Forecasting Methods and Models[J]. *Journal of Gansu Economic Management Institute*,pp.42-45 (In Chinese).

Zhong, J. , Ma, Y. , Tu, Y. , Li, X., 2016. Supply chain quality management: an empirical study. *International Journal of Contemporary Hospitality Management*, 28 (11), pp. 2446-2472.

BUSINESS MODEL FOR OCCUPATIONAL ACTIVATION OF ELDERLY PEOPLE VIA THE SERVICE E-MARKETPLACE PLATFORM – RESEARCH STUDY OF POLISH MARKET

Robert Kutera, Karol Lopacinski, Maja Leszczynska and Wieslawa Gryncewicz
Wroclaw University of Economics - ul. Komandorska 118/120, 53-345 Wroclaw, Poland

ABSTRACT

The authors address the issues of activating elderly people and improving their quality of life in the context of the possibility of increasing their effectiveness through the use of modern ICT solutions. The concept of the service e-marketplace platform for occupational activation of elderly people is presented and set in the context of Polish market conditions. Those entry data were gathered using three research methods: the extensive literature study, in-depth direct interviews and the survey dedicated to elderly people in Poland. On that basis the business model for implementation of such a platform for Polish market is proposed, what constitutes the main aim of the paper. The model includes the values provided to its users, the planned ways of achieving them, key market stakeholders and financial aspects following the Business Model Canvas methodology. The results of the research could be a guide for institutional stakeholders of the market on their way to reach their strategic goals in the area of activation of elderly users.

KEYWORDS

Occupational activation, elderly people, service e-marketplace platform, business model, market analysis

1. INTRODUCTION

The dynamic development of the information society influences the way of satisfying needs of a daily routine. The intensive expansion of information and communication technologies (ICT) determines also the development of electronic markets for the exchange of goods and services. While the e-market for goods has already reached its maturity, the service e-market is still in the development phase and looking for new development strategies, new business models. The service is meant as the process of contributing a context-specific value (Vargo and Lusch, 2016). This value is generated by the cooperation of service providers and customers within a common ecosystem, involving people, organisations, technology, and information resources (Maglio *et al.*, 2015). The phenomenon of service economy is emerging, which introduces its unique operating patterns, spatial distribution and the requirements of corresponding institutional environment (Zhou, 2016). It requires market entities to take a number of innovative activities in the face of emerging social and business challenges. The consequence of these changes is the development of the Life engineering discipline, which together with Business engineering strive to ensure the highest efficiency in meeting consumer needs (Oesterle, 2014). One of the tools that can play a key role in stimulating the synergy of these two disciplines are the service e-marketplace platforms (Kutera *et al.*, 2017).

One of the key challenges for the next several years is to face, especially in highly developed countries, the problem of aging (Moody, 2013; Rowe and Kahn, 2015; Szymańczak and Ciura, 2012) and its impact on the general quality of citizens' life. There are many factors that may affect the perception of the quality of life, including health conditions, financial status, social relationships and occupational activity. This last factor is very important and is conditioned by the other ones. It plays key role in shaping the national social and economic policy, in particular the pension system, where more and more people will be subjected to it in the coming years. Innovations in these areas require collaboration between government institutions, local governments, academics, and business practitioners. They are related in particular to the need for building new or redefining existing services and the corresponding business models (Kleinschmidt and Peters, 2017;

Witell *et al.*, 2016). The services, provided in a traditional way or electronically should provide a certain value to consumers in many dimensions. Consumers may not only be the final beneficiary of the service and get tangible results (work done), but they may also be involved in the value creation process. The determinants and the way of creating values in a conceptual dimension define business models. A business model can be defined as "a simplified and aggregated representation of the relevant activities of a company. It describes how marketable information, products and/or services are generated by means of a company's value-added component" (Wirtz *et al.*, 2016). In particular, it can describe the values and the planned ways of achieving them, key stakeholders and financial aspects. This structure is compliant with the Business Model Canvas (BMC) methodology that becomes the part of the canon of tools for analysts, managers, and researchers (Osterwalder, 2004). In the light of the rising importance of Corporate Social Responsibility (CSR) trends, both dimensions are important for the positive perception of new business initiatives and for building competitive advantage in a dynamic and highly unpredictable market.

The aim of this paper is to present and describe the business model prepared for the Polish market using the BMC methodology. This model was created as a result of the author's research work and the conclusions obtained from in-depth direct interviews and surveys with representatives of the target group.

The research results could be a guide for state and local governments, social organisations and businesses (key stakeholders of the market), on the way to reach their strategic goals in the area of activation of seniors.

2. RESEARCH METHODOLOGY AND CONTEXT

The research presented in this paper is an integral part of a three-year international project aimed at developing and launching a service e-marketplace platform. This platform serves to offer services dedicated to the elderly, offer services by the elderly, matchmake volunteers working for the elderly, activate elderly people through the support of social organisations.

The whole study is carried out in cooperation with existing social organisations and verified on the basis of field trials. The project covers both the technical part of developing and testing the proper software, as well as the business part aimed at creating a business model and the concept of commercialization.

Project research is carried out in accordance with the Consortium Research (Oesterle and Otto, 2010) methodology, which assumes the cooperation between researchers and practitioners within the framework of long-term research projects. The method is focused on the generation of scientific artefacts and their verification within iterative implementations. Each next iteration is enriched with previously created artifacts. On that basis the functional and non-functional requirements are produced.

In addition, three methods were used in parallel for the purpose of the research task that was related to the development and validation of the business model for the Polish market.

The first method was an analysis of academic and professional literature in order to build a broad spectrum of knowledge about business model development as well as to expand the context with the latest statistics about research area (Butryn *et al.*, 2015).

The second method used to develop the proposed concept of the e-marketplace platform in Poland was in-depth interviews (Brinkmann and Kvale, 2015) conducted directly in the form of meetings with seniors affiliated with senior clubs and Third Age Universities. This method was of a qualitative nature. Its purpose was to deepen the recognition of the opinions of people aged 50+ about the possibility of activating seniors, ensuring their independence and improving the overall quality of life using ICT. This part of research concerned exclusively the Polish market.

The study was conducted in twenty groups of 10 people according to the requirements and principles used in in-depth direct interviews. The surveyed groups consisted of active users of information technologies (primarily the Internet and mobile devices) or people who declared their willingness to participate in such activities. It was important to know the specifics of this type of activity and the barriers to its development. Only then it was possible to obtain interesting and valuable feedback, based on which the concept of the business model of e-marketplace platform application in Polish realities could be developed.

Therefore, the main objectives of the second research method were related to:

- recognizing the needs and expectations of seniors for the use of ICT in their daily lives,
- identification of the main causes of the use of the Internet and mobile devices by seniors,
- identification and evaluation Internet capabilities most commonly used by seniors,

• identifying barriers to using the computer and the Internet what are important for seniors,
• determination the range of services that activate seniors and ensure their independence.

The results of in-depth direct interviews proved to be very useful while building the final version of the business model of the e-marketplace platform in Polish realities.

The obtained results of qualitative research have also become the starting point for creating the questionnaire which was used in quantitative research. It was the third research method aimed at evaluating the developed concept of business model of service e-marketplace application in Polish realities. The questionnaire was addressed to people aged 50+ and included 20 questions about living and infrastructure conditions, Internet usage level and the perception of social and employment activation using ICT.

A detailed plan was defined and the study was finally performed between October and December 2016. The survey was conducted among seniors affiliated with senior clubs and Universities of the Third Age. The size of the required (minimal) study sample to obtain reliable results is 384 respondents. This requirement was met because the final number of properly completed questionnaires was 406. The main research objective was to determine the suitability of application the service e-marketplace platform business model in Polish market conditions.

A number of elementary science artefacts were developed so far to organize knowledge in the areas of service economy, social and economic policies, business model development, software engineering and integration, human-computer interaction. That work constitutes the basis for the preparation of the business model for occupational activation of elderly people. During the research process the authors address the issues of activating elderly people and improving their quality of life in the context of the possibility of increasing their effectiveness through the use of modern ICT. For this purpose, economic, social and technological determinants have been identified and described (Łysik *et al.*, 2015; Leszczyńska *et al.*, 2016; Butryn *et al.*, 2015), the model of delivering an IT solution for activation of elderly people (Kutera *et al.*, 2016) and the implementational aspects in the context of non-functional (Kutera and Gryncewicz, 2016; Maciaszek *et al.*, 2016) and functional requirements (Rot *et al.*, 2017), have been defined on the basis of the target group analysis in the pilot implementation in Switzerland and Germany.

3. KEY FINDINGS

The research in the form of series of in-depth direct interviews was conducted on a group of 406 individuals aged 50+. The study sample consists of 76% of women and 24% of men. A vast majority had high or secondary level of education: each of these groups constituted 45% of the sample. 84% of respondents received pensions. Nearly 7% worked under a regular employment contract and 6% had part time job. Others ran their own company. As regards housing, nearly 64% of them declared that they lived in flats and 36% in detached houses. About 53% lived with their spouses or partners. 35,7% lived alone. The following conclusions were reached:

1. Modern-day Polish senior citizens want to activate themselves in communities and they want to plan and organize meetings, events and collective activities together and in an efficient way.
2. Seniors are eager to use ICTs, but due to their age, they don't possess sufficient digital competences.
3. Senior citizens own internet-enabled mobile devices but a vast majority of them use their smartphones only in a traditional way, i.e. they make voice calls and write text messages. A large group of elderly people do not use the Internet functions because they lack the necessary skills and knowledge. Furthermore, they do not trust the mobile Internet.
4. Senior citizens would like to use ICTs in the presence of somebody who will provide them with the technological and factual support and who will give them proper training so that they could operate freely in this environment (communication, shopping, transport, health services etc.).
5. Senior citizens have both the equipment and the Internet access at home; however, they are reluctant to use them because they are afraid that their safety and privacy will be violated (frauds, internet thefts).
6. People over 50 years of age who participated in computer trainings adopt a considerably more open attitude and they have fewer fears as to the ICT usage. There exists a need of and understanding for the issue of self-improvement in this field among the research participants. Senior citizens wish to develop their skills mostly in the area of the usage of the Internet and mobile devices.

7. Organisations such as senior citizens' centres and Third Age Universities in the majority of cases have such premises and organisational infrastructure in which it is possible to implement and use ICT platforms. The problem is the lack of technological infrastructure (equipment, software, Internet access).

8. Polish senior citizens have a lot of free time. They willingly gather in communities and declare the intention of mutual assistance. This can take the shape of volunteering and casual labour due to the fact that in most cases seniors' basic financing is secured in the form of their pension or retirement pension.

9. In the modern Polish society it is common to retire when a person is still intellectually and physically fit to perform their duties. Therefore, seniors have a significant intellectual capital, professional experience and skills, which can be applied in a creative manner and yet not in the form of a full-time employment.

10. Senior citizens have needs regarding various services designed to support their self-reliant lives at home. Nevertheless, they are unaware of the fact that they can fulfil these needs by ordering such services via the Internet. They are afraid of potential frauds committed by service providers. It is important for them that somebody verify service providers in terms of their trustworthiness.

On the basis of those research conclusions, leading assumptions have been formed for the creation of a business model of the application of the service e-marketplace platform in Poland. It is necessary:

- to provide senior citizens with a safe environment in which they will use the ICT platform,
- to activate seniors within the framework of such structures as: seniors' centres, Third Age Universities,
- to guarantee the continuing access (in person or by phone) to technical and factual support assistants,
- to secure financing of the technological infrastructure (equipment, software, Internet access) designed to ensure the continued use of the platform by senior citizens free of charge,
- to use senior citizens' natural need to self-organize and to provide mutual assistance,
- to enable senior citizens to offer their services in the form of casual labour,
- to enable organisations trusted by senior citizens (senior citizens' centres, Third Age Universities) and senior citizens themselves to verify the providers of services for the elderly through opinion systems in which the customers evaluate the service and leave their comments after its performance,
- to create mechanisms of secured forms of payment made by seniors to service providers via a third party.

The assumptions underlying the construction of the business model presented above have also been reflected in previous research achievements, which are briefly described in the next section.

4. BUSINESS MODEL

The research artefacts produced so far and the assumptions concerning the business model based on the direct interviews allowed to define a high-level concept of the business model designed to activate senior citizens by the service e-marketplace platform. The concept specifies the main roles of stakeholders engaged in the activation of senior citizens and key relations between the roles, including the activities performed by one of the parties for the other, and all the financial flows facilitating proper functioning of the model under market conditions. A graphic depiction of the model is presented in Fig. 1.

The central part of this model is the service e-marketplace platform, which is provided by the IT Service Provider - a vendor of particular cloud Software-as-a-Service (SaaS) solution (Maciaszek *et al.*, 2016). This entity is responsible for the creation and configuration of the platform, the on-going technical support and system maintenance and, in return, receives proper remuneration. The platform offers the possibility of easy, non-invasive integration to external Internet services (client services) which provide information about occupational opportunities. It is aggregating data from various client services. It provides key functionalities connected with browsing, ordering, coordination, performance and verification of services. It also facilitates the management of membership and identity via its authentication service, which is compliant with the Single Sign On standard (Kutera and Gryncewicz, 2016). Suppliers provide elderly people with professional services and they obtain from the platform concrete benefits e.g. the possibility to use business-oriented IT tools and the access to a wide group of consumers. In return, suppliers are obliged to pay the subscription or commission fee. In this group, service providers represent the management of the organisations which perform services and they are responsible for defining both the services and the conditions of their performance. They are also in charge of the staff management and of allocating tasks to performers, who are responsible for performing the service to a given requestor. Requestors and volunteers constitute a group of customers. These are mostly elderly people or people working to the benefit of elderly people e.g. care givers. Requestors attempt to acquire a service which will match most accurately their expectations and which will be performed in a given place and time, established in the process of appointment coordination with the other party (supplier). On the other hand, volunteers search for the possibility to engage themselves in volunteering projects or to perform a free of charge one-time service to the requestor, who specifies their need for a particular work. It is worthwhile to mention that the roles of the requestor and of the volunteer may be performed interchangeably by the same person, depending on the context. In the case of tasks whose performance is hampered by the health condition, an elderly person uses the services provided by professionals or volunteers and, at the same time, he or she provides other elderly people with voluntary services which correspond to his or her current state of health. Such a solution meets the aforementioned natural need of senior citizens which has been identified in the course of quantitative research, namely the need to self-organize and to provide mutual assistance.

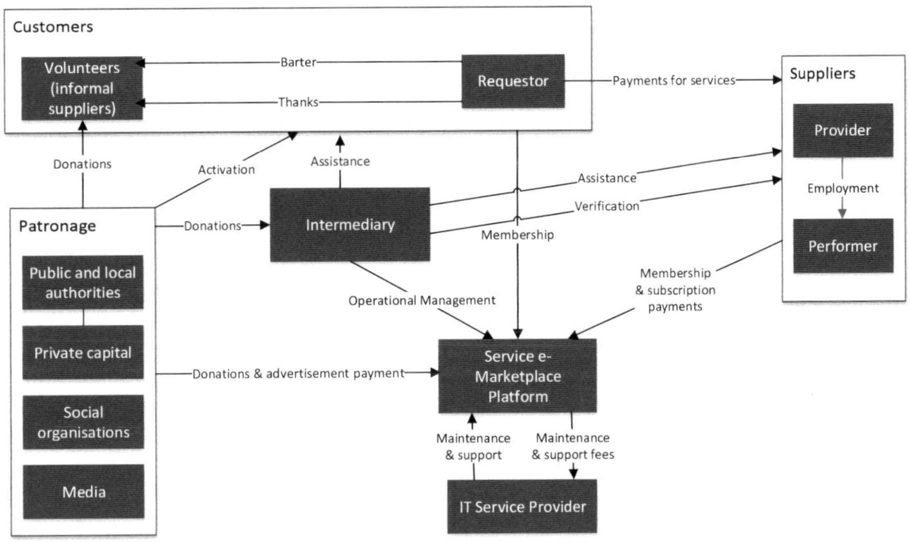

Figure 1. The business model for occupational activation of elderly people with service e-marketplace platform

It is the intermediary who plays a crucial role in this model. Intermediary's key task is to create a safe environment for senior citizens, in which they can use the ICT platform. Furthermore, the intermediary organizes the market by supporting the customers and suppliers in particular transactions. It also provides users with technological and factual support and they could be responsible for the performance of the party's duties. In the second case, the intermediary, while acting on behalf of the consumer, orders the service via the platform and negotiate the conditions of performance as well as define the demand for the service and choose the most adequate provider among the volunteers. The intermediary, apart from rendering short-term assistance, plays a significant role in administrating the Internet platform and in verifying the quality of professional services and service providers. It also participate in the process of stimulating the market by carrying out promotional activities on and outside the platform. The function of intermediary may be performed by the already existing communities and organisations activating senior citizens, such as senior citizens' centres and Third Age Universities. To make this possible, it is necessary to ensure public and private sources of funding. Apart from the funds obtained from subscription fees, the resources are contributed by the patronage group composed of the public and local authorities and by private donors, whose statutory objectives match the objectives of this business model by focusing on the professional activation of senior citizens. This group, together with the media and social non-governmental organisations, plays an important role in promoting and activating elderly people with the cooperation of the intermediary.

Such a business model takes the subjective dimension of the market centred around the service e-marketplace platform and is designed to activate elderly people in their professional careers. Defined roles and relations make it possible to understand the functioning of the market. However, what constitutes an intrinsic element of each model is a unique set of values provided by the said model in the form of services, as mentioned in the introduction to this paper. Therefore, it seems appropriate to complement the model with its formal representation, which helps to identify and systematize information in its key areas. The aforementioned BMC tool has been applied here (see table 1).

Table 1. The business model canvas for occupational activation of elderly people with service e-marketplace platform

<table>
<tr>
<td rowspan="2"><u>Key Partners</u>

Service providers

Social organisations

Public/local authorities

Private sponsors

IT service provider</td>
<td><u>Key Activities</u>
Assistance in matchmaking requestors with volunteers and suppliers
Membership management
Buying and selling services
Operational management
IT maintenance and support
Recruiting volunteers
Verifications of quality of services</td>
<td rowspan="2"><u>Value Propositions</u>
Selling own skills,
Lifelong learning
Additional incomes from helping others,
"Good feeling" and positive reputation
Support in necessary works,
Social participation and inclusion
Independency,
Improved quality of life.</td>
<td><u>Customer Relationships</u>
Intermediary office with personal assistance
Remote assistance via call center
Complaints handling</td>
<td rowspan="2"><u>Customer Segments</u>

Elderly people

Volunteers</td>
</tr>
<tr>
<td><u>Key Resources</u>
Intermediary employees
Volunteers
Performers
Intermediary office and equipment
Provider offices and equipment
Technical infrastructure
Donations</td>
<td><u>Channels</u>
Web site
Intermediary office
helpdesk Service
Cold calling
Word-of-mouth marketing
Social events</td>
</tr>
<tr>
<td colspan="3"><u>Cost Structure</u>
IT Support & maintenance fees
Intermediary employees' salaries
Operational costs</td>
<td colspan="2"><u>Revenue Streams</u>
Donations
Membership & subscription payments
Advertisement payments</td>
</tr>
</table>

Customer segments gather groups of people who share similar characteristics and who are targeted by activities. In this model, reaching retirement or pre-retirement age constitutes the criterion of similarity for one of the groups and it entails the need of professional activation in order to maximally prolong the professional life. The second group gathers volunteers.

Customers are offered a certain value, i.e. a set of services important for them. They also can sell their own skills acquired in the professional lifetime. The fact that the platform facilitates the performance of services for elderly people results in the possibility to generate an additional income and, most of all, to develop a good feeling through helping others and to build one's own reputation in the immediate surroundings. Belonging to the community centred around the platform makes it possible to avoid social exclusion. On the other hand elderly people who are in need can find a person or organisation who will render the necessary assistance to them. Thus, they will be able to be independent and they will be able to improve their quality of life due to the possibility of receiving help, both chargeable and free of charge, in the areas in which they are not self-reliant irrespective of the reason of the said dependency.

Channel is the way in which a value is offered to a customer. There exist communication channels, distribution channels, sales channels; in other words channels are points of contact between the customer and the platform/intermediary. The key channel is a webpage. Available interactive tools facilitate a direct contact with the intermediary and help to solve problems. Moreover, there exists a helpdesk available by phone in order to support all the users. The intermediary runs an office in which direct customer service is provided and in which customers who don't have the access to the Internet and computer or who are afraid to use the application on their own at home can easily utilize the platform. This meets the need of a continuing access to technological and factual support trainers in the area of the application of ICT. The said need was identified as a result of the in-depth direct interviews. The platform is also promoted via many communication channels, including cold calling, the word-of-mouth marketing and social events.

Another area are the relations formed with the customers when value propositions are being presented to them. Two basic forms of contact are proposed here: personal and direct relations with the customer service employees in the office and a remote contact via the helpdesk centre. It is very important to listen carefully to the customers and pay attention to their opinions. Such an approach results in the possibility to report complaints connected with the services and in the quick decision path of handling such complaints.

Providing the customers with a proper value proposition should generate revenue streams. The business model is of a pro-social character and therefore the elderly people will not pay for the platform usage. This meets their wishes from the interviews. The fees in the subscription or commission model will be paid by service providers. However donations from the public and local authorities and those companies whose CSR objectives match the objectives of the platform will make up a significant part of the budget.

Each business needs tangible and intangible assets, which are necessary to provide a value for customers. In that case, these are mostly people, who provide customer service and who perform services. Given the need for the existence of the customer service office, it is necessary to rent premises and purchase the office equipment. Moreover, the computer equipment and software constitute a significant asset which facilitates the functioning of the platform in the Internet environment and which meets all the formal requirements.

Apart from the resources, each business model needs proper activities required for its functioning. Selected key activities tending toward providing values are presented here. What comes to the fore is supporting the end users in the process of selling or buying services or in recruiting to volunteering projects by providing tools for searching through the offers, ordering and coordinating the dates. All the parties can manage their calendars and the service providers gain a set of tools for defining the offer and for personnel management. The application is enhanced with the tools for the intermediary, who can actively participate in the purchasing process through matchmaking the providers and customers. Moreover, the intermediary is responsible for the operational platform management and for responding immediately to all the market and technological incentives. To this end, the intermediary will use a dedicated ICT tool. Moreover, verifying service providers and the quality of performed services constitutes the essential activity conducted by the intermediary. Thanks to the application and due to authentication solutions, the users can manage their digital identity in a complex and safe way. For elderly people, the sense of security is an important determinant when it comes to the usage of the Internet applications, what was repeatedly emphasized in the interviews.

In the light of the model assumptions, the support given to the partners – entities, whose broadly understood participation is necessary to offer value propositions, is very important. They play two crucial roles in the model: on the one hand they provide resources, especially financial ones, necessary for the functioning of the business model in practice (public/local authorities and private investors) and on the other hand, they support the process of activating elderly people (public/local authorities, social organisations, the media). The IT Service Provider, already mentioned in this paper, is also an important partner as they provide both the application and its maintenance, and, if the need arises, they develop the application further.

When the customers generate revenue streams, the internal resources and activities generate the structure of costs. The expenses are mostly related to the development and maintenance of the application and to the cost of salaries paid to employees engaged in the work for the business venture. There are also costs of the office equipment and rents. There is no need to finance the promotion of the platform as such expenses are borne by the partners, especially by the media, who have assumed media patronage of the endeavour.

5. CONCLUSION

The issue of the quality of life of elderly people acquires special importance in the face of the adverse demographic forecast. One of the steps in the right direction to cope with these rather pessimistic trends is occupational activation of elderly people in order to prolong their active participation in the labour market. New forms of service distribution facilitate the aforementioned process. The business model of the service e-marketplace platform, which was proposed as a result of the research work and in-depth direct interviews with seniors, assumes the transfer of the processes of ordering and coordinating the services, which so far have been organized in a traditional way, to the virtual reality. The said transfer makes it possible to verify the service providers, to respond quickly to the market needs, to match the offer to the expectations and to enhance the trust in the system among the prospective customers. Supplying the market with an advanced platform which integrates providers of services for people 50+, employers who wish to hire seniors in part-time jobs on a commercial or voluntary basis, and service recipients, constitutes a complex response to the needs of the target group. Moreover, it provides environmental integration of elderly people and helps to build capital of confidence in service providers and employers. The intermediary renders assistance to seniors in the field of price negotiations, settlements and verification of service providers and employers. The model also takes into account the impact which the patronage exerts on the functioning of the service e-marketplace by providing ongoing financing and by promoting an active approach adopted by seniors on the labour market. The latter aspects also constitute a key determinant of success of the endeavour, whose self-financing capabilities are limited due to its pro-social character.

The model was evaluated partially in the series of iterative implementations in the Swiss and German market conditions and the feedback is quite positive. Seniors, especially the older ones, address the anxiety of using ICT-based platform, however the demographic change and the greater share of early retirees with higher ICT skills should lead to the gradual assimilation of this solution to everyday life in the next few years. The key role is played by the intermediary, whose extent of engagement is dependent on the level of digital awareness and competences of the society and should be regulated before the implementation. That is why such a model is applicable to many different settings, in different countries and environments. For

Poland there is a strong need to extend the role of intermediary and assist seniors in their first steps of taking part in the platform-centred community. The model is a pioneering initiative of such a large scale. Some undertakings aimed at promoting the volunteering among seniors are already running e.g. ProjectsAbroad for Elderly or RetiredBrains.com, however none of them use ICT platform as a core transactional tool.

ACKNOWLEDGEMENT

The paper is a part of the ActGo-Gate project funded by the AAL Agency awarded on the basis of the agreement number AAL6/1/2015.

REFERENCES

Brinkmann, S. and Kvale, S., 2015. *InterViews: Learning the craft of qualitative research interviewing*, Sage, LA, USA.

Butryn, B. et al, 2015. The Application of PEST Analysis to the Creation of the Profile of na IT Product Designed to Activate and Support Senior Citizens in Poland", in *Proceedings of the 4th ICTRS*, Rhodes, Scitepress, pp. 109–115.

Kleinschmidt, S. and Peters, C., 2017. Fostering business model extensions for ICT-enabled human-centered service systems, in *13th International Conference on Wirtschaftsinformatik (WI)*, St. Gallen, Switzerland.

Kutera, R. and Gryncewicz, W., 2016. Single sign on as an effective way of managing user identity in distributed web systems. The ActGo-Gate project case study, *Informatyka Ekonomiczna*, Vol. 40 No. 2, pp. 25–43.

Kutera, R. et al, 2016. The model of delivering an IT product designed to activate and support senior citizens in Poland, *Annals of Computer Science and Information Systems*, Vol. 9, 2016, PTI, pp. 195–202.

Kutera, R. et al., 2017. Towards an Architecture of Electronic Service Market System - requirements analysis and evaluation, *Annals of Computer Science and Information Systems,* in press.

Leszczyńska, M. et al., 2016. The impact of macroenvironment on senior's digital activation in Poland, *Organization Review*, No. 9, pp. 65–71.

Łysik, Ł. et al., 2015. Social Collaboration Solutions as a Catalyst of Consumer Trust in Service Management Platforms - A Research Study, in Abramowicz, W. (Ed.), *Business information systems: 18th International Conference, BIS 2015, Lecture Notes in Business Information Processing*, Vol. 208, Springer, Cham, pp. 220–232.

Maciaszek, L. et al., 2016. Integrated Service E-Marketplace for Independent and Assisted Living – Business and Software Engineering Challenges", in Shishkov B. (ed) *Business Modeling and Software Design. BMSD 2016. Lecture Notes in Business Information Processing*, vol 275, pp. 221–231.

Maglio, P.P. et al., 2015. Commentary-Toward a Research Agenda for Human-Centered Service System Innovation, *Service Science*, Vol. 7 No. 1, pp. 1–10.

Moody, H.R., 2013. *Abundance of life: Human development policies for an aging society*, Columbia University Press.

Oesterle, H., 2014. Business oder Life Engineering?, *HMD Praxis der Wirtschaftsinformatik*, Vol. 51 No. 6, pp. 744–761.

Oesterle, H. and Otto, B.,2010. Consortium research, *Business&Information Systems Engineering*, vol. 2/5, pp. 283–293.

Osterwalder, A., 2004. The Business Model Ontology-a proposition in a design science approach.

Rot, A. et al., 2017. Design and Assessment of User Interface Optimized for Elderly People. A Case Study of Actgo-Gate Platform", in *Proceedings of 3rd ICT4AWE International Conference*, Porto, Portugal, SCITEPRESS, pp. 157–163.

Rowe, J.W. and Kahn, R.L., 2015. Successful Aging 2.0. Conceptual Expansions for the 21st Century, *The Journals of Gerontology: Series B*, Vol. 70 No. 4, pp. 593–596.

Szymańczak, J. and Ciura, G., 2012. Aging in Polish society, *Infos – socio-economical issues*, No. 12, pp. 1–4.

Vargo, S.L. and Lusch, R.F., 2016. Institutions and axioms. An extension and update of service-dominant logic, *Journal of the Academy of Marketing Science*, Vol. 44 No. 1, pp. 5–23.

Wirtz, B.W. et al., 2016. Business Models. Origin, Development and Future Research Perspectives, *Long Range Planning*, Vol. 49 No. 1, pp. 36–54.

Witell, L. et al., 2016. Defining service innovation. A review and synthesis, *Journal of Business Research*, Vol. 69 No. 8, pp. 2863–2872.

Zhou, Z., 2016. The Basic Features of Service Economy Development Trend, *Springer Singapore*, available at: http://link.springer.com/chapter/10.1007/978-981-287-901-1_6/fulltext.html.

TOWARD OPTIMIZATION OF MARITIME TRAINING ON COMMUNICATIONS: A PILOT STUDY

Yushan Pan, Guoyuan Li, Steinar Nistad and Hans Petter Hildre
Department of Ocean Operations and Civil Engineering, Norwegian University of Science and Technology
Aalesund, Norway

ABSTRACT

Intelligent machines and advancing IT technologies enabling operators on a ship's bridge can work together with the platform and other vessels via communications channels. Even though research has addressed on the importance of "readback" skills in maritime communication, chaos communications in reality dismiss those "readback" skills. Due to poor design of communications channels, interactive relations between a group people and systems are overlooked. This paper records a case that took place in one of the offshore oilfields at Sea, which due to poor communications, resulted in unsafe operations. We adapt actor-network theory (ANT) to analyze and characterize weakness points of interaction relations between human and human communications as well as human and machine communication for maritime operations. We suggest that more training on communications, focusing on communications in interaction relations, would help enhancing safety concerns in safety critical working environments.

KEYWORDS

Design research driven, communications, and training

1. INTRODUCTION

Many researchers have investigated how to design for collaboration from different perspectives. For example, researchers have explored systems requirements (Sommerville et al. 2012) and conducted ethnographic studies on work practices in different workplaces, such as health care (Bardram 1998), the London underground (Heath & Luff 1991), onshore crane operations (Haavik 2014), and offshore operational systems (Bailey et al. 2006; Bøgh Andersen 2000). All these studies investigate users work with computer systems in situ, but do not address how technologies can be used if information is blended when performing tasks. In addition, those studies do not address how maritime training can be built up based on identified technical problems. In an offshore study, one researcher concludes that physical and information spaces are not designed well and should be improved to reflect a richer understanding of work routines on board (Pan 2016). That study does not account for insufficient communication and the management and organization of communications procedures, both of them also influence offshore operations.

This paper uses field studies on a ship's bridge of an offshore supply vessel. The communications systems are chosen in twofold. First, we use communication systems to identify technical problems in design. Through those technical problems in design, we suggest how to find out interactive relations between human and communications channels. Second, we use those interactive relations to suggest that maritime training should focus on those interactive relations. Communications should be trained to the points of interactive relations. We choose communications channels because when one vessel communicates with an oil platform, other irrelevant vessels around the platform should not be able to hear these messages. However, in reality, such communications are disordered, and all of vessels around the platform can hear the messages. These issues caused such serious mistakes that two vessels almost collided. Hence, to increase safety in offshore operations, frequent communication is a typical problem that needs to be solved. Second, insufficient management and organization of the functionalities of communications systems result in problems when designing systems. It is important to reformulate current understanding in maritime domain to better support cooperative work in maritime training. Hence, this article aims to discuss how to optimize maritime training on communications.

2. RELATED WORK

Researchers concern on communications issues from sociology perspective. Researchers use a micro-analytical approach to identify the work practices that speakers display in pre-scripted user-device interaction, such as airline operation center and air traffic control (Goodwin 1995; Goodwin 1996; Goodwin & Goodwin 1996), emergency centers (Baker et al. 2005; Tracy 1997; Tracy & Tracy 1998; Tracy & Anderson 1999), London underground control room (Heath & Luff 1992), cockpit interaction (Nevile 2001; Nevile 2004; Nevile 2005b; Nevile 2005a; Nevile 2006; Nevile 2007; Nevile 2008), and bridge team interaction (Bailey et al. 2006; Froholdt 2016). For example, researchers use the method of conversation analysis to check whether marine operators have done "readback" during their communications (Froholdt 2016). A readback loop in a communication process is that everyone repeats itself again when a person who receives or sends a message to other person. All those studies mainly address on how social orders of work practice are conducted. In addition, those studies also address on how such orders of work practices can shed lights on design of technology. If we bring "readback" into the maritime training, however it is nothing new in maritime domain. Studies in social orders of work practice do not point out a direction where should we focus on maritime training.

We do not focus purely on social work in communications. We also have different opinions of how social activities can shed lights to organize safety manners in maritime operations. We have interests on how to develop and plan engineering work to embrace suggestions from social orders of work practices to improve maritime communications. However, there is a few studies in the research field of maritime communications, focusing on training and providing technical supports (Bøgh Andersen 2000). Because of 'how-to' solution for trainers does not provided, researchers argue that sociologists have interested in raising up questions rather than providing technical how in their academic radar (Arminen 2001). Hence, in this paper we firstly use actor-network theory to analyze work practices of maritime communication through a fieldwork. Secondly, we suggest how to reframe the communications channels to unpack points where maritime training can take place. The aim is to providing a direction for upcoming engineering studies to understand how maritime communications can be improved.

3. THEORY AND METHOD

Actor-network theory (ANT) (Latour 1990) becomes a natural theoretical lens to scope these relations in this article because it gives voice to technological artefacts (Cordella & Shaikh 2003). That understanding expands our understanding of how an interactive relation is created if human beings interact with other human beings in addition to using some materials (Law 2009). This is important for categorizing interactive relations, since incompatible interests from actants may result in breakdowns during maritime communications, and this makes the network visible. The translation of interests may then be inscribed into a medium, be it a technology, work plan, procedure for training purposes. The actants may support the translation to perform an enrolment (Ingold 2001). To understand how people, use communications systems in situ, fieldwork was conducted in half a year of 2015. Operators were presented with the purpose of the study and gave informed consent, which is requested by Norsk samfunnsvitenskapelig datatjeneste (NSD). During the fieldwork, one of the researchers was also invited to have dinner with the operators on multiple occasions. Hence, there were many opportunities for interviews after observing on the ship's bridge.

From the very beginning of offshore operations, an offshore vessel has to wait far away from a platform. The platform gives orders to specific offshore vessels. An onshore center also coordinates with offshore vessels to serve specific platforms. Pathological communications in offshore operations occur in the following fragments of dialogue. The conversations are in English, but sometimes also mixed with the Norwegian and Danish languages. Those languages are translated into English in this article.

4. THE CASE

At the beginning, the communication was between an offshore vessel - Victore Princess (VP), and the oil platform. Bridge operators on the VP send their greetings to the platform "Good day, this is VP". Platform operators reply to the VP then has to responses even though VP asks a further question "We are ready to work with you. Can we go now?". Suddenly, the onshore center interjected into this communication and requested VP to report its current position at sea. The VP answered that request. However, in this communication, the bridge operator on the VP did not confirm whether or not this response came from the platform. The bridge operator sent an order to the engine room and started to approach the platform. A few minutes later, the platform replied. However, this reply was to another vessel, Seabed Vivian (SV), rather than VP. Platform operators then asks the vessel to come in for operations, however, they do not confirm who they meant to (SV or VP). This causes misunderstandings between platform and two vessels (see Figure 1).

Figure 1. Four vessels are waiting for their tasks (Photo credit to Teknisk Ukeblad)

Although VP tried to ask whether the platform was calling SV, no reply came from Seabed Vivian. And we observed that SV is trying to approach the platform. Moreover, it was nearer to the platform than VP. The platform did not call SV immediately to stop it. Instead, the platform guided VP to approach its crane #3. However, the operator of crane #3 did not notice that two vessels were coming toward him at the same time from different directions. The bridge operator on VP did not report this issue, even though he saw it. Instead, the bridge operator continued his own work. At the same time, the onshore center called VP to move its position. The bridge operator on the VP did not realize that changing direction in this manner would cause a problem later on. Then, the bridge operators on VP just managed to perform dynamic positioning operations to properly position. There were quite a few spaces between the two vessels - both vessels were under crane #3, and they almost stopped at the same time. At this moment, all the communications were disordered. No one can recognize which order applied to whom, when, and for what reason, nor the originator of orders. In Figure 2, we show how VP's communications are organized. Our analyses and discussions open up a direction of how maritime communication should be planned towards to a possible optimization manner.

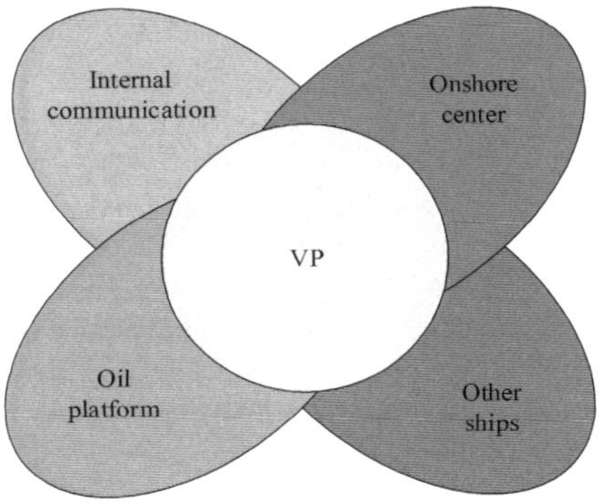

Figure 2. A blueprint of good communication for an offshore vessel

5. OPTIMIZATION OF COMMUNICATIONS TRANING

If looking at the communications from an ANT point of view, each cooperative task between platform-vessel and onshore-vessel can be seen as a network. Such network is not able to create a space for communication between platform and onshore center. However, even though operators on VP enrolled in networks, these networks were different, because they translated to different interests during operations. For example, the onshore order caused confusion to the bridge operator when the platform did not reply to VP. When onshore requested VP to change its direction a bit, it resulted in no space to give way for SV. Onshore may have the power to request vessels to do some actions; however, orders only apply to its own state vessels. Norwegian onshore has no right to order SV – a Danish vessel. Hence, networks become visible due to several breakdowns caused by different interests. When VP called the platform, whether or not the platform replied, they are in the same interactive relation. The reason is because they have the same interest in this network—safely positioning the vessel under the platform. This is a communication process between the vessel and the platform. Another interactive relation involves onshore and VP. This interactive relation is different than the former one, because such a relation occurs when the order is sent from onshore. Even though the operator on VP enrolled in both networks, the interest is different. The first interactive relation is built upon the safety purpose and the second may not be. When SV was participating in the network, the platform intended to ask them to stop. However, the request was sent to VP. This caused an illegal interactive relation, because the network is permitted. The responder should not be VP. If SV replied, there should be a network that involves only the platform and SV, since VP has no action it can take in that network, and of course, it should not be an actor there.

After the shouting from the platform, VP and SV were in the same network. The purpose was to know what was wrong. This is an interactive relation, which is different than the other interactive relation between VP and the platform, as well as the interactive relation between SV and the platform. The former interactive relations were about two actors in different networks. While both offshore vessels were in the same network, their interests were quite different than the latter ones—how to solve the safety problem and move the offshore vessel away. When crane #3 operator coordinated work with VP, the communication should be blocked to SV. In the meantime, crane #2 operator should be clear to whom he was talking.

To promote good communications, based on the previous sections where we characterize interactive relations and define their relationships, we apply this process from an evaluation perspective to promote where to communicate and how to improve. First, communications training should be planned with purpose. From the ANT perspective, every time the bridge operator works with communications systems to communicate with a relevant person/system, the network may change dynamically from the original interest to a new one. In addition, if there is a barrier between different languages and no confirmation of who is talking, the network is invalid, since interests may conflict from time to time during operations. Humans may not know that they are going into an unsafe situation, but they continue to work on the same task, because they may think others are in the safety loop of an operation. For example, the bridge operator did not know why he needed to stop the first time and change the ship's direction. The operator of crane #3 never knew that the operator of crane #2 was also participating in the network and cooperates with bridge operators. These problems are caused by current poor communications. When communication becomes network-based, a basic rule of control during communication is necessary.

Thus, we understand communication training should focus on group communications rather than a simple assemblage of collective communications of each individual maritime operator. The communications systems should be based on a concept of the composition of relationships among interactive relations. With such network-based understanding of interactive relations, maritime trainers should learn about that training course is not only designed to teach maritime operators an institutional set, such as using institutional style of communication (Froholdt 2016). Moreover, maritime training should foresee that human mistakes happen at anytime and anywhere on board. It satisfies that communication channels could have some weakness since developers are also humans. Most importantly, maritime trainers should know how to train operators to face different situations. Hence, this challenges current communications training. In current communications, everyone seems to wear the emperor's new clothes, doing their own stuff. However, people may notice what is going wrong when using communication channels and do their best to minimize its negative effects. For example, the bridge operator turns down the communications channels from time to time. Trainers know that this is a problem, but they may struggle with how to introduce this problem to the training processes.

Given that the communications channels are cooperative, each communications channel should be separately autonomous as interactive relations. Interactive relations could guide the training of communication. In this manner, the weakness of the communications are supported based on the training on interactive communications. Since communications training are conducted with specific purposes, indicating where to train and how to train. It would be better than just saying "readback" is enough (Froholdt 2016). In that case, it is possible to control communication messages which can be sent and received with a fixed route and which cannot.

For example, when human actants have different and incompatible interests, it will result in dynamic network changes. However, such dynamic changes do not apply to interactive relations, even though categorizing interactive relations is based on the network's interest. Interactive relations follow the same interests in a network. And such a network should be creatable. For example, the operator of crane #2 created a communication with both offshore vessels when they got stuck under the crane #3. We cannot say this is an interactive relation, because the interest in this network on each side is extremely different. Even though this network is created, and even if interests in this network can be translated into a compatible one, the interactive relation is still illegal. We cannot invert the causes and consequences of an event. The network that involves crane #2 and both offshore vessels is the result of poorly designed communications systems, which lead to incorrect communications. The operators in the case tried to manage the communication chaos. However, some opportunities to solve problems were missed, such as confirming a vessel's name, reporting another vessel's activities in the same oilfield area, and barriers caused by different languages. Researchers propose that "readback" (Froholdt 2016) can help with solving communication chaos, clarifying who's who (Nevile 2001) in maritime operations. However, when a network was created between the bridge operator on VP and the platform, the bridge operator mistakenly thought that onshore calling was a response from the platform. Although "Readback" can contribute in dismiss misunderstanding between human and human, it seems not a rule of thumb for maritime operators to follow in reality. The bridge operator did not know his reply went to onshore. Even though an order coming from the platform is different than one from onshore, the operator just followed orders without any doubts. As we interviewed the bridge operator, he expressed that he did not see any difference between orders that come from both onshore and oil platform.

As discussed above, interactive relations follow the interests of networks. Hence, the relationship between different interactive relations also needs to be investigated in networks as well. For example, the outcome from the interactive relation between the platform and VP should be considered by the bridge operator when he receives a request from onshore. Such notification should inform communications systems on the offshore vessel that the onshore request is an outcome that comes from a different interactive relation between the bridge operator and onshore. Another example is the irrelevant relations between crane #2 and both offshore vessels. As an outcome from the interactive relation between crane #2 and unknown vessel under crane #1, it should be impossible to link the interactive relation between crane #3 and both offshore vessels, VP and SV. Hence, maritime training on communications should be based on the relationships between interactive relations.

This is important for providing safe operations from a technical perspective to help operators and maritime trainers have an idea of how to bring cooperative work, as relationships between interactive relations, into training. Operators like systems that run and respond in accordance with their expectations. In that case, they can combine their interactions with other tools and systems they use regularly and begin using it quickly without a lot of help or instruction (Maceli 2011).

6. CONCLUSIONS

In this article, from the evaluation of current communications systems use in situ, the interactive relations are characterized by using the theoretical lens of actor-network theory to conceptually support maritime training purpose. A cooperative system, such as communications systems, should be considered a network-based system. Communication training should not simply be treated as a "readback" regulation that focuses on information exchanges. Multiple human beings who interact with part or whole systems to perform their tasks should also be considered. Hence, it should not be considered training a person working with a system and offering an output to others. This paper differs with other studies that discuss training communications for cooperative work through the interactive relations between human and human. The paper wants to promote training of a cooperative communication and evolve it within an overall maritime operations based on the relationships of interactive relations. Hence, in the future, we will further investigate run experiments to investigate how communication training can be improved, focusing on interactive relations between human and human as well as human and machine.

ACKNOWLEDGEMENT

This research is supported by the project "Integrated marine operation simulator facilities for risk assessment" funded by MAROFF, Knowledge-building Project for Industry, Norway (project nr.: 234007/O70).
The authors would like to thank Arnt Håkon Barmen and Jon Palmstrøm for their valuable discussion.

REFERENCES

Arminen, I., 2001. Workplace studies: the practical sociology of technology in action. *ACTA SOCIOLOGICA*, 44(2), pp.183–189.

Bailey, N., Housley, W. & Belcher, P., 2006. Navigation, interaction and bridge team work. *Sociological review*, 54(2), pp.342–362.

Baker, C., Emmison, M. & Firth, A., 2005. *Calling for help: language and social interaction in telephone helplines* A. Benjamins, ed.,

Bardram, J., 1998. Designing for the dynamics of cooperative work activities. In *Proceedings of the ACM 1998 Conference on Computer Supported Cooperative Work*. ACM, pp. 89–98.

Bøgh Andersen, P., 2000. *Communication and work on maritime bridges*,

Cordella, A. & Shaikh, M., 2003. Actor network theory and after: what's new for IS research?

Froholdt, L.L., 2016. "I see you on my radar": displays of the confirmatory form in maritime technologically mediated interaction. *Sociological review*, 64, pp.468–494.

Goodwin, G., 1996. Informatings and announcements in their environment: prosody within a multi-activity work setting. In Y. Engeström & D. Middleton, eds. *Prosody in conversation: interaction studies*. Cambridge University Press', pp. 436–461.

Goodwin, G., 1995. "Seeing in depth", Social Studies of Science. In M. Lynch & W. Sharrock, eds. *Harold Garfinkel: Four-Volume Set*. SAGE, pp. 237–274.

Goodwin, G. & Goodwin, M.H., 1996. Seeing as a situated activity: formulating planes. In *Cognition and communication at work*. Cambridge University Press, pp. 61–95.

Haavik, T.K., 2014. Sensework. *Computer-Supported Cooperative Work*, 23(3), pp.269–298.

Heath, C. & Luff, P., 1992. Collaboration and control: Crisis management and multimedia technology in London underground line control room. *Comput. Supported Coop. Work*, 1(1), pp.24–48.

Heath, C. & Luff, P., 1991. Collaborative activity and technological design: Task coordination in London Underground control rooms. In *Proceedings of the Second European Conference on Computer-Supported Cooperative Work*. pp. 65–80.

Ingold, T., 2001. Beyond Art and Technology: The Anthropology of Skill. *Anthropological Perspectives on Technology*, pp.17–31.

Latour, B., 1990. On actor-network theory. A few clarifications plus more than a few complications. *Finn Olsen "Om aktor-netvaerksteroi. Nogle fa afklaringer og mere end nogle fa forviklinger" - Philosophia*, 25(3), pp.47–64.

Law, J., 2009. Actor network theory and material semiotics. In *The New Blackwell Companion to Social Theory*. pp. 141–158.

Maceli, M., 2011. From Human Factors to Human Actors to Human Crafters: Principles Supporting Design in Use. In *Human Factors in Computing Systems*. pp. 1–4.

Nevile, M., 2008. Being out of order: overlapping talk as evidence of trouble in airline poilt's work. *Advances in Discourse Studies*, pp.36–50.

Nevile, M., 2004. *Beyond the black box: Talk-in-interaction in the airline cockpit*, Aldershot: Ashgate.

Nevile, M., 2005a. Checklist complete. Or is it? Closing a task in the airline cockpit. *Australian review of applied linguistics*, 28(2), pp.60–76.

Nevile, M., 2005b. Integrity in the airline cockpit: embodying claims about the progress for the conduct of an approach briefing. *Research on language and social interaction2*, 37(4), pp.447–480.

Nevile, M., 2006. Making sequentiality salient: and-prefacing in the talk of airline poilts. *Discouse studies*, 8(2), pp.279–302.

Nevile, M., 2007. Talking without overlap in the airline cockpit: precision timing at work. *Text and Talk*, 27(2), pp.225–249.

Nevile, M., 2001. Understanding who's who in the airplane cockpit: poilt's pronominal choices and cockpit roles. In A. McHoul & M. Rapley, eds. *How to analyse talk in institutional settings: A case book of methods*. Contiuum, pp. 57–71.

Pan, Y., 2016. Design of Digital Environments for Operations on Vessels. In A. De Angeli et al., eds. *COOP 2016: Proceedings of the 12th International Conference on the Design of Cooperative Systems, 23-27 May 2016, Trento, Italy*. Cham: Springer International Publishing, pp. 123–138.

Available at: http://dx.doi.org/10.1007/978-3-319-33464-6_8.

Sommerville, I., Lock, R. & Storer, T., 2012. Information Requirements for Enterprise Systems. In *Large-Scale Complex IT Systems. Development, Operation and Management*. Springer, pp. 266–282.

Tracy, K., 1997. Interactional trouble in emergency service requests: a problem of frames. *Research on language and social interaction*, 30, pp.315–343.

Tracy, K. & Anderson, D.L., 1999. Relational positioning strategies in calls to the police: a dilemma. *Discouse studies*, 1, pp.201–226.

Tracy, S. & Tracy, K., 1998. Emotion labour at 911: a case study and theortical critique. *Journal of Applied Communication*, 26, pp.390–411.

QUALITY OF WORK SYSTEM AND HSEQ CULTURE: VIEWS ON ICT BASED ON REVIEW, CASES AND TENTATIVE LIST OF FUTURE KEY FACTORS

Seppo Väyrynen
University of Oulu, Industrial Engineering and Management, Finland

ABSTRACT

This paper starts with a review on the studies of the author's team addressing work system analysis and development. Ten key approaches utilized for 20 years are presented. My team's own cases are mainly describing the information and communication related to work systems, and the innovative network for assessing Health (H), Safety (S), Environment (E) and Quality (Q) capabilities in an ICT-supported way. In addition to the team's own studies generally, and two cases more specifically, relevant scientific literature is reviewed. Other researchers' contributions, utilized for the team's studies and for future outlines of key factors forwards while promotion of quality of working life is concerned, are described. ICT provides organizations with many new opportunities to improve and innovate their work systems.

KEYWORDS

Work system, management system, HSEQ, individual participation, organizational participation, communication

1. INTRODUCTION

This paper is addressing interactive context, resources and conditions for work and particularly their connection with the provision of information and communication needed to manage manufacturing and services companies. The following approaches have been my team's usually utilized prerequisites in the studies for analyzing, assessing and developing work: (1) Humans at work are not isolated from Contextual Factors, (2) Work system (WS) is a concept describing the context, (3) Concerning WS, Information (I) and Communication (C) are essential practical enablers, including IC technology (T) (4) and so are Ergonomics, (5) and Design science as theories, (6) and further need to be mentioned TQM (Total Quality Management) and Stakeholders, (7) Emphasizing Experimentation, (8) and Implementation, (9) and a key role of Participation in both the points 7 and 8 (10) Finally, Addressing both desired (by promotion) and undesired (by prevention) outcomes of WS is important. Some examples of these kind studies of quality of work systems (QWS) and culture comprise Kirvesoja et al. (1999), Väyrynen (2005), Väyrynen et al. (2006), Väyrynen & Nevala (2010), Rajala & Väyrynen (2011), Reiman & Väyrynen (2011), Väyrynen et al. (2012), Väyrynen et al. (2014), Väyrynen et al. (2015), and Väyrynen et al. (2016).

The role of employees at its best, to gain driving forces for both social and technical performance, comprises participation in processes (e.g., Wilson & Haines 2000). The psychosocial preconditions for the success of participation include real involvement, confidence (trust) and motivation (Wilson & Haines, 2000). So, naturally the full utilization of individual participation within WSs and processes for desired outcomes needs a lot of shared I and wise C, intra- and inter-organizationally.

Additionally, if we tried to achieve success within macro context, too, I would propose the following issues related to the high performance business model according to Deshamps & Nayak (1995). They emphasize all the key stakeholders: customers, employees, and owners (shareholders). Their company cases show that employees as well need high positive interest by company and chief executives though we usually think that the last ones pay their attention mainly to shareholders. Actually, high attention is needed to all listed stakeholders, and one can think executives need to work like they are employed by all the above mentioned groups, and in a balanced way. Stock price growth was the highest if the attention is high and balanced: the so-called virtuous circle is fed most effectively. So, satisfied owners will make the necessary investments in terms of pay and benefits, productivity improvement, and work environment to increase employee satisfaction. In their Harvard book, Deshamps & Nayak (1995) continue that satisfied employees will work hard to provide the goods and services that increase customer satisfaction. Virtuous circle analogy shows according to its ideal path of functioning that satisfied customers will provide the loyalty, higher sales, and profits that will boost owner satisfaction even further. I think that the emphasis of this article on QWS can be seen to have a role in keeping the circle in continuous run. The high level of WS and sharing information, and communication within it, and with stakeholders as well, are not of importance only to employees but to owners and customers, too, and further to the society and the globe. In an important way they contribute to high performance and sustainable business by supporting the subjective and objective prerequisites of well-being at work for and by all employees.

2. INFORMATION AND COMMUNICATION – A KEY ENABLER OF QUALITY OF WORK SYSTEM AND CULTURE

ISO as the organization for international standardization has published a standard for a WS (ISO, 2004). In the research literature, most often a WS of five components (human (person, employee), organization, task, technology, work environment) is presented (cf. Smith & Sainfort 1989; Karwowski et al. 1994; Smith & Carayon 1995; Genaidy et al., 1999; Carayon & Smith 2000; Väyrynen, 2005; Väyrynen, 2006; Väyrynen & Nevala 2010; Carayon et al., 2014; Väyrynen et al., 2014). The products (artefacts) – i.e. the technology - are used as a tool to transform various inputs into various desired outputs within the frame of an organization (business or public sector) and other contextual components. This model of intended activity with a purpose can also be used to describe the context of product uses other than work. As said, I see I and C as essential factors and contributors of WSs. C enables interaction that exists and "operates" between and within system components.

The following definition of C guides the current study: "a process by which information is exchanged between individuals through a common system of symbols, signs, or behavior", and " the technology of the transmission of information (as by print or telecommunication)" (The Merriam-Webster, 2017). In general, in intra-organizational WSs, and even more so in the cross- and inter-organizational contexts, the channels and flow of I and C are essential for effective businesses and the individuals within them. (e.g., Väyrynen et al., 2014) Such C is today more and more enabled, aided, mediated and supported by T. Though face-to-face C is important, ICT should as well be more explicitly taken into account in the WSs. T has been considered bringing both pros and cons to C. The above mentioned study tried to promote the pros of T in terms of its potential to improve both the quality and quantity of C. For instance, the Health, Safety and Environment ICT (HSE ICT) relates significantly to C while fulfilling the tasks of reporting and the collection of data, data storage, information processing, and distribution of information to decision makers inside the organization (Kjellén, 2000).

The following industrial expressions of the role of C at work show many essential aspects: First, according to Reason (1997), C problems fall into three categories: 1. System failures, in which the necessary channels of C do not exist, or are not functioning, or are not regularly used; 2. Message failures, in which channels exist, but necessary information is not transmitted; 3. Reception failures, in which channels exist, the right message is sent, but it is either misinterpreted by the recipient or arrives too late.

Second, Hugnes & Ferrett (2003) emphasize the role of C while creating and maintaining:" The safety culture of an organization is the product of individual and group values, attitudes, perceptions, competencies and patterns of behavior that determine the commitment to and the style and proficiency of, an organizations health and safety management. Organizations with a positive safety culture are characterized by communications founded on a mutual understanding about the importance of safety and by confidence in the efficacy of preventive measures."

Third, an increasing trend within current work organizations is moving jobs at multiple sites. It means that employees are mobile, visiting many distributed sites with face-to-face communication situations, while at the same time frequently using mobile ICT as an essential tool during their work tasks and shifts. One example of this kind of business situation is short-haul truck driving (Reiman et al., 2010).

Fourth, it is worth to mention that Saari (1984) showed in his analysis that disturbances in the information processes of a WS and human communication comprise an important factor behind accidents at work.

Fifth, Glendon et al. (2006) concluded, that in highly demanding or busy work situations such as safety critical situations, communication factors typically include ones of language, hierarchy, authority, avoiding conflicts, fears, attitudes, behavior styles, rigid role differentiation, the complexity of the tasks, the impersonality of the media, C via IT or within team where each member can see and hear each other, among others.

Sixth, to guarantee an optimal C in a WS, in addition to the intra- and intergroup interactions of employers, managers and supervisors, and employees. C with external stakeholders is important, too. Fluent and frequent contacts with and between internal and external stakeholders can be provided only by increasing the role of C technology. Dul et al. (2012) show a lot of strategic and wise visions for ergonomics and human factors related, eg., to various stakeholders affecting and affected by modern businesses.

Concerning the WS, my assumption is that qualitatively (and quantitatively) enhanced C has power to increase desired and correspondingly decrease the undesired outcomes of the WS. Glendon et al. (2006) suggest looking at even more and specific topics within industrial organizations, such as the hierarchy, team structure, team performance, centralization degree of the teams and networks, attitudes, and the quality of C. The latter strongly relates to the roles and systems of ICT in company and individual levels, too. More precisely, Glendon et al. (2006) encourage developers to study the following aspects: with an adequate dissemination of top-down communications…, but also bottom-up communications…, ease worker relations…, reduced status distinctions operate through encouraging communication, sharing ideas, and promoting greater concern and trust among workers.

3. INTEGRATED MANAGEMENT WITHIN A FINNISH INDUSTRIAL NETWORK: CASE HSEQ ASSESSMENT PROCEDURE AND ITS ICT SUPPORT

Networking is a typical solution for companies of different sizes to combine and manage their contributions in a competitive way in contemporary business environment. It is typical that employees from several supplying companies or contractors, and independent workers, work simultaneously for the same production e.g. in process industry where big companies collaborate with suppliers, big companies act as customers of suppliers. The suppliers are often of smaller size but in spite of that they and their employees have a very important role in the value network.

The quality features of WS and culture within this kind of supply network are often the ones typical of maintenance activities in manufacturing or similar ones supporting the processes or special situations of companies. Lind-Kohvakka (2015) has concluded that the maintenance-related risk assessment and management has to be holistic, so that WS factors relating to technology, human and organizational viewpoints are considered. The risk assessment and management procedures must also take into account the WS's conditions, surrounding activities and structures, as well as fault manifestation in practice. The analyses may also need to pay attention to post-maintenance WS safety. Maintenance operations are conducted basically in all industrial environments, indoors and outdoors. The risks vary greatly, depending on the operating environment and conditions, and on the task involved. Some typical risk factors are poor system maintainability, defective task safety planning and shortcomings at the sites of industry. Väyrynen et al. (1994) described the conditions in the chemical process industry where maintenance includes many physically heavy tasks. Production employees working in the control rooms of process industry have, generally speaking, much better physical work conditions. The WSs in maintenance and operation are really different, and so are often the conditions at the same factory for day workers vs. night shift workers. (see as well Bergh et al., 2013).

The amount of the above style way of production or supporting processes and tasks, carried out at so-called shared workplaces, has increased. It means that supplying companies' employees work in the same premises (shared WS, multi-employer) than the purchasing company's own people do. The situations mentioned have set up new requirements for managing Health, Safety, Environment and Quality, HSEQ, issues and achieving desired results within that framework. Those requirements are partly regulation-based. On the other hand, they are voluntary, business-driven, promotional ones. Large-scale process industry companies in northern Finland have developed, in collaboration with R&D experts' institutions (Väyrynen et al., 2012, 2016) and started to apply HSEQ Assessment Procedure (HSEQ AP) for measuring and evaluating suppliers. The objective of HSEQ AP is to ensure that outside employees in shared workplaces have knowledge and skills good enough of HSEQ to operate in the principal customer companies' premises. HSEQ AP, run by the consortium consisting of customer companies and their development partners, is a tool and procedure for evaluating suppliers' HSEQ capabilities. One characterization of many supplying companies is multi-site style work and business. In addition, the sites' WSs are very varying concerning conditions and culture. The needs and features of ICT are then specific.

Generally, H, S, E and Q issues belong to the key factors of company's contemporary holistic control, assurance and management measures. Integration of all "additional" aspects of Q is the practical, rational, feasible and cost-effective model. Integrated Management Systems (IMS, cf. Wilkinson & Dale, 2007; Zülch et al. 1998) are used to assure customers that products and services satisfy requirements for "basic" quality (Q). Further, responsible organizations have also to be concerned the working environment and well-being of their employees (HS), the impact of operations on the local community, and the long-term effects of their products and activities (E).

HSEQ management comprises planning, organizing, control, monitoring and review of the measures. Multi-employer HSEQ management can be effectively arranged by a proper participation of all employers including contractors, and employees. Both managerial and labor commitment to HSEQ-oriented culture should be a part of the business and all work activities. Inner and outer auditing of HSEQ approach is in the key role for maintaining the high level of it. In Q maintenance, and in continuous improvement, sharing good practices and applying benchmarking procedures are as well important. Many of both core and assisting suppliers (N=200, around) have been assessed according to the HSEQ AP. An increasing share of Finnish manufacturing and service industries is utilizing HSEQ AP as a prerequisite factor of guaranteeing success in network collaboration. Diverse facts, figures, observations are needed of HSEQ indicators for HSEQ management in companies. That means HSEQ AP is effectively supported by ICT system (Väyrynen et al., 2015). Practical ICT tools of HSEQ Assessment System (HSEQ AS, Figure 1), as part of the procedures provide stakeholders with relevant HSEQ information and communication. Additionally, the ICT system via web sites and many journal articles and conference presentations describe the key features of HSEQ AP, but as well show some key results which act as the evidence of the positive effects of utilizing HSEQ AP (e.g., trend of average accident frequency rate, trend of overall satisfaction concerning service supplies, opinions in focus groups and questionnaires within companies). Though research needs to be continued. HSEQ AP is effective, I think, in both occupational risk prevention and quality promotion.

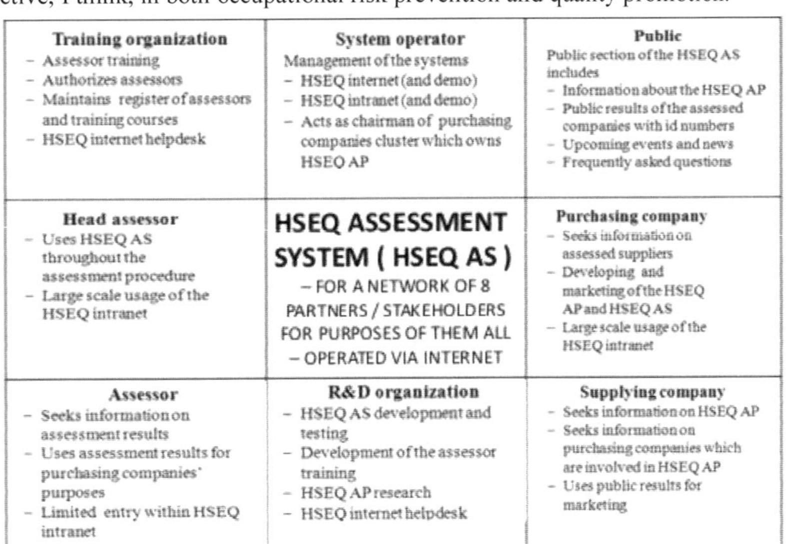

Figure 1. The HSEQ AS acts as mechanism to enable producing and sharing information within the HSEQ AP cluster companies and stakeholders (modified from Väyrynen et al., 2015)

As one representative of the clusters stakeholders we who come from the R&D organization described the near future of the ICT-supported HSEQ AS in the following way (Väyrynen et al., 2015, 794-795):

Better understanding and information sharing practices between purchasers and suppliers are mutually beneficial. They clearly define the HSEQ responsibilities for both business sides. All this also results in benefits to society and to individual employees. In general, organization- and personnel-related HSEQ, sustainability, social responsibility, and well-being at work applications seem to have more diverse possibilities in the future business and employment contexts. In addition to organization-centeredness, more features of employee-centeredness with a high level of usability are possible and are needed for enhancing innovativeness. These features could be valuable in enhancing contributions not only to individuals, but also to organizations. HSEQ AS is unique in its ideas and dimensions, which is why network management in a holistic context is not an easy job. The field of substances linking today's and tomorrow's needs is satisfactorily covered by HSEQ AP. However, full utilization of HSEQ AP requires more sophisticated and more employee-oriented new solutions. More opportunities, especially related to ICT, are waiting to be developed and implemented. In the near future, the ICT solutions and services available on the market will be completely different from simply recording days and presenting sick leaves and accidental injuries. Worldwide, the application of ICT to support national health-care services is rapidly expanding and increasingly important (ITU, 2014). ITU with the other key global organizations published a toolkit that is a landmark in understanding what eHealth is, what it can do, and why and how it should be applied to health care today. The Toolkit might provide a model for promoting a good and innovative practice of HSEQ to be recommended for being implemented widely, nationally and internationally.

HSEQ AP, supported by ICT, like other contemporary systems related to WSs, has many strengths, but for the future success it has to be developed continuously, e.g., to better meet the just mentioned and other emerging and future issues: needs, challenges and opportunities (Figure 2).

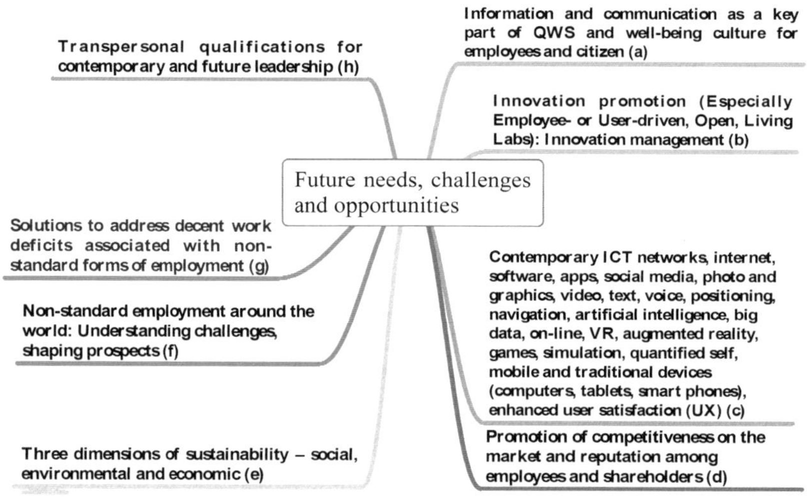

Figure 2. Future needs, challenges and opportunities to be addressed as key factors forwards while promotion of quality of working life via ICT is concerned (a) Väyrynen et al. 2014; b) Svensson & Nilsson, 2008; Danish…; 2009; Goffin & Mitchell, 2010; den Ouden, 2012; e) ISO, 2010; Zink & Fischer, 2013; Niskanen, 2012; Thatcher et al., 2016; ILO, 2016 f) ILO, 2016; g) ILO, 2016; h) Coyne, 2016)

4. CONCLUSION

ICT in use for QWS and well-being culture for employees and work organizations is at its best while all people of an organization are involved in relevant dialogue, and supported, in their work roles (manager, expert, supervisor, "ordinary" employee). It is not enough if there are only single interactional processes of the supervisors and subordinates, or every individual alone or within a small circle is dealing with his / her own information and communication about his / her own WS. Additionally, more and more often not only open intra- but even inter-organizational solutions are needed. Then solutions like HSEQ AP & AS are needed.

The described contemporary features of WS and the roles of IC and ICT in this paper are mainly based on my team's own studies, experiences, and results. Though, other selected literature about above features and roles used as sources during development is reviewed, on the other hand, and as well utilized is literature that shows future starting points, needs and opportunities in the field of work. The last mentioned are important both specifically concerning HSEQ AP of purchaser & supplier value network, and generally: The future aspects presented in this paper are aimed to enhance the utilization of ICT in the work context. Inclusive and innovative sharing of essential business and work knowhow for all individuals, organizations, communities, and globe is more and more needed, and possible. ICT can be in important traditional, and innovative new roles in guaranteeing the conditions where all employees – irrespective of their employment arrangement being standard or so-called non-standard – could be productive and benefit from decent work in the world of sustainable development.

REFERENCES

Bergh, M. et al., 2013. Occupational Safety Climate and Shift Work. *Chemical engineering transactions*, Vol. 31, pp. 403-408. DOI:10.3303/CET1331068

Carayon, P. & Smith, M. 2000. Work organization and ergonomics. *Applied Ergonomics*, Vol. 31, pp. 649-662.

Carayon, P. et al., 2014. Human factors systems approach to healthcare quality and patient safety. *Applied Ergonomics*, Vol. 45, pp. 14-25.

Coyne, S. 2016. Sustainable Leadership; Rewire Your Brain for Sustainable Success. *Transpersonal Leadership Series: White Paper Three.* Routledge, Taylor & Francis Group. (https://www.crcpress.com/rsc/downloads/WP-TL3-2016_Transpersonal_Leadership_WP3_r1.pdf, (10 Jan 2017)

Danish Enterprise and Construction Authority. (2009). *INSIGHT into user-driven innovation.* Programme for User-Driven Innovation,

Den Ouden, E. 2012. *Innovation Design. Creating Value for People, Organizations and Society.* London, Springer-Verlag.

Deschamps, J-P. & Nayak, P. 1995. *Product juggernauts.* Boston: Harvard business school press.

Dul, J. et al., 2012. A strategy for human factors/ergonomics: developing the discipline and profession. *Ergonomics*, DOI:10.1080/00140139.2012.661087.

Genaidy, A. et al.,1999. Principles of work system performance optimization: A business ergonomics approach. *Human Factors and Ergonomics in Manufacturing*, Vol. 9, No. 1, pp. 105–128.

Glendon, A.I. 2006. *Human Safety and Risk Management*, 2nd ed., CRC Press, Taylor & Francis Group.

Goffin, K. & Mitchell, R. 2010. *Innovation Management: Strategy and Implementation using the Pentathlon Framework*, 2nd Ed, Palgrave Macmillan.

Hughes, P. & Ferrett,E. 2003. *Introduction to health and safety at work*, Oxford, UK: Elsevier Butterworth-Heineman,

ILO. 2016. *Non-standard employment around the world: Understanding challenges, shaping prospects*. International Labour Office, Geneva. ISBN 978-92-2-130386-2 (web pdf, 8 Jan 2017).

ISO (International Organization for Standardization). 2004. *Ergonomic principles in the design of work systems*. ISO 6385. International Organization for Standardization, Geneva, Switzerland.

ISO (International Organization for Standardization). 2010. *Guidance on Social Responsibility*. ISO 26000. International Organization for Standardization, Geneva, Switzerland.

ITU. (2014). *National eHealth Strategy Toolkit 2012*. Retrieved from http://www.itu.int/pub/D-STR. (8 Jan 2017)

Karwowski, W. et al.1994. Integrating people, organizations, and technology in advanced manufacturing. *Human Factors and Ergonomics in Manufacturing*, Vol. 4, No.1, pp. 1–19.

Kirvesoja, H. et al., 1999. Implementation criteria for videophone system used in telemedicine: A case in Finnish health care, *Human-Computer Interaction: Communication, cooperation, and application design*, Lawrence Erlbaum Associates Publishers, pp. 271–275.

Kjellén, U. 2000. *Prevention of Accidents through Experience Feedback*, New York: Taylor & Francis.

Lind-Kohvakka, S. 2015. *Application of Accident Information to Safety Promotion – Case Industrial Maintenance*. In Väyrynen, S., Häkkinen, K., Niskanen, T. (Eds.), Integrated Occupational Safety and Health Management - Solutions and Industrial Cases. Springer, Production & Process Engineering. Cham, Heidelberg, New York, Dordrecht, London, (pp 25-37.

Niskanen, T. 2012. A Finnish study of self-regulation discourses in the chemical industry's Responsible Care programme. *Business Ethics: A European Review*, Vol. 21, No.1, pp. 77-99.

Rajala, H.-K. & S. Väyrynen, S. 2011. Participative design science approach on the optimum work system: an argumentative review-based model with a case. *Theoretical Issues in Ergonomics Science*, Vol. 12, No. 6, pp. 533-543.

Reason, J. 1997. *Managing the risks of organisational accidents*, Aldershot, England: Ashgate Publishing Limited.

Reiman, A. & Väyrynen, S. 2011. Review of Regional Workplace Development Cases: A Holistic Approach and Proposals for Evaluation and Management, *International Journal of Sociotechnology and Knowledge Development*, Vol. 3, No. 1, pp. 55-70.

Reiman,A. et al.,. 2010. Short haul drivers' work and different work environments outside the cab – New tool for two-way assessments, *Proceedings of the IADIS International conference ICT Society and Human Beings*, Freiburg, Germany.

Saari, J. 1984. Accidents and disturbances in the flow of information, *Journal of Occupational Accidents*, vol. 6. 91-105.

Smith, M. & Sainfort, P. 1989. A balance theory of job design for stress reduction. *International Journal of Industrial Ergonomics*, Vol. 4, pp. 67-79.

Smith, M. & Carayon, P. 1995. New technology, automation, and work organization: Stress problems and improved technology implementation strategies. *International Journal of Human Factors in Manufacturing*, Vol. 5, pp. 99-116.

Svensson, L. & Nilsson, B. (Eds.). 2008. *Partnership As A Strategy For Social innovation And Sustainable Change*. Santerus Academic Press Sweden, Stockholm.

The Merriam-Webster Dictionary. 2017. Available: http://www.merriam-webster.com/dictionary/ (8 Jan 2017)

Thatcher, A. et al.,2016. This Changes Everything: Macroergonomics and the Future of Sustainability. *Proceedings of the Human Factors and Ergonomics Society 2016 Annual Meeting*. 870-874. DOI: 10.1177/1541931213601199

Väyrynen, S., et al. 1994. Some links between accidents, postural load and accessibility in chemical plant maintenance. *Safety Science*, Vol. 18, No.2, pp. 125-133.

Väyrynen, S. 2005. *Review of Machinery Risk Prevention Through Efforts Expended on Design, Management, Quality, Ergonomics and Usability*. Project Reports of the Work Science No 20, Oulu: Oulu University Press, ISBN 951-42-7822-4.

Väyrynen, S. et al. 2006. User-Centered Development of Video Telephony for Servicing Mainly Older Users: Review and Evaluation of an Approach Applied for 10 Years. *Human Technology*, Vol. 2, No. 1, pp. 8-37.

Väyrynen, S. & N. Nevala, N. 2010. VIDAR as a tool in ergonomic development: Double utilisation model and work system cases. *Proceedings of the 8th International Conference on Occupational Risk Prevention ORP2010*, Valencia, Spain, May 5-7, 2010. An interactive CD-ROM edited by P. Mondelo, W. Karwowski, K. Saarela, A. Hale, & E. Occipinti, 10 p

Väyrynen, S., et al. 2012. A 15-year development path of actions towards an integrated management system: Description, evaluation and safety effects within the process industry network in Finland. *International Journal of Strategic Engineering Asset Management*, Vol. 1, No.1, pp. 3–32.

Väyrynen, S. et al., 2014. Review, Framework and Likert-scale Survey for Improving Intra-Organisational Communication of Finnish Case Companies. *Proceedings of The Fourth International Conference on Advanced Collaborative Networks, Systems and Applications, COLLA 2014,* Seville, Spain. pp. 12-20.

Väyrynen, S. et al. 2015. *ICT as a tool in industrial networks for assessing HSEQ capabilities in a collaborative way*. In: Encyclopedia of Information Science and Technology, Ed. Khosrow-Pour, M., 3rd ed., vol. 10. Hershey, PA: IGI Global, pp. 787–797.

Väyrynen, S., et al. 2016. *HSEQ Assessment Procedure for Supplying Network: A Tool for Promoting Sustainability and Safety Culture in SMEs*, Chapter 5, In: Ergonomics and Human Factors in Safety Management, Eds: P. Arezes & P.V. Rodrigues de Carvalho. CRC, Taylor & Francis Group, Boca Raton, FL, USA, pp. 83-108.

Wilkinson, G. & B. G. Dale, B.G. 2007. *Integrated management systems*. In: Managing quality, 5th ed., Eds. B. G. Dale, T. van der Wiele & V. V. Iwaarden, Chichester, UK: Wiley-Blackwell, pp. 310-350.

Wilson, J. & Haines, H. 2000. *Participatory Ergonomics*, In: Karwowski, W. (Ed.). International Encyclopedia of Ergonomics and Human Factors. London, Taylor & Francis. Vol. 2, pp. 1282-1286

Zink, K. J. & Fischer, K. 2013. Do we need sustainability as a new approach in human factors and ergonomics? *Ergonomics*, Vol. 56, No. 3, pp. 348-356.

Zülch, G. et al., 1998. Arbeitsschutz-Managementesysteme—Betriebliche Aufgabe der Zukunft. *Zeitschrift fur Arbeitswissenschaft*, No. 2, pp. 66–72.

BARRIERS TO E-GOVERNMENT IMPLEMENTATION: MULTIPLE CASE STUDY IN PUBLIC SECTOR

Syed Iftikhar H. Shah[1] and Dr. Muhammad Irfanullah Arfeen[2]

[1]*Director (IT), Ministry of IT, Pakistan*

[2]*Postdoctoral Fellow, United Nations University (UNU-EGOV), Guimaraes, Portugal, and Assistant Professor, QASMS, Quiad-i-Azam University, Islamabad*

ABSTRACT

An e-Government is an effective mechanism that may lead to good governance, improve public service delivery, transparency, paperless environment and enhanced efficiency of employees working in public sector. Despite huge investment in e-Government projects, the success rate of e-Government projects is questionable. This research attempted to explore common barriers to implementation of e-Government projects. Multiple case study as a research method has been adopted for our research work. Three (3) case studies have been conducted in different departments involved in implementing e-Government projects. Sixteen barriers found so far are concerned with organizational, political, socio-technical, behavioral and financial aspects that affected implementation of e-Government projects. Among those six barriers such as lack of ownership of the beneficiary government entities, government staff resistance, in-adequate ICT HR policy, frequent transfer/posting of staff, in-adequate vendor experience and lack of financial resources have been found common in the case studies conducted in three Government entities. Moreover, the barriers have been prioritized depending upon feedback from the stakeholders involved in implementing e-Government projects and then validated through a survey. The findings are further analyzed and suggestions have been recommended to overcome those barriers for smooth implementation of e-Government projects in the public sector. The study provides valuable guidelines for whom who are in the process of implementing e-Government projects in the country particularly in developing countries.

KEYWORDS

E-Government implementation barriers, Ownership of project, user resistance, ICT HR policy, Case study

1. INTRODUCTION

Almost all the countries in the world are attempting to take benefit of Information Communication Technologies (ICTs) through its maximum use in every area of life. Government of each of the country concerned has taken an initiative to involve ICT in their policy matters for its utilization in order to improve, reform and modernize the Government works. An e-Government is the use of ICTs in the public sector to improve its operations and delivery of services to its citizen (United Nations, 2012; Bjorn and Fathul, 2008; Kumar and Best, 2006). Mrinalini (2007) defined e-Government as "Use of ICTs to transform the efficiency, effectiveness, transparency and accountability of informational & transactional exchanges within government, between govt. to govt. agencies of National state, Municipal & Local levels, citizen & businessman and to empower through access & use of information.". It also refers to infrastructure capable for the provision of government citizen services to local community through electronic means (United Nations, 2012; Okot-Uma, 2001). Despite countries of the world are spending ample amount of money from their respective annual budget to implement e-Government projects, however, failure rate of e-Government projects implementation is too high (Arfeen et al., 2017; Bjorn and Fathul, 2008; Eynon and Margetts, 2007; Heeks, 2006). Satyanarayana (2004) stated that E-government projects play an important role to bring benefits to government.

According to European Commission (2012) the benefits of e-Government projects include proper record keeping, fast tracking, save time, gain flexibility in terms of time and place, better control over the process, save cost, increase users trust and enhance quality of services & transparency. The implementation of e-government to achieve such benefits is challenging task. The government reform efforts leading to e-government has been facing various barriers regarding implementation of e-Government project. Such stories have already been published since long time. Past research revealed that implementation of e-Government projects were facing different barriers such as leadership failures, lack of ownership from the beneficiary organization, lack of financial resources, digital divides & choice, organizational inflexibility, lack of knowledgeable & skilled workers, Return on Investment (ROI) justification, security and privacy issues, government entities staff resistance, social issues, fear from Bureaucracy, lack of user training, poor technical design, organizational culture, high employee turnover rate (Abuali, Alawneh and Mohammad, 2010; Schwester, 2009; Mrinalini, 2007; Eynon and Margetts, 2007; Bjorn and Fathul, 2008; Ezz and Themistocleous, 2005), lack of internal political desire, lack of overall vision and strategy, lack of self-interest, lack of strong change management, lack of effective project management and in-adequate technological infrastructure (United Nations, 2012; Shyu and Huang, 2011; Hossan, Habib and Kushchu, 2009). These barriers to implementation of e-Government projects invite researchers' attention to address the matter globally particularly in developing countries. The outline of the paper is as follows:

First Section addressed the relevant research work under the heading "Background/Literature Review". This section contains literature regarding what is e-government, barriers to implementation of e-Government projects, failure ratio due to barriers and causes of these barriers. This section also explains the gaps in the existing literature leading to research questions need to be addressed. **Second Section** explains the research methodology adopted to carry out our research work. **Third Section** encompasses the detail case studies of the three (03) government entities referred to as 'Entity-X', second as "Entity-Y", and last as "Entity-Z" to maintain anonymity. A short brief about the three government entities profiles, project objectives, projects budget, projects schedule, projects goals/objectives achieved. Detail of interviews conducted leading to data collection and analysis has been documented and suggestions/recommendations were also mentioned in **Section Four.** The **last Section** concluded our research work and presented our findings in the area under research.

2. BACKGROUND AND LITERATURE REVIEW

Not all the e-government projects implementation has ever success. There were several barriers to e-Government projects which led to e-Government project failures. The barrier means factor that create a hindrance for governments to develop/implement e-government project in the government entities (Rabaiah and Vandijck, 2011; Schwester, 2009). World Bank (2009) reported that e-government projects failure rate was higher than 50%. Heeks (2001) reported that 35% were total failures, 50% were partial failures and 15% were successes in e-Government projects. Lessa, Negash and Belachew (2012) reported that e-Government projects failure rate was round about 60%. The failure rate of e-Government projects implementation is too high (Zukang, 2012; European Commission, 2012; Rabaiah and Vandijck, 2011; Bjorn and Fathul, 2008; Eynon and Margetts, 2007; Heeks, 2001).

E-government projects failure rates were too high. Consequently, handsome governments' spending to take e-Government initiative ended with minimal success and disappointment. It affects stakeholders concerned leading to de-motivation on their part. Different barriers to e-Government projects may lead to e-Government project failures (Zukang, 2012). Several research studies those have been conducted in the past to determine the causes of failure of e-Government projects explained the phenomena; however, the failures of e-Government projects is still questionable. In this research, three (03) government entities those have attempted to adopt in e-government in their respective domain and initiated related projects were selected as unit analysis for multiple case study to explore causes of failures of e-government projects.

Past research findings explained that poor change management, lack of reward and recognition system in the government entities, minimal user involvement and excessive users resistance towards system usage as barriers to e-government projects (Shyu and Huang, 2011; Abuali, Alawneh and Mohammad, 2010; Hossan, Habib and Kushchu, 2009; Mrinalini, 2007). Other researchers found that lack of ownership and buy-in of the beneficiary government entities as one of the barriers to e-government projects in the government entities. (United Nations, 2012; Nikhar, 2012). Government staff usually was of the view that technology used in e-Government projects might shorten the existing strength of government staff, therefore they were against the e-Government projects (United Nations, 2012; Shah et al., 2011a; Khosrow-pour, 2008; Enyon & Dutton, 2007). Government staff resistance was also found a vital source to create hindrance for successful implementation of e-Government projects. Lack of financial resources was also considered as one of the major barriers to implementation of e-Government projects in government entities particularly in developing countries. Researchers added that governments of the countries should make financial investment for healthy and successful e-Government programmes. They further added that responsible government entity for e-Government projects should also demonstrate tangible output of the e-Governments projects to all the relevant stakeholders and such entities should also highlight that ROI associated with e-Government projects consist of time and cost saving regarding service delivery request (Rabaiah and Vandijck, 2011; Enyon & Dutton, 2007).

3. RESEARCH QUESTIONS

Following research questions are used to limit the research work.

Q1. What are common barriers regarding implementation of e-Government projects in different government entities?

Q2. Which common barriers regarding implementation of e-Government projects in different government entities are of top priority?

Q3. Do lack of ownership of the beneficiary government entities and in-adequate ICT HR policy are two major barriers regarding implementation of e-Government projects in different government entities?

Q4. What are the potential suggestions/recommendations to overcome barriers regarding implementation of e-Government projects in government entities?

4. RESEARCH METHOD

A case study approach was adopted to explore barriers to implementation of e-Government projects in three government entities. Case study may assist to look into a modern trend within its real-life circumstance (Shah et al., 2011; Yin, 2003). Montealegre (1999) of the view that case study looks to be a finer strategy for conducting an enquiry in contextual setting of organizations in less developed countries (Montealegre, 1999). Yin (2003) and Benbasat et al (1987) recommended case study as a research strategy in order to investigate the phenomena under research to explore the barriers where little theory is available. According to Creswell (2013) "The multiple case study method explores a real-life, contemporary bounded system over time, through detailed, in-depth data collection involving multiple sources of information... and reports a case themes". Semi-structured interviews of employees in three e-Government projects beneficiaries (Entity-X, Entity-Y and Entity-Z), executing and sponsoring government entities were conducted which include senior management, Projects Directors and other project team members and regular staff/employees.

Secondly, shareable/un-classified documentation related to e-Government projects relevant government entities (including beneficiaries, executing and sponsoring government entities) were also used as a source of information.

Thirdly, a survey based on closed questions was conducted. The sample size was 130 staff/employees of three e-Government projects beneficiaries (Entity-X, Entity-Y and Entity-Z), executing and sponsoring government entities belonging to different Sections/Wings. The objective of the survey was to explore the priority of common barriers to implementation of e-government projects found during the interviews of employees.

Our research attempted to explore the barriers to implementation of e-government projects due to which e-Government projects success is minimal. The common barriers and potential suggestions/recommendations to overcome these barriers to implementation of e-Government projects in government entities from interviewees' and priority levels of these barriers to implementation of e-government projects have been documented after rigorous analysis and are explained.

5. MULTIPLE CASE STUDY

Three (03) government entities are selected to conduct case studies who are involved in implementing e-Government projects on the basis of the following criteria: firstly, the implementation of e-Government projects in these government entities are completed; secondly, staff of these government entities do not accept the systems; thirdly, projects are closed without achieving the set goals/objectives. The relevant stakeholders in each case were willing to share the barriers to implementation of these e-Government projects. Moreover, relevant documents were available for research study.

The detail about the three studied government entities is as under:

Table 1. Detail about three studied government entities

Entity- Profile	Entity-X	Entity-Y	Entity-Z
Entity- Goals	The goal of the organization is to formulate food and agriculture policies, economic coordination of food, grain and agriculture; it includes procurement of food grains, fertilizer, work on price stabilization of agriculture, internal liaison and economic studies for framing above said policies.	The goal of organization is to launch projects for city development and maintenance, availability of indispensable necessities, further expansion of city with the passage of time, to keep city and its environment clean, acquire land and undertake works in specified area, planning and execution of development schemes, procure plants machinery instruments and material, enter into contracts, carry out studies, surveys and research removal of any works obstructing in the above mentioned projects and schemes.	The goal of organization is to manage development of water and power resources of the country. The organization has different subsidiaries. There was minimal automation of the existing business process neither in the host organization and nor in its subsidiaries organization. The common business processes within the organization deals in Inventory Management, File movement, Finance & Budgeting, Human Resource and project management etc.
Total cost of the E-government project as project charter	160 million	175 million	56 million
Actual cost/expenditure	70 million	128 million	36 million
Time period as per project charter	40 months	31 months	24 months
Actual period	67 months	65 months	72 months
Start Date	October, 2004	December, 2004	August, 2004
Goals / Objectives set	The development and implementation of the different software including customized Enterprise Resource Planning (ERP) solutions, Internal office automation and communication, information exchange gateway, File/Document management, workflow and content management, development and data center.	The development and implementation of the software including customized Enterprise Resource Planning (ERP) solutions to improve service delivery to citizens,provision of IT infrastructure in the said organization offices and building back office capability required for e-services delivery to citizens, online capability to register and track complaints, ensure transparency in government-public interactions, building digitized databases and implementing two-way communication to facilitate e-services delivery to citizens.	The organization decided to automate the existing business processes that might enable it to integrate its work processes, resource and information requirements to implement its operating procedures efficiently.
Goals / Objectives achieved	The expected benefits were not achieved from project. No single software module is in use. No formal quality testing and user acceptance of any deliverable has been given.	Different software modules were developed and deployed at the said government entity. However, no single software module is in use. No formal quality testing and user acceptance of any deliverable has been given.	The said government entity existing business processes are automated without the involvement of users of system. There was lack of ownership and poor change management, Vendors developed the software solution without having in-depth knowledge of the said entity. However, project is behind schedule, and usage of the automated system was minimal.

6. DATA COLLECTION, ANALYSIS AND FINDINGS

6.1 Analysis of Barrier to implementation of e-Government Project in Studied Government Entities

Barriers to implementation of e-Government projects were assessed through data triangulation based on the information provided by the top management, end users, and project team, staff of executing agency and sponsoring agency of these e-Government projects (including senior management, project directors, project managers etc) and extracted from the relevant documents (including projects description document, technical and user manual, minutes of the steering, coordination, change control committee and implementation committees, post monitoring visit reports, projects working papers) and communication documents and so on. The determination of barriers to implementation of e-Government projects is based on (i) understanding of implementation of e-Government projects, (2) each participant's barriers to implementation of e-Government projects (examined and validated through other sources, for example, implementation of e-Government projects documentation, technical and user manual, minutes of the steering, coordination, change control committee and implementation committees, post monitoring visit reports and relevant stakeholders informal communication, (3) a comparison of barriers to implementation of e-Government projects with the approval of relevant stakeholders (including project directors, monitoring officers and project manager of the beneficiary government entity).

The following barriers to implementation of e-Government projects were identified as follows:

Table 2. Barriers to e-government projects reported by interviewees' during the case study

Barriers to e-Government projects	Entity-X	Entity-Y	Entity-Z
Lack of Vision and Strategy		✓	✓
In-adequate Software Vendor Experience and knowledge about government entities existing business processes	✓	✓	✓
Poor Change Management	✓	✓	✓
Poor Government Entities Organizational Structure	✓	✓	✓
Lack of Financial Resources	✓	✓	✓
Poor Contract Agreements Signed with Vendors	✓	✓	✓
Lack of Skills and Knowledge of Staff	✓	✓	
Government Staff Resistance	✓	✓	✓
Lack of Political Support	✓	✓	✓
Lack of Ownership of the Beneficiary Government Entities	✓	✓	✓
In-adequate ICT HR Policy	✓	✓	✓
Frequent transfer/posting of staff including users of the e-Government projects and senior management	✓	✓	✓
Resistance to Re-engineering of Government entities processes	✓		✓
Communication Gaps between Relevant Stakeholders	✓		✓
Lack of User Training	✓		✓
Lack of IT & Security Policies and Guidelines including Standard Operating Procedures (SOPs)	✓		✓

Sixteen barriers to implementation of e-Government projects concerning organizational, political, socio-technical, behavioral and financial aspects are found. Among the sixteen barriers found so far, the following six e-Government implementation barriers are common in three case studies:

1. Lack of ownership of the beneficiary government entities
2. Government staff resistance
3. In-adequate ICT HR policy
4. Frequent transfer/posting of staff including users of the e-Government projects and senior management
5. In-adequate software vendor experience and knowledge about government entities existing business processes
6. Lack of financial resources

6.2 Survey

The questionnaire for survey was given to 130 staff/employees of three e-Government projects beneficiaries (Entity-X, Entity-Y and Entity-Z), executing and sponsoring government entities belonging to different Sections/Wings which have involvement in the development and implementation of e-Government projects in the said three government entities. The objective of the survey is to validate the priority of common barriers to implementation of e-Government projects found during the interviews of staff government entities. Only 93 usable questionnaires were received. The response rate was 71.54%.

The survey result Table, placed below, indicate six common barriers to implementation of e-Government projects found in our research, mean value (calculated based on frequency) and their priority level:

Table 3. Priority Level of common barriers to e-Government projects

Common barriers	Mean	Priority Level
Lack of ownership of the beneficiary government entities	4.80	1
Government staff resistance	4.59	2
Frequent transfer/posting of staff including users of the e-Government projects and senior management	3.71	3
In-adequate software vendor experience and knowledge about government entities existing business processes	3.20	4
In-adequate ICT HR policy	2.77	5
Lack of financial resources	1.92	6

It is observed from the above table that survey result validates the individuals' opinion recorded during their interviews.

6.3 Suggestions/Recommendations

In order to mitigate the above-mentioned barriers to implementation of e-Government projects, suggestions/recommendations were compiled for the Ministry of IT in Pakistan. The suggestions/recommendations were based on the interviews, lesson learnt reports of the e-Government projects in these entities, other relevant projects documents and past e-Government projects staff experiences.

The success of the e-Government projects can be maximized through mitigation of the following:

- **i.** Top management may provide sufficient resources to the e-Government projects for successful implementation.
- **ii.** Top Management may focus on effective change management
- **iii.** Users of the e-Government projects should be involved in the initial stage.
- **iv.** Top Management may arrange awareness programs regarding the e-Government system for its users.
- **v.** Government of country may formulate an IT cadre along with comprehensive IT HR policy regarding permanent IT professional positions with job security, market based/competitive packages, categorization of IT jobs, standardized selection criteria and clear carrier path for successful development and implementation e-Government programmes.
- **vi.** Government of a country may formulate a strategy framework for transfer/posting of government staff, including users of the e-Government projects, and especially senior management which will be based on clear and defined targets/goals such as successful development and implementation of e-Government projects.

vii. Concerned entities may ensure full coverage of mandatory points including software firms' relevant background and experience in the Request for Proposals (RFPs) for tendering of development and implementation of e-Government software systems.

viii. In case of limited financial resources, Planning Department of the country may work with the relevant stakeholders in order to identify the lists of priority and non-priority projects and then competent forum may approve the provision of required financial resources to only priority projects for successful and in-time development and implementation of e-Government projects and non-priority projects may be put on till the provision of financial resources.

7. CONCLUSION

The research work adopted a case study approach in order to identify the barriers to implementation of e-Government projects in three different government entities Entity-X, Entity-Y and Entity-Z. The case study findings lead to the conclusion that sixteen barriers to implementation of e-Government projects were found. Among these sixteen barriers, six e-Government implementation barriers were common in three case studies. Moreover, the barriers have also been prioritized depending upon feedback from the relevant stakeholders involved in implementing e-Government projects in three government entities. The priority levels of these common barriers were validated through a survey. The six common barriers as per priority level were lack of ownership of the beneficiary government entities, government staff resistance, frequent transfer/posting of staff including users of the e-Government projects and senior management, in-adequate software vendor experience and knowledge about government entities existing business processes, in-adequate ICT HR policy and lack of financial resources were further analyzed and discussed. The study also made suggestions/recommendations on the part of interviewees to overcome these barriers for smooth implementation of e-Government projects in a country. The common barriers to implementation of e-government projects basically validated the findings already explained in the past research except 'lack of /in-adequate ICT HR policy' barrier to implementation of e-Government projects. It is also hoped that this research work will be useful source to provide guideline for researchers wishing to explore barriers to implementation of e-Government projects in government entities in a country. The said case studies were conducted in a single Asia Pacific country and it is proposed that same studies may be performed in at least two other counties in order to explore the above mentioned six common barriers to implementation of e-government projects. One country will be from Asia Pacific region and the second country will be selected from a different region. This study has some limitations. The empirical findings focused only on e-Government projects at Federal government level in Pakistan. Nevertheless, this study provides the ground realities of e-government initiatives in Pakistan.

ACKNOWLEDGMENT

This paper is a result of the project "SmartEGOV: Harnessing EGOV for Smart Governance (Foundations, methods, Tools) / NORTE-01-0145-FEDER-000037", supported by Norte Portugal Regional Operational Programme (NORTE 2020), under the PORTUGAL 2020 Partnership Agreement, through the European Regional Development Fund (EFDR).

REFERENCES

Abuali A., Alwaneh A., and Mohammad H. (2010) "Factors and Rules Effecting in e-Government", *European Journal of Scientific Research*, vol. 39(2), pp. 169-175.

Arfeen, M. I., Shah, S. I. H. & Iqbal, J. (2017), "Assessment of Federal Government Websites" 17th European Conference on Digital Government – ECDG 2017, Lisbon, Portugal, June 12th – 13th, 2017

Benbasat I., Goldstein D. K. and Mead M. (1987) "The Case Research Strategy in Studies of Information Systems", *MIS Quartely*, vol. 11(3), pp. 369-386.

Bjorn F., & Fathul W. (2008) "E-Government Challenges & Role of Political Leadership in Indonesia: the Case of Sragen", *Proceeding of 41st Hawai International Conference on System Sciences*. pp. 1-10.

Creswell, J. W. (2013). Qualitative inquiry and research design: Choosing among five approaches. Thousand Oaks, CA: Sage.

Enyon R. and Dutton W. H. (2007) "Barriers to Networked Governments: Evidence from Europe", Prometheus: *Critical Studies in Innovation,* vol. 25(3) pp. 225-242.

Enyon R, and Margetts H. (2007) "Organizational Solutions for Overcoming Barriers to E-Governments", *European Journal of ePractice*, available at www.epracticejournal.au, accessed on 5th January, 2013,

European Commission (2012) "E-Government Benchmark Framework 2012-2015", available at http://ec.europa.eu/", accessed on 5th January, 2013

Ezz I. & Themistocleous M. (2005) "Investigating the Barriers to G2G Adoption", eGovernment *Workshop '05 (eGov05),* Brunel University, West London UB8 3PH, UK.

Heeks, R. B. (2006), "Implementing and managing e-Government: An International Text". London: Sage Publications.

Heeks R. (2001) "Understanding E-Governance for Development", *iGovernment working paper series*, Institute for development policy and management, University of Manchester.

Hossan, C.G., Habib, M.W. & Kushchu, I, (2009) "Success and Failure Factors for E-Government Projects Implementation in Developing Countries", *a study on the perception of government officials of Bangladesh*, in Usha, G. (Eds), E-Governance: Policy and Perspectives, Amicus Books, ICFAI university press, Hyderabad, pages 136-151 Chapter 6.

Khosrow-Pour (2008) "*E-government Diffusion, Policy and Input: Advance Issues and Practices*", Information Resources Management Association (IGT), USA.

Kumar R. & Best, M. L. (2006) "Impact and Sustainability of e-Government Services in Developing Countries: Lesson Learned from Tamil Nadu India", *the Information Society: An International Journal*, vol. 22(1), pp. 1-12

Lessa L., Negash S., Belachew M. (2012) "From Failure to Success: Using Design-Reality Gap Analysis as a Mid-implementation Assessment Tool for e-Government.", *6th International Conference on Theory and Practice of Electronic Governance,* pp. 34-48.

Montealegre R. (1999) "A Case More Case Study Research Implementation of Information Technology in Less-developed Countries", *Journal of Information Technology for Development*, vol. 8(4), pp. 199-207.

Mrinalini S. (2007) "E-Governance in India: Dream or Reality?", *International Journal of Education and Development using Information and Communication Technology,* vol. 3(2), pp. 125-137.

Nikhar N. (2012) "Countries Serious About E-Government Need to Tap Private-Sector Support", available at http://www.thejakartaglobe.com/opinion/countries-serious-about-e-government-need-to-tap-private-sector-support/507595#Scene_1, accessed on 8th January, 2013

Okot-Uma R.W. (2001) "Electronic Governance: Re-inventing Good Governance", London, U.K.: Commonwealth Secretariat.

Rabaiah A. and Vandijck (2011) "A Strategic Framework of E-Government: Generic and Best Practice", *Electronic Journal of E-Government*, vol. 7(3) pp.241-258

Satyanarayana J. (2004) "*E-Government The Science of the Possible*", Eastern Economy Edition Printice-Hall of India, New Delhi, India.

Schwester R. (2009) "Examining the Barriers to E-Government Adoption", *Electronic Journal of E-Government*, vol. 7(1), pp. 113-122.

Shah I. H S., Khan Z. A., Bokhari R. H. and Raza A. M. (2011) "Exploring the Impediments of Successful ERP Implementation: A Case Study in a Public Organization", International Journal of Business and Social Science, vol. 2 (22). Pp. 289-296.

Shah I. H S., Bokhari R. H. and Hassan S., Shah M. H., Shah A. M. (2011a) "Socio-Technical Factors Affecting ERP Implementation Success in Pakistan: an Empirical Study", Australian Journal of Basic and Applied Sciences, vol. 5(3). Pp. 742-749.

Shyu H. P. S., and Huang H. J. (2011) "Elucidating Usage of E-Government Learning: A Perspective of the Extended Technology Acceptance Model", *Government Information Quarterly- Elsevier*, vol. 28(4) pp. 491-502.

United Nations (2012) "e-Government Survey 2012" available at www.unpan.org/e-government, accessed on 7th January, 2013.

Yin R. K. (2003) "Application of Case Study Research", 2nd ed., Applied Social Research Method Series, Vol. 34, Sage, Thousand Oaks, CA, USA.

World Bank (2009) "How Do Manual and E-Government Services Compare? Experiences from India", available at http://siteresources.worldbank.org, accessed on 5th January, 2013.

Zukang, S. (2012). E-Government Survey 2012: E-Government for the People. New York: Department Economic and Social Affairs, United Nation.

NARRATIVE-BASED MANAGEMENT IN SOCIO-ECONOMIC SYSTEMS

Olga Shabalina[1], Aleksandr Davtian[2], Natalya Sadovnikova[1], Danila Parygin[1] and Dmitry Erkin[1]
[1]*Volgograd State Technical University, 28 Lenin Ave., Volgograd, 400005, Russia*
[2]*Moscow Institute of Physics and Technology, 9 Institutsky Lane, Dolgoprudny, 141701, Moscow region*

ABSTRACT

Socio-economic system management is commonly considered as a two-stage process: the first stage is associated with the analysis of the system and establishment of goals and objectives, while the second stage has to do with the development of management strategies for achieving the goals and objectives. Existing modeling approaches to socio-economic system management are classified in terms of goal setting or the development processes of the management strategy and are based on the assumption that a predefined general goal is priory achievable and that the strategy to achieve the goal definitely exists. In real time, socio-economic system management is implemented in a continuously functioning system and its interaction with the continuously changing environment. The subject-object relationship in socio-economic systems can lead to reconsideration of priori goals, their achievability, strategies of their successful achievement and even the necessity of achieving the goal itself.

This paper describes a goal model presented as a structurally ordered space with its elements as formal representations of objectives as heterogeneous, possibly non-numeric objects. The goal space is built as an insertion of the initial set of objectives to a lattice. The lattice properties allow dynamically building the goal space without losing the manageability of the system.

Subject-object relationships in socio-economic systems are described as narrative manifestation and socio-economic system management is considered as narrative in nature system activities aimed at changing the system state in a goal space for achieving the general goal. The principles of narrative-based management approach are described. An implementation of this approach is presented and a management support system (MSS) is developed.

Unlike existing approaches to socio-economic systems management, using mathematical methods for finding the optimal management decisions represented by a formal model, in a proposed approach the mathematical methods are used to monitor the results of management process in which the responsibility for the actions of participants of the process lies in the participants themselves. The results of the activities leading to the impossibility of achieving the general goal are recompensed by the modification of the goal space without losing its structural coherence, and thus the proposed approach ensures the system's observation and management and the achievement of the management goal in terms of dynamically changing goal-setting.

KEYWORDS

Socio-economic system management; narrative; dynamic goal setting; goal space; management support system

1. INTRODUCTION

The quality of management in socio-economic systems significantly affects the quality of life, well-being and security of modern society in general. Ineffective management can lead (and sometimes leads) to disastrous consequences. Therefore, the development of management approaches that provide sustainable system development and lead to the achievement of management goals is a key issue in socio-economic system management research.

Goal-setting is a fundamental stage in socio-economic system management. Unlike the technical systems, which are based on deterministic laws relating to natural phenomena and their properties and goal of their functioning are once and for all given by the system developer, socio-economic systems are entropic and unrepeatable, with the human factor playing a crucial role in the system behavior. Socio-economic system management is implemented in a continuously functioning system and its interaction with the continuously changing environment. The subject-object relationship in socio-economic systems can lead to reconsideration of priori goals, their achievability, strategies of their successful achievement and even the necessity of achieving the goal itself.

Managing socio-economic system without taking into account the influence of dynamic subject-object relationship on the goal setting process can lead to the loss of system manageability and finally, to the "raison d'etre" of the system itself.

2. MODELING APPROACHES TO SOCIO-ECONOMIC SYSTEMS MANAGEMENT

Socio-economic system management is commonly considered as a two-stage process: the first stage is associated with the analysis of the system and establishing goals and objectives while in the second stage, management strategies for achieving the goals and objectives are developed. Correspondingly, existing modeling approaches to socio-economic systems management are classified in terms of goal setting or the development processes of the management strategy.

System management goals are most commonly represented as a goal tree, i.e. as a reduction of the general goal to objectives (sub-goals), the cumulative achievement of which leads to the achievement of the general goal. The goal hierarchy is preferably based on the system organizational hierarchy. Using the goal tree model means that the goal structure is not being changed during the system development and management problem is considered as a problem of achievability of priori defined general goal.

The modeling approaches to management strategy development are commonly based on system structural and/or behavioral models. Both quantitative and qualitative modeling approaches are used to represent socio-economic systems. Graph-theoretical approach is widely used for study and analysis of structural and behavioral properties of a system (Christensen and Albert, 2007). The vertices of the graph, depending on the purpose of modeling can represent the system components, processes determining the system behavior, various factors affecting the dynamics of the system development, etc., and the arcs can reflect information, management, technological and other relations between them. Graph-theoretical models are based on the idea of a metric space, and thus such models limit the system structure description by binary relations, that significantly narrow the ability of the models to reflect the characteristics of socio-economic systems as systems with complex heterogeneous structure and a high degree of uncertainty behavior caused by the human factor.

Simulation techniques and qualitative modeling methods (Kim, 2006, Morecroft, 2007, Papageorgiou and Hadjis, 2011, Motlagh O. et al, 2013) provide wider opportunity in terms of reflecting the properties of complex socio-economic systems. In most cases, these models are focused on forecasting the socio-economic system behavior and selecting management activities for achieving the goal. System behavior in such models is described as the system state dynamics in state-space system representation. System management in these cases means selection of system development trajectory on the predefined set of its states, resulting from the initial state to a predetermined goal state, being unchanging during the system functioning. In general, these approaches are based on the assumption that the predefined general goal is priory achievable and the strategy to achieve the goal definitely exists.

3. NARRATIVE-BASED APPROACH TO SOCIO-ECONOMIC SYSTEMS MANAGEMENT

3.1 Goal Model for Dynamic Goal Setting

Socio-economic system management is a dynamic process aimed at the general goal achievement, wherein achieving certain objectives can depend on the achievement of the others. For managing the system under such conditions, a goal model should reflect the relations of the goals' availability and allow calculating the dynamics of achieving objectives in the given relations. The goal model reflecting such properties can be represented as a set with relations of objects availability:

$$Goal = < Objectives, Ach >, \quad (1)$$

where $Objectives$ – a set of objectives;

Ach – a binary relation of the set.

Elements $objective_i \in Objectives$ and $objective_j \in Objectives$ are related to ach_{ij}, if $objective_j$ becomes available only after achieving $objective_i$, i.e. $objective_i$ is a basis for $objective_j$. The goal structure corresponding to (1) is shown in Figure 1.

Graph representation (1) is the most common representation of binary relations, describing system static structures. However, the organization of dynamic goal-setting implies the possibility of changing the current objective without the loss of system manageability, i.e. actions performed by the system should not lead to changes, destroying its structure and inappropriate system behavior in relation to management actions.

To maintain the system manageability with dynamic goal setting, any changes in the goal setting must not change the structure of the already achieved objectives but should include them into the current goal space, i.e. the goal model should be structurally ordered. To reflect this property (Shabalina et al, 2016.), the initial set of objectives $Objectives$ with the given order Ach is embedded in the smallest algebraic structure (lattice):

$$GoalSpace = < Objectives^S, \leq > \qquad (2)$$

where $Objectives^S$ – structurally-ordered set of objectives;

$\leq$ – partially-ordered relations of the set.

In the new structure $GoalSpace$ built on the structure $Goal$, new elements can appear (the least upper and the greatest lower bounds of the substructures, e.g. $objective_{4+5}$ in Figure 2), providing its structural wholeness and thereby composing a goal space. The structural ordering of the lattice can detect underdetermined and / or hidden objectives, ensure the wholeness of the goal representation and the ability to select the current objectives within the given goal structure.

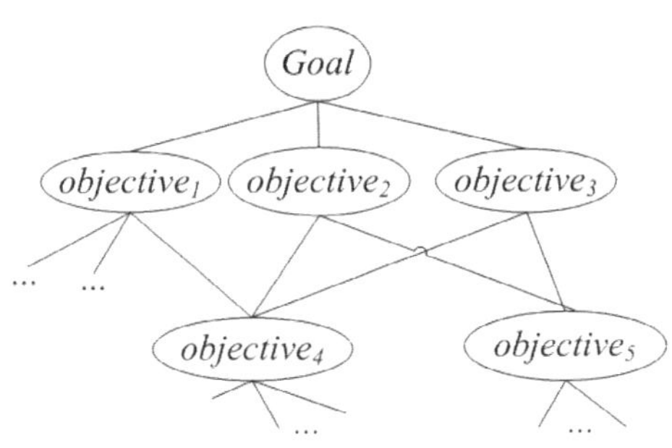

Figure 1. Goal structure

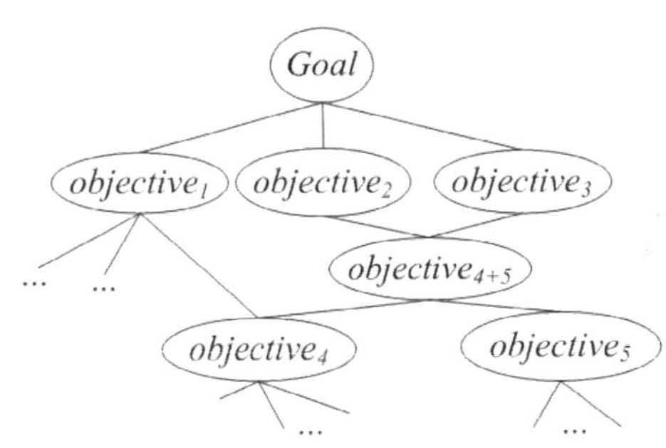

Figure 2. Goal space (Hasse diagram)

The lattice extendibility property allows decomposing the goal space in such a way that each objective can be replaced by the corresponding goal subspace. The lattice divisibility allows taking into account the goal setting dynamics and redefining/removing objectives without losing the whole goal space. Thus, the goal model, represented by a lattice, provides the ability to support the dynamic goal setting dependently on the current understanding of a manager who is responsible for achieving the general goal.

3.2 Narrative-based Socio-Economic Management Method

Socio-economic system management is considered as organization of activities leading to the achievement of the general goal. The general goal bearer (manager) is responsible for the development of the management strategy, and has the final say in making management decisions.

In socio-economic systems, there is no way to determine whether the chosen strategy leads to the achievement of the general goal or not. There are no priori known "right" solutions; there is only the manager's belief that if the solution he had chosen is followed, the goal will be achieved. Any management strategy chosen by the manager determines the future state of the system, and the future state exists in the present as its imagination by the manager, i.e. as a narrative. The achievement of the general goal depends on the management strategy chosen by the manager, management decisions selected for the strategy implementation, activities of people assigned to perform the strategy, and the result of those activities.

The interpretation of subject-object relationships in socio-economic systems as manifestation of narrative allows applying narrative approach to the systems management. The following principles of narrative management of socio-economic system are suggested:

1) socio-economic system management is considered as narrative in its sense aimed at changing the system state in a goal space for achieving the given general goal;

2) the system state dynamics depends on the results of subject-object interactions in the goal space;

3) the subject-object relationship changes not only the priory defined management goals but even targets the orientation of the subjects and objects;

4) manager's activities are limited by his level of responsibility and competence;

5) the results of system activities leading to the impossibility of achieving the general goal are recompensed by the modification of the goal space without losing its structural coherence.

The narrative-based management method comprises the development of an initial goal management strategy and system activities aimed at achieving currently accessible objectives in dynamically changing goal space.

At the first stage, structural analysis of the general goal is carried out (Parygin et al, 2015, Sadovnikova and Gnedkova, 2013) and the management strategy, represented as a set of objectives connected by the relations of their achievability of the objectives, is established (Sadovnikova et al, 2016.). This management stage comes within the scope of competence of the manager, and it is his responsibility to take management decisions. The initial goal structure is used for building a goal space. This stage requires professional knowledge in the field of lattice theory; therefore, it is performed using a management support system (see Section 4). From the manager's point of view, the goal space is also a final structure in which some new elements appear. The interpretation of these elements as hidden / underdetermined objectives is within the scope of the manager's competence.

The goal space built on the goal structure is considered as a strategic plan for managing the system development. The management process is implemented as development of decisions aimed at achieving currently available goals. Generating a set of available objectives in the goal space is also implemented in the management support system.

For each available objective, the necessity of its achievement is firstly defined. The decision is made by the manager after analyzing the current state of the system, the environment and other factors that could influence the decision. If the objective is considered unnecessary to be achieved, it is removed from the goal space. If the objective is identified as necessary to be achieved, the manager determines its achievability at the current time. The assessment of the goal's achievability is based on the verification of the adequacy of resources (finances, time, etc.) for achieving the goal. This stage is implemented in the management support system.

If the objective is defined as achievable, the manager generates a set of tasks that lead to achieving this goal. The tasks are ranked by importance in terms of their contribution to achieving the goal.

If the objective appears unachievable at the current time, its achievement is delayed, and other achievable goals are considered. Achievement of other objectives can result to making the delayed goal achievable. Otherwise, it means that the current goal structure will not lead to achieving the general goal, and the current goal space should be analyzed and somehow rebuilt.

For each achievable goal, the manager organizes the implementation process corresponding to the tasks. After each task is implemented, the manager evaluates the results and decides whether the goal is achieved or not.

Each goal achievement leads to changing the system state on the goal space and the possible appearance of new available objectives. The management process continues until the general goal is achieved.

If at some point in time the current set of objectives $Objective_{cur}$ becomes empty, it means that the chosen system development strategy does not lead to the achievement of the general goal, and it is necessary to modify the current goal space and/or even to rethink the general goal itself.

The management process described above is shown in Figure 3.

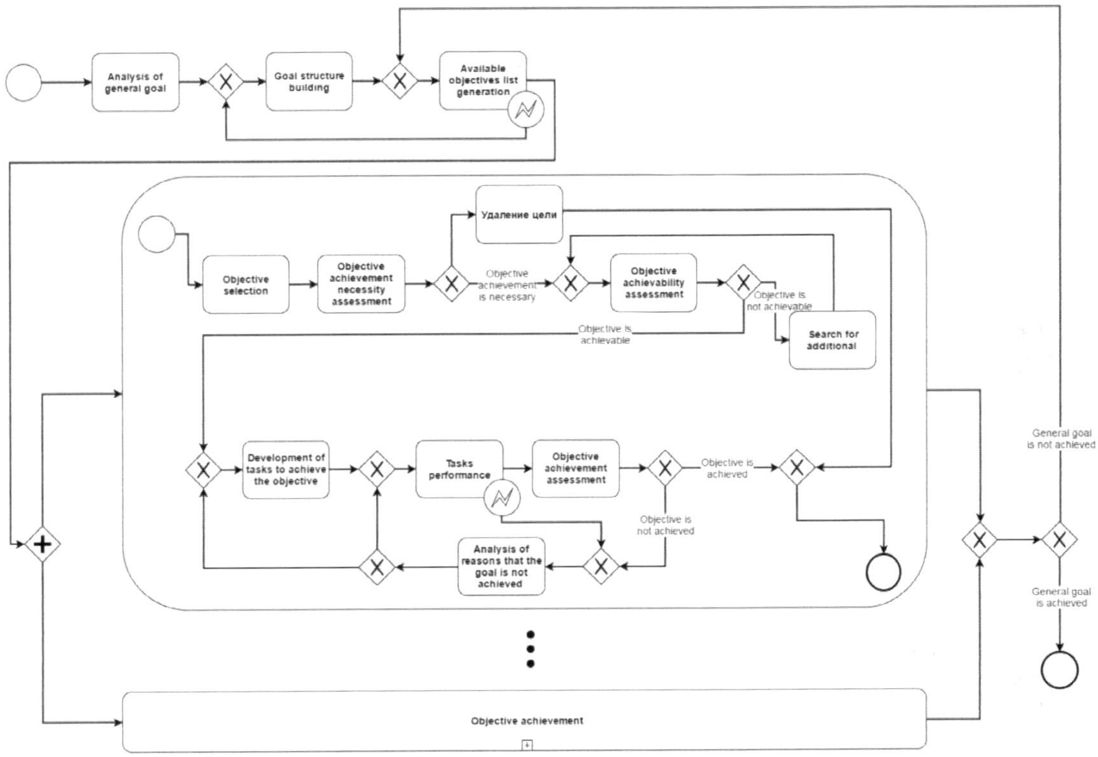

Figure 3. Narrative-based management process (BPMN notation)

4. NARRATIVE-BASED MANAGEMENT SUPPORT SYSTEM

To support the suggested approach to the socio-economic systems management, a management support system (MSS) is developed. The MSS integrates a set of subsystems, each of which is implemented as a standalone system designed to solve corresponding management problems. The MMS architecture is shown in Figure 4.

The goal achievement strategy management subsystem is developed using the lattice-theoretical approach, which allows operating with structurally ordered system models [12]. This subsystem implements the functions of building goal spaces and generates a set of available objectives in the goal space based on idempotent calculus.

The management strategy development subsystem allows analyzing the current state of the socio-economic system, its environment, available recourses and decision making support in defining the management strategy leading to achieve a general goal.

The objective achievability assessment subsystem implements a fuzzy hierarchical assessment method [14]. The objective is described as functionally weighed hierarchy of factors influencing the objective achievement (human and time resources, current conditions of system functioning, etc.). The possibility of achieving the objective with the given factors is defined depending on lower level factor values given by their membership functions.

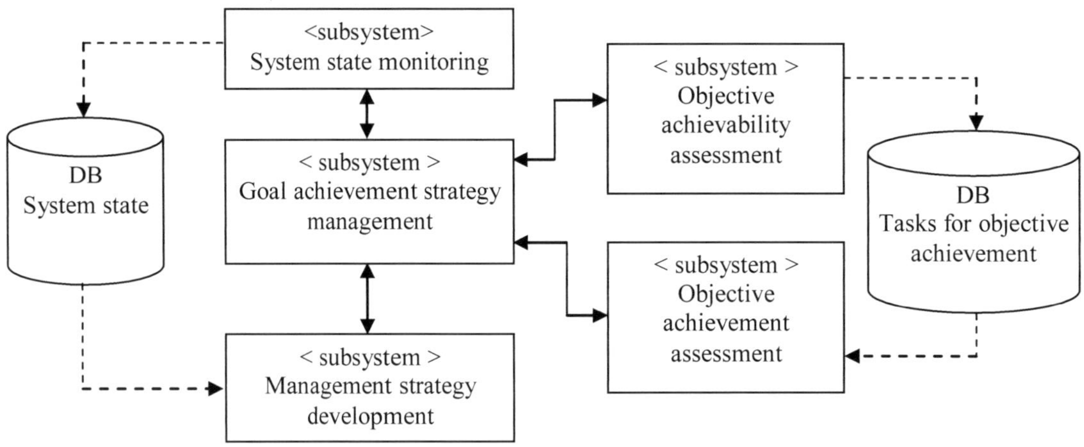

Figure 4. Management support system structure

The objective achievement assessment subsystem is intended for analysis and assessment of indicators of the task's performance. The manager selects/creates a set of tasks that, in his opinion, lead to achieving the objective and ranks them in terms of their contribution to achieving the objective; so each task is associated with its significance coefficient. The objective achievement is defined as the convolution of the estimates of the result of performing each task, taking into account the importance of its contribution. The final decision to consider the objective as achieved or not is made by the manager.

The state system monitoring subsystem comprises the functions of collecting qualitative and quantitative data from heterogeneous sources (mobile apps, social networks, sensors, etc.), indicating the current state of the system and its environment, data preprocessing and visualization.

5. CONCLUSION

In modern approaches to socio-economic systems management, mathematical methods are mostly used to find the optimal management decisions represented by a formal model. The possibility of achieving the management goal in such cases is based on the assumption that the system model is soluble, i.e. the conditions of the functioning system do not change, all the participants of the management process adhere to the roles prescribed by the model and follow the model regulations. In real life, the actions performed by the participants in the system are not predetermined, they are formed in the functioning process of the system; they change the properties of the system and its environment and determine the system status and the dynamics of the goal-setting. Therefore, the use of models based on predefined properties and behavior of the system, given by the initial conditions, are limited by time, until the system properties have not qualitatively changed.

In a proposed approach to the organization of socio-economic systems management, the mathematical methods are used to monitor the results of management process in which the responsibility for the actions of participants of the process lies in the participants themselves. The results of the activities leading to the impossibility of achieving the general goal are recompensed by the modification of the goal space without losing its structural coherence, and thus the proposed approach ensures the system's observation and management and the achievement of the management goal in terms of dynamically changing goal-setting.

ACKNOWLEDGEMENT

The reported study was funded by RFBR according to the research projects No. 16-07-00353_a, No. 16-07-00388_a.

REFERENCES

Christensen, C. and R. Albert, R., 2007. Using graph concepts to understand the organization of complex systems. *International Journal of Bifurcation and Chaos in Applied Sciences and Engineering*, volume 17 issue 07, pp. 2201-2214.

Kim, W. 2006. Improving strategic management with the fundamental principles of system dynamics, *System Dynamics Review*, 21(4), 329 – 350.

Morecroft, J., 2007. *Strategic modeling and business dynamics: a feedback systems approach*, John Wiley and Sons.

Motlagh, O. et al, 2013. An agile FCM for real-time modeling of dynamic and real-life systems, evolving systems. *Special issue on temporal aspects in fuzzy cognitive maps*. DOI: 10.1007/s12530-013-9077-6.

Papageorgiou, G. and Hadjis, A., 2011. Strategic Management via System Dynamics Simulation Models, *World Academy of Science, Engineering and Technology*, p.227-232.

Parygin, D. et al, 2015. Cognitive and ontological modeling for decision support in the tasks of the urban transportation system development management. *Proceedings of the Fifth International IEEE Conference on Information, Intelligence, Systems and Applications*, Corfu, Greece, pp. 1-5.

Sadovnikova, N. et al, 2016.Ontology-based Urban Transport System Modelling for Dynamic Goal Setting & Decision Making. *Proceedings of the Sixth International IEEE Conference on Information, Intelligence, Systems and Applications*, Chalkidili, Greece, pp. 1-5.

Sadovnikova, N. and Gnedkova, E., 2013. Scenario forecasting of sustainable urban development based on cognitive model. *ICT, Society and Human Beings 2013: Proceedings of the IADIS International Conference.* Prague, Czech Republic, pp. 115-119.

Shabalina, O. et al.., 2016. A Lattice-Theoretical Approach to Modeling Naturally Ordered Structures. *Proceedings of the Information Technologies in Science, Management, Social Sphere and Medicine (ITSMSSM 2016)*. Tomsk, Russia, pp. 151-161.

THE SOCIAL IN TECHNICAL ATTACKS – QUESTIONING THE BIFURCATION IN THE FIELD OF INFORMATION SECURITY

Jukka Vuorinen[1] and Pekka Tetri[2]
[1]*Economic Sociology, Department of Social Research, University of Turku, Finland*
[2]*Oulu University Secure Programming Group, University of Oulu, Finland*

ABSTRACT

This paper examines the social in information security. We argue that there is always a social aspect in technical information security attacks. By using Erving Goffman's sociological concept of "frame", we analyse the social in different illustrative contexts, in which technical attacks are compared with social engineering attacks. Through examining the concept of normality, we found that social engineering attacks and technical attacks can resemble each other. In both attack forms, the intruders can hide their actions in the flow of normality. Thus, we question the fertility of information security's bifurcation into the two separate branches (technical/social). Instead of thinking the technical as separated and free of the social, we argue that the social is present everywhere in the field of security, including the technical side as well. All security is social in the first place.

KEYWORDS

Keywords: social engineering, frame, normality, fabrication

1. INTRODUCTION

In this paper, we examine the social as part of technical attacks and argue that the social element can work similarly in technical and social engineering attacks. The main body of research in the field of information and cyber security asserts a fundamental bifurcation between technical (or technological) and social security. The bifurcation concerns as much the guidance of "making" security – how practitioners are guided by standards and frameworks – as well as academic research on information security. Firstly, there is the technological side of security, which refers to hardware and its counterpart software. Secondly, there is the social side of security, in the form of human behaviour, which also covers a vast array of activities and roles from human as end-users and administrators to humans as the creators and designers of technology and code (Gupta and Sharman 2009).

However, in terms of information security research and its emphasis, the two branches of bifurcation are not treated equally. Since the emergence of computers, computer security has been considered mainly as a technical issue (Baskerville 1993) as if technology driven systems call for security that is based on technology. The emphasis on the technological branch of security is affirmed by security frameworks and standards such as PCI DSS (Payment Card Industry Data Security Standard) that consists of 12 requirements, of which 11 are technology-driven and only one requirement is about people which thus refers to the social element.

Recently, softer approaches to information security have emerged. These approaches are based on the inclusion of social aspects (see Loch, Carr and Warkentin, 1992; Adams and Sasse, 1999; Siponen, Baskerville and Heikka, 2006; Gupta and Sharman, 2009). Thus, the social layer is certainly acknowledged in the field. Moreover, the social pertains to a variety of specific issues. For example, security policy compliance issues (Bulgurcu, Cavusoglu and Benbasat, 2010; Siponen and Vance, 2010), insider threat (Colwill, 2009), or computer abuse (Willison and Warkentin, 2013), all include a significant social aspect. The currently fashionable notion of the human element as the weakest link of security (Nohlberg, 2009; cf. Adams and Sasse, 1999) affirms and re-establishes the bifurcation as well. The social level – the human factor – opens a road for accidents and security incidents which then take place at the technical level. In social engineering, vulnerability comes with the social element that affects the technical side of security (Mitnick and Simon, 2011; Tetri and Vuorinen, 2013). In other words, a human element is used as an attack vector in order to make the attack on a technological system possible.

In this paper, we argue that there are similarities between social engineering and technical attacks. Technical attacks and defence for technical attacks contain a social aspect. More precisely, the social and technology are not merely intertwined (see Carter and Grover, 2015) but are inseparable. The layers of security (social, physical, technical) are anything but isolated. Rather, they form a machinery in which the levels are mixed (Vuorinen and Tetri, 2012). We argue that technical attacks include a significant social aspect as well. In order to make sense of the overarching social side in security, we use the sociological concepts of the frame, fabrication, and normality. Through these concepts, we can examine the social and the social construction of reality. Then, we are able to analyse social engineering that is the most obvious actualisation of the social in the field of information security and compare social and technical attacks through examples of phishing, Stuxnet worm, Heartbleed bug, honey pots and log manipulation. Finally, we question whether it is fertile to make a division between social and technical attacks in the first place.

2. THE FRAME, FABRICATION, AND NORMALITY

Sociologist Erving Goffman (1986) argues that everyone applies a "frame" – a set of thoughts – that answers the question of "what is going on here?" So, "I am typing" or "I am reading" are frames that describe the activity of the self. However, the frames are not solely limited to the activities of self but there are frames that relate to other actors, including both material and human actors. For example, "she sent a message", "a security patch is installed", or "it is raining", are frames – descriptions and accounts – of what is going on. Goffman's ideas pertain to the tradition of social constructionism which means that reality is always (partly) intersubjectively constructed (e.g. Blumer, 1986; Berger and Luckmann, 1990). For example, it is normal to scream and shout in a rock concert but it is not normal to act in such a way in a formal meeting with a client. Normality is, thus, a social construct. There is no "normal" without the social.

In this sense, the Goffman's frames can be considered as ontological work in which reality – in the sense of "what is going on" – is constituted. Here, the term "ontology" refers to the field of philosophy instead of the field of information system science in which ontology is understood, not as a process, but as a static map (e.g. Vuorinen, 2014, p. 24). Goffman's frames are not static but a product of constant ontological work that can change. The interpretation of a situation can alter quickly. For example, in context of traffic, a normally driving car that accelerates quickly can turn from a non-dangerous car to a serious threat from a pedestrian point of view. In such a case, the ontological status of a car changes (Woolgar and Neyland, 2013).

Goffman examined mainly face-to-face interaction. In this microsociological approach, face-to-face communication and binary relations reside in the focus. Nonetheless, the concept of frame can be applied to a broader context as well. In terms of groups and organisations, frames function in the intersubjective manner: frames can be commonly shared but they are also open to dispute. Whereas in quickly changing situations the frame (what is going on) can be in dispute, the suggested course of action – "what should be done" – is even more prone to disagreement. In the ideal case of consensus, everyone answers the questions of "what is going on here" and "what should be done next" in a similar way.

In terms of frames, intersubjectivity works on different levels. In addition to sharing the same frame between different subjects, we constitute frames on information that is communicated intersubjectively. Slightly differently put, frames are shaped in interaction with others. Importantly, it is not merely human subjects that provide information for frames. For example, a firewall log can offer information that provides material for the constitution of frame. In fact, a log is a frame in itself as it tells what has happened. In case of rain, the raindrops bring or "express" information of "raining". Therefore, different actors, humans and non-humans take part in the process of frame creating. In simple terms, there are different actors that carry out *ontological work*. By including material actors to the process of constitution of reality, we approach the viewpoint of sociomaterialism (in philosophy of science see Serres (2007); in sociology see Latour (1999, 2005), Suchman (2005); in information system science Scott and Orlikowski (2014) and Introna (2013, 2015)).

However, while some frames can be accurate and valid, other frames can fail to tell correctly what is going on. For example, it can simply be that there is not enough information to build an overarching accurate frame. When a computer is used, the frame is likely to be reduced at the level of "use of computer" instead of thinking of all the processes that take place using the computer. In other words, the frame is a simplified, incomplete version of what is happening. The frame fails to be accurate in terms of details. Alternatively, some information can be overlooked and interpreted wrongly. This means that the construction of the correct frame fails. Nonetheless, in such case, there is a frame constructed and applied but the frame is flawed.

In addition to mistakes and the lack of information, there is another source of false frames, namely, fabrication (Goffman 1986). In terms of security research – compared to overlooked information or improperly interpreted data – fabrication provides a more interesting case of frame. The frames that pertain to security become intriguing especially in cases in which information for the construction of frames is manipulated in a deceptive way (see Tetri and Vuorinen, 2013; Vuorinen, 2014). In other words, deceptive information is fed in order to tamper the thought of what is going on here.

In terms of communication, fabrication is misleading information. Interaction is used as the channel of communication through which the frame is fabricated – polluted by false information – into a form that benefits the attacker. This kind of an attack materializes in the form of phishing emails that seek to create a false frame. For example, such an email can say that your email account has exceeded a critical limit and suggest that you should log on immediately using a provided link that in fact directs you to a phishing site. Of course, the sender of this mail is only interested in your username and password – perhaps in hijacking your email account. Another popular scheme include providing false URLs for the victim to click, and instead of doing what the message says, it actually fetches malware, installs it on the victim's computer undetected by modern anti-virus software and becomes part of a botnet – to be used in further attacks, for example distributed denial of service attacks, or ddos attacks. In fabrication, attacker's frame is sought to be kept in the dark and the false interpretation of situation is imposed on the dupe. In such case, in Goffman's (1986) terms, the frame is fabricated. In other words, the cues offered to interpret and construct a frame are intentionally made different from what is really going on. Phishing, which is considered a social engineering technique, is not only technique which is based on fabrication. In fact, many of SE-cases include some fabricating elements, pretexting for example. (Tetri and Vuorinen, 2013.)

Nevertheless, how convincing phishing emails are depend on how the false narrative – the fabricated frame – is constructed. Fabrication seeks to propose a frame that can be true; the point is that the proposed frame is treated as a true one. We argue that the more normal the fabricated frame seems, the more likely it works. There is power in familiarity and normality. For example, this is the case in the modern CEO frauds[1], phishing e-mails. These types of frauds rely on the fact that people trust other people they know in real life (in this example, your colleague). Spoofing mimics the email address of someone the dupe knows, someone from the organisation. attacked@mycompany.com sends an email to the dupe, also working for mycompany.com, seems reliable. Co-workers communicate via email, ask for favours and transfer files. In fact, it would be odd to suspect if the email was spoofed, unless the message itself was very off. In this example, the attacker creates the frame using technology, yet the attack is based on trust between people, and people trusting technology. Technology can be hijacked, controlled, but also used as a fake narrative, in which the outside attacker only seems to be inside, even when they are not.

In terms of information security, the power of the normal should be noted. Normality is based on the social, in the sense that different social systems consider different things and customs normal. A visit to a strange culture can make you see your own normalities. The normal is powerful and possibly deceitful as it does not trigger any alarms. Normal things are approached with natural attitude (Berger and Luckmann, 1990). In a sense, the normal in its mundanity and continuously repeated refrain makes everything invisible, imperceptible. Normality can hide things because there is nothing alarming about normality. In security, normality is something that lays a pavement for threats. The threats do not come in isolated packages but are constituted through relations. Figure 1 summarises the construction of frame and the effect of normality.

[1] see https://krebsonsecurity.com/2017/02/irs-scam-blends-ceo-fraud-w-2-phishing/#more-37923

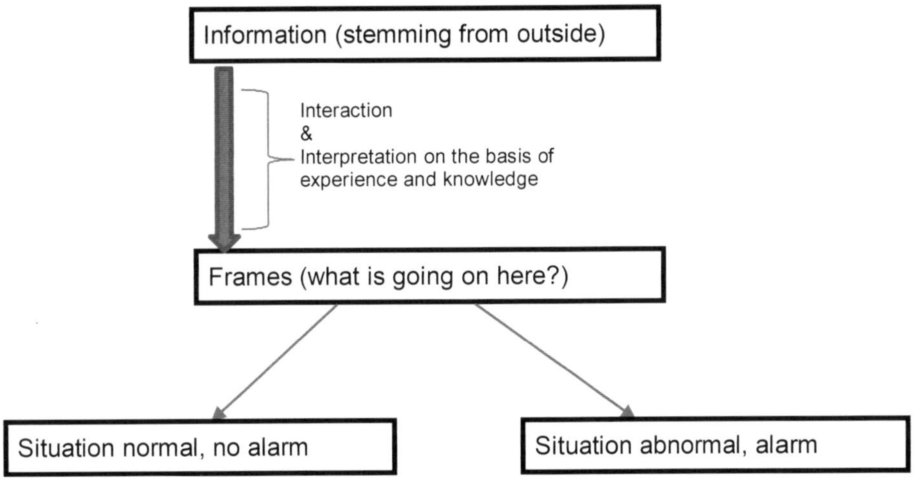

Figure 1. The construction of frame and alarm

However, normality does not concern merely the human side of information and cybersecurity. We argue that normality – what is treated as normal (partly a social construction) – extends to technical attacks as well. In the following section we deal with this subject.

3. THE SOCIAL IN TECHNICAL ATTACKS

As shown above, in SE, false trust between people is created through different frames. A false narrative is fed for the dupe to believe in. Similarly, technology can facilitate a false frame – carry out ontological work – or be the canvas for a false narrative. For example, in the network environment, trust is mediated with certificates, authentication, and tokens. In other words, a certificate carries out ontological work of "what is going on here?" It is a system of trust mediated by IT artefacts. Generally, in "man in the middle attacks", a trusted position – the channel in the middle – is occupied by a third party (e.g. Callegati, Cerroni and Ramilli, 2009). Differently phrased, attacker can use the systems of trust in order to achieve the goals of an attack. For example, the notorious Stuxnet virus used a stolen certificate, so that it would be considered legitimate code.[2] Here, a piece of technology, a malicious code, fools a technological system by pretending to be something else – pretending to be a normal, non-alarming case. Stuxnet, which was targeted to destroy Iranian centrifuges, acted as a normal code but made slight changes, powerful enough, to break the centrifuges. It can be then argued that Stuxnet attack was as social as it was technical. It used familiarity and normality to hide its true targets.

In the practical field of cybersecurity, the defenders can also play the same game of creating false frames that seem legit for the attacker. A honey client crawls through malicious websites pretending to be a normal browser, while it collects information about malicious websites (Wang, 2009). Another example is implanting faked credentials, that are flagged as stolen, and then tracked. These fake and tracked credentials are examples of honey tokens. An analogy of the previous could be tracking money, or marked notes. Once the money is used, the trackers can then pinpoint where the money went, and possibly track down who took it and used it. The idea is not to block it from happening per se, but to follow the trail. The attacker does not realise that they are using marked goods which make their own actions trackable. Again, normality is used. In above, the entire term "honey" refers to something that is made look tempting but is actually something else, a precious looking object that is used to allure and capture intruders without losing anything valuable. The ontological work takes place as the frame of honey is fabricated. In other words, how the temping features of a honey object are constituted.

Yet another defender technique using frames would be to deploy a honey net in the actual network. It is isolated from the actual goods and assets of the defender, so the attacker can roam freely, thinking they have

[2] see https://arstechnica.com/tech-policy/2011/07/how-digital-detectives-deciphered-stuxnet-the-most-menacing-malware-in-history/

successfully intruded the target while being trapped, monitored, and analysed. The gist of the matter is that for both sides create the frame seems valid. The key in fabrication is not technology, or devices that monitor, isolate, and analyse but the idea of the frame, which is based on the social. The narrative is built using technology. However, in the narrative technology and the frame (the social) are inseparable, neither will exist without the other. The technical and the social are entangled.

Trust is also created between technological devices. A company laptop is trusted to its user, and the laptop itself is trusted in the network. It is an entity that is allowed to enter the perimeter and use the services which it has been assigned privileges. The laptop itself might have security controls, such as antivirus, or other software. From a server, new updates are propagated into the laptops that are trusted. For example, group policies can be enforced to all of the machines. While this is all daily administration, it is another example of frame, where technology trusts technology.

The relations of trust can be as complex as the number of nodes in the network, people, services, and every single entity that functions in it. People trust people and machines, machines trusts other machines and people (after they log on with proper credentials). With thousands, or tens, or even hundreds of thousands of entities, endless amounts of traffic (both machine logs and network traffic logs), as well as endless frames, it only takes one frame that works for the attacker to get in.

Sometimes, the entire foundation of a trust system can fail. This was the case with the Heartbleed vulnerability. The discovery of Heartbleed vulnerability– or the Heartbleed Bug – in 2014 disclosed severe and critical problems and flaws in OpenSSL library. The problem in the vulnerability is in the very core of the information security procedures –the *trusted* library was vulnerable, which has (without repair) tremendous consequences. “This weakness allows stealing the information protected, under normal conditions, by the SSL/TLS encryption used to secure the Internet. SSL/TLS provides communication security and privacy over the Internet for applications such as web, email, instant messaging (IM) and some virtual private networks (VPNs).” (Heartbleed.com). Furthermore, attacks can be carried out “without leaving a trace”. OpenSSL library was vulnerable to begin with, however, it was trusted, as it was an unknown vulnerability (until it became known). As long as people are not aware of vulnerabilities, they do not exist, and therefore, they can be trusted. It is especially dangerous, when they regard security controls that function on the basis of trust. Ontologically, there are some things we need to know and trust. Otherwise we can never trust anything, especially security controls. Good programming is difficult in the sense that programs are supposed to do what they are supposed to do meaning that secure programming includes that they do not do anything else, except what they’re supposed to do. Applications calling other libraries might assume that those libraries are safe. In the case of OpenSSL it was not the case.

At the moment when *unknown* vulnerability became known vulnerability, trust was shattered in terms of frames. The library was trusted and the frame was “we are safe if we use these services” although the great potential to be abused was there all the time. Furthermore, exploiting the vulnerability, left no traces. This means that there were no material, hints or log files left in order to fix the assumption of what is going on here. Yet, this was not a fabrication but simply overlooking risks because this vulnerability was unknown.

Logs are also known to be targets of forgery and being tampered with. The security people rely on logs to find out “what really happened” or is happening. Therefore, the logs must be relied on to tell the truth. However, attackers can target the logs themselves, injecting malicious code in a browser (should the server itself still remain tamper-proof). An example of log injection, in which a new log entry is injected (https://capec.mitre.org/data/definitions/93.html):
“%0D%0A[Thu%20Nov%2012%2011:22]:Info:%20User%20admin%20logged%20in”
may appear as:"[Thu Nov 12 12:11:22]:Info: User admin logged in”

Logging can be also evaded, leaving no clear trace of the attacker. Such a problem existed in Microsoft’s IIS servers. The below example illustrates how, technically, attackers bypass controls and become invisible for the included transactions (http://www.webappsec.org/projects/articles/082905.shtml):

Attack Request
GET /?id=<insert 4095 A's>
User-Agent: Mozilla/4.0 (compatible; MSIE 5.01; Windows NT 5.0)
Host: TestServer

Logged Response (IIS 5.0 with default logging)

2005-08-10 17:21:29 172.16.10.3 - 172.16.10.111 80 GET /Default.asp ... 200 Mozilla/4.0+(compatible;+MSIE+5.01;+Windows+NT+5.0)

Logged Response (IIS 6.0 with default logging)
2005-08-10 17:09:54 172.16.10.116 GET /Default.asp ... 80 - 172.16.10.3 Mozilla/4.0+(compatible;+MSIE+5.01;+Windows+NT+5.0) 200 0 0

The point of logging examples is to illustrate that the systems provides insights to a human, answering "what is really going on?", while the attacker can dupe the victim by crafting requests that alternate the logs into something different or evade logging altogether. The dupe has to be aware of this problem of not knowing when evidence can be trusted. Narratives are created between humans, between human-machine, machine-machine interaction. This is one of the biggest challenges for security; how can one really trust anything, or in other words, how can one evaluate the frame and how is it done reliably? Even security controls play a part of storytelling and are used against the dupe.

All in all, ontological work – the construction of frames – is carried out socially and technically. However, the two levels are mixed and blended into each other in ways that makes it impossible to isolate them. What is the technical and the social in logs? What is the technical and the social in Stuxnet? What is the technical and the social in Heartbleed vulnerability? It is difficult to point solely to the technical. The technical comes with the social. Technologies can run own their own – yet, they are initiated socially. Moreover, the attack techniques – both social and technical – resemble each other. Both can seek to hide themselves in normality (as is the case with Stuxnet and log tampering).

4. CONCLUSIONS

The social extends much deeper into the "technical" level than it is assumed by the bifurcation statement in the field of information security. Both levels address the problem of normality in very similar manner. Whether the case was about a successful social engineering attack or an act of breaking into an information system, both cases are enormously difficult to detect because the marks they leave on the surface of the normal flow are imperceptible or very subtle. Of course, there are unsuccessful cases, in which the attackers are not able to mix in the stream of normal; they act visibly strange and are noisy. The hiding game into the veil of normality is on as much at the technical level as it is in the sophisticated social engineering attacks. In other words, the fabrication of the frame (the thought of what is going on here) is entirely possible at both levels. As the hiding game is played, the defenders have to constantly struggle with different techniques to check the validity of their frame. However, they have a chance to take the initiative as in all "honey" cases.

In this light, it should be clear that the division between the technical and the social is not fertile in terms of understanding information security and how it works, and how it is made. Rather, the two are intertwined and blended together in several different ways in the field of information security. Fundamentally, security is social and discursive; it seeks to find normality in order to spot abnormal activity. The key in becoming imperceptible is to appear normal – to impose a fabricated frame, to hide in normality. This concept aligns the social and technical. Security is social and discursive. The technical side – which for so long time has been treated separately from the social and is seen as the pinnacle of security – is always merged with the social.

REFERENCES

Adams, A. and Sasse, M. A. (1999) 'Users are not the enemy', *Communications of the ACM*, 42(12), pp. 40–46.

Berger, P. L. and Luckmann, T. (1990) *The social construction of reality: a treatise in the sociology of knowledge*. Anchor Books, New York, USA

Blumer, H. (1986) *Symbolic interactionism: Perspective and method*. University of California Press, Oakland, California, USA.

Bulgurcu, B., Cavusoglu, H. and Benbasat, I. (2010) 'Information Security Policy Compliance: An Empirical Study of Rationality-Based Beliefs and Information Security Awareness.', *MIS Quarterly*, 34(3), pp. 523-548.

Callegati, F., Cerroni, W. and Ramilli, M. (2009) 'Man-in-the-Middle Attack to the HTTPS Protocol', *IEEE Security & Privacy*, 7(1), pp. 78–81.

Colwill, C. (2009) 'Human factors in information security: The insider threat - Who can you trust these days?', *Information Security Technical Report*, 14(4), pp. 186–196.

Goffman, E. (1986) *Frame analysis: an essay on the organization of experience*. Northeastern University Press, Boston.

Gupta, M. and Sharman, R. (eds) (2009) *Social and human elements of information security: emerging trends and countermeasures*. Information Science Reference, Hershey, PA, USA.

Introna, L. (2013) 'Epilogue: Performativity and the becoming of sociomaterial assemblages', in Vaujany, F.-X. de and Mitev, N. (eds) *Materiality and space: organizations, artefacts and practices*. Palgrave Macmillan, Houndmills, Basingstoke, Hampshire, UK, pp. 330–342.

Introna, L. (2015) 'Algorithms, Governance, and Governmentality: On Governing Academic Writing', *Science, Technology & Human Values*, 41(1), pp.17-49.

Latour, B. (1999) *Pandora's hope: essays on the reality of science studies*. Harvard University Press, Cambridge, MA, USA.

Latour, B. (2005) *Reassembling the social: an introduction to actor-network-theory*. Oxford University Press, Oxford, UK.

Loch, K. D., Carr, H. H. and Warkentin, M. E. (1992) 'Threats to Information Systems: Today's Reality, Yesterday's Understanding.', *MIS Quarterly*, 16(2), pp. 173–186.

Mitnick, K. D. and Simon, W. L. (2011) *The art of deception: Controlling the human element of security*. John Wiley & Sons, Hoboken, New Jersey, USA.

Nohlberg, M. (2009) 'Why Humans are the Weakest Link', in *Social and Human Elements of Information Security. Emerging Trends and Countermeasures*. Information Science Reference, New York, USA.

Scott, S. V. and Orlikowski, W. J. (2014) 'Entanglements in practice: Performing anonymity through social media', *MIS Quarterly*, 38(3), pp. 863–893.

Serres, M. (2007) *The Parasite*. University of Minnesota Press, Minneapolis, MN, USA.

Siponen, M., Baskerville, R. and Heikka, J. (2006) 'A Design Theory for Secure Information Systems Design Methods.', *Journal of the Association for Information Systems*, 7(11), pp. 725–770.

Siponen, M. and Vance, A. (2010) 'Neutralization: New Insights Into The Problem Of Employee Information Systems Security Policy Violations.', *MIS Quarterly*, 34(3), pp. 487-A12.

Suchman, L. (2005) 'Agencies in technology design: Feminist reconfigurations', available at: <www.lancs.ac.uk/fass/sociology/papers/suchman-agenciestechnodesign.pdf>.

Tetri, P. and Vuorinen, J. (2013) 'Dissecting social engineering', *Behaviour & Information Technology*, 32(10), pp. 1014–1023.

Vuorinen, J. (2014) *Parasitic Order Machine. A Sociology and Ontology of Information Securing*. Annales Universitatis Turkuensis. Available at: <http://urn.fi/URN:ISBN:978-951-29-5868-9>.

Vuorinen, J. and Tetri, P. (2012) 'The Order Machine - The Ontology of Information Security', *Journal of the Association for Information Systems*, 13(9), pp. 695–713.

Wang, K. (2009) 'Open Source Honeyclient: Proactive Detection of Client-Side Exploits', in Oram, A. and Viega, John (eds) *Beautiful Security*. O'Reilly Media, Sebastopol, CA, USA, pp. 131–146.

Willison, R. and Warkentin, M. (2013) 'Beyond Deterrence: An Expanded View Of Employee Computer Abuse.', *MIS Quarterly*, 37(1), pp. 1–20.

Woolgar, S. and Neyland, D. (2013) *Mundane governance: ontology and accountability*. Oxford University Press, Oxford, UK.

THE USE OF SMARTPHONE AND MOBILE APPLICATION AMONG OLDER ADULTS IN MALAYSIA

Chui Yin Wong[1], Rahimah Ibrahim[2], Tengku Aizan Hamid[2] and Evi Indriasari Mansor[3]

[1]*Universal Usability and Interaction Design (UUID) SIG, Faculty of Creative Multimedia, Multimedia University, 63100 Cyberjaya, Malaysia*

[2]*Malaysian Research Institute on Ageing (MyAgeing), Universiti Putra Malaysia, 43400 Serdang, Selangor, Malaysia.*

[3]*Department of Computer Science, College of Computer & Information Sciences, Prince Sultan University (PSU), Riyadh, Saudi Arabia*

ABSTRACT

Malaysia will become an ageing nation in 2035. With the popularity of smartphone available in the current mobile market, it is undeniable to ignore the needs of smartphone and its mobile application by older adults. Previous literature studies describe the mobile phone use, in particular related to feature phones among older adults in Malaysia. There are limited studies illustrating the smartphone usage among older adults in Malaysia. This paper aims to fill the literature gap by investigating the smartphone trend and its mobile apps among the older adult population. A survey was conducted with 44 older adults aged 60-74. The findings reveal that majority own a smartphone these days as compared to feature phones. By and large, they prefer Android phone (84.1%) and the top mobile apps use are messaging (i.e. Whatsapp), video (i.e. YouTube), photography, utility, social media (i.e. Facebook) apps. The major problems raised by older adults using mobiles are battery finished fast, small keypad, complicated and difficult to use. This study gives insight and implication to mobile operators of smartphone usage for grey market and also mobile designers or developers for their mobile apps development.

KEYWORDS

Smartphone, older adults, elderly, mobile application and Malaysia

1. INTRODUCTION

There is a rising ageing population worldwide. Malaysia as a developing nation is not spared from becoming an ageing nation by 2035 (Bernama, 2016; Daim, 2016). With the prevalence of smartphone unfolding in the current mobile communication market, older adults whom are generally classified as 'laggards' (Essén and Östlund, 2011) in adopting new mobile technology trend eventually have to migrate into smartphone trend as a 'silver' mobile adopters. However, the elderly, age 60s and above, were not borne in the 21st century digital era. Majority are more familiar with the feature mobile phone, and not smartphone user interface. With the birth of iPhone in 2007 marks as the era of 'smartphone', almost nobody buys a feature phone anymore after 10 years later (Tan, 2017). Therefore, the elderly also cannot escape from migrating into 'silver smartphone users' in the 'grey market' cohort. Otherwise, they will be drifted away in the 'mobile technological' tidal wave and be left behind from using the current mobile communication technologies. As age changes, older adults experience decline in cognitive, motor, perceptual abilities (Fisk, Roger, Charness, Czaja and Sharit, 2009; Wong, Khong and Thwaites, 2010), not to mention their struggle to adopt a total new interaction mode of mobile technology. Having said this, the elderly are generally perceived as 'techno-phobic' in up taking a new technology (Haederie, 2011; Fisk, Roger, Charness, Czaja, and Sharit, 2009). As the elderly age, changes in skin integrity, vibrotactile sensitivity, visual perception and motor control affect the screen and keypad use, especially make it harder for them to see a smartphone screen, type a message on a small and compact virtual keyboard, and use more complicated mobile applications.

Previous literature review described a study of smartphone use in Malaysia (Osman, Talib, Sanusi, Tan and Alwi, 2012), but the study targeted the general populations and not specific for older adults. Few studies on mobile phone with elderly were conducted before 2014. The findings may not be relevant and applicable to the latest trend of mobile industry as it changes rapidly in the local mobile landscape. In addition, there are also lack of smartphone studies for older adults, especially in the context of smartphone usage and interaction in Malaysian context. To address this gap, this paper aims to investigate the smartphone usage and its mobile application among the older adults population in Malaysia.

2. LITERATURE REVIEW

This sections review some literature on mobile phone related studies to understand how older adults use the mobile phone, the problems and also expectation in needs.

2.1 Related Work on Mobile Phone Studies

There have been numerous literature studies conducted on mobile phones from the disciplines of human-computer interaction and interaction design. Kurniawan (2008) found out older adults were passive users and they treat mobile phones as a means for security (i.e. emergency) rather than communication device. This situation most likely has changed by now with the popularity of Whatsapp and other free messaging mobile applications on smartphone. In another study conducted by Kurniawan (2006), older women has lower usage of mobile phone as compared to their male counterparts. They used mobile phones for the purpose of security concern rather than casual talks, and they rarely used text messages (SMS). The problems faced by older women using mobile phones are physical design (display, mobile size, buttons, colour, mobile shape and backlight) and functionalities (memory aid, operational complexity, layout and shortcuts).

There is a dearth of literature on mobile phones usage and trend in local studies. Md. Nasir, Hassan and Jomhari (2008) conducted a survey of mobile phone use by 176 Malaysian elderly. The usage patterns from the results showed that majority are on pre-paid scheme as compared to post-paid scheme, and many used a mobile phone for more than 2 years. In general, the problems of using the mobile phones were small and rubbery buttons, complexed menus arrangement, difficult to understand, complicated and impossible to recall functions, the shape and size of mobile phone is too small to hold and bulky, using mobile phones for limited purposes such as calling or SMS (short-messaging system) in emergency situations, small screen size and displays to see the font size, buttons and characters are too small to press numbers wrongly, complicated functions and unclear instructions how to proceed to use a certain function (Md. Nasir, Hassan and Jomhari, 2008; Wong, 2011).

To find out the issues, purposes and context of use for mobile device among the older people, Azuddin, Abd. Malik, Abdullah and Mahmud (2014) conducted focus group studies on 11 older adults aged 65 years old and above in Malaysia. The findings summarise the mobile phone usage as four categories, which are mobile usage purposes, mobile usage applications, mobile usage issues, and mobile usage context. In terms of mobile usage purpose, older adults' main interest to use mobile devices were to communicate with their children, followed by friends, business and work, and emergency. It was learnt that the most frequent mobile usage are calling and SMS. The older adults face several issues such as (i) mobile design (small font size and button, not familiar with slide or touch screen interaction mode, complexities of menu design, preferably in Malay language rather than English, do not feel secure to use mobile banking); (ii) cognitive decline (memory difficulties of remembering own mobile phone number) (iii) motivational (i.e. fear of using mobile applications, not familiar out of calling and SMS, refer to help from grandchildren to use some features on mobile phone (iv) physical impairments or decline in motor skills, vision and hearing (i.e. eyesight problems in viewing message and save contact numbers), (v) circle of support (lack of support or training from family members, friends or any experts). It also showed that older adults who have high educational background are more conversant in adopting latest and newest mobile technology as they usually have experience using computers.

As the study was conducted before the wide spread of smartphone, the usage of mobile phone most likely refers to feature phones, and it is not applicable and relevant to the current smartphone trend for elderly. For instance, there are no more rubbery or metallic buttons on smartphone as it is a touchscreen-based user interface. The screen size of a smart phone is no longer an issue as it has varieties of mobile screen size in the current mobile device market. In addition, the font size of the screen can be adjusted easily, and it has now more options of different font sizes for better viewing. For complicated menu and user interface problem, smartphones these days no longer distinguish younger generations and older adults by designing separate mobile phone device. These days the smartphone is 'one size fits all' user interface concept, which means they can choose either Standard mode or Easy mode (with simpler user interface). This indicates that older adults do not like to be 'differentiated' or 'categorized' as 'laggard' users by using a so-called 'senior phone'.

Previous literature studied mobile phone by elderly, and the data collection was backdated in 2008. The findings may not be applicable to the smartphone usage and trend for the elderly by now. There are limited studies of smartphone usage in Malaysian context. Osman, Talib, Sanusi, Tan and Alwi (2012) conducted a survey with 1814 respondents on the trend of smartphone and its usage in Malaysia. However, the study mainly describes the smartphone usage in general, and only 0.9% (16 out of 1814) respondents fall under the age more than 57 years old. Thus, the study indicated that the design of mobile device is the prior important factors for choosing a mobile phone for young generations, and not for the older consumers. In addition, Wi-Fi capability is not pertinent to the older consumers (age more than 57 years old). In overall, the findings of the study was done in 2012, and most of the content is not relevant to today's smartphone era. For instance, the study also revealed that Instant messaging acts like a complimentary to SMS (short messaging services) rather than as a substitution of SMS. This is contrary with the current communication landscape where Whatsapp is the main communication tool across all the age groups mobile users regardless age concern. The findings also summarized that the smartphone is yet to be fully utilized by the consumers. It was suggested that user training, proper redesign of the mobile applications, user support should be prevalent to improve usability and user acceptance of the future smartphones.

Mohadis and Ali (2014) conducted a study to investigate the barriers of using a smartphone among the elderly in Malaysia. The study conducted semi-structured interviews with 21 elderly to understand the barriers in using smartphones among the elderly population. The barriers of adopting smartphone among non-smartphone users are 'not affordable', 'no interest', 'no necessity', 'lack of knowledge', 'vision, cognitive, hearing and motor impairment' that deter them from using a smart phone. It is also interesting to learn that prior experience of using feature phones did not help to transfer the technology experience to using a smartphone. This is due to the interaction mechanism between feature phone and smartphone is very different. Elderly are generally familiar with the 'pressing' interaction mode on hard keypad as compare to a total different interaction mode of using 'swiping', 'sliding', 'touching' on a touchscreen user interface. The change from previous alphanumerical hard key button keypad to QWERTY virtual keyboard makes it difficult for the elderly to type SMS, or any messages. The change of user interface and interaction mode somehow deters the elderly to adopt using smartphone. However, some findings of this study may not be applicable in the current smartphone scenario such as pricey and fixed standard mode of screen user interface.

3. RESEARCH METHOD

The study conducted a cross-sectional survey using questionnaire on the topic of 'Mobile Phone Usage for Senior Citizens'. The targeted groups were Malaysian young old adults, age 60 to 74 years. Fisk et. al. (2009) classified two (2) groups of older adult. The first group is classified as 'young old adults', age range from 60 to 74 years old; whilst the second group is 'old-old adults', age range from 75 years old and above. The reasons of choosing young old adults because this group has high potential of adopting new mobile technology such as smartphone and mobile applications (apps) as compared to the old-old adults. In addition, the mobile operators are more interested targeting this 'young older adults' cohort as potential 'grey market' users.

Due to time constraint, the survey was conducted at University of Third Age (U3A) Orientation Day in Universiti Putra Malaysia's Serdang campus in Selangor on August 2015. Although the older adults population is largely concentrated in rural areas in Malaysia than urban areas (Wan-Ibrahim and Zainab, 2014), it is believed the older adults residing in urban areas are more susceptible to adopt smartphone and its mobile apps based on their daily needs and financial support as compared to older adults living in rural areas. Moreover, it is noted that Selangor state shows the highest concentration of older adults (age 60 and above) residing in the state (4.36% ageing population) as compared to other states in Malaysia (Department of Statistics Malaysia, 2011; Yaakob, Masron and Masami, 2009). Apart from this, Selangor state has shown its statistics of mobile phone ownership, which is 9.02 million users (Department of Statistics Malaysia, 2015). The reason of choosing U3A participants is the members' involvement in lifelong learning courses for older adults in Malaysia.

4. FINDINGS

The result of the survey illustrates an overview of smartphone usage and mobile apps among older adults in Malaysia. This helps to provide insight and information for mobile operators and mobile apps developers.

4.1 Demographic Profiles

The survey received a total of 73 respondents from age 49-82 years old (mean=62.18, SD=6.848). After filtering, the final number of respondents for young old adults (age 60-74 years old) is 44 (mean=65.16, SD=4.324). Table 1 describes the demographic profiles of the respondents in general. In terms of gender, there are 39% male, and 61% female from the total 44 respondents. There are 3 major ethnics in Malaysia, who are Malay, followed by Chinese and Indians. The respondents show 68% Chinese, 27% Malay, and 5% Indians. The result here is not proportionately representing the right ethnicity ratio for Malaysian population. However, this survey was not collected for the purpose for inference statistical analysis rather than descriptive analysis. Nevertheless, it is a small-scale survey and majority of the current membership in U3A are Chinese.

Table 1. Demographic Profiles of Older Adults

Descriptions	**Percentage (%)**	**Number (n)**	**Descriptions**	**Percentage (%)**	**Number (n)**
(a) Gender			(b) Ethnicity		
- Male	38.6	17	- Malay	27.3	12
- Female	61.4	27	- Chinese	68.2	30
			- Indians	4.5	2
(c) Marital Status			(d) Educational Background		
- Single	22.7	10	- Primary school	4.5	2
- Married	63.6	28	- Upper secondary	47.7	21
- Divorce or Separated	2.3	1	- Tertiary education (college/ university)	40.9	18
- Widowed	11.4	5	- Others	6.8	3
(e) Occupation			(f) Health Status		
- Still working	18.2	8	- Excellent	4.5	2
- Retired	77.3	34	- Good	63.6	28
- Never work before	4.5	2	- Fair	31.8	14
(g) Languages			(h) Monthly Income		
(i) Bahasa Malaysia (BM)			RM12,000 and above	2.4	1
- BM Speaking	88.6%	39	RM5000-9999	2.4	1
- BM Written	81.8%	36	RM3000-4999	26.8	11
- BM Reading	75.0%	33	RM2000-2999	24.4	10
(ii) English (Eng)			RM1000-RM1999	14.6	6
- Eng Speaking	95.5%	42	Less than RM1000	2.4	1
- Eng Written	95.5%	42	No more income	24.4	10
- Eng Reading	81.8%	36	Don't know	2.4	1
(iii) Mandarin					
- Mandarin Speaking	43.2%	19			
- Mandarin Written	34.1%	15			
- Mandarin Reading	29.5%	13			
(iv) Tamil					
- Tamil Speaking	6.8%	3			
- Tamil Written	4.5%	2			
- Tamil Reading	4.5%	2			
(v) Others (e.g. Cantones,					
Hokkien, etc.)	6.8%	3			
- Others Speaking	2.3%	1			
- Others Written	2.3%	1			
- Others Reading					

Since Malaysia is a multi-racial with diverse cultural society, Malaysian speak different languages and dialects depending on their ethnicity and family background. For Malaysian society, Malay language (Bahasa Malaysia) is the national language, whilst English is well-spoken by the older adults, especially those received British educational system before Malaysia's independence from Britain in 1957. Many Malaysians, especially older adults are able to speak multiple languages. As such, there is no surprise that majority of the respondents (95.5%) are able to speak and write English well due to their age-related educational background. Unexpectedly, English reading skill is not tally with the English-writing skill, which could be some older adults deem themselves of able to write simple English phrases, but may not be able to read English articles in-depth. It is surprised that the second highest spoken and written language is Bahasa Malaysia (Malay language), which is 88.6% of respondents are able to speak, 81.8% for written, and 75% for reading the language itself. This is due to those who joined U3A are considered having at least secondary education. Although there are 68% respondents are Malaysian Chinese, only 43.2% of the respondents are able to speak Mandarin, and 34.1% can write, and 29.5% can read Mandarin. Malaysian Chinese has a unique language background as many have diverse family and ancestors backgrounds from China, thus Mandarin is not a compulsory language in their daily life. Many Malaysian Chinese are able to speak their dialects such as Hokkien, Cantonese and so forth. Similarly, only 6.8% of the respondents are able to speak Tamil, 4.5% writing and reading Tamil respectively. The percentage is small as compared to other languages because of small sample size of Malaysian Indians participating in this survey, and mostly Malaysian Indians speak Tamil in Malaysia. Other languages count for 6.8% speaking in different dialects such as Cantonese, Hokkien, Arabic. This implicates that majority has no issue of using English as the smartphone interface main language except for those Chinese-or-Tamil-educated.

For occupation, there is no surprise that 77% of respondents had retired. According to Minimum Retirement Act 2012, Malaysia Ministry of Human Resources had announced that the minimum retirement age had increased from 55 to 60 years old for Malaysians, especially government servants (Ministry of Human Resources, 2013). There is no restriction for those who are working in private sector, or having own business. The finding also shows that 18% respondents are still working, which could be some of them have their own business. Only 5% respondents replied they have never worked before, most likely are housewives.

In terms of monthly income, many have retired as described in occupation profile, there is no surprise that 24.4% indicated no more income at their old age. Having said this, it is interesting to learn that there are few clustered groups who still receive monthly income such as government servant retirees, who are entitled for their monthly pension. Unexpectedly, 2.4% earning a monthly income of RM12,000 and above, which is very high income for the older adults. This is an exceptional case because the person is still employed in a high position in corporate sector. In a nutshell, the elderly have some minimum income from their pensions or allowance from children to sustain their daily living, including mobile expenses. For the health status, majority considered themselves in good health (64%). None of them claimed their health status as poor. This could be a good sign as majority of older adults are still physically active except deterioration on eyesight, and memory to recall and learn new things.

4.2 Mobile Status for Older Adults

In terms of mobile ownership, all 44 respondents owned a mobile phone. It was found that the average years of owning a mobile phone was around 12.42 years. There are few older adults owning a feature phone these days with only 18.2% respondents own a keypad phone. On contrary, 86.4% respondents have a smartphone. This could be due to the current market is occupied by all kinds of smartphone brands with touchscreen interfaces. It is more difficult to find and buy a feature phone in a mobile phone shop than smartphone devices. Apart from this, the average months of owning the current mobile phone is 30.68 months. Table 2 explains the mobile status for older adults.

Table 2. Mobile Status for Older Adults

Descriptions	**Percentage (%)**	**Number (n)**	**Descriptions**	**Percentage (%)**	**Number (n)**
(a) Current Mobile Brand			(b) 'Who Purchase the mobile phone		
-Samsung	31.8	14	for older adults?'		
-Lenovo	18.2	8	-Themselves	36.4	16
-Apple iPhone	15.9	7	-Children	27.3	12
-Xiaomi	6.8	3	-Spouse	13.6	6
-Oppo	6.8	3	-Relatives	9.1	4
-Asus	6.8	3	-Others (i.e. corporate phone, gift)	7	3
-Nokia	4.5	2	-Son or daughter-in-law	4.5	2
-Huawei	4.5	2	-Friends	2.3	1
-Blackberry	4.5	2			
(c1) Used other brand before	86	38	(d)Features use on Mobile:		
-Yes	14	6	- Making calls	95.5	42
-No			- Message	86.4	38
			- Photo-taking	77.3	34
(c2) Previous phone brand			- Communication App (Whatsapp,	75.0	33
based on 'Yes' (c1):			Facebook)		
-Nokia	65.9	29	-Alarm clock	63.6	28
-Samsung	25	11	-Calendar	59.1	26
-Motorola	20.5	9	-Video-taking	54.5	24
-Blackberry	13.6	6	-Internet browsing	54.5	24
-Sony	9.1	4	-Phonebook	52.3	23
-Apple iPhone	4.5	2	-Email	47.7	21
-HTC	4.5	2	-Torch light	40.9	18
-MSN Windows Phone	2.3	1	-GPS	38.6	17
-Lenovo	2.3	1	-Emergency	36.4	16
-LG	2.3	1	-Music	36.4	16
			-Notetaking	29.5	13
			-Setting Configuration	20.5	9
			-Games	18.2	8
			-Radio	15.9	7
			-Mobile banking	11.4	5
			-Health monitoring	4.5	2
			-Others	2.3	1
(e)Use of Mobile apps:			(f) Frequent Contacts:		
-Messaging apps (Whatsapp,	79.1	34	-Friends	79.5	35
WeChat)	55.8	24	-Children	75	33
-Video apps (i.e. YouTube)	55.8	24	-Spouse	68.2	30
-Photography apps	55.8	24	-Relatives	50	22
-Utilities apps	53.5	23	-Neighbours	20.5	9
-Social Network apps (i.e.			-Parents	11.4	5
Facebook, Skype)	44.2	19	-Maid	11.4	5
-GPS apps	27.9	12	-Others	9.1	4
-Budget Calculator apps	16.3	7	-Caregiver	6.8	3
-Mobile banking apps	16.3	7	-Grand children	2.3	1
-Mobile games apps	7.03	3			
-Mobile shopping apps	4.7	2			
-Health monitoring apps	2.3	1			
-Others	14	6			
-None					
(g) Types of Mobile			(h) Internet Service (data plan) on		
Subscription Plan:			mobile:		
-Prepaid	39	17	-Yes	69.8	30
-Postpaid	61	27	-No	25.6	11
			-I don't know	4.7	2
(i)Who pay bill			(j)Problems using mobile phones:		
-Myself	81.8	36	-Complicated and difficult to use	31.7	13
-Children	11.4	5	-Expensive	26.8	11
-Spouse	4.5	2	-Small keypad	41.5	17
-Relatives	2.3	1	-Danger to health	24.4	10
			-Battery finish fast	53.7	22
			-Other reasons	9.8	4

5. DISCUSSION

The background of older adult's population in Malaysia is not homogeneous and they have different interests and demands on the smartphone usage and its application. However, there are few requirements in common such as use of FREE communication apps like Whatsapp has replaced SMS (short messaging system). Instead of using SMS, Whatsapp has become the top use of messaging app feature for using a smartphone. This is because it is free as compared to SMS, which requires extra charges from mobile operators. Unlike the previous literature done in mobile phone studies for elderly, SMS was deemed as the top 2 feature use for older adults. On contrary, this study reveals the importance of using Whatsapp as one of the core reasons of adopting smartphone for the older adults in order for them to be in touch with their children, old friends, peers, professional networks via media-sharing and connection. Both the video apps such as YouTube (55.8%) and Photography apps (55.8%) are also considered well-received. Social-network apps (e.g. Facebook, Skype) (53.5%) is also quietly commonly used by them.

For the current brands of mobile phones ownership (Table 2), the finding indicates that Samsung is still the top favourite brand (31.8%) among the older adults. All the mobile phones are Android OS, except Apple iPhone. Those who choose Apple iPhone are considered more financially-able to purchase such a pricey smart phone. In terms of 'who purchase the mobile phone for older adults', the result reveals that majority of mobile phone is purchased by 'themselves' (36.4%), followed by children (27.3%). It shows that the older adults have their own preference and sense of authority to choose the type of mobile phone they like. However, many of the older adults also have no idea what types of smartphone they would like to buy, and most of the time their children are the one to give or buy one for them as a gift, or passing down to them from their old smartphone. There is no surprise that the top previous brand of mobile phone is Nokia (65.9%). It shows an interesting result that Nokia brand used to be the number one brand for many people, including the older adults. Unfortunately, Nokia did not keep themselves abreast with the latest smartphone mobile technology, and they were too late to enter the smartphone playground, and became obsolete. It is learnt that some current mobile phone brands such as Oppo, Xiaomi and Vivo are not 'existed' in the market yet until 2011.

In terms of problems using mobile phones, the older adults find that the battery finished faster using a smartphone as compared to their previous experience of using feature phones. Majority lack of knowledge that mobile apps running behind the scenes causing the consumption of battery power. They find it hard to type on virtual keypad, and some of them blamed themselves of their 'fat' fingers. They still prefer the tactile sensation and accuracy of touching the hard keypad on feature phone. In addition, they also express it is complicated and difficult to use smartphone interface and navigate the mobile apps as compared to feature phone.

Nonetheless, there are limitation of studies. The education backgrounds of the 44 respondents are considered quite well-educated for the local context. This could be due to those who attended University of Third Age (U3A) orientation are those who had received education during their younger age, and also they are residing in Klang Valley (Selangor and Kuala Lumpur) as compared to those residing in other states or rural areas. Basically, they are eager to learn and pursue their life-long learning after their retirement. Compared to the general statistics from Department of Statistic Malaysia (2011), the general education background for older adults are generally average. Majority did not study up to tertiary education level. At those days, those older adults who received tertiary education are considered as an elite group. Thus, this study only represent the sub-cluster group of older adults' population from the country. As a result, the findings of this preliminary study reflect on the general knowledge and skillsets of this sub-cluster group of older adults from U3A.

6. CONCLUSION

To conclude, this paper depicts the use of smartphone and mobile apps features among sub-cluster group of older adults in Malaysia. It is undeniable that older adults have become the new adopter for smartphone and mobile applications. For mobile operator and smartphone developers, we cannot ignore their needs and difficult of use in using a smartphone due to their age-related decline. The smartphone apps need to design in such a way to allow simplicity and intuitive user interface to cater for the older adults. Due to the length of this paper, future studies will discuss how their prior product experience influencing the adoption of smartphone.

ACKNOWLEDGEMENT

This research is supported by Fundamental Research Grant Scheme (FRGS) [FRGS/1/2015/SS05/MMU/02/2] and UPM Putra Grant (UPM/700-2/1/GP-IPS/2013/9390400). The authors like to express gratitude to Malaysian Ministry of Education (MOE) and University of Third Age (U3A) for allowing the participants to join the survey during the U3A Orientation event.

REFERENCES

Azuddin, M., Abd Malik, S., Abdullah, L. M. and Mahmud, M., 2014. Older People and Their Use of Mobile Devices: Issues, Purpose and Context. *The 5th International Conference on Information and Communication Technology for the Muslim World (ICT4M) 2014,* pp.1-4, IEEE.

Bernama (2016). *Malaysia 'ageing nation' in 2035, faces huge socio-economic challenge.* [Online] Available at: https://www.malaysiakini.com/news/326990 (Access on 7 January 2017).

Daim, N., 2016. *Malaysia to become 'ageing nation' by 2035.* [Online] Available at: http://www.nst.com.my/news/2016/03/134562/malaysia-become-ageing-nation-2035 (Access on 7 January 2017).

Department of Statistics Malaysia, 2011. *Population Distribution and Basic Demographic Characteristic Report 2010.* Putrajaya, Department of Statistics Malaysia.

Department of Statistics Malaysia, 2015. *Social Statistics Bulletin Malaysia 2015.* Putrajaya: Department of Statistics Malaysia, pp. 58.

Essén, A. and Östlund, B., 2011. Laggards as Innovators? Old Users as Designers of New Services & Service Systems. *International Journal of Design,* 5 (3), 89-98.

Fisk A.D., Rogers W.A., Charness N., Czaja S.J., Sharit J., 2009. *Designing for older adults: Principles and creative human factors approaches (2nd ed.).* CRC Press, Florida, USA.

Haederie, M., 2011. *Technology Fear Stops Older adults from Logging On.* [Online] Available at: http://www.aarp.org/technology/innovations/info-08-2011/elderly-fear-of-technology.html (Access on 7 January 2017).

Kurniawan S. (2006) An Exploratory Study of How Older Women Use Mobile Phones. In: Dourish P., Friday A. (eds) UbiComp 2006: Ubiquitous Computing. UbiComp 2006. Lecture Notes in Computer Science, vol 4206. Springer, Berlin, Heidelberg

Kurniawan, S., 2008. Older people and mobile phones: A multi-method investigation. *International Journal of Human-Computer Studies,* 66 (12), 889-901.

Md. Nasir, Hassan, H. and Jomhari, N., 2008. The Use of Mobile Phones by Elderly: A Study in Malaysia Perspectives. *Journal of Social Sciences,* 4 (2), pp.123-127.

Ministry of Human Resources, 2013. *About Minimum Retirement Age: Why Enact the Minimum Retirement Age?* [Online] Available at: http://minretirementage.mohr.gov.my/general/about-minimum-retirement-age/ (retrieved on 22 February 2017).

Mohadis, H. M. and Ali, N. M., 2014. A Study of Smartphone Usage and Barriers Among the Elderly. *2014 3rd International Conference on User Science and Engineering (i-USEr).* Selangor, Malaysia, 109-114.

Osman, M. A., Talib, A. Z., Sanusi, Z. A., Tan, S-Y, Alwi, A. S., 2012. A Study of the Treend of Smartphone and its Usage Behavior in Malaysia. *International Journal on New Computer Architectures and Their Applications (INJCAA),* 2 (1), 275-286.

Tan, K. H., 2017. *The iPhone is 10.* [Online] Available at: http://www.thestar.com.my/tech/tech-news/2017/01/09/how-the-world-has-changed-thanks-to-the-iphone/ (Access on 9 January 2017).

Wan-Ibrahim, W.A. and Zainab, I., 2014. Some Demographic Aspects of Population Aging in Malaysia. *World Applied Sciences Journal,* 30 (7), 891-894.

Wong, C.Y., 2011. Exploring the Relationship Between Mobile Phone and Senior Citizens: A Malaysian Perspective. *International Journal of Human-Computer Interaction,* 2 (2), 65-77. KL: CSC Journal.

Yaakob, U., Masron, T. and Masami, F., 2009. Spatial Distribution of Senior Citizen in Peninsular Malaysia 1991-2000. *The Journal of Ritsumeikan Geographical Society*, 21, 59-69.

ASSESSING ICT USAGE IN INDONESIAN SMALL AND MEDIUM ENTERPRISES TOWARDS POVERTY ALLEVIATION USING SUSTAINABLE LIVELIHOODS ASSETS

Fathia Prinastiti Sunarso
MSc Candidate in ICTs for Development, The University of Manchester, UK

ABSTRACT

Poverty alleviation is one of the most pressing agenda that have been listed explicitly in many international development goals. In Indonesia, the establishment of small and medium-sized enterprises (SMEs) has been long associated with economic growth and development, eventually resulting in poverty reduction. Despite its dominance in domestic economic activities, Indonesian SMEs are still facing many problems, such as lack of information and technological support, inhibited financial access, and difficulties in marketing and sales. Some ICT initiatives have been underway to address these problems and to enhance Indonesian SMEs. Using sustainable livelihood assets pentagon, we examine how ICT affects the five capitals that are needed to sustain SMEs in the long run. It is found that while some government-led and SMEs-led initiatives have been taken to advance SMEs in social, financial, and physical capital, some other livelihood assets such as human and natural capital are still left far behind. It is then must be understood that ICT itself is not a solution, but rather an enabler to enhance SMEs' sustainability.

KEYWORDS

Poverty alleviation, SMEs, livelihood assets, ICT

1. INTRODUCTION

Poverty alleviation has become one of the main objectives for many countries in the past few decades. It has been explicitly listed as one of the development goals in both Millennium Development Goals (MDGs) and Sustainable Development Goals (SDGs). A lot of efforts and policies have been implemented in order to achieve such target, with most of them focuses on the economic aspect of poverty.

One of the most common attempts to lift people from poverty line is through the establishment of small and medium-sized enterprises (SMEs), despite its initial purpose whether it is intended to address poverty issues directly or not. SMEs play a vital role especially in developing countries by creating source of employment, exporting growth, and improving income distribution (Tambunan, 2008; Ongori & Migiro, 2010). However, SMEs continuously face many challenges in order to survive and promote economic growth. To address these challenges, several solutions have suggested that there is a need to adopt the use of information and communication technology (ICT) to increase SMEs efficiency and competitiveness (Ongori & Migiro, 2010), and eventually leads to further economic benefits and poverty reduction.

This paper aims to assess to what extent the use of ICTs can help to enhance SMEs in order to alleviate poverty in Indonesia. The assessment will use literature review through one of the variations of sustainable livelihoods framework (SLF), namely the livelihoods assets pentagon, which contains the five livelihoods assets that are in need to be sustained in order to create sustainable livelihoods (DFID, 1999; GLOPP, 2008). SLF was chosen as it offers an analytical tool to manage the complexity and decode all the factors that affect livelihoods, and therefore has been used widely in poverty alleviation research (DFID, 1999; Carney, 2003). Moreover, SLF uses a more development-centric approach, making it more open to changes and flexible to be implemented within the local context (GLOPP, 2008; Heeks & Molla, 2009).

The structure of this paper is as follows. First, I will give a literature review in regard to poverty alleviation as one of the major international development goals and an overview of the sustainable livelihood framework. The next section will be focusing on the case study of ICT usage in Indonesian SMEs using SLF, as well as how it can improve the livelihoods of the poor in Indonesia. The final part of this paper will consist of conclusions and discussions to further achieve poverty alleviation goal in Indonesia.

2. LITERATURE REVIEW

2.1 Poverty Alleviation as International Development Goals

Poverty alleviation as one of the major international development goals was listed first out of the eight Millennium Development Goals (MDGs) in year 2000. The target was to reduce the world's population who lived in extreme poverty and hunger by half in the span of fifteen years (United Nations, 2013). By 2010, this target has been achieved, with poverty rate declining from 47% in 1990 to 22% in 2010 (United Nations, 2013). As the MDGs reaching expiration in 2015, the Sustainable Development Goals (SDGs) were established to carry the momentum from the MDGs and extending the goals towards a more sustainable, unified, and socially-inclusive targets (Sachs, 2012; SDG Fund, 2014). However, there are some differences in regard of how poverty alleviation will be measured in SDGs compared to its predecessor. In SDGs, poverty must be eradicated in all of its forms; rather than focusing heavily on economic aspect; SDGs also take social issues such as gender inequality, education opportunities, and social exclusion into account (World Bank, 2016).

2.1.1 Indonesia's Poverty Alleviation and SMEs

In Indonesia, small enterprises are defined as enterprises with total assets ranging from IDR 50 to 500 million or annual revenue of IDR 300 million to 2,5 billion (Bank Indonesia, 2008). Medium enterprises then defined as enterprises with assets or annual revenues ranging respectively from more than IDR 500 million to 10 billion and more than IDR 2,5 to 50 billion (Bank Indonesia, 2008). Both are the dominant players in Indonesia's domestic economic activities, forming more than 90% of all firms and thus become the main provider of primary and secondary income for many households (Tambunan, 2008a; Tambunan, 2008b). SMEs also have been credited as a robust shock-absorber in Indonesia during the economic crisis in 1997/1998, due to its flexible nature to modify production processes while being less dependent on formal markets and formal credit sources, unlike larger enterprises (Berry et al, 2001; Tambunan, 2008). Data from Central Statistics Agency of Indonesia shows that there has been a steady increase in the number of SMEs in Indonesia, from 36.8 million units in 1998 to 56.5 million units in 2012 (BPS, 2014). It can also be noted that SMEs have been providing employment for an average 85.3 million people per year from 1998 to 2012 (BPS, 2014). Parallel with this, there has been a sharp decline on poverty rate in Indonesia in the same period, from 65.3% to 11.8% (World Bank, 2016).

Aside from economic growth, SMEs in Indonesia also act as pioneers of development for villagers, as they are mostly spread throughout the rural area and thus have special significance in enhancing rural economies (Tambunan, 2008; Mourougane, 2012). The establishment of SMEs then have indirectly contributed to further progression of Indonesia's social issues, such as the empowerment of women, advancing youths' education, and enhancing the poor's resistance towards shocks (Vandenberg, 2006; Tambunan, 2008). Despite these contributions, SMEs in Indonesia are still facing many challenges to expand and push further growth. Several main problems that have been observed from Indonesian SMEs are lack of financial access, difficulties of marketing and sales, and insufficient information and technological support (Tambunan, 2008; Muafi et al, 2012; Irjayanti & Azis, 2012).

3. RESEARCH FRAMEWORK AND METHODOLOGY

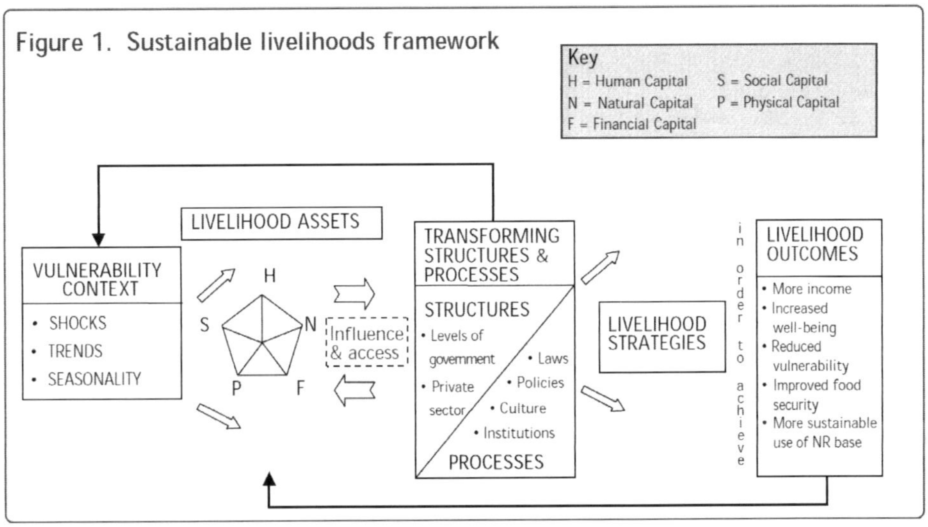

Figure 1. Sustainable livelihoods framework (DFID, 1999)

This study will be conducted through literature review from previous research and open-sourced data using the Sustainable Livelihood Framework (SLF). SLF is a tool to analyze and enhance our understanding about the livelihoods of the poor (DFID, 1999). SLF presents various internal and external elements that affect people's livelihood, as well as the objectives and priorities for development from the perspective of poor people (DFID, 1999; Carney, 2003). In this context, SLF requires us to think beyond the technical issue and approach the poor with a certain degree of recognition that they already have access to poverty-reducing assets and created their own strategies to cope with vulnerability (Carney, 2003; Duncombe, 2007; Morse & McNamara, 2013, pp. 40). Only when a livelihood is resistant to stresses and shocks and maintains to enhance its capabilities and assets without sacrificing natural resources, it is said to be sustainable and thus capable to lift people from poverty line (DFID, 1999).

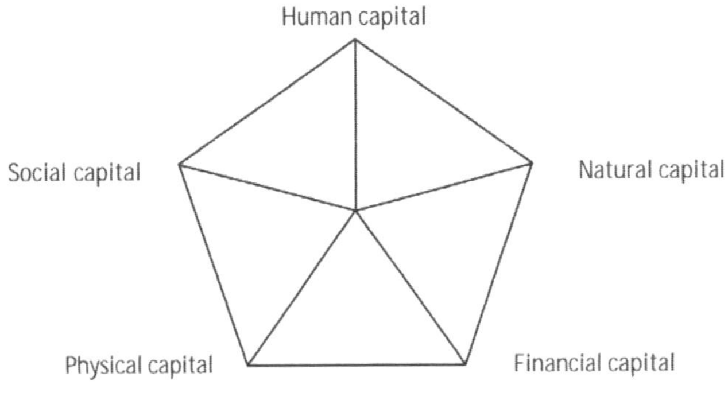

Figure 2. Livelihood assets pentagon (DFID, 1999)

In this paper, we will be focusing only on the livelihood assets pentagon. The livelihood assets pentagon consisted of five interdependent elements that reflect people's strength to alter these assets into sustainable livelihoods (DFID, 1999; GLOPP, 2008). The first asset is the human capital, which described as all the skills, knowledge, and good health that enable people to pursue livelihood strategies (DFID, 1999; Duncombe, 2007). The second asset is the social capital, which refers to all the social resources such as norms and extended networks in social organizations that generate actions in order to pursue livelihood strategies (DFID, 1999; Duncombe, 2007). The third asset is the natural capital, which defined as the natural resource stocks such as land, trees, and water that are vital for the livelihood of the poor (DFID, 1999; Duncombe, 2007). The fourth asset is the physical capital, which contains the physical infrastructures that are essential to support livelihoods, such as clean sanitation, affordable transportation, and technology (DFID, 1999; Duncombe 2007). Lastly, the fifth asset is the financial asset which stands for monetary resources, such as savings or credits that can be accessed by people to sustain their livelihoods (DFID, 1999; Duncombe, 2007).

4. ASSESSING THE USE OF ICT IN INDONESIAN SMES USING THE LIVELIHOOD ASSETS PENTAGON

4.1 Human Capital

The quality of human resource in Indonesia has been an issue for a long time, and digital literacy is not an exception in this matter. In terms of basic information technology skills, Indonesia only ranked 63rd out of 139 countries as the result of low quality educational system and secondary education enrollment, and adult illiteracy (World Economic Forum, 2016). This condition often leads to organizational resistance in the process of ICT adoption (Kartiwi & MacGregor, 2007; Muafi et al, 2012; Maryeni et al, 2012). For example, only 5% of SMEs located in Yogyakarta use IT for transaction because the workers feel that they do not have the skill to use IT and therefore do not need it at all (Muafi et al, 2012). Another study conducted in 179 SMEs in West Java, DKI Jakarta, and Bali province found out that SMEs owners and staffs feel that it is "too difficult" to incorporate ICT into their business process (Kartiwi & MacGregor, 2007). Even in some cases where ICT have been implemented, it is often that the adoption process takes a long time, with many trial-and-error processes due to the SMEs owners' lack of IT knowledge and strategy (Sarosa & Zowghi, 2003; Maryeni et al, 2012).

4.2 Social Capital

Indonesian SMEs still rely heavily on local markets and have difficulties in exploring their own markets, mostly depending on their trade partners to promote and sell their products (Tambunan, 2008). However, in some of the cases Indonesian SMEs have identified the way to boost their market share using ICT. A study in five of Indonesia's largest cities (Jakarta, Surabaya, Medan, Yogyakarta, and Banda Aceh) found that mobile food vendors use mobile phones to keep them informed about daily market conditions, especially regarding location information, menu preordering, customer recommendations, and special events (Dawood et al, 2010). These food vendors use mobile phones to alert regular customers via text messages about their availability and gather information about public events such as open concerts, state fairs, or public rallies to set up their pop up stores (Dawood et al, 2010). Another study in the city of Bandung and Makassar shows that rather than using formal business associations and co-operatives, SMEs owners are more inclined to discuss business matters through their own self-formed networks, usually by using mobile phones (Anwar, 2015). It has been shown that mobile phones are becoming increasingly important to SMEs owners, as it functions as primary business contacts storage and enabling word-of-mouth marketing, especially for SMEs that run service-based businesses (Anwar, 2015).

4.3 Natural Capital

Access to natural resources has become an issue for Indonesian SMEs for a long time. Despite the dominance of traditional, agricultural business in Indonesian SMEs, agriculture in Indonesia still often characterized by small, landless farmers (LANDac, 2015). In an agricultural census conducted by Central Statistics Agency of Indonesia in 2013, it was found that there are 26.14 millions of farming households in Indonesia, owning an average of only 0.98 hectares of land (BPS, 2013; LANDac, 2015). The difficulty to gain raw materials access also happens in SMEs who runs manufacturing industries. In 2011, the Association of Furniture and Handicraft Rattan Indonesia in Borneo expressed the difficulties of obtaining raw materials of rattan, up to the point that they had to reject many orders because of it (Irjayanti & Azis, 2012). In addition to that, the scarcity and high fuel prices often lead to SMEs inefficient production and hampers product distribution (Tambunan, 2008; Irjayanti & Azis, 2012).

4.4 Physical Capital

As an archipelago country with more than 17,000 islands, the need of physical connectivity in Indonesia is higher than in other countries with more land. However, the lack of information access is still being suffered by the majority of Indonesian SMEs; and it is related directly to the lack of infrastructure in Indonesia (Muafi et al, 2012; Irjayanti & Azis, 2012). In terms of Networked Readiness Index (NRI), Indonesia's infrastructure and digital component aspects such as mobile network coverage, international internet bandwidth, secure internet servers, electricity production, and availability of digital content are still low, only ranked 105th out of 139 countries (World Economic Forum, 2016). Having realized about this, The Ministry of Communication and Information Technology of Indonesia launched the Indonesia Connected program, in which 35,280 kilometers of fiber-optic undersea cable named Palapa Ring will be implemented to boost connectivity by 2019 (Citizen Lab, 2014; Menkominfo, 2015). But the Palapa Ring project poses another issue of digital divide, as the project only covers the western islands of Indonesia such as Sumatra, Java, Borneo, and Mataram while leaving eastern islands such as Sulawesi and Papua behind (Citizen Lab, 2014).

4.5 Financial Capital

Evidences have suggested that one of the most challenging obstacles that Indonesian SMEs have to face is the lack of financial resources, especially for enterprises that are based on rural area (Tambunan, 2008; Irjayanti & Azis, 2012; Mourougane, 2012). Although there have been several government-led initiatives to provide financial access, the majority of SMEs still rely heavily on their own savings, money from family and relatives, or loans from informal financial institutions (Tambunan, 2008; Irjayanti & Azis, 2012; Mourougane, 2012). For instance, in 2009, more than 90% of SMEs based in Yogyakarta and Banten Province in Indonesia had no bank loans but rather using financial sources from family and friends (ADB, 2010). It is also should be noted that Indonesia has one of the lowest efficiency of financial intermediation among South East Asian countries, as a result of disproportionate information distribution (ADB, 2010; Mourougane, 2012). Most of Indonesian SMEs do not keep tracks of their financial report, making it difficult for banks and other formal financial institutions to assess the risks of lending credits to SMEs, and therefore make them charge higher interest rates or even reluctant to lend credits at all (Mourougane, 2012).

In order to address these pressing problems, a public credit bureau (*Biro Informasi Kredit* – Credit Bureau) has been established in Indonesia since 2006, with main task to collect and record credit and loan data into Debtor Information System and distribute them as Individual Debtor Information (IDI) History (Mourougane, 2012; Bank Indonesia, 2013). However, some of the information access in Credit Bureau is still restricted, with only commercial and large rural banks and non-bank credit card suppliers can access the information freely and thus inhibit the much needed transparency of financial access information (Mourougane, 2012).

5. RESULTS ANALYSIS AND DISCUSSIONS

All previous assessments regarding the five livelihood assets have suggested that lack of information access have become the common thread that inhibit Indonesian SMEs growth. This problem is related directly to the use of ICT. All the evidences have suggested that low level of information distribution have caused SMEs difficulties in almost every aspects, from the difficulty of gaining bank loans, trouble with innovation and keeping up with international product standards, to the struggle of selling and marketing products in an ever growing competition. In this respect, ICT applications can be used directly by SMEs to serve their information needs as well as helping them to make decision on daily basis (Duncombe, 2007).

Out of five livelihood assets that were assessed in this paper, two of them—social and financial capital—have been somewhat incorporating ICT to boost its effectivity and efficiency, with physical capital still on its way to be enhanced through the government-led connectivity initiative. In terms of human capital, the problem is related back to the motivation of using ICT itself; with low basic education and technological skills among the population, most of the SMEs owners have not yet understood how to exploit ICT for their benefits. The most extreme cases are found in terms of natural capital, where ICT initiatives have not yet been implemented to address the issue of lack of access.

As Indonesians already have a strong community-driven culture, it also can be suggested that the use of ICTs is implemented to strengthen social capital assets to open access into new markets. However, the application of ICT in regard to social capital needs to be more structured; as the current nature of information from within the SMEs self-formed networks are still scattered and disorganized, it will be better if the information are gathered and distributed through one devoted, formal channel.

The lack of physical infrastructure still poses as the main threat to the growth of SMEs. Infrastructure growth needs to be more even, especially in the eastern part of Indonesia where there are still little to no development of basic transportation and communication infrastructure. As Indonesia has a large area to be developed, the government could opt to collaborate and do partnerships with private sectors to build infrastructures.

The application of ICT to enhance SMEs, however, cannot be implemented successfully without any adjustment in institutional aspects in Indonesia. Perhaps the bigger problem that lies here is the lack of coordination between the livelihood capitals enhancement itself. While the five of them are definitely interconnected to each other, the use of ICT (or lack of) in all five capitals are coming from different actors with different drivers and visions. There has been no effort to align these enhancements of livelihood capitals, causing these assets to grow sporadically and disproportionately. In this matter, government should be acting as the initiators as well as regulators to both boost and control these ICT-enabled programs so these assets will achieve their true potentials to further sustaining SMEs and eventually reducing poverty.

6. CONCLUSIONS

This paper attempts to assess the relationship between ICT usages in Indonesian SMEs in order to reduce poverty using the livelihood assets. It is quite clear that the use of ICT is still far from enabling more efficient, effective, and therefore sustainable SMEs in the long run. It is then must be understood that ICT itself is acting more as enablers rather than the solution itself to enhance Indonesian SMEs; in the future, there needs to be a simultaneous effort both from the SMEs owners, government, as well as other private sectors to guarantee the sustainability of SMEs in the long run.

Further research proposed from this study can be done in the area where this study has limitations; for instance, as this study discusses SMEs in broader terms, perhaps future research should be focusing on specific SMEs industry with primary data to give more accurate and objective results of the actual condition in the real world.

ACKNOWLEDGEMENT

I would like to give my biggest gratitude to Allah SWT; both of my parents for always trusting and believing in me; Suci Fadhilah, one of my biggest and closest supporting systems during our study abroad in the United Kingdom; Indonesia Endowment Fund for Education (LPDP) as my generous sponsor; and to everyone who keeps supporting me.

REFERENCES

ADB, 2010. *Indonesia: critical development constraints,* Manila: Asian Development Bank.

Anwar, M., 2015. *Mobile Phones and the Livelihoods of Indonesian Micro-Entrepreneurs: Evidence of Capability Expansion.* Singapore, Pacific Asia Conference On Information Systems (PACIS).

APJII, 2014. *Profil Pengguna Internet Indonesia 2014,* Jakarta: Asosiasi Penyedia Jasa Internet Indonesia.

Bank Indonesia, 2008. *Undang-Undang Republik Indonesia Nomor 20 Tahun 2008 tentang Usaha Mikro, Kecil, dan Menengah.* Jakarta: Bank Indonesia.

Bank Indonesia, 2013. *Credit Bureau.* [Online] Available at: http://www.bi.go.id/en/moneter/biro-informasi-kredit/Contents/Default.aspx_[Accessed 20 December 2016].

Berry, A., Rodriguez, E. & Sandee, H., 2001. Small and Medium Enterprise Dynamics in Indonesia. *Bulletin of Indonesian Economic Studies,* 37(3), pp. 363-384.

BPS, 2013. *Jumlah Rumah Tangga Usaha Pertanian menurut Golongan Luas Lahan yang Dikuasai Tahun 2003 dan 2013.* [Online] Available at: https://st2013.bps.go.id/dev2/index.php/site/tabel?tid=21&wid=0 [Accessed 21 December 2016].

BPS, 2014. *Table of Micro Small and Medium Enterprises Progress Period 1997 -2012.* [Online] Available at: https://www.bps.go.id/linkTabelStatis/view/id/1322_[Accessed 15 December 2016].

Carney, D., 2003. *DFID's Sustainable Livelihoods Approach and its Framework: Progress and Possibilities of Change.* London: Department for International Development.

Chandy, L. & Gertz, G., 2011. *Poverty in Numbers: The Changing State of Global Poverty from 2005 to 2015,* Washington, DC: The Brookings Institution.

Citizen Lab, 2014. *Islands Of Control, Islands Of Resistance: Monitoring the 2013 Indonesian IGF,* Toronto: Canada Centre for Global Security Studies and the Citizen Lab.

Cornwall, A. & Brock, K., 2005. What do Buzzwords do for Development Policy? A critical look at 'participation', 'empowerment' and 'poverty reduction'. *Third World Quarterly,* 26(7), pp. 1043-1060.

Dawood, R., Jackson, S. J. & Yew, J., 2010. *Supporting the information needs of mobile microentrepreneurs in the developing world: the case of Indonesian food cart vendors.* London, ICTD '10 Proceedings of the 4th ACM/IEEE International Conference on Information and Communication Technologies and Development.

DFID, 1999. *Sustainable Livelihood Framework Guidance Sheets.* [Online] Available at: http://www.eldis.org/vfile/upload/1/document/0901/section2.pdf [Accessed 21 November 2016].

Duncombe, R., 2007. Using the Livelihoods Framework to Analyze ICT Applications for Poverty Reduction through Microenterprise. *The Massachusetts Institute of Technology Information Technologies and International Development,* 3(3), pp. 81-100.

Duncombe, R. & Heeks, R., 2005. *Information & Communication Technologies (ICT), Poverty Reduction and Micro, Small & Medium-scale Enterprises (MSMEs): A framework for understanding ICT applications for MSMEs in developing countries,* Manchester: Institute for Development Policy and Management (IDPM).

Easterly, W., 2008. How the Millennium Development Goals are Unfair to Africa. *World Development,* 37(1), pp. 26-35.

GLOPP, 2008. *DFID's Sustainable Livelihoods Approach and its Framework.* [Online] Available at: http://www.glopp.ch/B7/en/multimedia/B7_1_pdf2.pdf_[Accessed 28 November 2016].

Heeks, R. & Molla, A., 2009. Impact Assessment of ICT-for-Development Projects: A Compendium of Approaches. *Manchester Development Informatics Working Paper,* Issue 36.

Irjayanti, M. & Azis, A. M., 2012. Barrier Factors and Potential Solutions for Indonesian SMEs. *Procedia Economics and Finance,* Volume 4, pp. 3-12.

Kartiwi, M., 2006. Case studies of e-commerce adoption in Indonesian SMEs: The evaluation of strategic use. *Australasian Journal of Information Systems,* 14(1).

Kartiwi, M. & MacGregor, R. C., 2007. Electronic commerce adoption barriers in small to medium-sized enterprises (SMEs) in developed and developing countries: A cross-country comparison. *Journal of Electronic Commerce in Organizations (JECO),* 5(3), pp. 35-51.

LANDac, 2015. *Food Security And Land Governance Factsheet: Indonesia,* Utrecht: The Netherlands Academy on Land Governance for Equitable and Sustainable Development.

Maryeni, Y. Y., Govindaraju, R., Prihartono, B. & Sudirman, I., 2012. *Technological and organizational factors influencing the e-commerce adoption by Indonesian SMEs.* Denpasar, Management of Innovation and Technology (ICMIT), 2012 IEEE International Conference.

Mbuyisa, B. & Leonard, A., 2016. The Role of ICT Use in SMEs Towards Poverty Reduction: A Systematic Literature Review. *Journal of International Development.*

Menkominfo, 2015. *ICT Research and Development.* [Online] Available at: https://www.nict.go.jp/en/asean_ivo/4otfsk00001ver81-att/a1436766621134.pdf [Accessed 20 December 2016].

Morse, S. & McNamara, N., 2013. *Sustainable Livelihood Approach: A Critique of Theory and Practice.* London: Springer.

Mourougane, A., 2012. Promoting SME development in Indonesia. *OECD Economics Department Working Papers,* Issue 995.

Muafi, Gusaptono, R. H., Effendi, M. I. & Charibaldi, N., 2012. The Information Technology (IT) Adoption Process and E-Readiness to Use within Yogyakarta Indonesian Small Medium Enterprises (SME). *International Journal of Information and Communication Technology Research,* 2(1), pp. 29-37.

Ongori, H. & Migiro, S. O., 2010. Information and communication technologies adoption in SMEs: literature review. *Journal of Chinese Entrepreneurship,* 2(1), pp. 93-104.

Raphael, D., 2013. The Politics of Poverty: Definitions and Explanations. *Social Alternatives,* 32(1), pp. 5-11.

Sachs, J. D., 2012. From Millennium Development Goals to Sustainable Development Goals. *Lancet,* Volume 379, pp. 2206-2211.

Saith, A., 2006. From Universal Values to Millennium Development Goals: Lost in Translation. *Development and Change,* 37(6), p. 1167–1199.

Sarosa, S. & Zowghi, D., 2003. Strategy for adopting information technology for SMEs: Experience in adopting email within an Indonesian furniture company. *Electronic Journal of Information Systems Evaluation,* 6(2), pp. 165-176.

SDG Fund, 2014. *From MGDs to SDGs.* [Online] Available at: http://www.sdgfund.org/mdgs-sdgs [Accessed 6 December 2016].

SMRJ, 2008. *Small & Medium Enterprise Development Policies in 6 ASEAN Countries,* Tokyo: Organization for Small & Medium Enterprises and Regional Innovation, Japan.

Tambunan, T., 2008. Development of SME in ASEAN with Reference to Indonesia and Thailand. *Chulalongkorn Journal of Economics,* 20(1), pp. 53-83.

Tambunan, T., 2008. SME development, economic growth, and government intervention in a developing country: The Indonesian story. *Journal of International Entrepreneurship,* 6(4), pp. 147-167.

Tambunan, T., 2009. Promoting innovation in SMEs through transfer of technology: Lessons from a metalworking industry cluster in Indonesia. *Tech Monitor,* pp. 32-38.

United Nations, 2013. *Millenium Development Goals and Beyond 2015 Fact Sheet,* s.l.: UN Department of Public Information.

United Nations, 2016. *The Sustainable Development Goals Report 2016,* New York: United Nations.

Vandenberg, P., 2006. Poverty reduction through small enterprises: Emerging consensus, unresolved issues and ILO activities. *SEED Working Paper,* Issue 75.

World Bank, 2015. *Enterprise Surveys 2015: Indonesia,* Washington, DC: The World Bank Group.

World Bank, 2016. *Poverty & Equity: Indonesia.* [Online] Available at: http://povertydata.worldbank.org/poverty/country/IDN [Accessed 15 December 2016].

World Bank, 2016. *Poverty Overview.* [Online] Available at: http://www.worldbank.org/en/topic/poverty/overview [Accessed 1 December 2016].

World Bank, 2016. *World Development Indicators 2016 Highlights: Featuring the Sustainable Development Goals,* Washington, DC: The World Bank.

World Economic Forum, 2016. *Global Information Technology Report 2016.* [Online] Available at: http://reports.weforum.org/global-information-technology-report-2016/economies/#economy=IDN [Accessed 20 December 2016].

DESIGN BEST. AN INTEGRATED E-COMMERCE AND E-LEARNING INNOVATIVE PLATFORM TO PROMOTE EDUCATION FOR ITALIAN DESIGN SYSTEM (PRODUCT & PROCESS)

Dalia Gallico
Università San Raffaele Roma, Via Daverio 7 Milano – via Val Cannuta 247 Roma, Italy

ABSTRACT

DesignBest concept is born as response to the necessity to create a virtual community (a square) about italian design matters. The extraordinary achievement of communities demonstrated the enormous potentials of technologies in supporting communication and self-production of contents to create strong communities. The program proposes to apply technologies to support a marketplace and to build a community around the education of Italian design.
Leveraging the development of ITC technologies, the program integrates innovative web technologies 2.0, in order to:
1) Create, applying the most advanced web technologies 2.0, an environment where all active users (designers, design students, etc..), vendors or buyers, can develop ideas, concepts, events, opinions, about Made in Italy Design, joining potentials of vendors, designers, students, amateurs and curious;
2) Explain Culture of Project, display products' characteristics, allowing the user/buyer to interact to capture the extra value of the product;
3) Use buyer's auto profiling and geo localization data to increase the offer and create feed-back flows which could be translated into networking;
4) Create data exchange with the logistic platform to assure the quality of logistic performance expected from the market;
5) Enable the sale of Design objects between the Italian SMEs (small, medium enterprises) and the potential buyers around the world (the business will focus mainly on the following markets: Brazil, Russia, India, China, Canada, USA, Mexico, Japan, Arab Emirates) trying to support Design SMEs in:
- Reach the "critical mass" needed to build a wide catalogue of "Made in Italy" Design learning corses
- Have access to an alternative sales channel, since they cannot bear investments in IT by themselves
- Take advantage of DesignBest international visibility to reach new markets
- Have access to e-commerce in an easy way (without problems related information technology structure, order management, invoicing, payment and shipment, returns and complaints management)
- Leverage some supporting services to international sales and marketing(information, advice, training, data bank, market analysis, etc)
- Spread the Italian Design culture through a platform of e-learning addressed to foreign companies and universities.
Critical success factors of the project are:
- A wide adhesion of Italian design schools to the marketplace, where they can offer part of their own catalogue (also ad hoc courses) exploiting a new channel (e-commerce) and entering on new markets;
- The ability to attract the Design community (lovers, designer, students)

KEYWORDS

Higher Education, Design of societal systems – rethinking, Managed Learning Environments (MLEs), Learning Theories and Approaches, E-Learning Models. E-commerce

1. INTRODUCTION

Design industry plays a main role in the Italian productive system and it contributes significantly to support the trade balance (the value of design export in 2016 was of about 15 mld € between jeweller's craft and furniture accessories).

Lombardy, with its districts and SMEs, is the sector leader in Italy with an export that, only in terms of furniture accessories, is closed to 2 bln of €, of which more than 950 mln € made in Milan (around 11,3% of total Italian production).

Design is, therefore, an Excellence recognized to our country in all the world, although there are still few structures supporting internationalization of the e-commerce and e-learning of design education.

Università San Raffaele Roma decided to cooperate to start an initiative called Design Best aiming to support SMEs' commerce (above all abroad) related to Italian design sector and to spread in the world the Italian design culture.

Institutions MISE Economic Ministery and the Municipality of Milan and, recognizing to Milan the pre-eminence of design in Italy, showed interest for the initiative.

2. DEFINITION OF THE PROGRAM IN THE TECHNOLOGICAL AREA FRAMEWORK. GENERAL AND SPECIFIC PROJECT GOALS

Università Telematica San Raffaele Roma, Web Mobili, Politecnico di Milano, Accademia di Brera, Gaia, and companies Empsol, Nemos Solutions, Neptuny, Tefen, Moviri, with economic support of MISE Economic Ministery (Industria 2015) and the Municipality of Milan decided to join together and to take part to the public competition (as "proposer players") in the field "house system" in the objective area "strategic market" coverage with the intent of developing together e-commerce and e -learning market intelligence solutions.

The project mainly covers the topics:

- Development and application of cooperative technological solutions for management of global transactions and orders and customer relationship management.

- Development and application of technologies and tools to create contents and communication format being multi-lingual and multi-culture, customized and flexible;

- Development and application of integrated tools and solutions of business and marketing intelligence

The program aims to design, build and test a prototype for an integrated platform that could support SMEs of "Made in Italy" Design to win globalization challenges with e-commerce and long life learning. The platform provides access to an alternative channel sales that is also a different way to communicate, train and promote Made in Italy Design.

DesignBest's specific objectives:

A. Provide the information technology to support SMEs doing e-commerce and e-learning. As a matter of fact, in this field, 80% of SMEs are craftwork companies

- Many SMEs do not develop e-commerce and e-learning because economic costs and risks are too high;

- If the project's actors support the starting investment, barriers to entry in e-commerce and e-learning can be significantly reduced.

B. Develop an Internet support for the "Made in Italy" design world community. The community consists of people who seek and appreciate Italian Design both for products and for culture. The concept could be taken as an "umbrella" to link different activities, such as e-commerce, training, business supporting operations and market intelligence.

- A remarkable part of on-line sales is addressed abroad (for example, more than two-thirds of "clothing" turnover has foreign origins).

- One single SME usually does not have a strong and known brand to compete in the global market.

- Advertising investments (on different media) are expensive, especially when it is international marketing.

- Web marketing has many chances to succeed but it is also really complex and characterized by frequent changes and development

- If SMEs are not able to widen to international markets, they can't take advantage of the opportunities related to globalization process

- Sales channel for SMEs consists of distributors and retailers, so SMEs and customers are not directly linked; the consequence is a low visibility and acknowledgement for SMEs which are not able to analyze potential markets

- New technologies will allow a constant analysis of the community to fill the gap; important information about customers' needs will be available for companies which will take part in the role of vendors

- The Brand of the marketplace, related to the concept of Made in Italy (synonymous with quality, innovation, elegance, beauty and design), becomes synonymous with reliability for the sector

- Building a single channel it is possible to develop media campaigns (offline and online), which give an exclusive brand image also to little known and small companies

- As a community, it is possible to exploit economies of scale buying media space (especially online, eg.: AdWords, etc.) to ensure visibility

C. Provide solid and specific services to companies on foreign trade

- Italian SMEs usually are not able to approach new markets/countries because they do not know local laws and rules, local market needs and characteristics, etc.

- Often SMEs have to deal with bureaucracy and export issues (contracts, customs regulation, documents required)

- A shared platform can be a reference point where SMEs find help and support for foreign trade, as well as contents and experience related to the field. The platform can be also a way to create a chain in foreign trade

D. Broaden the "Made in Italy" Design culture around the world

- Italian Clothing and food&wine sectors are already popular around the world whereas Design is not known enough at present time

- Design products are the highest performance of "Made in Italy", which means elegance and innovation. Sometimes they can be compared to a "work of art", but they are still not popular enough around the world

- Italian companies have the leadership and they are the benchmark for Design around the world

- The e-learning platform, supported by new technologies, is the best way to let University and companies know about culture and contents of Italian Design

The project development is based on an integrated platform made by main modules, linked together by the concept of the community for Design Made in Italy.

The community mission is so be to involve everyone is interested to the subject such as simple beauty admirer, people attracted by trendy and glamour in general, aspiring designers or collectors.

According to modern theories of web marketing (web 2.0) this is possible when the contents are shared and created by users (for example Wikipedia, Facebook, You Tube), not when they come only from the top to the bottom.

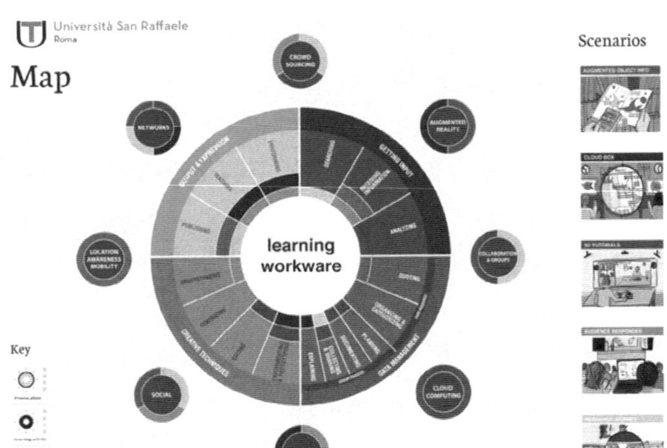

Figure 1. The "mandala" of "customisez" contents

This requires the use of basic elements from new technologies, connected in a new way, innovative and unique. In this context companies, users/buyers, supporting organizations, simple lovers or aspiring designers are all together a big laboratory of ideas and content, where the four functional elements described below are the engines of value creation.

3. E-LEARNING PLATFORM TO DEVELOP CULTURE OF MADE IN ITALY DESIGN AROUND THE WORLD

A virtual research laboratory promotes design culture, distance relationships and creation of ideas shared from all design system. This pattern aims to communicate to the world, history, concepts, design art, building brand awareness and benefits for all chain companies and linked industries (including exhibitions, events, eg).

The pattern supports a network of creativity, giving visibility to companies who will benefit through talent scouting and through an open window on creative concepts worldwide.

The concept is able to involve different kind of users:

- "amateurs" who have the opportunity to widen their knowledge and test their creativity
- "aspiring professionals" who have the opportunity to start training on specific subjects, or add something new in a context of high visibility
- "professionals" who can improve their competences
- "linked", meaning all professionals , like innovation project managers, who want to learn more about design, start to be creative and know more about design industry
- companies, which can observe what is being done, look for human resources and new talents.

The project contains also a platform for e-learning with different characteristics according to the target countries. The platform covers topics "Design for Business and Business for Design" such as:

- Market and design marketing
- Networks for sharing innovation
- Research and innovation for materials and technology
- Design and Environment
- Brand Protection and legal aspects

The platform has to support creativity through technology, allowing the building of contents with a bi-directional process. Concerning to background part of training and spreading information, DesignBest provides SMEs an experimental system based on narrowcasting technologies.

The work packages to reach the objective of the stream have been :

1 - Market solutions scouting: This activity analyzes the market solutions (national and international) available about the E-learning solutions, focusing on different variables of analysis to orient the identification of the best solutions for the Design Best e-learning platform

2 - User Requirements Analysis: This activity had 1 carried out the users requirements through structured interview to the key users identified for each functionalities area of the E-learning platform. Afterwards the result from the interviews will be elaborated to define the necessary functional requirements of the Portal

3 - Functional specification: This activity designed the set of functionalities area of the E-learning platform. Information architecture will be define as well as interface and interaction aspects. The latter will be define in a beta version successively harmonized through the activity

4 - e-Learning platform development: This activity analyzes the technological solutions available moving from the result of the market solutions scouting national and international planned for each module to define the overall architecture of the design Best Platform, focusing on open source scenario requirements, interoperability aspects and diffusion level of technological standards

5 - Content production: aims at producing a scientific program, multimedia contents in different languages. New and scientific program will be collected, in order to define coherent and innovation program.

6 Validation: This activity defines first a validation plan to verify the consistency between the result carried out from the activity and the result carried out from the activity .During the validation will be define actions to get more consistency, where a gap will be pointed out

7 - E-Learning platform test and update on collected feedbacks: The activity objective is the definition of a coherent testing plan, able to ease the introduction of the E-learning platform in the real business contexts of the different actors involved in the testing phase. The PL aims at defining organizational, commercial and technical support processes, able to assist educational relationships based on the services delivered by the platform.

4. TECNOLOGICAL APPLICATIONS AND CHARACTERISTICS

As part of the project devoted to the dissemination of high quality material in Design, Uni San Raffaele University, the portal "design.unisanraffaele.gov.it" is designed to allow easy and flexible access to a big potential user. In this sense, the portal is based on some of the most widely used, reliable and functional tools in the field of content management, electronic commerce, and technology training. Inside the portal, the Joomla and virtuemart platform is integrated in conjunction with Moodle for the sale and use of online courses.The implementation of the online sales system for the design.unisanraffaele.gov.it site is concerned with the Moodle, Joomla and VirtueMart platforms. The latter is an add-on for Joomla cms that allows you to extend its capabilities to create and manage an e-commerce portal.This tool, in conjunction with an API implementation, enables the integration of Moodle courses with the sale and purchase auto-subscription.

The basic component of Virtuemart covers the basic features of an on-line shop (online catalog submission, file download, cart), but add-ons that implement additional functionality such as product search or preview in. The shop management allows you to modify the seller and related product information by entering basic information (name, identifier), advanced (weight, unit of measure, size, related products) and images (Picture of the article).

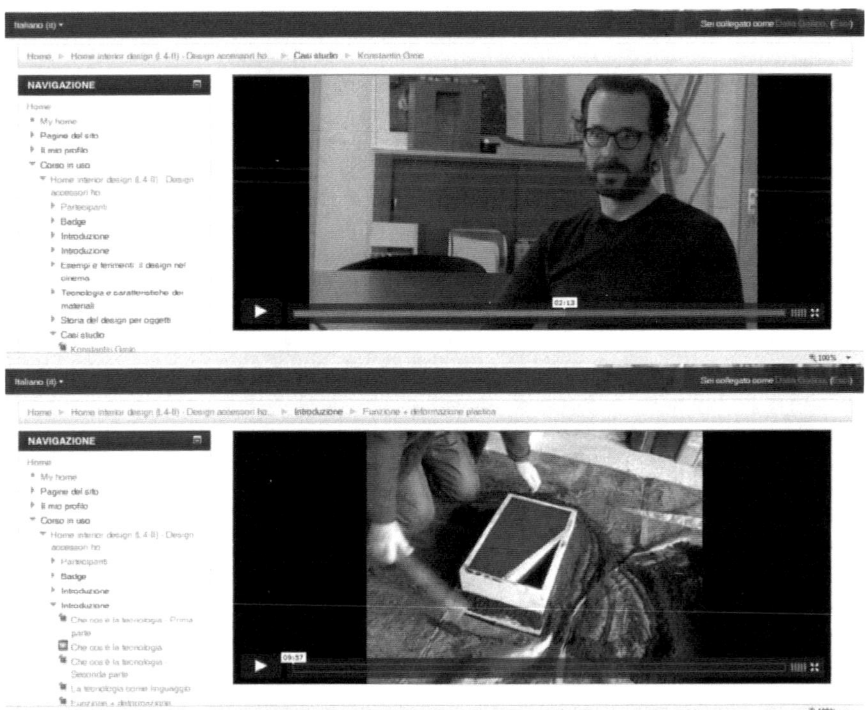

Figure 2. A dedicated plug-in for video lesson tracking

Streaming video with Vimeo provider. Always in order to increase the portability of the contributions and to exploit the potential offered by streaming video, it has been chosen to use a professional broadcast service. In particular, the solution envisaged the adoption of Vimeo and Vimeo Pro service providers, which enabled complete portability of any type of device, including mobile (smart phones and tablets), otherwise unavailable through any dedicated server Owned properties that the University had or could have had. A dedicated plug-in for video lesson tracking Vimeo's adoption has allowed another goal to be achieved.

The Vimeo platform, in fact, automatically exports some information about the access by authorized users of the video contributions stored therein. Such information, intercepted "application" through appropriate web services, can be used for "fine" tracking of these teaching contributions.To this end, a proprietary plug-in (Video Content) was developed, compatible with Moodle (verse 2.6), able to query the Vimeo platform and make available all the information about accessing, advancing, and completing the View of each video contribution. Additionally, this plug-in has made it possible to make full use of all those useful features for tracking and evaluating the didactic activity of the trainees. In fact, in addition to providing "raw" data on the video resource usage, the teacher-editor can set different criteria to define the "completion of the activity": "The student must see the activity to complete it", "the student must end the video view to complete it", "the student must enjoy the video for more or equal duration of the video.

5. COMPETITIVE ADVANTAGES W.R.T THE STATE-OF-THE-ART EXPECTED IMPACTS OVER THE INDUSTRY AND OVER SPECIFIC EDUCATION COMPANIES

The project brings high improvement concerning technology and organization and allows to differentiate from competition systems of other countries.

With regard to technology, the difference is be done by web 2.0 technologies, used to build a virtual environment that will enable bottom-up creativity; support the development of sophisticated experience systems representing design as an interaction for example with interactive tables and walls or texters.

The logistic platform needs to develop advanced information management systems to create a single virtual warehouse.

Today production chain is made by many small companies usually hand-crafted. The project brings development and new elements for companies that will be able to improve their processes and take advantage of new technologies, all with the purpose of changing today's innovation processes and supply chain.

The creative process will be radically changed due to new technology allowing users to participate and develop a real bottom-up creative network. Today, creative processes involve one person or small groups, tomorrow it will be the many-to-few allowing companies to test a wide range of ideas, concepts, format, design in a very short time and obtain directly information market needed to business development.

The project plans to develop prototypes fully scalable, which may, after testing, be taken as a model to create real and complete platforms.

These models could be used also for other Made in Italy sectors, such as fashion, art and media.

The main Italy's competitors on design are France, Sweden and Germany. Compared to those competitors, the project purpose is to be the first mover and create an advantage which competitors could not reach.

The programme impacts all companies taking part of the initiative (vendors); to be more precise those of home design objects, home furnishing accessories, jewellery and trinkets:

- Knowledge development of marketing intelligence in the BRIC Brazil, Russia, India and China, NAFTA Canada, USA, Mexico, ME Middle East, above all United Arab Emirates and Japan Markets;
- Widen the reach of medium and small companies, over such markets, with positive outcomes on sales and sector employment;
- Increase of talents network through training programs and expansion of the surplus value perception supporting the spread of Made in Italy design culture;

Companies of sectors involved, are an important part of the Made in Italy export:

- About volumes, the Italian goldsmith industry is second only to the Indian, at the same level of the Chinese one, double of United States, and at least 10 times above the first European competitor, Spain. Instead, from a qualitative point of view it is absolutely the first player, and the trade balance, shows, historically, a positive credit balance around 2.8 billion of Euro, with the production value of almost 6 billion Euro. United States are the main country buyer, followed by various European countries, but China and the Middle East are in strong rising. In this sector operate about 10.000 companies of which 8.500 craftsman and 1.500 industrial, for the total of about 47.000 employed;
- Design industry, with home furnishing accessories production, is another important part of our balance of trade.Trade surplus for this sector amount to about 9 billion Euros, including crosswise sectors such as wood carving, glass and ceramics manufactory. Companies involved are tens of thousands, with a number of employers around 120.000, 80% of these companies have hand-crafted structure Information data processed by Federorafi/ISTAT.
- Italy produces also "design culture", there are many and qualified educational programs, as IED, Istituto Europeo di Design, and others are SPD, Scuola Politecnica di Design, the Design Degree at Politecnico,

ISAD, NABA or the Domus Academy, all placed in Milan; the ISIA in Florence, Faenza ed Urbino; Fabrica, related to Benetton Group, or the Interaction Design Institute situated in Ivrea. This educational offer is not addressed only to talents of Italian market but also to the international one. It may seems that Italian position as a worldwide design leader for contents production could be penalized by spreading and exporting skills. The truth is that the country is strengthened by the network, first of all the laboratory allow to share new ideas developed through cultural exchange and this means on-going improvement for Made in Italy design concept. Secondly, talents trained in Italy become real ambassadors of our design, able to spread our products' value proposition in other countries.

Chains can benefit of direct and indirect positive outcomes on their competitiveness:

- Direct outcomes:
  - Through an active presence on the website vendors will widen their operational horizon, being directly in touch with their customers. This is an opportunity to increase sells volumes and also the chance for companies which are not big enough to use marketing methods based on web 2.0. Companies will be able to make the most of active participation of users, bidirectional relationship, opened system, easy access, and collect information for their innovation processes and marketing;
  - Through services helping internationalization processes, companies will find easier to enter new booming markets and they will find instruments to reduce risks.
- Indirect outcomes:
  - Distant learning activities, as well as contents directed to users and generated by users through web 2.0 will increase international awareness of value offered by Italian design.

Both direct and indirect outcomes will have the consequences:

1. Increase sales volumes, first for vendors linked to the platform, secondly for all Italian producers
2. Improve of margin product due to design's culture spread
3. Increase of employment levels due to higher sales volumes

6. CONCLUSION

Exploitation of research and industrial skills and excellences.Skills development involves, among the others, the next fields:

- Advanced communication media, based on web 2.0 technologies, suitable to support B2C sale for home furnishing accessories, design objects, jewellery and trinkets;
- Analytical instruments able to produce channels analysis and customer segmentation in automatic way;
- Logistic organizational models with high performance driven to offer a worldwide service at top level, also flexible and affordable.

New technologies allows to create communities with a lot of users sharing contents. An example, among many others, is given by Wikipedia, Facebook, eBay, Del.icio.us, LinkedIn. This proves that management technologies can do more and more. The project aims to use these technologies for the marketplace development to build a community on the Italian design concept.

Related to growth of ICT technologies, the project allows the development and joining of innovative technologies web 2.0, able to:

1. Create a place where all users are connected, both vendors and buyers, could develop ideas, contents, events, opinions, all related to design Made in Italy. Advanced technologies web 2.0 will join potential of vendors, design students, interested people and keen on design;
2. Translate the characteristics of products in a way that user/buyer can exactly understand and feel the additional value of the product just through the web (experience interaction);
3. Use buyer's profile and location data to increase the offer and create return information flows which could be translated into marketing information available for vendors;
4. Create data exchange with the logistic platform able to assure the quality of logistic performance expected from the market

The final product is unique and knowledge, concepts and system supports developed can be used later in other contexts to support the Italian Industry.

Figure 3. Layout of E-learning portal Design Best

REFERENCES

Bentley, T. (1998). *Learning beyond the classroom: Education for a changing world.* London: Routledge.D'Andrea A., Ferri F., Fortunati De Luca L.

Gallico D, (2016). *Rapporto nazionale sul Design nelle imprese italiane (dalla A alla Z)* isbn 9788868741518 Logo Fausto Lupetti editore

Gallico D, Giacobone T (2011). *Adi lombardia design codex 001-il paesaggio dell'innovazione*. Bologna:Logo Fausto Lupetti editore

Gallico D (2013). *Contam-Innovation Cinquecento icone tra design, cultura e innovazione.* Bologna:Logo Fausto Lupetti editore

Guzzo T (2009).*"Mobile Devices to support advanced forms of e-Learning"* Handbook of Research on Multimodal Human Computer Interaction and Pervasive Services: Evolutionary Techniques for Improving Accessibility. Editor: Patrizia Grifoni, IGI Global Dillenbourg, P., Baker, M., Blaye, A., & O'Malley, C. (1996). The evolution of research on collaborative learning. In E. Spada & P. Reiman (Eds.), *Learning in humans and machine: Towards an interdisciplinary learning science.* Oxford, UK.

Grew, P., & Pagani, E. (2005). Towards a wireless architecture for mobile ubiquitous e-learning. *Workshop on Learning Communities in the Era of Ubiquitous Computing*, Milan, Italy.

Haythornthwaite, C., Kazmer, M.M., Robins, J., & Shoemaker, S. (2000). Community development among distance learners: Temporal and technological dimensions. *Journal of Computer Mediated Communication.*

Hamdani, M. (2012)*Advance principles for visual aesthetics in designing the contents of e-learning*

Majid Hamdani, Mohammad hosseinpour, Rio Sumarni Bt. Sharifuddin Science Series Data Report, No.6, volume 4, Horton, W, Horton K *"E-learning Tools and Technologies"* (2003) Wiley Publihing Köse, U. *Artificial Intelligence Applications in Distance Education* International Book Editorship Masterman, E., Jameson, J., & Walker, S. (2009). *Capturing teachers' experience of learning design through case studies* Distance Education, 30(2): 223–238.

Masterman, L. , *The challenge of teachers' design practice* Chapter accepted for H. Beetham & R. Sharpe (Eds.), Rethinking Pedagogy for the Digital Age, 2nd edition. London: Routledge.

McGreal, R., & Roberts, T. (2001). *A primer on metadata for learning objects*. Retrieved from http://www.elearningmag.com/issues/Oct01/learningobjects.asp.

Pathak, A. (2005) *Medium is the Message: Web-based Lecture Presentations in Distance Education* ISSN 1347-9008 Asian J D E vol 3, no 2, pp 13 - 22.

Paz González-Brignardello, M. (2008) *E-Learning Uses of Concept Maps* Published in "Concept Mapping: Connecting Educators" Proc. of the Third International Conference on Concept Mapping A. J. Cañas, P. Reiska, M. Åhlberg & J. D. Novak, Eds. Tallinn, Estonia & Helsinki, Finland

Ramadhanie, M. A. *Design and Implementation of Learning Object Ontology for e-Learning Personalization* Ramadhanie, M. A, Siti Aminah, A. Nizar Hidayanto, Adila A. Krisnadhi. (7-8 Dec 2009) *Proceeding International Conference on Advanced Computer Science and Information Systems (ICACSIS*), University of Indonesia, Depok, pp. 427-433 staf.cs.ui.ac.id 20

Reyna, J (2009). Developing quality e-learning sites: A designer approach. In *Same places,different spaces. Proceedings ascilite Auckland 2009*. http://www.ascilite.org.au/conferences/auckland09/procs/reyna-1- poster.pdf Riedling, E. & Riedling, K, ."*An E-Learning Platform with a Deliberately Simple Design"* (2003).

VISUAL ANALYSIS FOR VOTING RELATIONSHIPS IN JOSEON DYNASTY, KOREA

Seongmin Mun[1,2], Gyeongcheol Choi[2], Sangkuk Lee[3] and Kyungwon Lee[4]
[1]*UMR 7114 MoDyCo - CNRS, University Paris Nanterre, France*
[2]*Life Media Interdisciplinary Program, South Korea*
[3]*Department of History, South Korea*
[4]*Department of Digital Media, South Korea*

ABSTRACT

History studies involve discovering new facts based upon the records as well as understanding relationships between historic events and figures. However, a vast amount of resources, background knowledge and time would be required for empirical historical research. *The Genealogy of the Kwon family* and *Annals of the Joseon Dynasty*, both of which are applied in this study, are particularly difficult to comprehend without sufficient knowledge about their terminologies and backgrounds. However, a vast amount of resources, background knowledge, and time would be required for empirical historical research. On the other hand, visual analysis enables users to easily understand information and the relationships between data. We propose an analysis method that visually describes voting relationships based on historical records, for a clear and cognitively beneficial understanding (URL: http://202.30.24.167:3008/bubble). Our visualization method is divided into two parts: First, it refines the database by selected options, such as by color and category. In the second part, users can confirm the details of this result with a bubble graph. These two parts are synchronized and describe the differences results based on the user's selection. In a case study of users' feedback and expert opinions, we verified the effectiveness and usability of our visualization method.

KEYWORDS

Visualization, Voting relationship, Bubble-graph, Historical data mining, Joseon-Dynasty

1. INTRODUCTION

Prior to being established as an individual academic discipline, historical studies was understood as a subset of other literature or interpreted from a religious perspective. Modern historical studies were established in the 1800s after German historian Leopold von Ranke argued that history is a study based on strict criticism of ancient records. History is thereby a discipline which empirically examines historical records in order to understand facts and the relationships between cause and effect. An empirical study is a method that identifies regularities and patterns through the objective analysis of historical records. As contemporary historical research methods are also based on empirical studies, precise understanding of time periods and objective attitudes toward research are considered essential. It remains difficult for researchers to stay objective during the entire study process, since understanding extensive historical records in order to precisely understand the exact time period requires a great deal of time and effort. Visualization analysis can thus enable users to better understand data by automatically analyzing accumulated data as well as offering a visual presentation. This analysis method can contribute to historical studies in the following ways. First, it shortens the time it takes to study historical records because of its automated method. Second, it improves the objectivity of studies through analysis based on mathematical algorithms. Third, visualized study results help users analyze and understand the results more effectively.

2. PURPOSE AND BACKGROUND

Current historical studies provide insufficient understanding of the link between present events and the past. "Modern" has been regarded as a conflicting concept from "Traditional," which has led to a binary perspective when attempting to understand the "traditional" (pre-modern) period. This phenomenon generally appears during events such as the confrontation between political powers in the late Goryeo to early Joseon dynasty (Hyungoo Min 1974), conflicts between the Meritorious Elite and Neo-Confucian Literati in the early Joseon dynasty (Soogeon Lee 1979), challenges in coterie politics in the late Joeson dynasty (Sogkjong Chong 1983: Seongmoo Lee 2000), and through confrontational understanding between colonized Koreans and Pro-Japanese Koreans during the Japanese colonial period (Dongmyung Kim2006). However, since binary voting relationships in modern society share certain characteristics with those in the pre-modern period, they must be analyzed as an extension of voting relationships in pre-modern society. Therefore, we aim to discover the factors affecting binary voting relationships in the Joseon dynasty by analyzing historical records from the pre-modern period, annals of the Joseon Dynasty, and genealogy of the Kwon family; we also provide a visual representation of our findings.

3. RELATED WORK

Research to understand voting relationships through visualization, as well as integrated visualization studies are a growing trend. Adam Perer in CHI 2008, Francisco G. de Borja in SIBGRAPI 2015, Manjai Lee in Human Computer Interaction Korea and Hanmin Choi in Journal of Society of Design Convergence are ideal examples of previous research for our work.

Adam Perer analyzed the voting patterns of US senators with a network visualization tool, which was verified by political science experts in his article "Integrating Statistics and Visualization: Case Studies of Gaining Clarity" using exploratory data analysis. Figure 1 (a) illustrates the results of Perer's work.

Francisco G. de Borja studied the political history of brazil by the visualization of political data in " CivisAnalysis: Interactive Visualization for Exploring Roll Call Data and Representatives' Voting Behaviour." He designed a visualization tool that gave citizens a unique view of the country's political history. Figure 1 (b) shows the results.

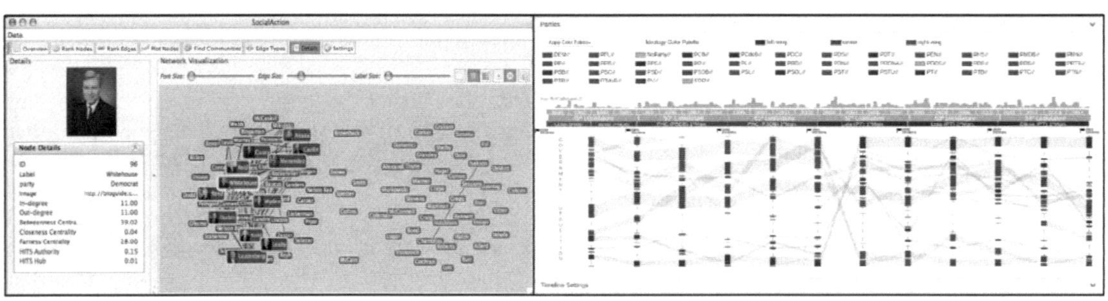

(a) (b)

Figure 1. (a) Integration of statistics and visualizations by Adam Perer, (b) visual result by Francisco G. de Borja

Manjai Lee visualized UN voting record as public data to help everyone figure out the meaning of public data using proper visualization techniques. In his paper, to improve the weak point of the existing social graph visualization, he propose Friend-Matching, Friend-Rival Matching, and Bubble Heap algorithms in his paper. Figure 2 (a) shows the results.

Hanmin Choi proposed Interactive Visualization method that can be analyzed relations between nations in various viewpoints such as period, issue which is used total 5211 of the UN General Assembly voting data. He conducted a comparative experiment between Social Network Graph and Proximity based Circular Visualization. As a research result, he found that Proximity based Circular Visualization can be better to see analysis result by each node and Network Graph Visualization can be better to see analysis patterns for the nations. Figure 2 (b) suggests its results.

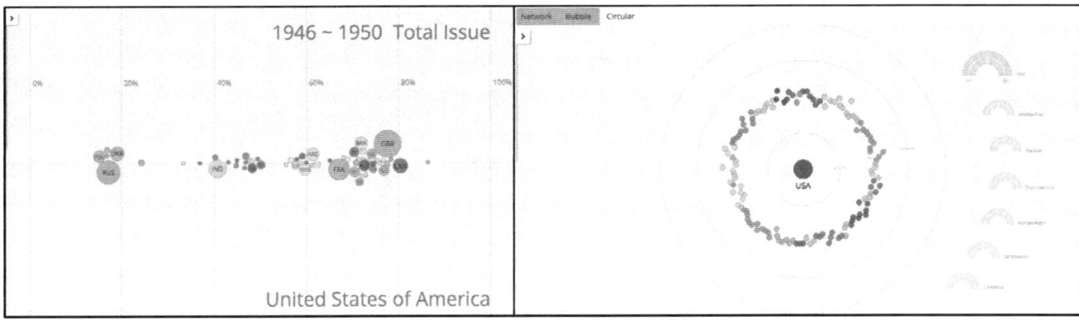

(a) (b)

Figure 2. (a) Visualization of UN voting record by Manjai Lee, (b) interactive visualization by Hanmin Choi

4. USER TASKS AND DESIGN OBJECTIVES

We have refined voting relationship data with historians, linguists, and statisticians, focusing on a figure known as Geojeong Seo, including the historical agendas he supported and the voting results of these agendas. As he was a central figure who belonged to the power group in the Joseon Dynasty, we created data by assuming that individuals who were similar to Geojeong Seo belonged to a power group, while those showing few similarities would belong to a less powerful political group. Meanwhile, the Kwon family genealogy contains records of individuals related to Geojeong Seo by blood and their degree of consanguinity. This study explores a visual method to analyze voting relationships based on this data, and aims to discover factors affecting binary relationships between figures in the Joseon Dynasty. The tasks and visualization design objectives of our project are as follows.

Task 1: Calculating the similarity between each individual and Geojeong Seo for each agenda.

As we presumed that high similarities between an individual and Geojeong Seo would suggest that the individual also belonged to a power group, we calculated the similarities between the voting patterns of each individual utilizing a Phi coefficient and then visualized the results.

Design Objective: We should create an axis that indicates similarity levels in order to mark the relationships on it.

Task 2: Classifying agendas into specific categories to present voting relationships.

The total number of agendas in this research is 93, which includes different topics such as state affairs, royal family, diplomacy, politics, and customs. Based on our assumption that the nature of agendas would influence the relationships between individuals, we aim to visually represent these relationships in multiple ways, according to both overall and classified agendas.

Design Objective: Users should be able to select each classification that will illustrate different aspects of voting relationships according to each category.

Task 3: Presenting figures based on the degree of kinship.

Blood ties are highly likely to be a critical factor influencing the relationships between individuals. According to our hypothesis, blood relations will have a significant impact on the voting patterns of the characters. We visually explored voting relationships according to their kinship.

Design Objective: We need to visually distinguish relationships that involve blood relations from those that do not.

5. VISUALIZATION

To satisfy the three objectives described above, we followed Lee's(Lee & On, 2015) Bubble-heap graph design methodology in that only the X-axis is used to see the relationship between the central figure and the surrounding figures. A complete visualization, developed based on java script, can be found here http://202.30.24.167:3008/bubble. Through this visualization, we analyzed the voting tendency data of Joseon Dynasty, Korea by classified agendas and the effect of blood relations on voting tendency through color.

5.1 Phi coefficient

The agenda data in our research also contains personal opinions, which are represented as in favor (1), against (−1), and neutral (0). The phi coefficient, a measure of correlation used when two variables are divided by two quantitative categories, was applied in our study.

$$Phi\ coefficient = \frac{n_{11}n_{00} - n_{10}n_{01}}{\sqrt{n_1 * n_0 * n_0 * n_1}}$$

After calculating the relationships between individuals based on this formula, we provide a visual representation of the results. Figure 3 illustrates the relationships between the individuals calculated based on the overall agenda. The visualization we propose is shown in the x-axis. The individuals represented by each node are located along the axis, ranging from 0% to 100%.

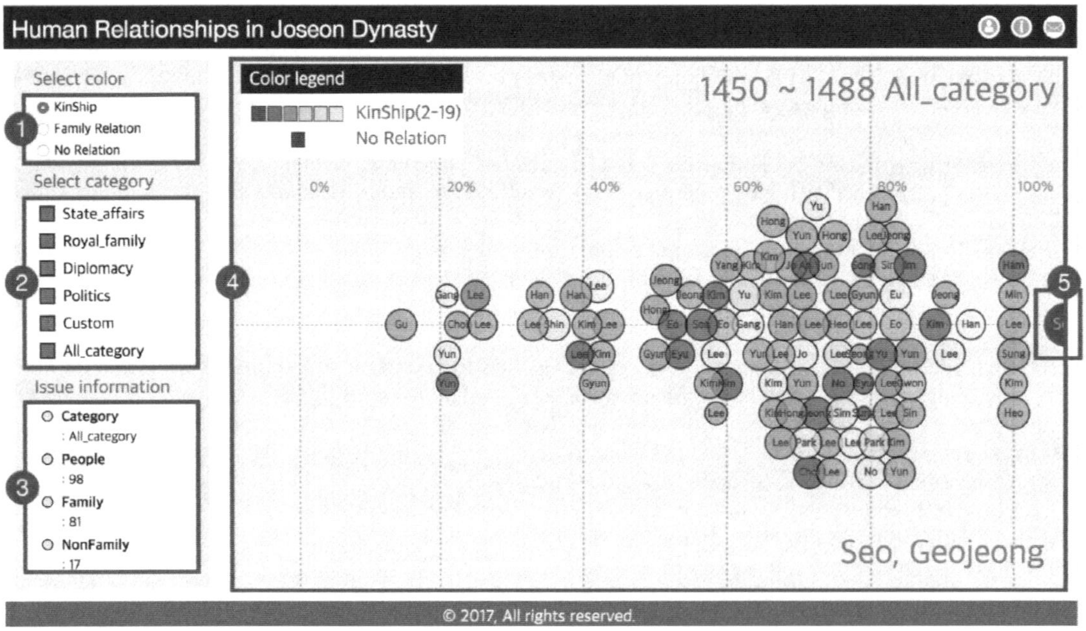

Figure 3. Voting relationships visualized based on the overall agenda

In the upper left area of visualization, there is a function to select different colors according to the relationship (blood, kinship). And you can select the category of the agenda in the middle (area 2). Also, in the bottom (area 3), we provide brief information by selected agenda. The main part of visualization (on the right side) shows the similarity by voting pattern between the central figure and the surrounding characters. Area 5, located in the right side of the main view, represents Geojeong Seo who was central figure in the Joseon Dynasty, Korea. If the voting tendency is completely consistent with Geojeong Seo, the figure located in line of 100%, or not in 0%.

5.2 Categorizing each issue

Agendas were classified as state affairs, royal family, diplomacy, politics, and customs, each of which was represented visually along with the overall agenda. We created a function to select each category in order to indicate changes in the relationship between individuals according to the nature of agendas. Figure 4 shows the relationship between individuals for each category, in the order of state affairs, royal family, diplomacy, politics, customs, and overall agenda.

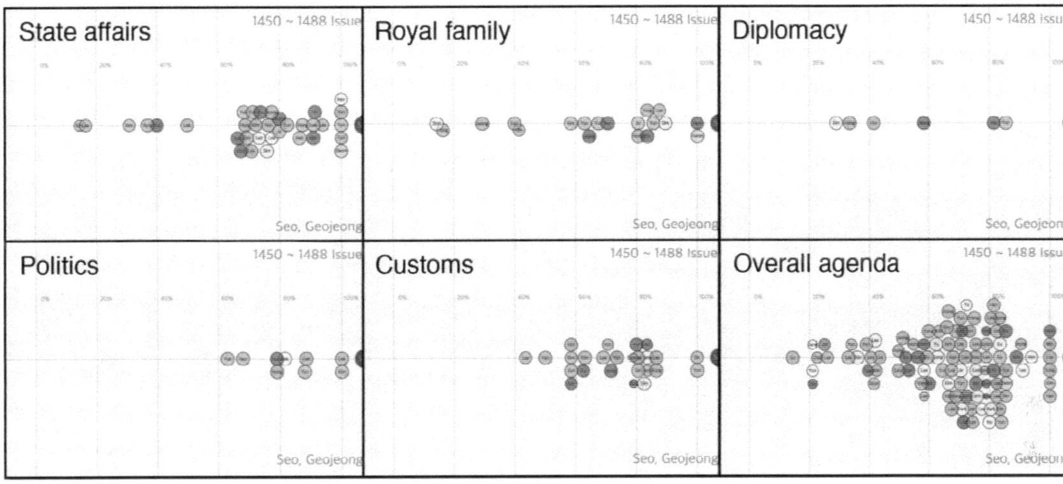

Figure 4. Relationships between individuals and Geojeong Seo reflecting kinship

5.3 Family relationship

We have also assumed that kinship would be a significant factor in voting patterns. Individuals who were related to Geojeong Seo by blood are represented in red, as shown in figure 4. The color became darker if they were more closely related. Individuals who were not related to Geojeong Seo by blood are represented in gray.

6. EVALUATION

We conducted scenario and user studies to evaluate the effectiveness of our interactive visualization method and its usability. In the scenario studies, we worked with historians who studied the history of the Joseon Dynasty and possess expert knowledge about it. In the user study, we surveyed 22 people to evaluate our visualization method. The 22 people were either undergraduate students or professionals in data analysis who had a deep understanding of visualization and visual analysis.

6.1 Usage scenario for the visual analysis

We tested our visualization method based on three scenarios, drawing answers from our visualizations in order to find the solutions for each scenario.

- **Scenario 1: Is there a difference in voting patterns if the nature of agenda changes?**

Figure 4 shows the relationships between individuals for each category: state affairs, royal family, diplomacy, politics, and customs. This figure shows that politics and customs categories are leaning toward the right side, while the other categories show a relatively even distribution from 0% to 100%. Thus, we discovered that voting patterns varied according to categories of agenda, and that the patterns became more similar to Geojeong Seo with regard to politics and customs agendas.

• Scenario 2: Will an individual show different voting patterns if the nature of agenda changes?

According to historians, Myunghoi Han was another individual who was as prominent as Geojeong Seo by the time Seo was commissioned. After identifying the relationship between the two based on our visualization, we found out that voting patterns of Han varied according to each agenda category. Figure 5 shows changes in the similarity level between Myunghoi Han and Geojeong Seo, according to different agenda categories. While Han shared a high similarity level of over 70% with Seo on agendas relating to state affairs and politics, this decreased to less than 50% for agendas relating to the royal family, diplomacy, and customs. Furthermore, in the overall agenda, the similarity level bounced back to 60%-70%. These findings indicate that the voting patterns of an individual varied according to the nature of agendas, as Han deviated from Seo's agenda with regard to the royal family, diplomacy and customs, but showed higher similarities with Seo in state affairs and politics.

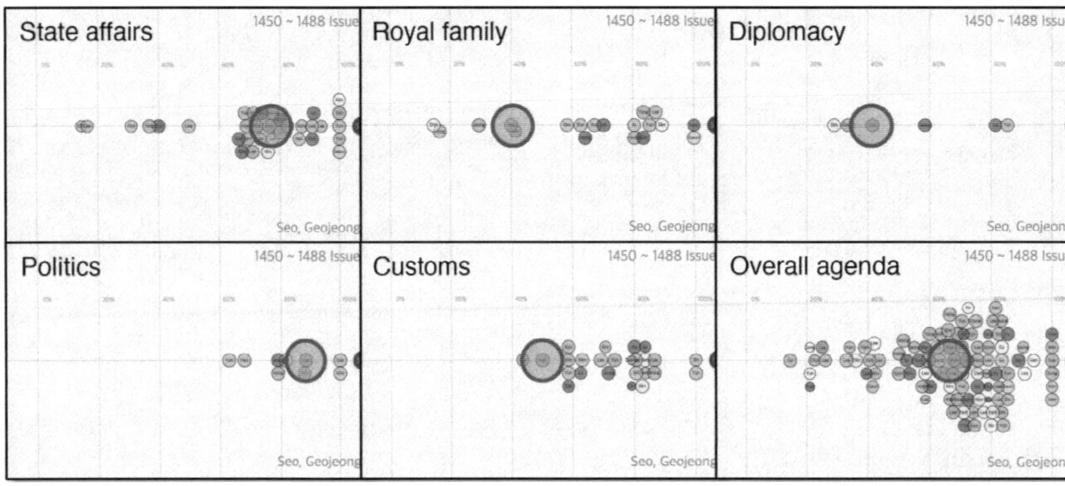

Figure 5. Similarity level changes between Myunghoi Han and Geojeong Seo, according to different agenda categories

• Scenario 3: Will kinship affect the similarity level in voting patterns?

The vast amount of previous studies suggests that blood relationships significantly influence voting relationships. We aimed to estimate the difference between individuals who were related to Seo by blood and those who were not, based on the same assumption. Figure 3 is a visualization of the overall agenda, which includes the largest number of relationships among the six visualizations. Each individual represented as a node is shown in red if they are related to Seo by blood and gray otherwise. We discovered that 81 out of the 98 people in our data were all related to Seo by blood, while the other 17 showed various distributions from 0 to 100. Thus, we could not determine whether kinship affected voting patterns in this particular case, and found that the majority of people who were commissioned at that time were related to Seo by blood.

6.2 User study

We performed an informal user study to evaluate our visualization method. We recruited 22 people, all of which have some experience in visualization. We first explained to them the basic concepts of our work and demonstrated the system functionalities. Then, we asked them to complete three exploration tasks with our system. Finally, we collected their feedback via a questionnaire and their opinions on the advantages and disadvantages of our system. Our questionnaire contained 13 questions in three categories: visual design, filtering, and system function. The answers are based on a five-level Likert Scale, where 1 means "Strongly Disagree,", 2 means "Disagree," 3 means "Normal," 4 means "Agree," and 5 means "Strongly Agree."

Table 1. Summary of the evaluation questions and results

Category		Questions	Rating
Visual design	Similarity	Q1: The similarity of the voting tendency between the central figure and surrounding characters is clearly shown through visualization.	4
		Q2: The blood relationship between the central figure and the surrounding characters is clearly shown through visualization.	4
		Q3: The kinship between the central figure and the surrounding characters is clearly shown through visualization.	3
	Issue	Q4: As the agenda changes, it can be confirmed that the voting tendency of the central character and other characters changed.	4
		Q5: It can be confirmed that the voting tendency of the characters is changed depending on the agenda selected.	4
	Color	Q6: It is easy to understand the blood relationship between characters through color.	4
		Q7: It is easy to understand the kinship of characters through color.	4
Filtering		Q8: It is easy to make changes by the agenda.	5
		Q9: It is easy to make a color change.	4
		Q10: Satisfied with the changed analysis results according to the selection.	4
System		Q11: Data analysis results are easy to recognize in one view.	4
		Q12: This visualization makes it easy to understand the voting patterns and blood relationships of the central figure and surrounding characters.	4
		Q13: This visualization makes is easy to explore data analysis results.	4

The results, summarized in Table 1, are very encouraging. For most questions, the median rating is above 4, which means that our system has fulfilled its design requirements and supports the major tasks. In particular, the only question with a rating 5 is Q8, which is about changing selection by agenda. During the free discussion, most users considered the functionality and interaction most satisfactory. One of them mentioned: "It's easy to understand the voting relationships between the central figure and surrounding characters." Another one said: "It is easy to make changes by agenda and color." On the other hand, the only question with a rating 3 is Q3, which is about showing kinship between the central figure and the surrounding characters. We need to improve the way to show kinship more easily.

7. CONCLUSION

The main significance of our research that it is an interdisciplinary study of historical studies, linguistics, statistics, and data visualization. Adopting a historical perspective that represents voting relationships as an extension of the past, we aimed to visually represent the relationships between individuals from past data and identify the factors affecting these relationships. We designed a visualization method in order to conduct this research and tested its effectiveness through three scenarios and a user study. The three key findings of this study can be summarized as follows.

First, the opinions on each five agenda will vary according to the nature of the agenda. Classifying the agendas in the Joseon Dynasty into state affairs, royal family, diplomacy, politics, and custom, the opinions regarding politics and customs showed a high similarity level of over 60%, and ranged from 0% to 100% in other the categories. Thus, it can be concluded that the nature of agendas influenced voting patterns.

Second, each figure individual indicated different opinions on different sets of agendas. As the nature of agendas influenced voting patterns, this can be used to discover the agendas that showed distinct gaps in opinions.

Third, blood relationships cannot be regarded as an integral factor that affects the similarity level of voting patterns. In one of our analyses, most of the individuals commissioned were related to Geojoeng Seo by blood. Although this implies that kinship itself is possibly a key factor for appointment to the state council, the relatively even distribution from 0% to 100% in our visualization suggests that kinship has no significant impact on the similarity level of voting patterns. Figure 3 shows the relationships between each individual and Seo in terms of overall agendas In addition, our work is unique in that it is an integrated research in historical studies, where empirical studies are of great importance. However, our findings should not be generalized since this was a cohort study focusing exclusively on the period when Geojeong Seo was commissioned to the state council. We thereby aim to expand the period covered in our future analysis.

REFERENCES

Journal

Claurissa Tuttle. et al., 2010. PedVis: A Structured, Space-Efficient Technique for Pedigree Visualization. *IEEE Transactions on Visualization and Computer Graphics,* Vol. 16, No. 6, pp 1063-1072.

Dongmyung Kim, 2006. Reorganization and agitation of Japanese imperialism in colonial Korea, *Dankook University Oriental Studies, Oriental Studies*, Vol. 39, No. 0, pp 147-157.

Hanmin Choi. et al., 2015, Proximity based Circular Visualization for similarity analysis of voting patterns between nations in UN General Assembly, *Journal of Society of Design Convergence*, Vol. 14, No. 4, pp. 133—150.

Hyungoo Min, 1974. The Review: Establishment of an influential family in the late Goryeo Period. *Research Institute of Honam, Junnam National University, Honan Culture Research*, Vol. 6, No. 0, pp 21-40.

Manjai Lee and Byung-Won On, 2015. Social graph visualization techniques for public data, *Human Computer Interaction Korea*, Vol. 10, No. 1, pp. 5—17.

Seongmoo Lee, 2000. The Review: Party strife in Joseon Dynasty, *Korean History Research Society, Reasearch of Korean History*, Vol. 111, No. 0, pp 241-247.

Sogkjong Chong, 1983. The Review: Study of Korean archives. *Daegu Historical Society*, Vol. 22, No. 0, pp 261-269.

Soogeon Lee, 1979. Generation of Yeongnam Sarim: Social foundation of Generation about Yeongnam Sarim. *Yeongnam University National Cultural Institute, National Cultural Studies*, Vol. 2, No. 0, pp 23-148.

Steve Kieffer. et al., 2016. HOLA: Human-like Orthogonal Network Layout. *IEEE Transactions on Visualization and Computer Graphics,* Vol. 22, No. 1, pp 349-358.

Conference paper or contributed volume

Adam Perer and Ben Shneiderman, 2008. Integrating Statistics and Visualization: Case Studies of Gaining Clarity during Exploratory Data Analysis, *CHI 2008 Proceedings. Visual Synthesis*, pp 265-274.

Francisco G. de Borja and Carla M.D.S. Freitas, 2015. CivisAnalysis: Interactive Visualization for Exploring Roll Call Data and Representatives' Voting Behaviour, *2015 28th SIBGRAPI Conference on Graphics, Patterns and Images*, pp 257-264.

Hyoji Ha. et al., 2015. Proximity Based Circular Visualization for Similarity Analysis of UNGA Voting Patterns, *IEEE International Symposium on Big Data Visual Analytics*.

Jasminko Novak. et al., 2014. histoGraph - A Visualization Tool for Collaborative Analysis of Networks from Historical Social Multimedia Collections, *2014 18th International Conference on Information Visualisation*, pp 241-250.

K. Dinkla. et al., 2015. Dual Adjacency Matrix: Exploring Link Groups in Dense Networks, *Eurographics Conference on Visualization (EuroVis) 2015*, Vol. 34, No. 3, pp 311-320.

Masahiko ITOH and Mina AKAISHI, 2012. Visualization for Changes in Relationships between Historical Figures in Chronicles, *2012 16th International Conference on Information Visualisation*, pp 283-290.

Oh-Hyun Kwon. et al., 2014. Proximity-based Visualization of UNGA Voting Data, *In Proc. International Workshop on Vision, Modeling, and Visualization*.

Y. han. et al., 2015. Visual Analysis of Proximal Temporal Relationships of Social and Communicative Behaviors, *Eurographics Conference on Visualization (EuroVis) 2015*, Vol. 34, No. 3, pp 51-60.

ATTITUDES TOWARDS SOFTWARE AS A WEAPON

Jantje A. M. Silomon and A. W. Roscoe
Department of Computer Science, University of Oxford, Oxford OX1 3QD, UK

ABSTRACT

Software permeates all aspects of modern life and is thus prone to abuse, either in the form of generic malware or as a targeted weapon against systems. Whilst some research and publications exist on this broad area of 'cyber weapons', the solicitation of public opinion through surveys is lacking. This paper presents the results of a questionnaire pertaining to attitudes and understanding of cyber weapons. The results of the study suggest that there is a significant difference between respondents employed in the 'military', 'academia', or 'other' professions.

KEYWORDS

Malware; malicious code; cyber weapon

1. INTRODUCTION

Cyber weapons, digital weapons, virtual weapons, and software as a weapon (SaaW) are terms often used interchangeably but remain highly ambiguous, with requirements and definitions varying even further. A very loose consensus of criteria across encompasses a type of malicious software that is a) employed against a specific target, b) has a very high level of sophistication, and c) is sponsored by an actor (state or non-state).

Although several papers, books, blogs and other media articles have been written on the broad area of cyber weapons, ranging from technical analysis and case studies to potential consequences for the international system, surveyed public opinion remains absent. Yet, this is highly important: interconnected digital systems are vital to modern society, from personal use for communication and consumer transactions to national energy supplies and security or international banking and trade. The advent of the Internet of Things (IoT) sketches out an even more data-driven and interconnected future, encompassing civilian aspects such as smart cities or military applications, with lines blurred far more extensively than before.

Each individual can be affected by SaaW, whether as a target, a stepping-stone to the target or mere collateral; equally, they can be a key component of SaaWs, from providing technical know-how or by merely being an unwitting resources; lastly, they can also affect public policy via debates and elections.

This paper therefore reports on the results of a questionnaire, which aimed to capture the current attitudes towards and understanding of SaaW. It presents the findings centred on three aspects, which can be summarised as a) the physicality of software, b) the concepts of weapons, and c) the understanding and implications of SaaW, also in regards to what extent there is a difference between groups of respondents (Academic, Military and Other).

2. RELATED WORK

The characteristics of SaaW and related weapons can be approached from multiple different perspectives, from firmly tying them to physical weapons that can be wielded (Rid & McBurney, 2012), centring on specific systems (Peterson, 2013) or aspects (Hakkarainen, 2014), or through a legal analysis (Blake & Imburgia, 2011; Schmitt, 2013; Schmitt, 2013a; Mele, 2013; Brown & Metcalf, 2014). Yet others attempt to create a wider framework (Herr, 2014; Herr & Rosenzweig, 2015) or a characterisation based on code analysis and reverse engineering (Wilson, 2015). Similarly, there has been a lot of technical work centred on malware detection and defence: from insider patterns (Agrafiotis, et al., 2015), botnet taxonomies (Khattak, et al., 2014), DoS/DDoS research (Radunovic, 2013) to specific vulnerabilities in standards; advanced persistent threats (APT)s providing insight on the capabilities have also been addressed (Liu, et al., 2013; Bhatt, et al., 2014; Roth, 2016). Yet wider public solicitation has not been explored.

In the nuclear domain, a parallel area of weapon discourse, questionnaires surveying public opinion on nuclear weapons reach as far back as 1945, with those carried out in the USA addressing issues from fall-out shelters and chances of nuclear war, to opinions on "first use", the arms race or development. Although the frequency and wording varies over time, common themes can be ascertained and analysed, as seen in Kramer et al. (Kramer, et al., 1983) examining nuclear-related survey data from 1945 to 1982.

In regard to the importance of the individual opinion, an analogy can be drawn to a discussion held in the nuclear domain several decades ago. In the early 1980s, the Harvard Nuclear Study Group published a book entitled *"Living with Nuclear Weapons"*. The first chapter addresses issues in the nuclear debate, highlighting the importance of the individual as *"each citizen is not just a target of nuclear weapons; each is also an actor in the nuclear drama*" (Harvard Nuclear Study Group, 1983) before giving examples. This is also true of the individual and SaaW.

Although there are additional parallels that can, and have been, drawn to the nuclear discourse (Alperovitch, 2011; Cimbala, 2011; Betts, 2013; Cirenza, 2015), key differences to SaaW arise from the nature of the weapons themselves. These range, for example, from fundamental aspects, such as physicality and immutability, to consequential ones, such as destructive potential, tangible evidence thereof, proliferation requirements and (historic) data availability. For SaaW, there is no clear, agreed-upon definition of what it is, or whether it can even exist – its nature is not only nascent but still very much in flux.

This questionnaire therefore explores the public opinion of SaaW and its differences to more traditional weapon concepts to supplement the academic and technical discourse. It further assesses to what extent work sectors, age and expertise within computer science/security (CS) or international relations/security (IR) affect these.

3. EXPERIMENTAL DESIGN

The formation of the questionnaire followed an iterative process, taking literature surveys, supervisor and colleague discussions, as well as feedback into account. It was approved under the Central University Research Ethics Committee (CUREC) of the University of Oxford (Ref: R46775/RE001). A pilot test was conducted with eight people to ensure the questionnaire was well set-up on the Bristol Online Survey system, ensuring the data was collected, stored and accessible as intended.

The questionnaire itself was online-based and was shared through a variety of means, such as social media, direct emails and word-of-mouth. It had an age requirement of 18, and the participants had to consent to their data being gathered anonymously. Aside from sourcing attitudes towards a SaaW, there was a contention that the work sector/experience will lead to different responses, in this case groups of Military, Academic and Other. Age and experience within CS or IR were also analysed.

Overall, the questionnaire contained 46 questions (Q1 being consent) and only fully completed ones were used for analysis, a total of N_{Tot}=96. A further 65 began the survey but did not complete.

It was divided into three main sections, following demographics and topic familiarity (Q2-Q7): the first part centred on weapons, their nature and constitution (Q8-Q16); the second part focussed on software, malware and understandings thereof (Q17-Q34); the final section brought SaaW together against the backdrop of international security (Q35-Q46) but will not be discussed here.

The majority of questions used the common five-point Likert rating scale, allowing for a 'neutral' response. The responses are not interval variables – the strongly disagree category does not, for example, imply a disagreement twice a strong as disagree – and the sample sizes are different. To ensure the robustness of the statistical analyses, Mann-Whitney U (MWU) tests were used to test differences in value ranking between two independent samples, as well as the non-parametric Kruskal-Wallis H (KWH) tests, performed to test median differences for more than two independent sample groups.

The open-ended questions, allowed for free-text responses but pose a greater challenge for analysis. For example, the term 'gun' can be understood in several different ways: colloquially is used interchangeably with 'pistol', 'side arm', 'firearm' or 'rifle' and others; it can also refer to pellet, water or other toy guns; in the military on the other hand, it refers to weapons that require a small group of people to use, such as artillery or a heavy machine gun. For the purpose of this paper, responses were grouped and labelled as 'firearm' to denote the use of an explosive charge to accelerate a projectile. The qualitative analysis conducted per question will be discussed in the relevant section.

4. RESULTS AND DISCUSSION

The key results are discussed here, with Table 1 in Appendix A showing a summary; results predominantly pertaining to the IR aspect of the questionnaire (Q35-46) will be presented in future work.

4.1 Respondent Profiles

The respondents were asked to provide their sector of work, with Figure 1 showing the main groupings. It should be noted that although the military personnel is analysed as a single group, their roles vary greatly, ranging from legal, to nursing or intelligence aspects. Similarly, the 'Other' group has a wide spread, ranging from IT professionals, education and finance/banking to hospitality, construction, and NGOs. For analysis, three groups were used: Military (N_{mil}=38), Academia (N_{aca}=19) and Other (N_{oth}=39). All but two respondents provided their nationality (Figure 2), with the largest number of respondents being British. One respondent stated dual nationality and was grouped with his first listed country.

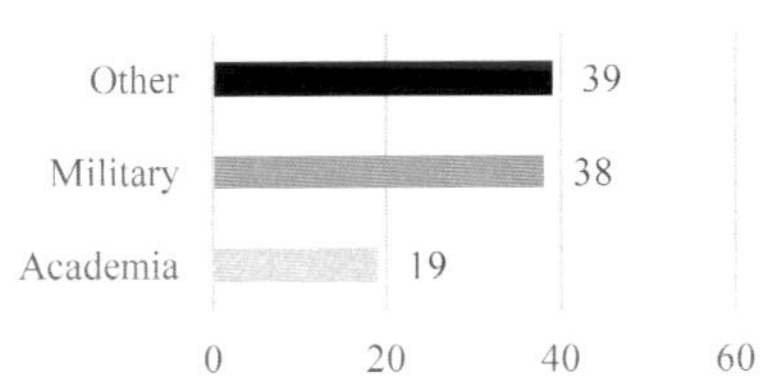

Figure 1. Sectors

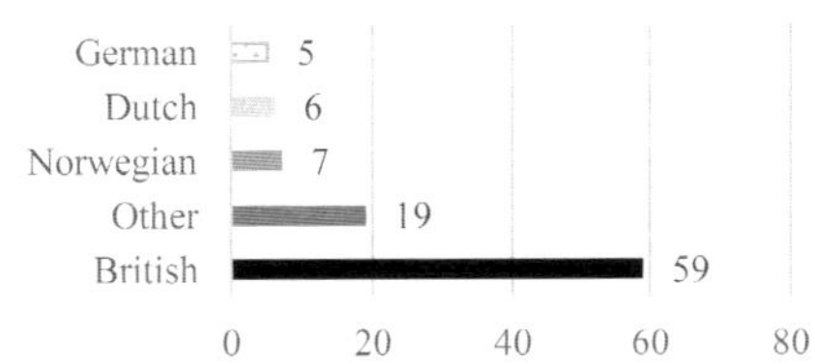

Figure 2. Nationalities

Two further preliminary questions were asked to self-rate the familiarity with the related topics of CS and IR, results are shown in Figure 3.

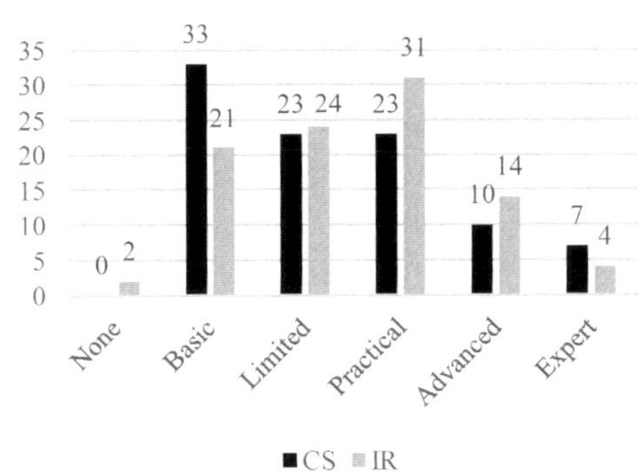

Figure 3. Familiarity with CS and with IR, respectively

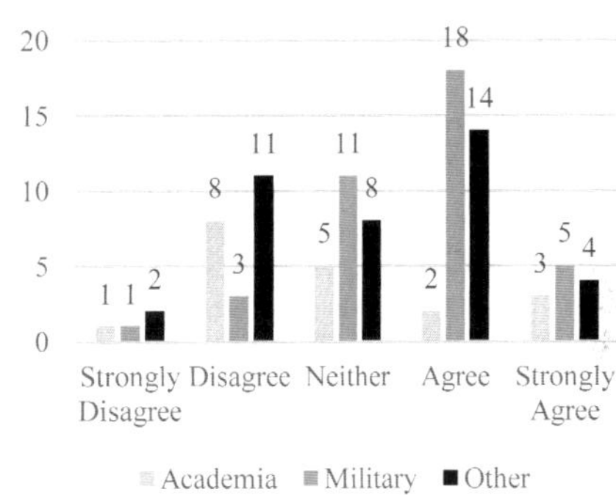

Figure 4. Software should be treated like any physical object or tool

4.2 Software and physical objects

The opinions on whether software should be treated like any physical object or tool were divided as seen in Figure 4. Based on background, there is a significant difference, with the Academic group tending to disagree more, the Military group agreeing and the Other group being indecisive. Performing a KWH test underlined this statistically ($H(2)= 6.44$, $p=0.04$); using MWU for *post hoc* analysis, Academic to Military differences remain statistically significant ($U=249$, $p=0.007$), however Military-Other ($U=556$, $p=0.05$) and Academic-Other ($U=220$, $p=0.49$) do not.

When suggesting a three-tiered classification of objects and software/malware (tool/dual-use/weapon), there is agreement (Figure 5). No statistically significant differences were found based on groups of background, age or expertise in CS or IR. This is relevant when considering to what extent current handling of weapons, nationally and internationally, is put in place; this includes prosecution of ownership or use, or international agreements or embargos. However, this does not address the technical challenge of how to differentiate 'good' from 'bad' or 'really bad' code, nor how to approach rapid transformation of technology.

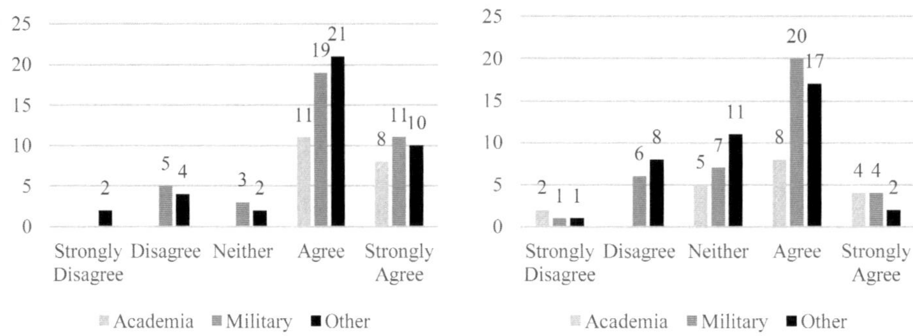

Figure 5. Three-tiered (sole weapon, dual use, situational) classification of objects (left) and software (right)

4.3 What constitutes weapons

Prior to seeking answers specifically related to software, several questions canvassed attitudes towards and beliefs held towards weapons to provide a basis for the discussion. Asked what a weapon was (Figure 6), a large proportion centred on harm and damage, with a small number of descriptions including 'amplifying violence', used to 'kill' or 'injure' and a single mention of 'defend' on its own. Overall, the perspectives are offensively driven, which is also reflected globally within the national and international legal system, with only few jurisdictions, such as Queensland in Australia, defining purely defensive measures, such as bullet proof vests as a weapon (Queensland Police, 03/02/2017).

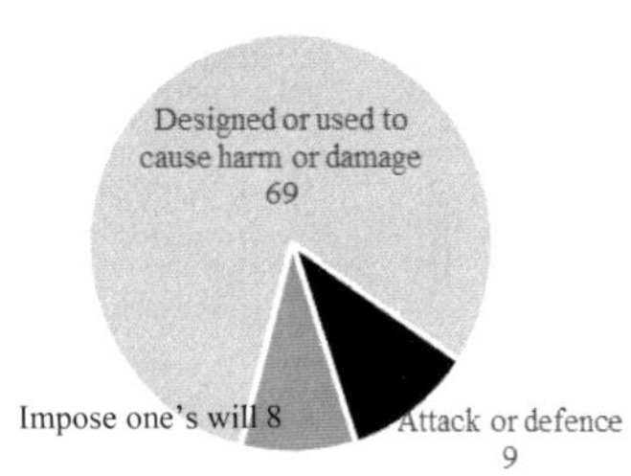

Figure 6. What is a weapon?

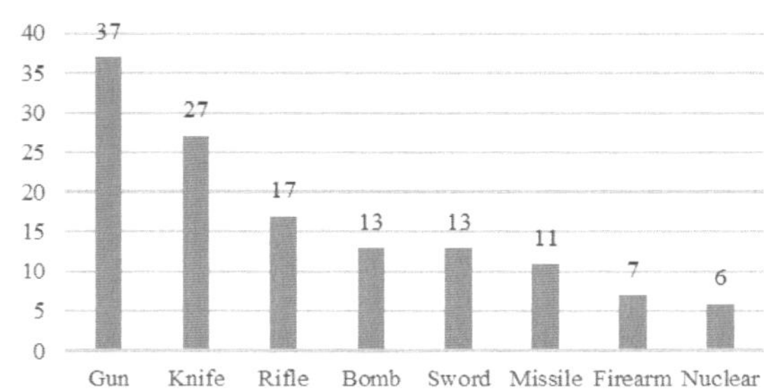

Figure 7. List of weapons

To clarify further, respondents were asked to list three different types of weapons each resulting in specific examples to general attributes. A total of 98 different responses were given including synonyms.[1] The most frequent single terms are shown in Figure 7; the most obscure response was the 'sharpened bones of a Hufflepuff' – a quote from fan-fiction *Harry Potter and the Methods of Rationality*, to exemplify that anything could be used as a weapon. There are four main axes into which the responses fall when examining the attributes:

- harm scale: intent, lethality, and target number
- range: close combat, short- or long-range
- means: physical, psychological, digital
- construction: bladed, projectile, explosive, bio-chemical, nuclear

Furthermore, responses highlighted the different terminology used, for example: computer-related weapons were referred to as 'computer', 'computer program', 'computer virus', 'computer hacking', 'malware', 'cyber', 'cyber weapon', 'IT' and 'software' (total of 18); combining bio-chemical weapons into

[1]Certain responses were standardised and/or combined; this includes spelling mistakes, merging of singular/plural responses, derivations and appending of 'weapon'.

one category yielded 10 responses; various uses of the human body accounted for 9 responses. Based on the above responses, it could be argued that weapons are part of *Familienähnlichkeit* (family resemblance) a philosophical idea first proposed by Wittgenstein encompassing things that have one essential feature in common but are in fact linked by several similarities without one feature common to all (Wittgenstein, 1953).

A majority of respondents believe that there is a difference between an object being a weapon and being used as one (Figure 8), and in a follow-up to explain their answer 78 responded, with two groups forming centring on either 'use' defining a weapon or the initial 'design' intent (Figure 9). No statistically significant difference was found based on groups of background, age or expertise in CS or IR.

Asked when an object becomes a weapon, the responses were similar to the reasoning given when explaining their previous answer, with most respondents giving the intent in design and/or use as answers, with varying keywords (Figure 10).

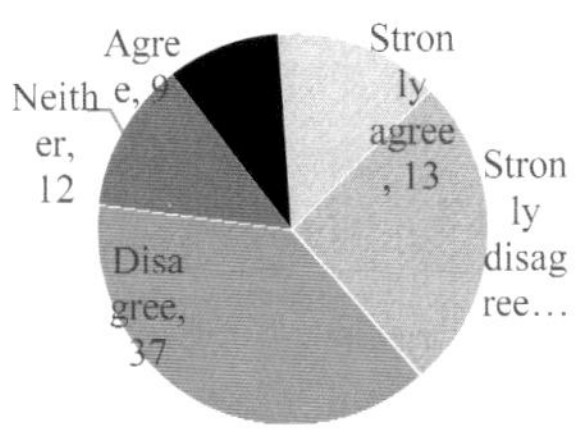

Figure 8. There is no difference between being a weapon and being used as one

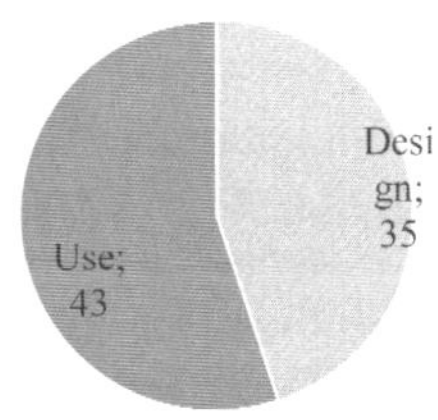

Figure 9. What makes a weapon

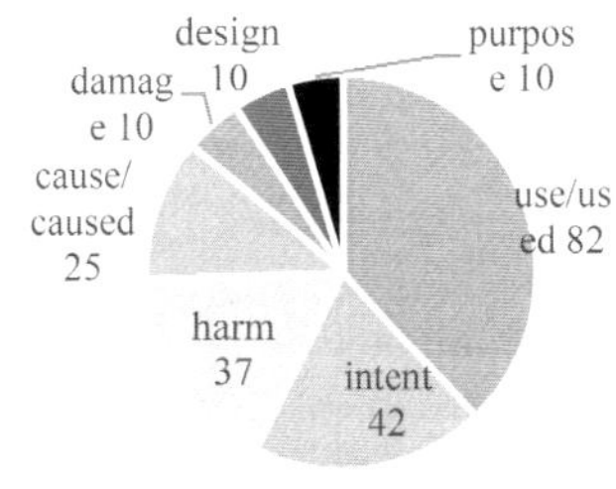

Figure 10. Keyword frequency of an object becoming a weapon

Aside from encompassing software/malware used offensively as a weapon, the use/design intent 'blanket' covers not only offensively used code and attacks, but also exploited vulnerabilities. From a UK legislative perspective, this is in line with the Computer Misuse Act (CMA): Section 1 covers vulnerability exploitation by focussing on obtaining data access regardless of method if not authorised by the data owner, however, knowing that the act is unauthorised is also vital.

4.4 Software/malware as a weapon

Opinions on whether malware is a weapon were split, but not statistically significant based on groupings of age, background or CS/IR knowledge. The majority agree or strongly agree that malware can be used as a weapon, and that it can sometimes be, or be used as, a weapon. However, there was greater variation in responses to the latter question based on background. More importantly, whether malware needs to cross a threshold to be considered a weapon was inconclusive, with the same number agreeing as disagreeing, indicating uncertainty.

The majority (83) believe malware can cause physical damage, with only 7 disagreeing. Of those in agreement, 11 mention 'Stuxnet' or 'nuclear' in their comments referencing the widely publicised attack in 2010. The majority disagree that software/malware is only a weapon if it causes physical damage (Figure 11), which would exclude damage to data confidentiality, integrity, and accessibility (CIA).

However, there is a difference in responses based on background KWH ($H(2)=7.57$, $p=0.02$), particularly between the Military and Other group MWU ($U=467.0$, $p=0.004$), with the Military being more cautious and tending to require more than a breach of CIA properties for software/malware to be a weapon. At the same time, there is agreement that software/malware causing damage to a living being, a structure or system (a 'cyber-physical attack') is a weapon, regardless of the type or severity of damage – even from the Military group, Figure 12.

Most disagree that the damage caused determines whether the software/malware is a weapon or not, regardless of the intentions of the attacker, however, there is some difference in opinion, particularly with those of Academic background. At the same time, there is no consensus on whether the reverse is true: does the intention of the attacker determines whether the software/malware is a weapon or not, regardless of the damage caused. However, the Academic group differs from the other two groups KWH ($H(2)=8.58$, $p=0.01$) by agreeing or strongly agreeing more often (MWU Academic-Military ($U=235$, $p=0.003$)), MWU Academic-Other ($U=237$, $p=0.005$). This deviates from common and legal perspective on crime, where a conscious decision to deprive or injure is an essential component of *mens rea* – a basis for establishing guilt.

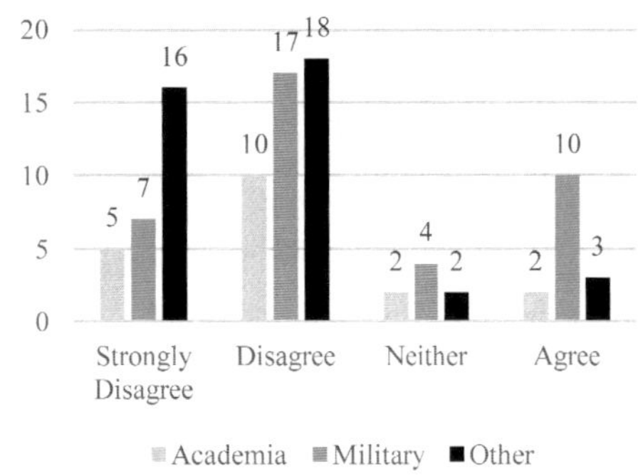

Figure 11. Physical damage is necessary for software/malware to be a weapon

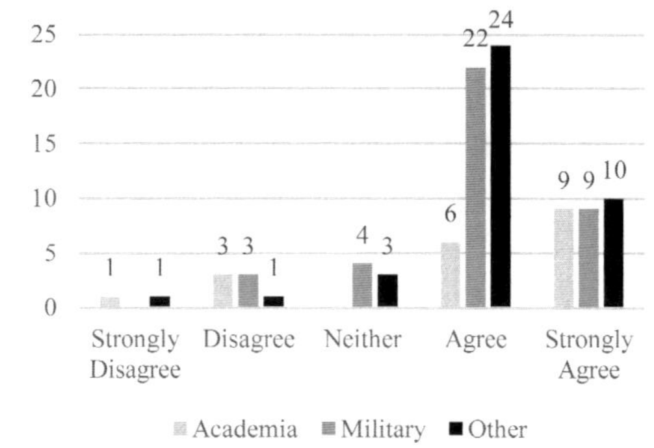

Figure 12. Software/malware causing physical damage is a weapon regardless of type or severity thereof

There is no consensus of whether it makes sense to approach software/malware attacks with (traditional) weapon terminology (e.g. 'warhead', 'trigger', 'payload') and/or measures (e.g. 'calibre', 'yield', 'range'). The responses to the terminology question are surprising to some extent, given that some language of that type is already employed within the literature, the IT field and public. Asked for additional comments, 32 responded arguing for and against keeping the terminology; the top reasons can be summarised as keeping those terms if it helps uniformity, awareness or understanding as language is often 'reused' (12). Those in favour of new terminology (13) suggested new terms centring on effect and output, stating the need for more flexibility and new words for new things. The remaining responses were unsure (5) or using a mixed approach (2).

5. CONCLUSION AND FUTURE WORK

This paper presented the results of an online questionnaire carried out to source public attitudes towards SaaW in order to supplement the academic and technical discourse. A total of 46 questions were asked, including consent and demographics, divided into three sections, with the first two centring on weapons and software/malware being discussed in this paper. Fully completed questionnaires were used for analysis, with respondents split by background Military, Academic and Other forming three groups.

Unsurprisingly, the opinions on what a weapon is varied greatly – yet there was also some consensus: around two-thirds consider it to be an object that is designed or can be used to cause harm or damage and are offensively driven. But when deciding whether malware is a weapon, opinions were split, as they were when asked if a threshold is needed for this to occur. Furthermore, Academics are more likely to disagree that software should be treated like any physical object, whilst Military respondents are more likely to agree and Others are indecisive – with the differences being statistically significant.

A clear majority believe malware can cause physical damage but there is disagreement as to what type of attack causes it to be a weapon: is it physical damage (to a living being, structure or system) or is an attack on CIA is sufficient? Whether the intent of the attacker or the damage (effect) caused is what makes software/malware a weapon is inconclusive: on the one hand, most disagree that damage matters regardless of intent; on the other hand, there is no consensus that intent is the decisive factor. In both cases the Academics deviate more, particularly on the second question where it is statistically significant.

Future work on this data should, from a statistical point of view, begin with the application of the (stringent) Bonferroni correction, however, this would have to be done per section/grouping of questions, as there are hierarchical/linked questions that are not fully independent. Furthermore, clustering between the groups could be of interest to examine similarity/overlap and consistency in responses, particularly with further analyses of the free-text responses.

The last part of the questionnaire centring on international relations aspects will be addressed in a future article, analysed in reference to theory and practice of that field, as well as implications thereof for the international system.

ACKNOWLEDGEMENT

We are very grateful to my colleagues for helpful discussions and assistance in the research reported, as well as all the respondents.

REFERENCES

Agrafiotis, I. et al., 2015. Identifying attack patterns for insider threat detection. *Computer Fraud & Security,* 2015(7), pp. 9-17.

Alperovitch, D., 2011. Towards establishment of cyberspace deterrence strategy. *3rd International Conference on Cyber Conflict,* pp. 1-8.

Betts, R., 2013. The Lost Logic of Deterrence. *Foreign Affairs,* 87(1), pp. 87-99.

Bhatt, P., Yano, E. T. & Gustavsson, P., 2014. *Towards a framework to detect multi-stage advanced persistent threats attacks.* Oxford, IEEE, pp. 390-395.

Blake, D. & Imburgia, J. S., 2011. 'Bloodless Weapons'? The Need to Conduct Legal Reviews of Certain Capabilities and the Implications of Defining them as' Weapons'. *Air Force Law Review,* Volume 66, pp. 157-207.

Brown, G. D. & Metcalf, A. O., 2014. Easier Said than Done: Legal Reviews of Cyber Weapons. *Journal of National Security Law & Policy,* Volume 7, pp. 115-138.

Cimbala, S., 2011. Nuclear Crisis Management and "Cyberwar" Phishing for Trouble?. *Strategic Studies Quarterly,* 5(1), pp. 117-131.

Cirenza, P., 2015. *An Evaluation of the Analogy Between Nuclear and Cyber Deterrence.* Stanford: Stanford University.

Hakkarainen, P., 2014. Cyber-Target Categorization. *Critical Infrastructure Protection against Cyber Threats,* 1(36), pp. 37-52.

Harvard Nuclear Study Group, 1983. *Living with nuclear weapons.* s.l.:Bantam Books.

Herr, T., 2014. PrEP: A Framework for Malware & Cyber Weapons. *The Journal of Information Warfare,* 13(1).

Herr, T. & Rosenzweig, P., 2015. Cyber Weapons & Export Control: Incorporating Dual Use with the PrEP Model. *Journal of National Security Law and Policy,* 8(2).

Khattak, S. et al., 2014 . A Taxonomy of Botnet Behavior, Detection, and Defense. *IEEE Communications Surveys & Tutorials,* 16(2), pp. 898 - 924.

Kramer, B. M., Kalick, M. S. & Milburn, M. A., 1983. Attitudes toward nuclear weapons and nuclear war: 1945–1982. *Journal of Social Issues,* 39(1), pp. 7-24.

Liu, S.-T., Chen, Y.-M. & Lin, S.-J., 2013. *A novel search engine to uncover potential victims for apt investigations.* Guiyang, Springer.

Mele, S., 2013. *Cyber-Weapons: Legal and Strategic Aspects,* Rome: Italian Institute of Strategic Studies 'Niccolò Machiavelli'.

Peterson, D., 2013. Offensive cyber weapons: construction, development, and employment. *Journal of Strategic Studies,* 36(1), pp. 120-124.

Queensland Police, 03/02/2017. *Category of weapons.* [Online] [Accessed 01 01 2017] Available at: https://www.police.qld.gov.au/programs/weaponsLicensing/licenceApplication/weapons/categories/categories.htm.

Radunovic, V. J., 2013. *DDoS - available weapon of mass disruption.* Belgrade, IEEE.

Rid, T. & McBurney, P., 2012. Cyber-weapons. *RUSI,* 157(1), pp. 6-13.

Roth, F., 2016. *APT Groups and Operations.* [Online] [Accessed 26 02 2017] Available at: https://docs.google.com/spreadsheets/d/1H9_xaxQHpWaa4O_Son4Gx0YOIzlcBWMsdvePFX68EKU/htmlview.

Schmitt, M. N. ed., 2013a. *Tallinn Manual on the International Law Applicable to Cyber Warfare.* s.l.:Cambridge University Press.

Schmitt, M. N., 2013. Cyberspace and international law: the penumbral mist of uncertainty. *Harvard Law Review Forum,* Issue 126, pp. 176-180.

Toorani, M., 2015. *On Vulnerabilities of the Security Association in the IEEE 802.15.6 Standard.* Puerto Rico, Springer, pp. 245-260.

Wilson, C., 2015. *Cyber weapons: 4 defining characteristics.* [Online] [Accessed 27 02 2017] Available at: https://gcn.com/articles/2015/06/04/cyber-weapon.aspx.

Wittgenstein, L., 1953. *Philosophische Untersuchungen.* Reprint 2003 ed. Frankfurt: Suhrkamp Verlag.

APPENDIX A

Table 1. Summary of responses for the multiple-choice questions post demographics; N_{Tot}=96

	Question	Str. Dis.	Dis.	Neither	Agree	Str. Ag.
8	What is a weapon?	Free-text responses				
9	Please list three different types of weapon:	Free-text responses				
10	An everyday object or tool (e.g. a cup, a chair, a shirt) can be a weapon.	8	11	10	29	38
11	An everyday object or tool (e.g. a cup, a chair, a shirt) can be used as a weapon.	3	0	2	33	58
12	There is no difference between an object being a weapon and an object being used as a weapon.	25	37	12	9	13
13	What turns an object into a weapon/when does an object become a weapon?	Free-text responses				
14	Weapons are only used offensively.	34	47	3	10	2
15	There are three types of objects: 1) those created for the sole purpose of being used as a weapon (offensively or defensively) 2) those created for dual use, either as a tool or a weapon, depending on the situation 3) those created to be used as a tool but that can situationally become/be used as a weapon. To what extent do you agree with the categorisation above?	2	9	5	51	29
16	If an object with an un-precedented destructive potential is created, but nobody is aware of it, it is still a weapon.	7	14	24	31	20
17	What is software?	Free-text responses				
18	Software should be treated like any physical object or tool.	4	22	24	34	12
19	What is malicious software (malware)?	Free-text responses				
20	All malware is equally dangerous.	25	52	9	5	5
21	On what basis should malware be classified?	Free-text responses				
22	Software and/or malware can cause physical damage.	3	4	6	46	37
23	All software has the potential to become malware.	5	23	31	29	8
24	Malware is a weapon.	2	13	20	40	21
25	Malware can be used as a weapon.	1	2	6	48	39
26	Malware can sometimes be/be used as a weapon.	6	9	13	47	21
27	Malware needs to cross a threshold to be considered a weapon.	12	34	15	34	1
27a	If you agree, what would you base the threshold on?	Free-text responses				
27b	Should that type of weapon be given a new name to reflect its potency, e.g. cyber weapon?	3	11	29	41	5
28	It makes sense to approach software/malware attacks with (traditional) weapon terminology (e.g. 'warhead', 'trigger', 'payload').	7	24	24	38	3
28a	And/or measures (e.g. 'calibre', 'yield', 'range').	10	21	25	39	1
29	Software/malware causing physical damage to a living being, a structure or system (a 'cyber-physical attack') is a weapon; software/malware causing damage to data integrity, accessibility and confidentiality is not a weapon.	28	45	8	15	0
30	Software/malware causing damage to a living being, a structure or system (a 'cyber-physical attack') is a weapon, regardless of the type or severity of damage.	2	7	7	52	28
31	The damage caused determines whether the software/malware is a weapon or not, regardless of the intentions of the attacker.	18	44	12	18	4
32	The intention of the attacker determines whether the software/malware is a weapon or not, regardless of the damage caused.	5	27	13	36	15
33	Software/malware can be separated into three types: 1) created for the sole purpose of being used as a weapon (offensively or defensively) 2) created for dual use, either as a tool or a weapon, depending on the situation 3) created to be used as a tool but that can situationally become a weapon	4	14	23	45	10
34	Most attacks by software/malware fall only into three categories: 1) Mere nuisance 2) Summary offences / misdemeanour / petty crime 3) Indictable offence / felony	3	8	25	48	12

ACCOUNTABLE AND RESPONSIBLE DISCLOSURE OF FINANCIAL OPEN GOVERNMENT DATA: OPEN SPENDING INITIATIVES ENHANCING CIVIC ENGAGEMENT

Martijn Hartog and Bert Mulder
eSociety Institute of The Hague University of Applied Sciences, Johanna Westerdijkplein 75, 2521 EN The Hague

ABSTRACT

This research focuses an optimal arrangement of open spending as added instrumental value to the accountability in communicating financial information towards citizens within The Netherlands. Open Spending is more and more of relevance in the Netherlands and is addressed as one of the key action points in the Open Government Partnership Action plan of The Netherlands. In order to adequately communicate financial information towards citizens, 5 arrangement variables of accountability (transparency, liability, verifiability, responsibility and responsiveness) as defined by Jonathan Koppell where explored and extended with the notion of social accountability. As social accountability mechanisms are geared towards public expenditure management processes - mechanisms that seek to directly involve ordinary citizens in processes of allocating, disbursing, monitoring and evaluating the use of public resources - have proved very effective since it is this resource flow that puts policy into action. From a viewpoint of the 'Civic Engagement Model' created by The World Bank, we reflected on the current formats of accountability in a focus group with six key actors from amongst others Dutch Ministries, Open State Foundation, Provinces and Municipalities and verified afterwards with delegates of the Open Knowledge Foundation. After empirical analyses current initiatives surrounding open spending within The Netherlands are lacking a clear goal, content and format and an adequate completion on a National level. This research also showed a twofold goal for further open spending developments, on one hand generating social accountability, civic engagement and clarifying financial Open Government Data by providing contextualised information.

KEYWORDS

Open Spending, OGD, government finances, transparency, accountability, civic engagement

1. INTRODUCTION

The Netherlands is shifting towards a participatory society in which citizens wish to decide and think with governmental bodies on policies and governmental influence. Open Spending is one of the solutions contributing to trust of citizens in government (Council for Public Administration, 2012:70; Scientific Council of Government Policy, 2012:27) and well discussed by Mayors and City Council Members in many Municipalities. The Council for Public Administration (2012) addressed, that structurally supplying government information to citizens will increase openness and transparency resulting in trust. This kind of openness is therefore a kind of representation or accountability. Without transparency citizens would not have sufficient insights in the operation of governmental bodies feeding the inability to fully participate with the government. According to the Ministry of Interior and Kingdom Relations (2014) expectations of citizens in governmental bodies has changed under the influence of ICT's, education, media, internationalization and individualization, shifting towards a participatory society in which citizens wish to decide, co-create. Also the HM Treasury of the United Kingdom mentions that a more informed citizen is a more empowered citizen, who has the right to ask the government concerning expenditure and results (2009:25), which is key according to Lathrop and Ruma (2010:19). It is assumed that a citizens' view on government is now demanding renewal on influence and participation (Scientific Council of Government Policy, 2012:170-171), when providing the right context and data on expenditure and results, citizens could there for be better informed and more empowered which is necessary for a participatory society.

2. RESEARCH METHODOLOGY

This research is built on an exploratory literature review, five expert interviews with National and International Open Spending researchers. Afterwards, the insights gathered from the literature and expert interviews where validated and conceptually explored in an elaborate interactive session with 10 key informants / leading experts from the related fields in The Netherlands: senior information advisors, (associate) professors IT & Design, policy advisor financial information management, programme leaders, developers, researchers of amongst others Open State Foundation, Ministry of Finance, Province of South-Holland, The Hague University of Applied Sciences, Municipality of The Hague and ProDemos.

3. OPEN SPENDING AND OPEN GOVERNMENT DATA

Open data ensures transparency and accountability. The assumption is that it can lead to more citizenship participation in the decision-making process and possible innovation in both government and public services (Davies, 2012). Openness and open data also have a positive impact on government processes and civic involvement (Meijer, 2013; O'Hara, 2012). According to Höffner, Martin and Lehmann (2013), the benefits of open data include:

- Citizens get to know more about government functions, making better accountability.
- It contributes to valuable information about the world.
- The government can function more efficiently.

According to the Dutch General Audit Office, open spending is about the provision of open data on public finances. For example, the planned and realized income and expenses, grants and information about procurement and contracts (General Audit Office, 2015:19). Open Spending can take place both at transactional level, with the reporting of individual transactions from a certain value, as at aggregated level, summing up individual amounts in categories. The Open State Foundation is a non-profit organization focused on promoting digital transparency in the Netherlands. They realize open spending for regional and local authorities by unlocking their financial data through the openspending.nl website. The release of those data is based on the CBS-Iv3 standard (Iv3 stands for 'Information for Third Parties'). The CBS-Iv3 Standard is a standard that indicates how governmental bodies should provide financial data to monitoring organization, such as the Financial Supervisor, the European Union, the Ministry of Interior and Kingdom Relations and Statistics Netherlands (CBS). This standard is used to communicate the figures of budgets, quarterly figures and annual accounts. Through openspending.nl, the Open State Foundation unlocks the financial data communicated by governmental bodies to the CBS, which allows comparing public government spending by municipalities, by households and by acreage.

3.1 Open Spending Developments

The United States and The United Kingdom have a leading position in the field of Open Data and Open Spending. This position was acquired by respectively President Barack Obama and Premier Cameron. Worldwide attention was paid to open spending, after President Obama signed the 'American Recovery and Reinvestment Act' of 2009. That memorandum introduced the concept of public accountability and transparency of the spending of federal funds in digital form. The federal open spending data have been available on USAspending.gov since 2008. In order to provide better insight into the expenses, the Digital Accountability and Transparency Act of 2014 (Data Act) was adopted in addition to the previous Federal Funding Accountability and Transparency Act of 2006 (General Audit Office, 2015:14-15). The Data Act aims to improve the insight into the expenses by:

- Providing direct expenses of federal services, where the expenses are linked to the policy.
- Developing data standards.
- Facilitating reporting obligations.
- Improving data quality by raising responsibility.

The Open Government Partnership (OGP) was established in 2011 to ensure that governments become more transparent, open to ideas from society and open to innovative technologies and accountability

(Ministry of Interior and Kingdom Relations, 2013). The World Wide Web Foundation was founded in 2009 by Web Inventor Sir Tim Berners Lee, promoting the Web as a fundamental public property. Recently, this organization released the Open Data Barometer Global Report (2015), which included the progress made by countries in the field of open data. The report describes a study of the willingness and impact of open data on the world:

– 'Readiness to secure benefits from open data, including the legal, political, economic, social, organizational and technical foundations that can support the supply and use of open data'.

– 'Impact of open data, measured through media and academic notions of data use and impact'.

Furthermore, the G7 as an intergovernmental forum consisting of seven leading industrial countries: Italy, Germany, France, Japan, Canada, United Kingdom and the United States established the 'Open Data Charter' in 2013. The purpose of this initiative is to standardize the open offer of data: 'open by default'. The G7 also seeks to ensure that data is reusable to all, so governments become more transparent and innovative.

3.2 Legislation and OGP Action Plan

Disclosure of government information can be placed in a passive and active manner. Passive, in this case, means that the citizens must submit a request to obtain government information. While active disclosure, entails government data that already has been made public, so citizens do not have to submit a request (General Audit Office, 2014). Since 1980, government information has been issued passively under the Information Act (WOB). The WOB regulates the disclosure of information that the government produces or collects for the purpose of carrying out its duties. If government data falls under the WOB refusal grounds, they will not be released (General Audit Office, 2014). In 2013, a new Open Government Act was initiated to replace the WOB stating that the government would be obliged not only to grant access to data as individual citizens ask (situation now) but also to actively make active data available for the whole society. This Act is currently in revision and process by the House of Representatives.

After The Netherlands joined the OGP in 2013, the ‘Vision Open Government’ and the ‘Open Government Action Plan’ were drafted in order to achieve the Open Government program of the Ministry of Interior and Kingdom Relations. The purpose of the Vision Open Government is to renew the government over a term of ten years or longer. In this vision, the purpose and underlying reasons for striving for an open government are described. In addition, it describes what projects and programs are intended for the realization of an open government (Ministry of Interior and Kingdom Relations, 2014). The objective of the Action Plan is defining actions in order to realize structural openness and transparency, as the following action describes: 'Financial transparency through open budget and Open Spending experiments' (Ministry of Interior and Kingdom Relations, 2016). This item includes the publication of the annual government budgets, amended budgets and accountancy information by the Ministry of Finance and all parties involved. Although adoption of open spending will take place in the coming years, the challenge lies in the implementation. In the near future, the Open State Foundation will organize pilots in the field of open spending with governmental bodies. All these initiatives indicate that open spending is a structural development and that a good form is important.

3.3 The Professional Iv3 Standard for Disclosure

The government-defined Iv3 standard, originally developed as a benchmarking tool for government, is repeatedly associated with and used as a basis for open spending. The Iv3 standard will play an important role, as all governmental bodies already have reports in that form. However, further consideration shows that the Iv3 standard, and thus the resulting information, has limitations in communication towards citizens. The exchange format was initially created as a means of exchanging information between professional stakeholders of the government. The aggregation level of the Iv3 standard is high and therefore does not have a direct meaning for citizens. For this reason, a number of levels have been added to the province of Groningen (still in pilot form). The question is whether the Iv3 standard can be sufficient even when municipalities use it as a window format to fill it with more detailed information. This would bring down the aggregation level, but not necessarily lead to meaningful information for the citizen.

In addition to a correct aggregation level, Iv3 data lacks insight into "meaningless" Iv3 data as different parties point out. The city council of the Municipality of The Hague believes that spending data gives insight into the finances of the municipality and thereby publicly accounts for the financial policy, provided that explanatory explanations of the figures are combined (Municipality of The Hague, 2013). The City Council also assumes that accountability must create a realistic image. This means that all relevant facts and circumstances must come to fruition. At the same time, those facts and circumstances must also be placed in the correct context (Council for Public Administration, 2012). At www.openspending.nl - the province of Groningen clearly shows the high level of aggregation and lack of context in the future.

4. (SOCIAL) ACCOUNTABILITY AND RESPONSIBILITY

Mark Bovens (2007) describes accountability as a collective name of different concepts: "In contemporary political and scholarly discourse 'accountability' often serves as a conceptual umbrella that covers various other distinct concepts, such as transparency, equity, democracy, efficiency, responsiveness, responsibility and integrity". According to Bovens, accountability is a broad concept. It is not an analytical but an evaluative concept and leads to responsiveness and willingness to act in a transparent way. Jonathan GS Koppell (2005) unraveled this kind of accountability on the basis of five different sub-concepts:

- Transparency.
- Liability.
- Controllability.
- Responsibility.
- Responsiveness.

Each of these forms of accountability has its own purpose and determinants for the organization. The same applies to a possible financial responsibility between governmental bodies and citizens: this is also determined by its goal, but that goal has its own character and demands its own organization. Governmental accountability to citizens has been described in the literature as social accountability, among others, by the World Bank. Social accountability is taken into account in various ways. In business, this concept is formulated in the standard 'social accountability 8000'. This describes how to keep in line with generally applicable social standards and values in the workplace (Social Accountability International, 2014). The SA8000 is an example of the possibilities of structured development of standards in social responsibility. However, it does not contribute to a better understanding of government responsibility towards citizens. Far more closely with citizens and governmental bodies, is the way in which the World Bank gives substance to social accountability and good governance (with the 'development' domain as an area of concern). Here, accountability 'civic engagement' has the central purpose: "Social accountability relies on civic engagement where citizens and civil society organizations access information about budgets, expenditures, and services and extract accountability" (Agarwal & Heltberg & Diachok, 2009).

4.1 Responsibility

Responsibility as one of the sub-concepts of Koppell (2005) implies that municipalities and provinces are bound by laws, rules and norms. Participants in our study mention that the unclosed data should explain what responsibility municipalities and provinces carry. This is the responsibility that they can influence from their task, and thus not imposed by, for example, the government or the European Union. Many amounts are budgeted or multi-annual allocated and therefore have a fixed destination. The available funds for citizens' wishes, for example a cycle path, are often unclear due to those reservations in multi-annual budgets. According to the professionals, clarity about 'shiftable money' should first be obtained, before accountability takes place in the context of open spending. The professionals state that it is important to map what financial resources the municipality has at its disposal and which of these are public resources. In addition to public resources, the municipality also manages money from other parties such as health insurance companies (who have purchased health care there), housing corporations and energy companies. The Ministry of Internal Affairs and Kingdom Relations maps these cash flows at the moment in the project: 'Cash Flows in the Neighborhood'. The question is whether public accountability applies to non-public funds. The public duties of a municipality are described in policy programs. In order to connect accountability and responsibility, this information must be made available together with the financial data.

The professionals make three different statements:

1. The unlocked data must show what the actual responsibility of the municipality or the province is.
2. Board members must first know how much of the local government fee is available for 'shifting' before responsibility is applied to open spending.
3. There must be research into public funds.

Interesting is that professionals notice that not all resources may 'fall under open spending', where professionals previously agreed that 'unlocking the entire financial administration is the best way to justify'. Again, here is the question of providing contextual information of the data as concluded in the preceding paragraph. However, this time to determine from what responsibility activities have taken place. With the remark of the previous point, it would be appropriate to provide financial information with three different types of contexts: 1) project information, 2) the financial structure and 3) information about accountability. The question is: How does the layout of this context enhance civic engagement?

4.2 Civic Engagement

Civic engagement entails participation of citizens in the public domain, with the aim of influencing decision making or pursuit of common goals (Spoor, 2005). Since the budget and spending process is a key element for the World Bank (like in this research), the impact of civil engagement takes place in this direction:

"[...] social accountability mechanisms geared towards public expenditure management processes - mechanisms that seek to directly involve ordinary citizens in processes of allocating, dispensing, monitoring and evaluating the use of public resources - have proven very effective since it is this resource flow that puts policy into action (The World Bank, 2013)".

Each step of financial accountability can make a significant contribution to civic engagement (see figure 1). According to Cornwall and John Gaventa, there are two solutions that improve the legitimacy problem between government and citizens: informing citizens about their interests through participation and the government explains more accountability. However, actions by citizens without government support lead to a 'voice without influence'. In addition, government efforts to increase responsiveness without consultation with citizens do not improve accountability. In the context of open spending, this means that in addition to publishing spending data, the government must involve citizens in the preparation of budgets: 'participatory budgeting' (Cornwall & Gaventa, 2001).

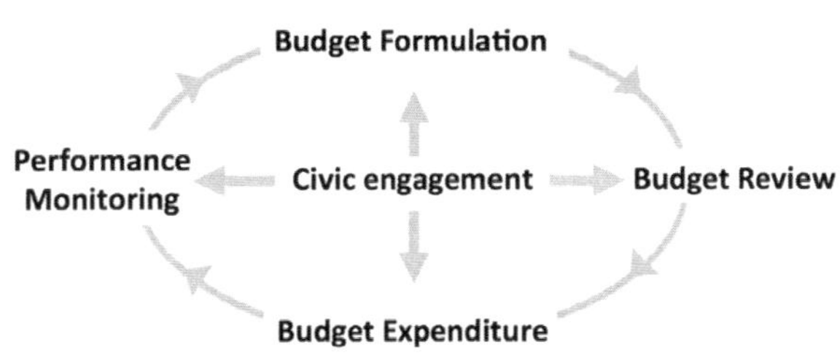

Figure 1. civic engagement achieved through participatory budgeting and open spending (The World Bank, 2013)

Budget formulation. This refers to citizen's involvement in the preparation of budgets.

Budget review. A process in which data relating to government spending and investment is accessed, investigated, monitored and disseminated. Social organizations hereby check that the budgets are in line with the social obligations of the government. They also analyze the effects of allocations of public funds in the budgets. They also translate field terms. Finally, they raise attention for citizens' budget issues.

Budget expenditure. Hereby, the government gives insight into the expenses incurred for citizens (open spending).

Performance Monitoring. This means that citizens monitor and evaluate the effectuation and performance of public services.

Based on this paragraph, it can be concluded that the purpose of existing financial reports in the public administration is to account for officials (professionals) within the domain and to compare the figures. For citizens, there is another purpose: civil engagement. That other purpose leads to other forms of reporting, so also another form of accountability: social accountability. In this way, 'social accountability' gives a possible completion closer to what citizens want from governments around accountability.

5. CONCLUSION

Accountability has a purpose and this purpose determines the design of this accountability. The same applies to a possible financial accountability between government and citizens, so-called social accountability. The purpose and design of this form of accountability are not explained by the governmental bodies. However, the literature research shows that civic engagement (civic participation) can be the goal of this social accountability. This is confirmed by the interactive session. In order to achieve this goal (civic engagement), institutional variables have been defined in this study. The five sub-principles of accountability of Koppell provide a starting point for determining these design variables. In order to investigate the usefulness of these sub-concepts as variables, professionals are interviewed, all active in the field of open spending. The visions of the professionals seem to differ. They state the following:

– Transparency. All professionals agree that this is a relevant variable. They believe that it has to be realized by making available an 'insightful and comprehensible report' on the one hand, but on the other hand also in the form of raw data.

– Liability. The professionals differ in this regard. On the one hand, some professionals think that citizens should be able to make the government liable, for example in the form of a 'Citizen Audit room'. (Also known as 'Armchair Auditors') On the other hand, one professional did not agree because then the citizens would pass the city council.

– Controllability. Here the professionals differ too. One professional had the opinion that the accountability is sufficiently understandable and therefore controllable for citizens. However, the other professionals do not agree. This is because the municipal accounts are too internal and thus not understandable for outsiders. However, they believe that context information, apps and newspaper articles (journalists research) increase the controllability of information.

– Responsibility. The professionals give different responses to this. However, all professionals agree that the responsibility domain (the task statement) must be accountable. One professional believes that in the current accountability the councilors do not have sufficient insight into the "shiftable" money. He said that this should be resolved before opening the open spending account.

– Responsiveness. All professionals agree that the government needs to answer questions that citizens have about accountability. In doing so, they provided various examples for facilitating this. First of all, the most frequently asked questions (via phone, email or web portal) and their answers can be collected on the website in the form of 'frequently asked questions' (FAQ). Secondly, citizens can be invited to participate in a jury based on a lottery, as usual in US jurisprudence. Finally, citizens can be actively involved in the preparation of budgets by releasing a percentage of the budget to spend freely by the citizens.

The five design variables do not give immediate effect to open spending, but they provide insight into the arrangement possibilities. Professionals provided concrete alternatives during the interviews. In order to further investigate the concrete implementation of open spending, a interactive session was held with material experts.

During this session, the experts concluded that the purpose, content and form of open spending have not yet been adequately elaborated. In order to prevent municipalities and provinces from giving their own input to open spending, they believe that it should first take place in national terms. They also concluded that the purpose of open spending is twofold:

– Provide insight into the actions of the government.
– Civic engagement by enhancing participation.

Insights are provided through the disclosure of government financial data, partly through open data. The figures are combined with explanatory information placed in the context. Civic engagement aims to stimulate and support citizen participation. According to experts, the two objectives may lead to two different structures and two systems:

– Open spending as justifying the existing public administration structure.
– Open spending as stimulating new forms of public administration.

In conclusion, in order to achieve open spending practically, further research is needed. This research must focus on national approaches for each of the possible types of open spending. For this it is important to determine what the purpose, content and form of open spending should factually concern. The study shows that the political pressure on financial transparency is high. The question is whether there is no risk of a deadlock when working on open spending under pressure, while essential institutional arrangement questions are not yet determined.

ACKNOWLEDGEMENT

This paper is related to the 'Government of the Future' research programmes with the Municipality of The Hague (2012-2018) and the Province of South-Holland (2013-2017) in The Netherlands. The opinions of the authors do not necessarily reflect the opinions of the governmental bodies. The authors would like to thank the interviewees for their constructive input.

REFERENCES

Agarwal, S., Heltberg, R. and Diachok, M., 2009. *Scaling- Up Social Accountability in World Bank Operations.* Retrieved from www-wds.worldbank.org.

Bovens, M., 2007. Analysing and Assessing Accountability: A Conceptual Framework. *European Law Journal,* Vol. 13, No. 4, July, pp. 447-468.

Cornwall, A. and Gaventa, J., 2001. Bridging the gap: citizenship, participation and accountability. *PLA Notes*, 40, pp. 32-35.

Council for Public Management [Raad voor het Openbaar Bestuur], 2012. *Gij zult openbaar maken: Naar een volwassen omgang met overheidsinformatie*. The Hague.

Davies, T., 2012. *How might open data contribute to good governance?*

General Audit Office [Algemene Rekenkamer], 2014. *Trendrapport Open Data*. The Hague.

General Audit Office [Algemene Rekenkamer], 2015. *Trendrapport Open Data*. The Hague.

HM Treasury, 2009. *Putting the frontline first: smarter government.*

Höffner, K., Martin, M. & Lehmann, J., 2013. *Linked Spending: Open Spending becomes Linked Open Data*. pp. 1-5, IOS Press.

Koppell, J., 2005. Pathologies of Accountability: ICANN and the Challenge of "Multiple Accountabilities Disorder". *Public Administration Review*, January/February, Vol. 65, No. 1, pp. 94-108.

Lathrop, D. and Ruma, L., 2010. *Open Government: Collaboration, transparency, and Participation in Practice*. O'Reilly Media Inc.: Sebastopol, CA.

Meijer, A., 2013. *Understanding the Complex Dynamics of Transparency.*

Ministry of Interior and Kingdom Relations, 2013. *Visie Open Overheid.* The Hague.

Ministry of Interior and Kingdom Relations, 2014. *Open Government Partnership Self-Evaluation Report The Netherlands.*

Ministry of Interior and Kingdom Relations, 2016. *Actieplan Open Overheid.* The Hague.

Municipality of The Hague, 2013. *Answers to written questions council member J.C. Sneller.*

O'Hara, K., 2012. *Transparency, Open Data and Trust in Government: Shaping the Infosphere*.

Open State Foundation, 2014. *On Open Data.*

Scientific Council of Government Policy [Wetenschappelijke Raad voor het Regeringsbeleid], 2012. *Vertrouwen in Burgers*. Amsterdam University Press: Amsterdam.

Social Accountability International, 2014. *Social Accountability 8000: International standard.*

Spoor, M. (ed.), 2005. *Globalisation, Poverty and Conflicts: A critical 'Development' reader.*

The World Bank, 2013. *Tools and Methods*. Retrieved from http://web.worldbank.org.

ONTOLOGY ALIGNMENT APPROACH TO SOCIAL NETWORKS TIES ESTABLISHMENT

Leandro Pupo Natale[1], Israel Florentino Santos[1], Adriana Valio[2] and Nizam Omar[3]
[1]Universidade Presbiteriana Mackenzie, Rua da Consolação, 896, São Paulo, Brasil
[2]Centro de Rádio, Astronomia e Astrofísica Mackenzie, Rua da Consolação, 896, São Paulo, Brasil
[3]Universidade Presbiteriana Mackenzie, Rua da Consolação, 896, São Paulo, Brasil

ABSTRACT

Due to its capacity of formal structuring, ontologies favor the sharing in web environment. At the same time, Social Networks seek to create a centralized, unique, and organized database for making recommendations for services, products, people, and virtual assistants. However, considering that each user has its own definition, it is necessary to have negotiated alignments between the parties for interaction without dissonance. Thus, this paper presents the implementation specificities of the Information Sharing and Knowledge model between pairs through the alignment of ontologies for corporate environments to establish an Ontological Social Network.

KEYWORDS

Artificial Intelligence, Knowledge Management, Ontologies, Social Networks, Semantic Web

1. INTRODUCTION

The advancement of the green economy in the pursuit of human well being and social equality with reduction of environmental risks and ecological scarcity [Brasil, 2008] has aroused in society the need for new collaborative semantic solutions by using Information and Communication Technologies (ICT). However, the information and data sharing between different sources are ambiguous in all domains involved. One of the most complex computational challenges is to analyze, integrate, and manage data to transmit some information and allow the extraction of knowledge from different databases [Seligman et al. 2010][Halevy et al. 2005][Bernstein and Haas 2008][Natale et al. 2008]

The Semantic Web represents an extension of the existing Web with the objective of assigning meaning to the data content allowing computational and human agents to interact cooperatively with each other [Berners-Lee and Hendler 2001]. Nevertheless, the integration of semantic metadata includes uncertainties in the process due to different formats of representation of metadata in different repositories [Ibrahim et al. 2013].

Several proposals for semantic integration have emerged in recent years with the aim of improving the representation of knowledge by enabling forms of content recommendation optimization [Brandão et al. 2013], among them, the structuring of concepts in hierarchical form [Freitas et al. 2008], space temporal information [Monclar et al. 2009][Leme et al. 2016], natural language processing for extracting relationships and grammar connectors [Wijaya et al. 2013], and using topic identification [Nolasco and Oliveira 2016]. In this context, this work presents the implementation of the method of aligning ontologies Web Knowledge Integration (WKI) defined by Natale [Natale and Omar 2016], which is based on the alignment of ontologies of each user, to subsidize the establishment of the ontological social network. Thus, automatically, negotiated, and individualized resource sharing occurs more between each user, because this sharing is subsidized in concepts among users rather than the coincidence of keywords [Natale 2017].

2. DEFINITIONS

The alignment of ontologies establishes the creation of methods capable of performing an automatic translation between the concepts between two ontologies [Noy and Musen 1999]. One-to-one directly established mappings can fully express the necessary conceptualization [Noy and Musen 1999]. To integrate ontologies in different domains, it is necessary to avoid incorrect combinations at the linguistic level. This occurs when ontologies in different languages are integrated without considering the grammatical particularities and the ontological level, and also when different concepts are aligned as equivalent or vice versa [Klein 2001][Gruber et al. 1993]. Figure 1a presents a simplified representation of similar concepts of two ontologies, demonstrating that an automatic integration process may not be sufficient for this task. Therefore, knowledge, represented through ontologies, must be integrated into a semantic layer, creating a meaningful relationship structure to avoid this kind of problem [Ehrig 2006].

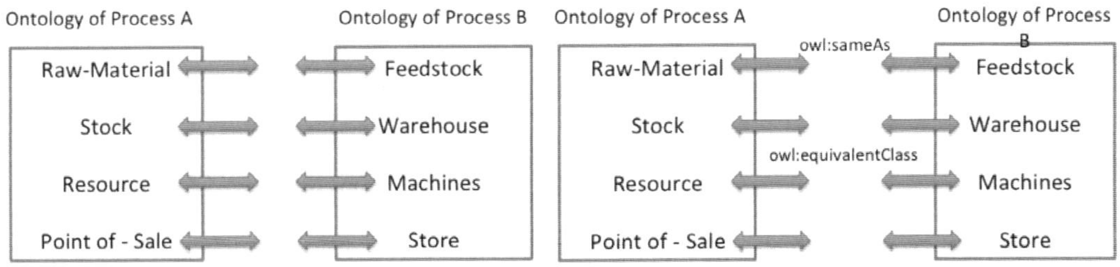

Figure 1. (1a) Example of Ontology with related concepts. (1b) Example of Ontology with semantic relationship align concepts [Uschold and Gruninger 1996]

Figure 1b shows a proposal in which the OWL language [bechhofer2009owl] is used to create meaningful relationships between the concepts of the two aligned ontologies. In this sense, there may be different types of ontology alignments, according to the process performed and its final result [Ehrig 2006][Euzenat and Shvaiko 2013][Otero-Cerdeira et al. 2015]:

- Combination: A combination can be established without there being a specific identification between the terms;
- Integration: A process that can be performed for ontologies of different domains, creating a new ontology from the original concepts.
- Matching: For alignments of this category there must be meaning matching between aligned entities, and relationships must be typed. This is the category adopted by this work, using structures of the Web Ontology Language (OWL) language as a form of relationships: *owl: equivalentClass, owl: equivalentProperty, owl: sameClass* and *owl: differentFrom.*
- Mapping: There must be a relational mapping between the axioms, concepts, relationships and instances of the treated ontologies.
- Merging: Alignment processes within this category should produce a new ontology containing the original concepts and relationships. Different from the category of Integration, here the original ontologies are altered.

The WKI is a taxonomy model of ontologies to be aligned, algorithms used for extraction and creation of ontologies, ontological alignment algorithms and a set of operators that promote the interaction of the creators of each ontology. This method works with a sequence of activities grouped by in synchronous and asynchronous processes, as shown in the activity diagram of Figure 2. This algorithm is used as the operational center within the platform architecture WProfile [Natale and Omar 2013].

The architecture of the WProfile platform is designed to manage a social network that allows the search and sharing of multimedia resources. Each multimedia resource present in the system is represented by a local ontology. The interaction of users seeking and sharing resources is carried out transparently in relation to local knowledge. This is possible through the ontological alignment model created by WKI.

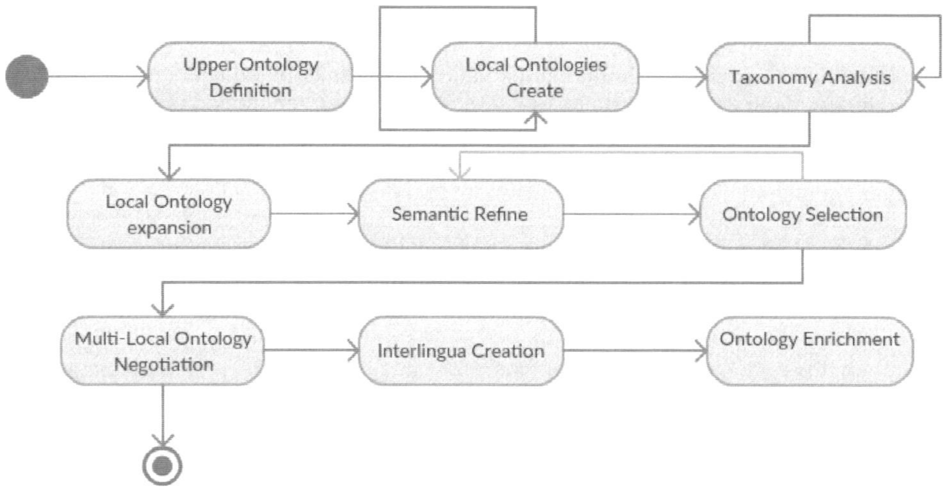

Figure 2. Activity Diagram of the WKI method [Natale, 2017]

3. BACKGROUND

This section presents different ontology alignment techniques from different domains [Ehrig 2006][Euzenat and Shvaiko 2013], which works with a process of merging structures [Ding et al. 2015][Hong and Kuo 2015], aligning structures and entities [Loia et al. 2013], alignment based on relations of Users on social networks and data sharing [Shklovski et al. 2015]. In the latter, however, one does not take into account the semantics of the terms [Shvaiko and Euzenat 2013][Asiaee et al. 2015].

The FIONA Method [Kachroudi et al. 2015] is based on relationships previously indicated or created by a specialist in the domain to be treated. These alignments, in this way, are established semi-automatically using representations described in RDF.

PROMPT [Noy and Musen 1999] performs the task of aligning ontologies through a structural analysis of concepts and their neighbors. The terms or concepts must be evaluated continuously, updating the alignment with new information inserted in the original ontologies. A specialist should oversee the entire alignment process to validate the entire process and make the necessary corrections.

Similarly, the ONIONS (ONtological Integration Of Naive Sources) method [Steve et al. 1997] only aligns ontologies of the same domain. In this same scenario, FCA-Merge [Stumme and Maedche 2001] uses a set of documents, from which it extracts concepts to be used as the initial elements of a merge process.

The SAMBO system uses medical ontologies described in OWL [Lambrix and Tan 2011] and additional tools that support the identification of similar concepts. One of the most useful tools in this context deals with a terminological search for comparisons in a list of words that compose the terms present in the ontologies. Additionally, this system also performs a structural analysis comparing the transitive relationships between two concepts that are related through is-a or is-a-part-of. Entities can also be enriched based on the knowledge provided by the Unified Medial Language System (UMLS) [Bodenreider 2004].

The PARIS algorithm [Suchanek et al. 2011] performs the alignment task from the relationship between the instances of classes present in an ontology. Running in an automated way, it has a probabilistic function of equivalence. Thus, when two instances are defined as equivalent the ontologies that have them share the same relationship. It should be emphasized that this algorithm has the potential to create optimal alignments from instances that have numeric information or unique identifiers. However, PARIS does not support ontologies that model events through heterogeneous relationships.

4. WEB KNOWLEDGE INTEGRATION METHOD (WKI)

Evaluating a collaborative and interactive scenario, the WKI method was created for the establishment of ontological alignments through negotiation of concepts carried out point by point. The WKI consists of a supervised and an automated phase. Within the supervised phase the activities of creation and expansion of the local ontologies occur, and negotiation of concepts forms the interlanguage of ontological integration of each user involved. The automatic phase allows the execution of inference processes of local and interlanguage ontologies to extend existing relationships.

The creation of local ontologies, interlanguage (integration ontologies), uses a multi-domain top-level ontology. This top-level ontology is based on the specification of entities defined by the Schema.org microformat pattern. Through this taxonomy the WKI defines basic ontological classes representing naturally established concepts: Person, Organization, Event, Place, and Creative Work, according to the general view shown in Figure 3. This type of modeling allows the creation of local ontologies in a supervised and standardized way, facilitating the creation of interlanguages in a more natural way.

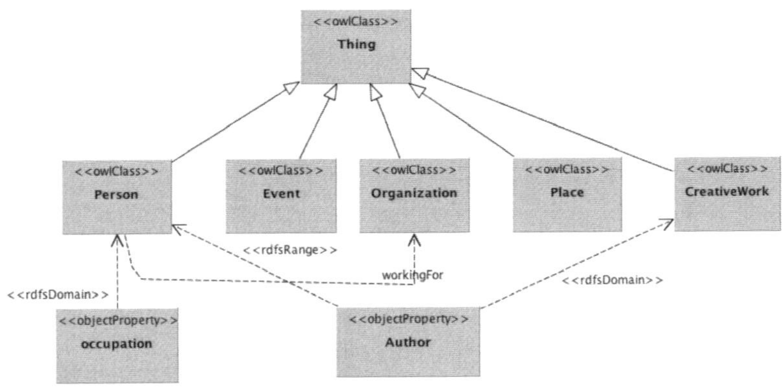

Figure 3. Top Level Ontology of WKI method [Natale, 2017]

After executing the WKI method, the multi-local negotiation of two ontologies produces a negotiated interlanguage, as exemplified in Figure 4. In this case each user has his own definition of the entity *TobySegaran*, for the user *Leandro*, he is a *Writer*, and for *Vanessa* a *Researcher*.

Following the activity of negotiating and establishing interlanguage, users negotiated that the *TobySegaran* entity represents the same concept in their ontologies. The interlanguage created, identified as *Vanessa_Leandro*, is created based on the "*owl: sameAS*" relationship denoting this equivalence.

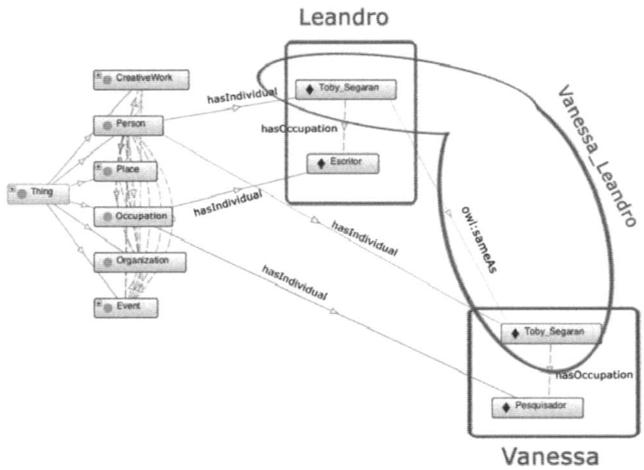

Figure 4. Ontology Aligment created by WKI method [Natale, 2017]

5. CONCLUSION

Environments that provide social interactions, among which, social networks, collaborative and / or collaborative learning and knowledge management systems, manipulate a large amount of data and heterogeneous resources. Creating ontologies as a representation mechanism of each user's knowledge and executing processes to establish alignments of these ontologies provide a better usability of such tools. For social bonds it can be created from relevant information to each user.

Negotiating the meaning of concepts among users for the establishment of interlanguages also enables the semantic integration of data repositories and heterogeneous resources based on higher-level ontologies. In this way it is possible to establish a dynamic semantic network between the different actors (human beings or systems) connected in a collaborative environment, allowing the sharing of multimedia resources through more relevant mechanisms in comparison to the simple search for coincidence of terms. This type of integration enables, through an ontological integration, the collaborative creation of a global ontology derived from local ontologies. This global ontology begins to be refined and evolves as local ontologies also evolve and, in this way, the interlanguage is broadened.

This model can be explored in future projects, analyzing the use of different tools and formats for the representation of knowledge. The use of only OWL and RDF languages to implement the metadata of a repository can be disadvantageous when implementing a project. This difficulty is associated with the mechanism required to access the repository, not following a traditional model such as databases. In this way future projects should explore new forms of knowledge representation and access to this data. Thus it will also be possible to measure the quality that each type of iteration provides for the integration of data repositories and resources.

REFERENCES

Asiaee, A. H., Minning, T., Doshi, P., and Tarleton, R. L. (2015). A framework for ontology-based question answering with application to parasite immunology. Journal of biomedical semantics, 6(1):31.

Berners-Lee, T. and Hendler, J. (2001). Publishing on the semantic web. Nature, 410(6832):1023–1024.

Bernstein, P. A. and Haas, L. M. (2008). Information integration in the enterprise. Communications of the ACM, 51(9):72–79.

Bodenreider, O. (2004). The unified medical language system (umls): integrating biomedical terminology. Nucleic acids research, 32(suppl 1):D267–D270.

Brandão, M. A., Moro, M. M., Lopes, G. R., and Oliveira, J. P. (2013). Using link
semantics to recommend collaborations in academic social networks. In Proceedings of the 22nd International Conference on World Wide Web, pages 833–840. ACM.

Brasil and ONU (2008). Programa das nações unidas para o meio ambiente.

Ding, G., Wang, G., Fan, C., and Chen, S. (2015). Schema matching based on source codes. In International Conference on Database Systems for Advanced Applications, pages 86–97. Springer.

Ehrig, M. (2006). Ontology alignment: bridging the semantic gap, volume 4. Springer Science & Business Media.

Euzenat, J. and Shvaiko, P. (2013). Classifications of ontology matching techniques. In Ontology matching, pages 73–84. Springer.

Freitas, C., Nedel, L. P., Galante, R., Lamb, L. C., Spritzer, A. S., Fujii, S., de Oliveira,
J. P. M., Araújo, R. M., and Moro, M. M. (2008). Extração de conhecimento e análise visual de redes sociais. SEMISH-Seminário Integrado de Software e Hardware, Belém do Pará, Brasil, SBC, pages 106–120.

Gruber, T. R. et al. (1993). A translation approach to portable ontology specifications. Knowledge acquisition, 5(2): 199–220.

Halevy, A. Y., Ashish, N., Bitton, D., Carey, M., Draper, D., Pollock, J., Rosenthal, A., and Sikka, V. (2005). Enterprise information integration: successes, challenges and controversies. In Proceedings of the 2005 ACM SIGMOD international conference on Management of data, pages 778–787. ACM.

Hong, J.-H. and Kuo, C.-L. (2015). A semi-automatic lightweight ontology bridging for the semantic integration of cross-domain geospatial information. International Journal of Geographical Information Science, 29(12):2223–2247.

Ibrahim, N. Y., Mokhtar, S. A., and Harb, H. M. (2013). Towards an ontology based integrated framework for semantic web. arXiv preprint arXiv:1305.7058.

Kachroudi, M., Chelbi, A., Souid, H., and Yahia, S. B. (2015). Fiona: A framework for indirect ontology alignment. In International Symposium on Methodologies for Intelligent Systems, pages 224–229. Springer.

Klein, M. (2001). Combining and relating ontologies: an analysis of problems and solutions. In IJCAI-2001 Workshop on ontologies and information sharing, pages 53–62. USA.

Lambrix, P. and Tan, H. (2011). Sambo-a system for aligning and merging biomedical ontologies. Web Semantics: Science, Services and Agents on the World Wide Web, 4(3).

Leme, L. A. P. P., Renso, C., Nunes, B. P., Lopes, G. R., Casanova, M. A., and Vidal, V. P. (2016). Searching for data sources for the semantic enrichment of trajectories. In International Conference on Web Information Systems Engineering, pages 238–246. Springer.

Loia, V., Fenza, G., De Maio, C., and Salerno, S. (2013). Hybrid methodologies to foster ontology-based knowledge management platform. In Intelligent Agent (IA), 2013 IEEE Symposium on, pages 36–43. IEEE.

Monclar, R., Tecla, A., Oliveira, J., and de Souza, J. M. (2009). Mek: Using spatial–temporal information to improve social networks and knowledge dissemination. Information Sciences, 179(15):2524–2537.

Natale, L. P. (2017). Busca e Compartilhamento de Recursos Multim´ıdia em Redes Sociais Ontológicas. PhD thesis, Universidade Presbiteriana Mackenzie.

Natale, L. P. et al. (2008). Utilização de banco de dados ontológicos e an´alise de redes sociais de cidadãos em sistemas de governo eletr^onico.

Natale, L. P. and Omar, N. (2013). Utilizac¸ ˜ao de bancos de dados ontológicos em integração de bases de dados heterog^eneas. In Proceedings of International Conference on Engineering and Computer Education, volume 8, pages 292–296.

Natale, L. P. and Omar, N. (2016). Knowledge integration in collaborative environments using supervised ontological alignment. In International Conference on Intelligent Systems Design and Applications, pages 945–954. Springer.

Nolasco, D. and Oliveira, J. (2016). Detecting knowledge innovation through automatic topic labeling on scholar data. In System Sciences (HICSS), 2016 49th Hawaii International Conference on, pages 358–367. IEEE.

Noy, N. F. and Musen, M. A. (1999). Smart: Automated support for ontology merging and alignment. In Proc. of the 12th Workshop on Knowledge Acquisition, Modelling, and Management (KAW'99), Banf, Canada.

Otero-Cerdeira, L., Rodríguez-Martínez, F. J., and Gómez-Rodríguez, A. (2015). Ontology matching: A literature review. Expert Systems with Applications, 42(2):949–971.

Seligman, L., Mork, P., Halevy, A., Smith, K., Carey, M. J., Chen, K., Wolf, C., Madhavan, J., Kannan, A., and Burdick, D. (2010). Openii: an open source information integration toolkit. In Proceedings of the 2010 ACM SIGMOD International Conference on Management of data, pages 1057–1060. ACM.

Shklovski, I., Barkhuus, L., Bornoe, N., and Kaye, J. (2015). Friendship maintenance in the digital age: Applying a relational lens to online social interaction. In Proceedings of the 18th ACM Conference on Computer Supported CooperativeWork & Social Computing, pages 1477–1487. ACM.

Shvaiko, P. and Euzenat, J. (2013). Ontology matching: state of the art and future challenges. IEEE Transactions on knowledge and data engineering, 25(1):158–176.

Steve, G., Gangemi, A., and Pisanelli, D. M. (1997). Integrating medical terminologies with onions methodology.

Stumme, G. and Maedche, A. (2001). Fca-merge: Bottom-up merging of ontologies. In IJCAI, volume 1, pages 225–230.

Suchanek, F. M., Abiteboul, S., and Senellart, P. (2011). Paris: Probabilistic alignment of relations, instances, and schema. Proceedings of the VLDB Endowment, 5(3):157–168.

Uschold, M. and Gruninger, M. (1996). Ontologies: Principles, methods and applications. The knowledge engineering review, 11(02):93–136.

Wijaya, D., Talukdar, P. P., and Mitchell, T. (2013). Pidgin: ontology alignment using web text as interlingua. In Proceedings of the 22nd ACM international conference on Information & Knowledge Management, pages 589–598. ACM.

VALUE CREATION THROUGH RELATIONSHIPS BUILDING ON PRIVATE AND PUBLIC SOCIAL MEDIA

Maxim Wolf[1], Julian Sims[1] and Huadong Yang[2]
[1]*Birkbeck, University of London, UK*
[2]*University of Liverpool, UK*

ABSTRACT

The qualitative multiple case study paper has two aims. One is the discussion of theoretical approach to theory building in Information Systems, specifically the power of Actor Network Theory in explaining IT and IS-use phenomena. The second aim is the investigation of "bottom-up" social media-use impact on traditionally "top-down" communication processes within Human Resource Management in organisations. The paper introduces a qualitative multiple case study which discusses actant networks – their emergence, maintenance and extensions within three organisations. The emergent networks in each case are compared and discussed from the view-point of value creation. The finding suggest that complex interconnected and dynamic networks result in greater potential for value generation than hereto assumed managed and controlled communication flows.

KEYWORDS

Social Media, Actor Network Theory, Case Study, Theory Building, Human Resource Management

1. INTRODUCTION

There are many papers discussing what constitutes theory, makes a good theory, how to build theory and how theory is applied, enhanced and created in the field of Information Systems (DiMaggio, 1995; Eisenhardt, 1989; Fox, 2000; Freese, 1980; Gregor, 2006; Merton, 1968; Sutton & Staw, 1995; Weick, 1989; Whetten, 1989).

This paper is concerned with theoretical foundations and practical implications for building theory in Information Systems (IS). It is using a multiple case study undertaken as parts of PhD research project investigating social media-use in Human Resource Management (HRM) process within three organisations to demonstrate the application of Actor Network Theory (ANT) for theory development.

HRM traditionally relies on top-down communication with employees (Ostroff & Bowen, 2016). Social media challenges these communication flows because of its "bottom-up"-use. The research is motivated by the question how bottom-up social media-use impacts on top-down HR communications.

The main contributions of the paper are three-fold: first, as one of first papers it applies ANT as an explanatory lens in social media research; second, extending theory on social media-use in organisations and challenging established top-down approach to communications; finally, practical implications for managers showing how social media can be used to create value by extending inter- and intra-organisational networks.

The contribution of (social) sciences lies in highlighting and explaining the genesis of relationships which influence actions and perspectives (Weick, 1989).

This paper adopts a *performative* view on IT-use as a process of social interactions (Cecez-Kecmanovic, Kautz, & Abrahall, 2014; Giddens, 1984; Jones & Karsten, 2008; Orlikowski & Scott, 2008; Sutton & Staw, 1995) and argues that ANT provides a valuable lens for understanding how IT-use and its outcomes are performed.

2. ANT

Actor-network theory goes beyond analysis of intra-human relationships and introduces non-human actors and relationships between all of these actors explain the "very nature of the society" (Latour, 1996, p. 369) thus assuming a socio-material nature of societies (Cecez-Kecmanovic et al., 2014). It focuses on the practices and actions of actants which build and maintain connections and paths between them (Fox, 2000).

The two defining terms "actor" and "network" are a confusing choice, especially in the domain of IS, where "actor" is often assumed to be a human (or a group) and "network" is understood as intra-connected set of entities (e.g. computer or social networks). An *Actor (or Actant)* in ANT is anyone or anything that can initiate or perform actions, independent of the presence or absence of motivation, free will or force. Ontologically, ANT assumes a "networky" nature of actants who build network chains to achieve certain ends. A *Network* in ANT allows connections between human and non-human actants beyond social networks (Latour, 1996).

Methodologically ANT is concerned with *how* societies are enacted through creation, maintenance and modifications of connections (Fox, 2000). The actor-networks are analysed through their length and density. ANT does not provide a differentiated picture in terms of connection strength, stability and "distance" (Latour, 1996). Applications of ANT neither require nor assume ANT to be the sole methodological framework used in a research project (Cecez-Kecmanovic et al., 2014). Other theories e.g. Critical Realism (Allen, Brown, Karanasios, & Norman, 2013), Communities of Practice Theory (Fox, 2000), or Social Exchange Theory (Emerson, 1976) provide tools for enriching ANT.

Application on ANT starts with the identification of *What* is the phenomenon and what properties, features and relationships make up the phenomenon. Once the argument for inclusion of concepts and variables in the theory has been made, the "arrows to connect the boxes" (Whetten, 1989, p. 491) need to be drawn. The ANT theorising process follows the connection paths to identify "networks" of connections building a more complex picture over time (Freese, 1980). This process aims at identifying the multidimensional connections, but not the strength or distance of these connections (Latour, 1996). In raw-ANT networks are dichotomous – actants are either connected or not, a network either exists or it does not.

The second vital element of theory is the *explanation*. Whetten (1989) argues that herein lies the difference between data and theory – data describe, theory explains. ANT questions the "organisation" as unit of analysis, instead, (non-) human actants and their interconnections become the focus. The theory is then aimed at explaining and predicting networks through description of *what* networks exist and *how* they grow (Fox, 2000).

3. ANT IN INFORMATION SYSTEMS RESEARCH

The domain of HRM is concerned with establishing and maintaining communications between management and employees, with the aim of creating a consensus about the expected employee behaviours in exchange for pay and benefits (Ostroff & Bowen, 2016). Social Media created new ways of communication, content creation and consumption, and changed social interactions around the world (Oestreicher-Singer & Zalmanson, 2013).

The aim of the study was to understand why some organisations leverage SNS to engage their employees in a dialogue, while others are failing or refusing to do so. The research project involved three large multinational organisations in the UK. The data was collected through semi-structured interviews with managers and employees. The interviews were transcribed and analysed using a qualitative data analysis tool NVivo.

Where, When and Who – the case studies settings

From two pilot case studies and literature (Wolf, Sims, & Yang, 2014), the initial framework assumed investigation of dialogic communication between Employer and Employees.

Dialogue assumes a bi-directional flow of communications, so that given two "participants" four types of engagement can be constructed (Figure 1): 1) both groups are engaged (social enterprise), 2) engaged employees, 3) neither group is engaged, and 4) engaged employer. These types represent "ideal types", and are, of course, non-existent in real life social settings (Freese, 1980).

Three organisations from squares 1, 2 and 4 have been selected and qualitative case studies in each of the organisations have been conducted (Wolf, Sims, & Yang, 2015). Each case study involved (1) data collection from public websites and (2) a series of 5-6 interviews.

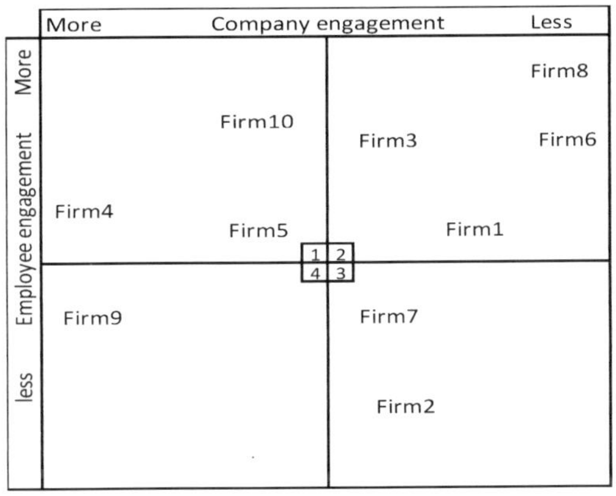

Figure 1. Social Media Engagement: Selection Matrix

Case 1: UKBank is an internationally operating financial services company with headquarters in London. Most the interviews were conducted in and with employees from the head office. The main tools used are Avature (a CRM-like system) for selection and attraction, and an internally developed chat. Externally, LinkedIn is used by recruiters, employees and alumni for attraction, broadcast and "socializing".

Case 2: UKConsulting is a technology consulting firm. The case study focused on the London office. There is a plethora of internal social media tools (from chat clients, to blogs and Facebook-like personal pages) used internally, as well as use of LinkedIn by managers, recruiters and employees.

Case 3: UKOutsourcing is a services company with contracts in several areas. The head office functions are distributed across the UK. Employees from London and Birmingham were involved in the study. An internal communication platform – Yammer is being used for inter and intra-team communications, but not to the expected extent. Externally, it is company policy to "monitor but not to engage" on twitter and co.

What – Social Media use in HRM – definitions and actants

Social Media has been defined differently in a variety of papers (Oestreicher-Singer & Zalmanson, 2013). Boyd and Ellison (2008) define "Social Networking Sites" (SNS) as web applications where (1) within a bounded system (2) connections between users are made explicit and (3) are traversable. Kaplan and Haenlein (2010) define Social Media as internet-based applications which allow creation of User Generated Content. In this paper, Social Media are defined to encapsulate previous definitions. First, Social Media require internet/network connectivity. Second, Social Media require combination of technologies such as mobiles, and software applications. Third, Social Media support interactions through content generation and sharing. Finally, these technologies and content are shared openly and available to a broad audience at low cost. Thus Social Media, is understood as an Information System which is created from a set of interconnected and integrated technologies, which are built on the technological foundation of media-rich internet technologies and on the ideological foundation of openness and transparency. The terms Social Networking Sites (SNS) and "Social Media" are used interchangeably.

HRM is concerned with the search for the source of competitive advantage (Barney, 1991; Guest, 2011; Miles & Muuka, 2011). Ostroff and Bowen (2016) describe HRM as something organisations "do": communications between the employer and employees. Focusing on the top-down message delivery that a (communication) strong system is high on consistency, consensus and distinctiveness.

A *distinctive* message would be sent from higher hierarchy levels. Additionally, *distinctiveness* is supported by utilisation of the media and technology to reach relevant audiences (Billington & Billington, 2012; Kaplan & Haenlein, 2010), subject matter expertise (Fieseler, Hoffmann, & Meckel, 2010), and strong emotional binding (Leonardi, Huysman, & Steinfeld, 2013).

Consistency implies consistency in space and over time. Consistency over time requires that the same content to be presented to potential, current and former employees (Ostroff & Bowen, 2016). The spatial dimension of consistency refers to organisational hierarchy, i.e. definition of goals and values by strategic management, communication and implementation of practices at mid-management level, and execution at the shop-floor-level (Boxall & Macky, 2009; Wright & McMahan, 1994).

Consensus is a shared understanding of a message (Edwards, 2010) and results in increased organisational performance (Sanders & Yang, 2015). Consensus is established at two levels – at inter-personal level among senders and recipients (Ostroff & Bowen, 2016) and at process level, through integration of the message content into activities (Kent & Taylor, 1998; Lawler, 1988; Walton, 1985). Bi-directional communication and information exchange, including provisions for employee voice, are paramount for consensus building and establishing of a shared understanding (Miles & Muuka, 2011; Ostroff & Bowen, 2016).

As this research is looking at levels of employees / management-sponsored engagement on Social Media, *engagement* is a bi-directional exchange of content. A "*management-sponsored*" actor is someone who acts with the permission and on-behalf of the management. This includes CEOs blogs, corporate twitter-accounts, and official LinkedIn pages.

Actants in the context of this paper have been identified as part of the data analysis. The human actors can be broadly grouped into two categories – those acting on their own behalf: Employees (former, current and potential), and those acting on behalf or in the name of the management: Managers and HR employees. The groups within each category differ in their behaviours and in their intentions.

Employees derive personal value from Social Media-use. They build, own and maintain personal relationships and act intentionally. Each group differentiates from the other by level of access and motivation for SNS-use. Employees (and Alumni) have access to internal SNS, candidates have no access. Employees use SNS to progress within the organisations (e.g. by accessing and amassing knowledge) and to maintain relationships with alumni. Alumni are driven by desire to maintain social contacts with their ex-colleagues. Candidates are motivated by the prospect of acquiring a position within the organisation.

Managers and HR professionals use SNS for the benefit of the organisation: Managers to promote corporate values and strategy, HR professionals to recruit and retain employees, or to create an "employer brand". The relationships are built "on behalf of" the organisations and are maintained even after an individual has left or changed roles. It is acknowledged that people working in HR are also employees. Whenever they act as such, they are recognised as belonging to the first category of human actors. This duality of individual action adds an interesting dimension to the complexity of the analysis and will be discussed further in this section.

As non-human actants the paper focuses on Public and Private SNS. The relationships and attitudes of human actors towards public and private SNS vary, as do constraints on who can access these SNS and how management supports and suppresses their use. This dimension of "openness and transparency" is impeded by the degree of access, (lack of) support afforded by private and public SNSs, and management influence.

Public SNS are available to everyone within and outside the organisation. Employees, HR and all other groups can communicate openly. For example, a job posted on the company's LinkedIn – page can be shared by employees with their contacts, can be commented on, candidates can ask questions, and HR can refer to it when talking to potential applicants. The SNS as "independent" actant provides a set of "features" which enable and restrain relationship building. For example, LinkedIn allows creation of "closed" groups, so that e.g. only employees and alumni can access the information published there, thus limiting the audience and number of contributors (i.e. "openness and transparency"). Additionally, the "reputation" of a platform influences its acceptance. Facebook is viewed as a "Social Media" and LinkedIn as a "professional tool": this implicitly sanctions access to the latter and discourages access to former. The audiences for different SNSs, as well as the responsibilities for corporate accounts within organisations vary. LinkedIn is a "recruitment tool" is "controlled" by HR, twitter and YouTube are "marketing tools" and are "managed" by Marketing.

How – Rhetorical Practices and Dialogue on Social Media

To achieve *consistency* alignment of HR communications at strategic level and top-down coordination are necessary (Ostroff & Bowen, 2016). Communications coming from a higher hierarchical level within organisations stand out and are more *distinctive*. However, feedback mechanisms need to be provided, to validate understanding of the message content and *consensus* among the recipients. As long as the management retains control over communication channels, such top-down approach might be possible. Social Media makes limiting access to communication channels, censorship of content and distinctiveness of messages difficult. The top-down control of communication channels (Figure 2) has rapidly changed.

Huang, Baptista, and Galliers (2013) noted that organisations lose control over the rhetorical resources, with boundaries between the rhetor and the audience becoming blurred. In case of Social Media-use in HR new audiences (Alumni and Candidates) are entering the space of corporate communications (Figure 2).

Social Media-use levels the playing field and gives employees more power and control about what is being said. This supports the creation of a *dialogue* – a conversation in which a power balance between all participating parties is maintained (Kent & Taylor, 1998). The idea of the balance of power goes back to Habermas' ideal speech situation which requires all parties to be true to themselves, have the same opportunity to participate and equal power to influence others, and also allows every statement to be questioned and debated (Leeper, 1996). How can SNS be used by the actants to create networks which support dialogue?

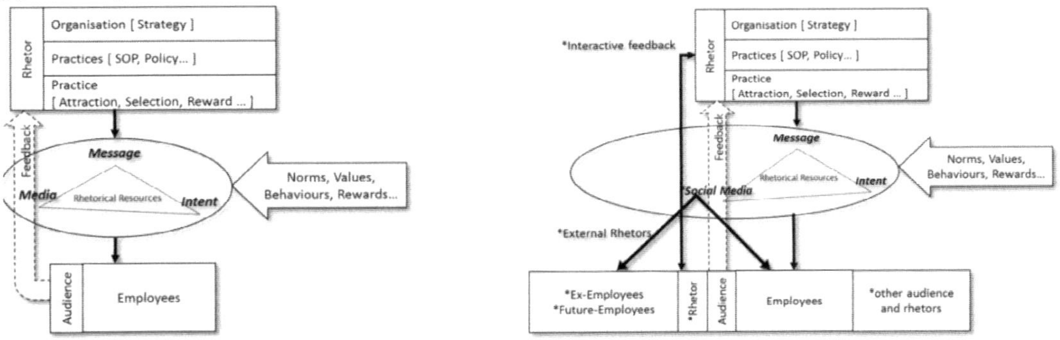

Figure 1. Changing Internal Rhetorical Practices: before and after Social Media (adapted from Huang et al., 2013)

Employee Networks are complex networks within and outside of organisations. The relationships within the organisations are three-dimensional: relationships on a professional level among employees, on a sub-ordinate level towards the management (or "the organisation"), and on the technological level with SNS.

Relationships between employees are based around the use of internal SNS. The prevalent argument for using internal SNS is the "ease of use" and "connectedness" – specifically teams working remotely report SNS-use allows them to "feel like a team". The applications are wide-ranging: from sharing documentation to organising internal events. Collaborative approaches include internal Wiki-Pages and open discussion and Q&A forums. In only one case the employees actively created content not project/product related content on internal SNS. In another case, employees refused to engage in content creation despite manager's encouragement.

The main motivation for SNS-use is "getting the job done": using internal SNS as productivity tools.

External SNS-use is motivated by maintaining relationships with colleagues and finding new employment.

Recruiter Networks are created on behalf of the organisation to engage with candidates.

Recruiters in all three organisations are using LinkedIn to discover information and to source candidates. Recruiters perceive LinkedIn as a productivity tool which they use because they believe it gives them additional value and improved performance. LinkedIn as an "actor" appeals to recruiters as an "enabler".

The recruiters create temporary relationships with potential candidates on LinkedIn. No one reported that these relationships would be maintained after a candidate has been hired. Much of the communication is in a "broadcast" mode – sharing job postings and other firm-relevant information to attract candidates. Notably, no recruiter shared the information on internal SNS. The content created and shared by recruiters is intended for the "outside" public, current employees are "expected" to discover that information on public SNS.

Manager Networks on internal social media are used to broadcast management messages. In one case HR unsuccessfully tried to encourage managers posting on LinkedIn to showcase the organisation's agenda.

HR managers encourage the use of private and public SNS, but have no strong relationship to either. Generally, top-managers appear to attribute some value to SNS-use while not using the tools themselves.

Why – Explaining value in Social Media use in HRM

The focus of the paper is the value creation through dialogue within the context of HMR as a communication system (Ostroff & Bowen, 2016). Dialogue between management and employees leads to a better agreement on the content of the messages (Sanders & Yang, 2015). The analysis therefore focuses on why in certain settings bi-directional communications emerge on SNS and fail in others. In an idealised situation, the relationships between actants are complex, direct relationships are re-enforced through use of SNS (Figure 3).

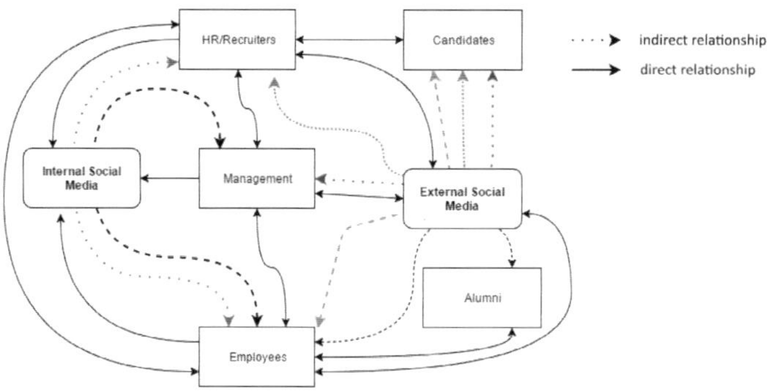

Figure 2. Relationships in HRM Actor-Network

External SNS provide transparent access to relevant information to different audiences, which contributes to creation of dialogue (Leonardi et al., 2013). It would connect employees, candidates, alumni, HR and management. Further, relationships between hereto unconnected actants – e.g. managers and candidates, can be created and the networks could expand further.

ANT explains social phenomena by showing how actants connect, and these connections are explaining the complex intra-social settings. However, ANT is not a valid tool to differentiate connections and to assess them other than dichotomously, other theories are required to make these differentiation (Latour, 1996).

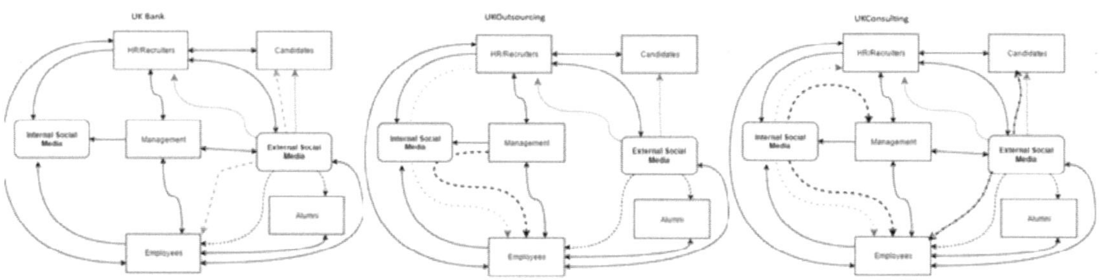

Figure 3. Organisation Networks: UKBank, UKConsulting, UKOutsourcing

UKBank the employees connect via SNS. They leverage internal and external tools to maintain and create connections with other employees, alumni and candidates (Figure 4). Management relies on the "broadcasting" platform (to which employees have no access) to inform the candidates about job offerings. Recruiters use SNS deviating from policy: instead of broadcasting jobs, they use SNS to personally connect with candidates. Employees use LinkedIn to create open groups which are not managed or sanctioned by the organisation.

Internal SNS are not leveraged by HR or management. It is "nothing but a messenger tool", there is no perceived additional value in using the tools for HR related communications.

UKConsulting the network is more complex (Figure 4). The firm is providing consultancy services in Social Media-use, and use of all types of SNS is encouraged. Management uses internal SNS to broadcast new policies, products, to allow Q&A sessions, etc. Employees leverage internal SNS to share and access product knowledge. Several tools are provided internally, there is mandatory training on how to use these tools.

Externally, LinkedIn is used by candidates, recruiters, employees and alumni to engage and maintain relationships. Groups on LinkedIn are maintained and managed on behalf of the management.

UKOutsourcing presents a picture different from the first two cases (Figure 4). The managers/employee relationships are top-down one-way. Only one tenth of employees are participating on an internal SNS. Management and HR are creating content and encouraging participation, however without adequate response.

Externally, LinkedIn is used to source candidates, but many recruiters do not engage with them online. Employees maintain their connections with alumni. There is no support for LinkedIn-use and managers are refusing to participate in employer-branding on SNS. The policy is: "we monitor, but do not engage".

4. DISCUSSION

Human Resource Management is about "resources" – creating valuable, rare and immutable configurations to achieve competitive advantage (Barney, 1991). Looking at the different associations in the three case studies, accessing similar internal, and the same external SNS: why are different associations created in each case?

From the management perspective, Social Media-use can increase employer brand (Juntunen, Juntunen, & Autere, 2012), innovation within the workforce (Wilson & Daniel, 2007), and create new value (Füller, Mühlbacher, Matzler, & Jawecki, 2009). These motivate management to support and encourage Social Media use, but from the third case study it is obviously not enough to motivate employees to participate in a dialogue with the management and to contribute to the creation of the consensus.

Agreeing with Huang et al. (2013), we found that social media allows new rhetors to enter the scene "bottom-up" without support from the management. Employees, alumni and candidates are accepting a more active, participative role in content creation and leverage the freely available public social media sites to engage, as do recruiters when it comes to their choice of communication media with the candidates.

UKConsulting, by encouraging use of social media, by providing training and removing limitations on what platforms can be used and are being used by both management (and HR) and employees, can create more complex and extensive associations between the multitude of actors involved.

Applying ANT as an analytical framework, the study showed that organisations that were identified as more "engaged" – that is management being more transparent in their communication flows, offering voice to employees and engaging them in the ongoing dialogue (which arguably leads to a stronger HR system) can create more complex and sophisticated networks and to support multiple pathways connecting actants. On the contrary, organisations with fewer paths and associations were characterised by weaker, less consistent and opaque communications and thus weaker HR systems.

Contrary to the established HR management view that communications require top-down management and control to deliver value, this study shows that complex, fuzzy, uncontrolled and dynamic networks create greater value than managed "lean" communication networks.

This paper focused only on "value" of social media-use as reported by the interviewees. Further research into linking complexity of actor networks to HRM outcomes (e.g. retention) would further benefit our understanding of social media impacts on HRM.

It is acknowledged that the three case studies cover but a small portion of organisations and that the studies provide a snapshot view. Longitudinal studies and studies in other organisations would expand and confirm (or possibly challenge) the findings from this study.

REFERENCES

Allen, D. K., Brown, A., Karanasios, S., & Norman, A. (2013). How Should Technology-Mediated Organizational Change Be Explained? A Comparison of the Contributions of Critical Realism and Activity Theory. *MIS Quarterly, 37*(3), 835-854.

Barney, J. (1991). Firm Resources and Sustained Competitive Advantage. *Journal of Management, 17*(1), 99-121.

Billington, M. G., & Billington, P. J. (2012). Social Media Tools for Leaders and Managers. *Journal of Leadership, Accountability and Ethics, 9*(6), 11-19.

Boxall, P., & Macky, K. (2009). Research and theory on high performance work systems: progressing the high-involvement stream. *Human Resource Management Journal, 19*(1), 3-23.

Boyd, D. M., & Ellison, N. B. (2008). Social Network Sites: Definition, History, and Scholarship. *Journal of Computer-Mediated Communication, 13*, 210-230.

Cecez-Kecmanovic, D., Kautz, K., & Abrahall, R. (2014). Reframing success and failure of information systems: a performative perspective. *MIS Quarterly, 38*(2), 561-588.

DiMaggio, P. J. (1995). Comments on" What theory is not". *Administrative science quarterly, 40*(3), 391-397.

Edwards, M. R. (2010). An integrative review of employer branding and OB theory. *Personnel Review, 39*(1), 5-23.

Eisenhardt, K. M. (1989). Building Theories from Case Study Research. *Academy of Management, 14*(4), 532-550.

Emerson, R. M. (1976). Social exchange theory. *Annual Review of Sociology*, 335-362.

Fieseler, C., Hoffmann, C. P., & Meckel, M. (2010). CSR 2.0 - Die Kommuniation von Nachhaltigkeit in Sozialen Medien. *Marketing Review St. Gallen, 27*(5), 22-26.

Fox, S. (2000). Communities Of Practice, Foucault And Actor Network Therory. *Journal of Management Studies, 37*(6), 853-868.

Freese, L. (1980). Formal theorizing. *Annual Review of Sociology*, 187-212.

Füller, J., Mühlbacher, H., Matzler, K., & Jawecki, G. (2009). Consumer empowerment through internet-based co-creation. *Journal of Management Information Systems, 26*(3), 71-102.

Giddens, A. (1984). *The Constitution of Society: Outline of the Theory of Structuration*: University of California Press.

Gregor, S. (2006). The nature of theory in information systems. *MIS Quarterly*, 611-642.

Guest, D. E. (2011). Human resource management and performance: still searching for some answers. *Human Resource Management Journal, 21*(1), 3-13.

Huang, J., Baptista, J., & Galliers, R. D. (2013). Reconceptualizing rhetorical practices in organizations: The impact of social media on internal communications. *Information and Management, 50*(2), 112-124.

Jones, M. R., & Karsten, H. (2008). Giddens's Structuration Theory and Information Systems Research. *MIS Quarterly, 32*(1), 127-157.

Juntunen, M., Juntunen, J., & Autere, V. (2012). Recruits/' Corporate Brand Co-creation Experiences of the Finnish Military Forces. *Corp Reputation Rev, 15*(2), 88-104.

Kaplan, A. M., & Haenlein, M. (2010). Users of the world, unite! The challenges and opportunities of Social Media. *Business Horizons, 53*(1), 59—68.

Kent, M. L., & Taylor, M. (1998). Building Dialogic Relationships Through the World Wide Web. *Public Relations Review, 24*(3), 321-334.

Latour, B. (1996). On actor-network theory: a few clarifications. *Soziale welt*, 369-381.

Lawler, E. E., III. (1988). Choosing An Involvement Strategy. *The Academy of Management Executive, 2*(3), 197-204.

Leeper, R. V. (1996). Moral objectivity, Jurgen Habermas's discourse ethics, and public relations. *Public Relations Review, 22*(2), 133-150.

Leonardi, P. M., Huysman, M., & Steinfeld, C. (2013). Enterprise Social Media: Definition, History, and Prospects for the Study of Social Technologies in Organizations. *Journal of Computer-Mediated Communication, 19*, 1-19.

Merton, R. K. (1968). *Social theory and social structure*: Simon and Schuster.

Miles, S. J., & Muuka, G. N. (2011). Employee choice of voice: a new workplace dynamic. *Journal of Applied Business Research (JABR), 27*(4), 91-104.

Oestreicher-Singer, G., & Zalmanson, L. (2013). Content or community? A digital business strategy for content providers in the social age. *MIS Quarterly, 37*(2), 591-616.

Orlikowski, W. J., & Scott, S. V. (2008). Sociomateriality:Challenging the Separation of Technology, Work and Organization. *The Academy of Management Annals, 2*(1), 433-474.

Ostroff, C., & Bowen, D. E. (2016). Reflections on the 2014 decade award: Is there strength in the construct of HR system strength? *Academy of Management Review, 41*(2), 196-214.

Sanders, K., & Yang, H. (2015). The HRM Process Approach: The Influence of Employees' Attribution to Explain the HRM-Performance Relationship. *Human Resource Management.*

Sutton, R. I., & Staw, B. M. (1995). What theory is not. *Administrative science quarterly*, 371-384.

Walton, R. E. (1985). From control to commitment in the workplace. *Harvard Business Review, 63*(2), 77-84.

Weick, K. E. (1989). Theory construction as disciplined imagination. *Academy of Management Review, 14*(4), 516-531.

Whetten, D. A. (1989). What Constitutes a Theoretical Contribution? *The Academy of Management Review, 14*(4), 490-495. doi:10.2307/258554

Wilson, H., & Daniel, E. (2007). The multi-channel challenge: A dynamic capability approach. *Industrial Marketing Management, 36*(1), 10-20.

Wolf, M., Sims, J., & Yang, H. (2014). *Social media utilization in human resource management.* Paper presented at the Web based communities and social Media 2014 conference (WBC 2014); 8th multi conference on computer science and information systems, Portugal, Lisbon.

Wolf, M., Sims, J., & Yang, H. (2015). *Theoretical Sampling – ALIAS: a Case selection framework for research on social media engagement.* Paper presented at the Annual Conference of the UK Academy of Information Systems, Oxford, 2015.

Wright, P. M., & McMahan, G. C., McWilliams, Abagail. (1994). Human resources and sustained competitive. *International Journal of Human Resource Management, 5*(2), 301-326.

A CONCEPTUAL FRAMEWORK OF LEARNING RELATIONSHIPS IN ONLINE COMMUNITIES

Bo Liang[1] and Debra L. Scammon[2]
[1]*Saint Vincent College, 300 Fraser Purchase Road, Latrobe, PA, USA*
[2]*University of Utah , 201 Presidents Cir, Salt Lake City, UT, USA*

ABSTRACT

A major gap in previous research in social learning in online communities is the lack of attention to the effects of relationships built among participants on the learning process. Within a thread in an online forum, posts can refer to previous posts. These connections present an opportunity to extend the learning process. We construct a conceptual framework of reference relationships. We propose that four key aspects of reference relationships are associated with the furtherance of the social learning process: engagement, sociality, and advanced levels of learning, and existence and strength of ties between posters.

KEYWORDS

Communities, social networks, social learning, reference relationship

1. INTRODUCTION

According to social learning theory, people learn in their social contexts. Previous research has found that social learning has significant effects on knowledge generation and decision making (e.g., Greene et al., 2010; Jayanti & Singh, 2009). As online communication becomes a large part of people's everyday lives, online social learning is attracting a great deal of attention among researchers (Cheung et al., 2013; Lai and Chen, 2014; Majchrzak et al., 2013; Panahi et al., 2013). A major gap in this line of research is the lack of attention to the relationships built among participants in online communities.

Following Walther (1996), we view social learning in online communities as a process in which participants not only learn from each other but also build relationships with one another through interactional activities such as making posts. Within online communities, participants create threads and within threads, participants make posts. When a post is made quoting or referring a previous post, a connection is built between the poster of the current post and that of the referenced post. Previous research in online contexts in communications and education has used message reference analysis to explore the role of reference relationships between posts in facilitating online learning (Bullen, 2007; Wise et al., 2006).

The essential feature of social learning is that people learn within social structures. This study aims to examine the factors associated with social learning in online communities. We are particularly interested in reference relationships between posters. We develop a conceptual framework that incorporates relationship measures into the understanding of social learning. Previous studies have used the number of friends listed on an individual user's friend list to measure the social influence of a user on other members in online communities. We argue that influence can be better understood by exploring the interactions between users. We propose that the actual interaction between users can be demonstrated by reference relationships. We then bridge the gap between theories (tie strength theory) and practices (reference relationships of posts).

2. BODY OF PAPER

2.1 Tie Strength and Online Social Learning

Tie strength measures the strength of relationships. Granovetter (1973) proposed that two types of ties develop in social relationships: weak ties and strong ties. Strong ties develop when one person has frequent and reciprocal contacts with others whose social circles overlap (e.g., relatives, friends). Weak ties are those shared between mere acquaintances or infrequent and nonreciprocal contacts (e.g., friends of friends). Tie strength plays an important role in linking individuals within social structures. Strong ties deepen the connections between members of the social network; members connected by strong ties are trusted sources of social and emotional support. Weak ties extend the reach of social networks and lead to the discovery and dissemination of new information.

Empirical research on information diffusion through online social networks has found that weak ties are responsible for disseminating novel information (Bakshy et al., 2012). In online education, researchers have proposed that computer-supported collaborative learning (CSCL) includes two major components: effective discussion and social interaction. Effective discussion is defined as elaboration of new ideas, comments, or opinions. Social interaction plays an important role in motivating group cohesion and belonging and thus is the first step for collaborative learning (Wegerif, 1998). Kreijns and Kirschner (2002) further developed this idea and proposed a theoretical framework for the positive association of social interaction and effective discussion in the environments of CSCL.

Social learning processes are "cyclically connected and socially construed" (Jayanti and Singh, 2009, p. 1061). People identify problems, generate knowledge, and then take actions. While taking actions, they may identify new problems and begin a new round of the learning process. During this cyclical learning process, individuals interact and develop relationships with one another. In the context of online forums, it is important to determine the role that the reference relationship has in social learning. Some posts are referenced in other posts, while others are not. Whether an individual post is referenced may facilitate or inhibit the building of relationships among users in online forums. A direct dialogue between posters builds a connection facilitating the development of a relationship between the two posters. Some consumers to make multiple and reciprocal posts to others, thus building strong ties with them, whereas other consumers make only a single nonreciprocal post to others, establishing weak ties with them.

2.2 Conceptual Framework

To explore how posters engage in an online social learning, we take a dynamic view to look at the patterns of referencing others by posters in an ongoing thread (see Figure 1). Specifically, we investigate new posters' engagement in an ongoing thread and across threads in the broader community over time. We examine the content of new posts in ongoing threads. We explore the ties between new posters and the posters they reference. This study considers the development of relationships over time by focusing primarily on analysis at the poster level.

In an ongoing thread, a new post may reference the thread initiator, a responder, or the group. The decision of who to reference influences the following posts in the thread. Common sense suggests that a responder will make a new post in response to the thread initiator or the group by providing information relevant to the question proposed by the thread initiator. The more interesting reference relationships are those between new posters and responders revealed in their discussions relevant to the question advanced by the thread initiator.

We view the decision by a new poster of who to reference as an initial decision. If the decision is to reference a responder (rather than the group), then a second decision is which responder to reference, a "stranger" or a "friend". A stranger is defined as a poster by whom the new poster had not been referenced directly in the ongoing thread. In this situation, the new poster is initiating a conversation with this stranger. A friend is defined as a poster by whom the new poster had been referenced directly in the ongoing thread. In this situation, the new poster is responding to this friend. We investigate the factors that influence a new poster's decision about who to reference. In the following section, we construct propositions for the dynamic development of reference relationships. We present the definitions of key terms used in this study in Table 1.

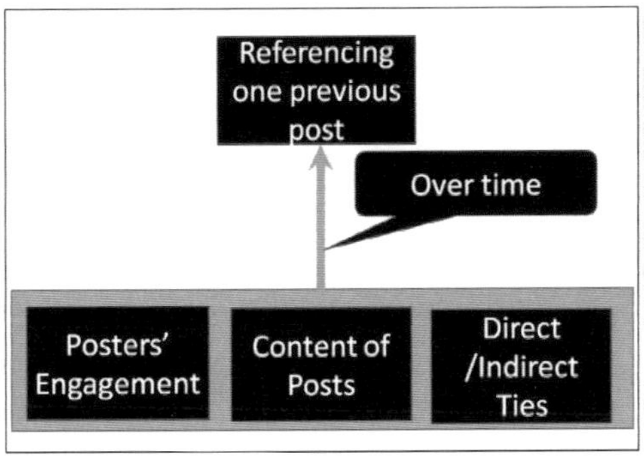

Figure 1. A conceptual framework of consumer online social learning process

Table 1. Definitions for key terms

Term	Definition
Post	A specific message made by a poster within a thread
Thread initiator	The poster who makes the first post within a thread
Responder	Any of the posters within a thread other than the thread initiator
New post	An incoming post into an ongoing thread
New poster	The poster of a new post
Referenced post	The post that a poster specifically mentions in the post
Referenced poster	The poster of a referenced post
New referenced post	The post referenced in a new post
New referenced poster	The poster of the new referenced post
Tie	A reference relationship between two posters

2.2.1 Dynamic Development of Posters' Engagement

Individuals frequently participate in multiple threads within a given community. Their activities in threads beyond the focal or ongoing thread can be a signal of their engagement in the community. Engaging in activities such as learning the rules of posting and reading and responding in threaded discussions in an online community take time and effort. Individuals may build trust by engaging in such activities. People are more willing to develop relationships with individuals whom they trust. Trust is a key mediator of the effects of relationships on learning (Wenger, 2006).

Researchers and practitioners have primarily used participation behaviors as a measure of engagement in online communities. Engaged users are defined as users who have high scores on variables such as frequency of site visit, number of page views, and number of posts made by users (e.g., Pawan et al., 2003; Ransbotham and Kane, 2011). For example, researchers have used the average number of posts per student to measure students' engagement in online threaded discussions (Pawan et al., 2003). Researchers have also used different participation behaviors to measure the level of engagement in online communities. For example, the number of threads initiated by one user is employed to measure the user's interaction with the community, whereas the number of posts made by one user is employed to measure the user's interaction with other specific users (e.g., Bateman et al., 2011).

Research suggests that a user's engagement in an online community positively predicts the user's activities and responses acquired from other users in the community. For example, the length of a poster's engagement in an online community positively predicts the number of threads read by the poster (Bateman et al., 2011). The log-in frequency of a user positively predicts the log-in frequency of this user's friends (i.e., users listed in this particular user's friend list in one community; Trusov). Research also suggests that as participants spend more time engaging in a discussion (e.g., responding to others) in an online community, they are more likely to contribute to knowledge collaboration (Rafaeli and Ariel, 2008; Tseng and Kuo, 2014).

Posters build trust of others by developing their relationships with other posters across threads in the community. We argue that a new poster's engagement in the community will be positively associated with the possibility of referencing a responder in the ongoing thread. We further argue that a poster's engagement over time in the ongoing thread indicates this poster's interest in the continued discussion in the thread. The poster with enduring engagement will be more likely to pay attention to messages posted by individual responders and thus reference the posts by individual responders. The early posters in the thread may focus more on the thread initiator, whereas the middle and latter posters may focus more on the topics discussed in which they take personal interest. Engaging in a thread longer also provides the poster more opportunities to build trust with the group and members in the group. Therefore, our first proposition is

Proposition 1: A new poster will reference a specific responder,

a: when the new poster has higher engagement in the community;

b: when the new poster has higher engagement in the ongoing thread.

In an online learning community, students tend to initiate a discussion when they have formed impressions of the community and members in the community. These impressions are formed through engagement in online activities in the community (Kreijns and Kirschner, 2001). Referencing a stranger indicates the new poster's intention to initiate a new conversation with a responder. We expect this will be more likely when the new poster has higher engagement with the community and with the ongoing thread. Therefore, our second proposition is

Proposition 2: A new poster will reference a stranger,

a. when the new poster has higher engagement in the community;

b. when the new poster has higher engagement in the ongoing thread.

2.2.2 Dynamic Development of Sociality and Advanced Learning

Jayanti and Singh (2009) articulate the consumer social learning process as a progressive inquiry-action process including four elements, (1) problem-focused experience, (2) inquiry, (3) knowledge generation (i.e., reflecting, reframing and exploring), and (4) action-focused experience (see Figure 2). Advanced levels of learning (inquiry and knowledge generation) may invoke critical thinking and thus encourage more interactions between posters, leading to reciprocal and frequent reference relationships between posters. Research has shown that posts containing questions and factual expertise are more likely to obtain more responses from users in online communities (Adamic et al., 2008; Joyce and Kraut, 2006).

Social learning is a cyclical process (Jayanti and Singh, 2009). Communication changes as relationships develop (Walther, 1992). According to the theory of cooperative learning, one speaker tends to clarify, justify, and elaborate attitudes, opinions, and beliefs in a dialogue (offline). Researchers in online education have suggested that students develop and elaborate their ideas and opinions when they reference others' posts in online threaded discussions (Bullen, 2007; Ingram and Hathorn, 2004; Wise et al., 2006). We argue that reference relationships established through previous posts may influence the content of following posts facilitating progress toward more advanced levels of social learning (e.g., knowledge generation). Posts involved in reference relationships (being referenced by others or referencing others) are more likely to contain content indicating advanced learning steps.

Written social communication is an important component of online communities (Ellison, 2007). There are two major types of social messages in online communities, social functional messages (e.g., greetings and gratitude) and expressive messages of personal feelings and emotion (e.g., happy; Chen and Wang, 2009; Ingram and Hathorn, 2004). Previous work on online education highlights the positive role of social communication in online discussion groups (Chen and Wang, 2009; Ingram and Hathorn, 2004). Social messages are off-task but "important in creating an environment that supports collaboration, such as introductions…" (Ingram and Hathorn, 2004, p. 225). We propose that an online community is a social networking environment in which participants learn from others as they develop reference relationships with others.

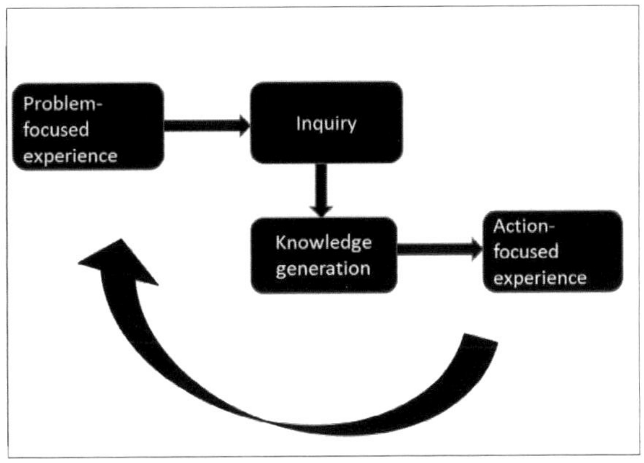

Figure 2. Consumer online social learning process

Referencing a specific responder shows that a poster is interested in not only the general topics under discussion in the ongoing thread, but also the specific topics raised by a responder. Based on the theory of reciprocity, when replying to an old friend, the poster is more likely to use social messages to demonstrate friendliness. Further, when responding to a specific responder, the poster is involved in a reciprocal dialogue with the other poster. This suggests a way of collaborative learning in which posters are exchanging more questions and knowledge. Figure 3 demonstrates a current post with a quote to a previous post on an online diabetes forum (personal information removed). In the current post, the poster provided further elaboration on the idea (diabetes self-management) posted in the previous post.

So, our third proposition is

Proposition 3: Posts that reference a responder include

a. more social statements;

b. more statements indicating advanced learning steps (e.g., inquires, knowledge).

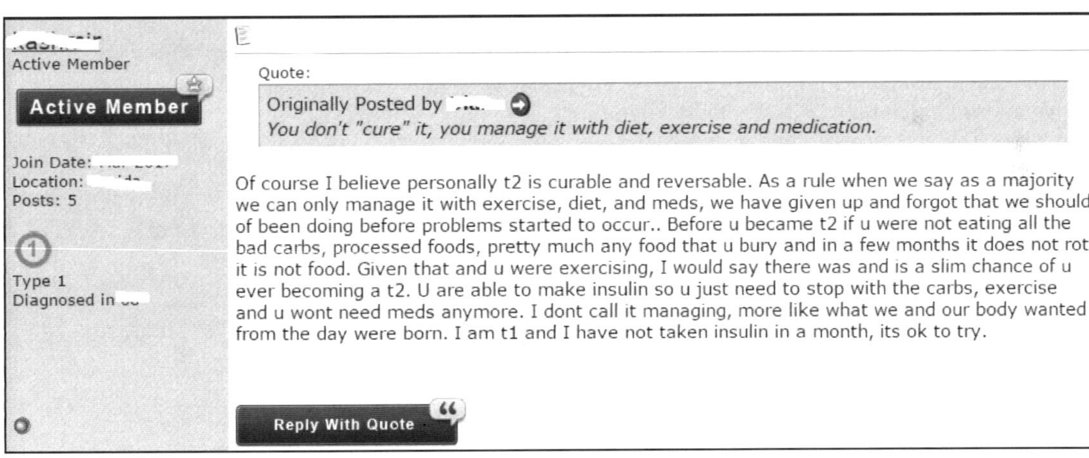

Figure 3. An example of a post with a quote for knowledge advancement

In an online community, old members create ties with new members by sending messages to the new members. In cognitive science, occasions in which more than one person is engaging in a conversation about an object are defined as joint attention. Initiating joint attention (IJT) occurs when a person directs another person's attention to the object. When the second person follows the conversation, this constitutes responding to joint attention (RJT). Previous work suggests that initiating joint attention requires greater cognitive control processes than does responding to joint attention (Redcay et al., 2012). Referencing a stranger, by whom the new poster has not been referenced in the ongoing thread, is a way to initiate a new conversation.

By engaging in this new conversation, the new poster can direct others' attention to specific topics and add new ideas or opinions to the discussion in the ongoing thread. Therefore, our fourth proposition is

Proposition 4: Posts that reference a stranger include more statements indicating advanced learning steps(e.g., inquires, knowledge).

2.2.3 Dynamic development of ties

Granovetter (1983) proposed four dimensions of tie strength: amount of time, intimacy (mutual disclosure), emotional intensity, and reciprocal services. Subsequent research has identified additional dimensions such as communication reciprocity and shared. We extended the work on tie strength in the context of online threaded discussions. Ties among two posters may be built over time in any thread in the community. Ties between posters established previously in other threads may influence the reference relationship of a new post in the ongoing thread. These prior ties may establish trust between the two posters. People are more willing to acquire and disseminate information with their trusted contacts. When a new poster has ties with a new friend in other threads in the community, trust may have been established facilitating reference to that new friend.

Transitivity assumes that if a chooses b as a friend and b chooses c as a friend, a will choose c as a friend. In this relationship, b is a shared contact connecting a and c. Transitivity plays an important role in distributing knowledge and strengthening ties in social networks (Brown and Reingen, 1987). In our study, transitivity can be a thread or thread initiator. In a thread, both a and b make posts, but neither of them references the other. The thread or thread initiator is a bridge linking a and b. We define a direct tie as the accumulation of reference relationships between two posters in a thread. We define a shared tie as a relationship in which two posters make posts but do not have any referencing relationships with each other in a thread.

Ties among two posters may be built over time in any thread in the community. Ties between posters established previously in other threads may influence the reference relationship of a new post in the ongoing thread. These prior ties may establish trust between the two posters. People are more willing to acquire and disseminate information with their trusted contacts. When a new poster has ties with a new friend in other threads in the community, trust may have been established facilitating reference to a new friend, that is, to a poster with whom no previous references in the ongoing thread have been made

We use an example to illustrate the development of ties between two posters across threads in the community(see Figure 3). Posters a and b may establish a tie in thread A. In the subsequent thread B, poster a may directly reference poster b who has not directly referenced a in the current thread B. We argue that it is the familiarity or the trust built between the two posters, a and b, in the previous thread A that leads poster a to initiate a conversation with poster b in the ongoing thread B.

The strength of ties in previous threads in the community can be measured along five dimensions: coexistence, directness, recency, reciprocity, and frequency. We present the definitions of the five dimensions in Table 2.

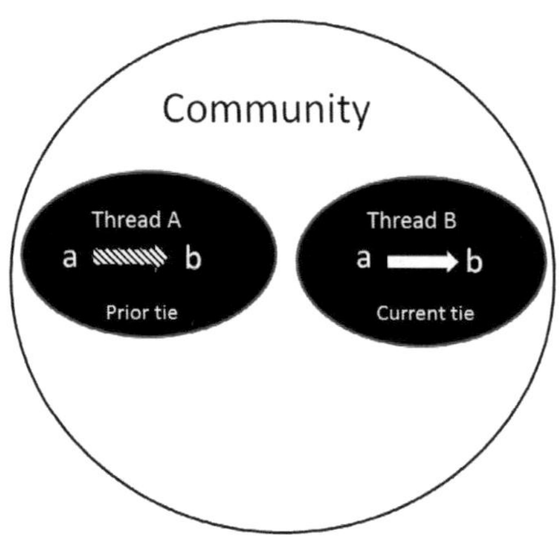

Figure 3. An example of ties in one other thread and the ongoing thread

Table 2. Definitions of dimensions of tie strength

Variables	Definition
Coexistence	whether the two posters (a and b) made posts in at least one other thread
Recency	length of time between when the most recent post was made between the two posters in one other thread and when the new post was made between them in the ongoing thread.
Directness	whether one of the two posters directly referenced the other in at least one other thread
Reciprocity	for direct ties, whether the two posters referenced each other in at least one other thread.
Frequency	for direct ties, how frequently (one time or multiple times) the two posters referenced each other in one other thread.

Strong ties lead to familiarity and trust between posters. We expect that a new poster will be more likely to reference a stranger with whom they have previously established a strong tie in other threads in the community. We propose that a strong tie (i.e., shared, direct, reciprocal, frequent, and recent ties) between two posters in one thread is positively correlated with the initiation of a conversation by one of the two posters in a subsequent thread. Therefore, our fifth proposition is

Proposition 5: A new poster who references a stranger in the ongoing thread has stronger ties with the stranger in other threads in the community than does a new poster who references a friend in the ongoing thread.

3. CONCLUSION

Social learning is a shared phenomenon. Previous research has primarily focused on how users are influenced by their online friends in terms of attitudes and behaviors (Ellison et al., 2007). A simple friend count is an insufficient metric for user influence (Trusov et al., 2010). To more fully understand how consumers learn through online social networks, we argue that it is important to understand specific features of a relationship. Our study enhances the present understanding of the mechanism of social learning in online communities by examining the pattern of referencing relationships in online learning networks, or Who-Referenced- Whom networks. From an ecological point of view, posters in one community are connected by engaging in a variety of activities in the community. A new poster's reference behavior in a specific thread is influenced by this new poster's network established in the community.

Our study demonstrates that the strength of ties between posters plays different roles at the macro and micro levels in reference relationships in ongoing threads. At the macro level, posters participate across threads in a given community. Posters' engagement in the community is demonstrated through engaging in a variety of activities such as initiating threads. These activities help posters form ties with the community. At the micro level, posters learn in one thread and establish reference relationships specific responders. Ties established in the community may drive posters to make new posts to particular responders, especially those with whom new posters have had ties in other threads. This illustrates how ties are built through the transitivity of relationships across threads.

Reference relationships are influenced not only by posters' ties established in the community demonstrated by their historical activities (e.g., engagement across threads in the community), but also revealed by the cognitive activities of participating in ongoing threads demonstrated by the content of new posts. These cognitive activities reflect an advanced step in the social learning process: knowledge generation. From this perspective, reference relationships advance learning in ongoing threads. Specifically, referencing a new friend in an ongoing thread reflects a new poster's intention to initiate a new conversation with this new friend. Such an activity may encourage the cultivation of fresh ideas and self-discovery in the learning process. In our study we assess strength of shared ties in threads other than the ongoing threads (intensity of social interactions between posters) along five dimensions: existence, directness, frequency, reciprocity, and recency.

Our study aims to provide a conceptual framework for future empirical study in consumer online social learning process. Our study suggests the potential factors related to reference relationships in an ongoing thread, including (1) posters' engagement in community activities and (2) posters' engagement in the ongoing thread, (3) ties between the new poster and new referenced poster in other threads, and (4) the content of posts reveal progressive cognitive activity advancing social learning. Future study is needed to empirically test to what extent these factor will influence referencing relationships in online communities.

REFERENCES

Adamic, L.A. et al, 2008, April. Knowledge Sharing and Yahoo Answers: Everyone Knows Something. *In Proceedings of the 17th international conference on World Wide Web*, pp. 665-674. ACM.

Bakshy, E. et al, 2012, April. The role of social networks in information diffusion. *In Proceedings of the 21st International Conference on World Wide Web*, pp. 519-528). ACM.

Bateman, P.J. et al, 2011. Research Note—the Impact of Community Commitment on Participation in Online Communities. *Information Systems Research*, 22(4), pp.841-854.

Brown, J.J. and Reingen, P.H., 1987. Social Ties and Word-of-mouth Referral Behavior. *Journal of Consumer Research*, 14(3), pp.350-362.

Bullen, M., 2007. Participation and Critical Thinking in Online University Distance Education. *International Journal of E-Learning & Distance Education*, 13(2), pp.1-32.

Chen, F.C. and Wang, T.C., 2009. Social Conversation and Effective Discussion in Online Group Learning. *Educational Technology Research and Development*, 57(5), pp.587-612.

Cheung, C.M. et al, 2013. Understanding the Continuance Intention of Knowledge Sharing in Online Communities of Practice through the Post-knowledge-sharing Evaluation Processes. *Journal of the American Society for Information Science and Technology*, 64(7), pp.1357-1374.

Ellison, N.B., 2007. Social Network Sites: Definition, History, and Scholarship. *Journal of Computer‐Mediated Communication*, 13(1), pp.210-230.

Granovetter, M.S., 1973. The Strength of Weak Ties. *American Journal of Sociology*, 78(6), pp.1360-1380.

Greene, J.A. et al, 2011. Online Social Networking by Patients with Diabetes: a Qualitative Evaluation of Communication with Facebook. *Journal of General Internal Medicine,* 26(3), pp.287-292.

Ingram, A.L. and Hathorn, L.G., 2004. Methods for Analyzing Collaboration in Online. *Online Collaborative Learning: Theory and Practice*, pp.215-241.

Jayanti, R.K. and Singh, J., 2010. Pragmatic Learning Theory: an Inquiry-action Framework for Distributed Consumer Learning in Online Communities. *Journal of Consumer Research,* 36(6), pp.1058-1081.

Kreijns, K. et al, 2002. The sociability of Computer-supported Collaborative Learning Environments. *Educational Technology & Society*, 5(1), pp.8-22.

Lai, H.M. and Chen, T.T., 2014. Knowledge Sharing in Interest Online Communities: A Comparison of Posters and Lurkers. *Computers in Human Behavior*, 35, pp.295-306.

Majchrzak, A. et al, 2013. The Contradictory Influence of Social Media Affordances on Online Communal Knowledge Sharing. *Journal of Computer-Mediated Communication*, 19(1), pp.38-55.

Pawan, F. et al, 2003. Online Learning: Patterns of Engagement and Interaction among In-service Teachers. *Language Learning & Technology*, 7(3), pp.119-140.

Panahi, S. et al, 2013. Towards Tacit Knowledge Sharing Over Social Web tools. *Journal of Knowledge Management*, 17(3), pp.379-397.

Ransbotham, S. and Kane, G.C., 2011. Membership Turnover and Collaboration Success in Online Communities: Explaining Rises and Falls from Grace in Wikipedia. *MIS Quarterly*, pp.613-627.

Rafaeli, S. and Ariel, Y., 2008. Online motivational factors: Incentives for participation and contribution in Wikipedia. *Psychological Aspects of Cyberspace: Theory, Research, Applications*, pp.243-267.

Redcay, E. et al, 2012. Look at this: the Neural Correlates of Initiating and Responding to Bids for Joint Attention. *Towards a Neuroscience of Social Interaction*, p.491.

Tseng, F.C. and Kuo, F.Y., 2014. A Study of Social Participation and Knowledge Sharing in the Teachers' Online Professional Cmmunity of Practice. *Computers & Education*, 72, pp.37-47.

Trusov, M. et al, 2010. Determining Influential Users in Internet Social Networks. *Journal of Marketing Research*, 47(4), pp.643-658.

Walther, J.B., 1996. Computer-mediated Communication: Impersonal, Interpersonal, and Hyperpersonal Interaction. *Communication Research*, 23(1), pp.3-43.

Wegerif, R., 1998. The Social Dimension of Asynchronous Learning Networks. *Journal of Asynchronous Learning Networks*, 2(1), pp.34-49.

Wenger, E. 2006. Communities of Practice: A Brief Introduction. Retrieved from http://www.ewenger.com/theory/index.htm

Wise, K. et al, 2006. Moderation, Response rate, and Message Interactivity: Features of Online Communities and Their Effects on Intent to Participate. *Journal of Computer‐Mediated Communication*, 12(1), pp.24-41.

BIG DATA ANALYTICS AND SMART CITIES: A LOOSE OR TIGHT COUPLE?

Ahmed M. Shahat Osman, Ahmed Elragal and Birgitta Bergvall-Kåreborn
Luleå Technical University- Department of Computer Science, Electrical and Space Engineering
971 87 Luleå, Sweden

ABSTRACT

Smart City (SC) is an emerging concept aiming at mitigating the challenges raised due to the continuous urbanization development. To face these challenges, government decision makers sponsor SC projects targeting sustainable economic growth and better quality of life for inhabitants and visitors. Information and Communication Technologies (ICT) is the enabling technology for smartening. These technologies yield massive volumes of data known as Big Data (BD). If spawned BD are integrated and analyzed, both city decision makers and citizens can benefit from valuable insights and information services. The process of extracting information and insights from BD is known as Big Data Analytics (BDA). Although BDA involves non-trivial challenges, it attracted academician and industrialist. Surveying the literature reveals the novelty and increasing interest in addressing BD applications in SCs. Although literature is replete with abundant number of articles about SCs applications harnessing BD, comprehensive discussion on BDA frameworks fitting SCs requirements is still needed. This paper attempts to fill this gap. It is a systematic literature review on BDA frameworks in SCs. In this review, we will try to answer the following research questions: what are the big data analytics frameworks applied in smart cities? what are the functional gaps in the current available frameworks? what are the conceptual guidelines of designing integrated scalable big data analytics frameworks for smart cities purposes? The paper concludes with a proposal for a novel conceptual analytics framework to serve SCs requirements. Additionally, open issues and further research directions are presented.

KEYWORDS

Big data, Big data analytics Frameworks, Smart cities

1. INTRODUCTION

The concept of smart cities (SC) emerged as a strategy to mitigate unprecedented challenges of continuous urbanization, while at the same time provide better quality of life to the citizens (Hafedh Chourabi, et al., 2012). City smartness is realized by means of the advances of Information and Communication Technologies (ICT) (YIN ChuanTao, et al., 2015) and as a result SCs are usually characterized by an extensive use of digital technologies in various city domains in combination with a holistic view of the city where different domains should be closed integrated. Furthermore, the diffusion of digital technologies in people's daily life has boosted human-to-human, human-to-machine, and machine-to-machine interactions. These interactions yield massive volumes of data, commonly known as "Big Data" (BD) and characterized by large and fast growing volumes of complex datasets, which go beyond the abilities of commonly known data management systems to accommodate. By analyzing these data volumes valuable insights and correlations can be extracted (Chun-Wei Tsai, Chin-Feng Lai, Han-Chieh Chao, & Athanasios V. Vasilakos, 2015). However, BD complexities result in non-trivial challenges when performing Big Data Analytics (BDA) processes (YIN ChuanTao, et al., 2015). Although literature is replete with articles addressing applications of BDA in different SC domains, detailed discussions on integrated BDA frameworks fitting SCs requirements are still needed. The lack of this type of articles is the primary motive for this research.

This article is a systematic literature review on BDA frameworks in SCs aiming at answering three basic research questions. RQ1: What types of BDA frameworks are available for the smart city context? RQ2: What are the functional gaps in the current available frameworks? Finally, RQ3: What conceptual guidelines for designing integrated scalable BDA frameworks, relevant for smart city contexts, can be found in the literature? The literature review analyzed 30 articles addressing BD applications in SCs. The review process followed the widely known framework proposed by Vom Brocke.

This paper is organized as follows: Following this introduction a presentation of key the concepts of big data, data analytics, and smart cities are given. After this, the scope and method of the literature review is presented together with a discussion of the findings. Thereafter, the main contribution of this paper, i.e. a proposal of a novel conceptual BDA framework for SCs is described followed by recommendations for future research directions. The paper ends with a summary and conclusion.

2. TOPIC CONCEPTUALIZATION

In this section, the fundamental concepts of the study, "big data" and "smart cities", are reviewed for better understanding for the challenges of harnessing big data analytics in various SC domains.

2.1 Big Data (BD)

Big data (BD) is a natural crop of the advanced digital artifacts and their applications. Sensors, mobiles and Social Media Networks are examples of modern digital technologies that have permeated our daily lives. Penetration of these technologies in our lives yields unprecedented massive volumes of data known as "Big Data". The term "Big Data" refers to the continuously growing datasets to the extent it is difficult to manage using traditional relational database management systems. BD is commonly characterized by the four Vs: Volume, Velocity, Variety and Veracity (Figure 1).

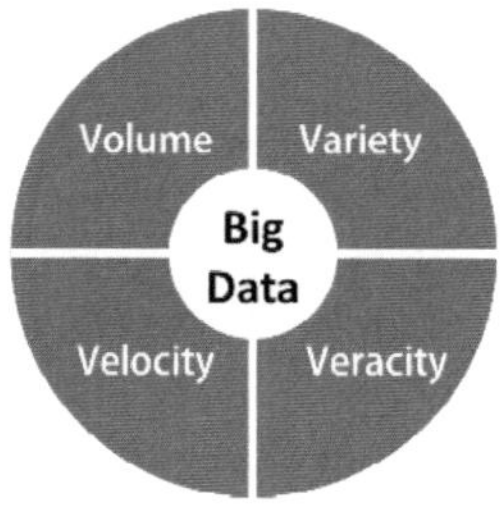

Figure 1. Big data 4Vs

Volume of BD, as outlined before, goes far beyond the size of traditional operational databases or data warehouses. Traditional databases usually grow to the order of gigabytes or terabytes. Volumes of BD are big enough to the extent that new measuring units are required such as Petabyte (10^{15}) and Exabyte (10^{18}).

Velocity of BD refers to the high rate of data streaming into hosting platforms. In addition to the high rate of incoming data, velocity raises important question about data aging, i.e. for how long these data will be valuable. In some cases, real time analysis of streaming data is critical. For example, real time analysis for video streams captured by traffic surveillance cameras is critical to predict traffic jams and prevent bottlenecks.

Variety refers to the complexity of BD formats. BD is mostly composed of semi-structured and unstructured data, e.g. text data files and images, and stream data, e.g. geospatial data streams. This is in addition to traditional structured data. Usually, the ratio between structured data to other data types is estimated by 20% to 80%, respectively. We believe that the adjective "big" will fade over time. The self-evident meaning of "data" will intuitively be extended to include all data types mentioned above.

Veracity refers to the trustworthiness of the data. Incorrect data will definitely lead to misleading analytics. Therefore, there is a need to ensure that the data is correct as well as the analyses performed on the data are correct, especially in the case of automated decision-making, where no human is involved.

In fact, the above four V's are not the only characteristics of BD. Value, Variability and Visibility represent another set of dimensions. However, the first four are the most commonly known ones. These V characteristics bestow a wild nature to BD compared to the traditional structured data.

The chain of activities for extracting values out of BD is known as BD value chain (H. Gilbert Miller & Peter Mork, 2013; Curry, 2016) or BDA (Chun-Wei Tsai, et al., 2015). Although BDA involves non-trivial processes and many challenges due the wild nature of BD. However, BDA holds an unprecedented opportunity to shift the traditional methods of information extraction into new dimensions.

2.2 Big Data Analytics (BDA)

To deal with the challenges of BD, platform scalability is the intuitive solution. There are two commonly known scaling approaches: vertical and horizontal scaling or known as scale up and scale out, respectively.

Vertical scaling means empowering the processing platform with additional computing resources (memory, CPUs, disk space, etc.), to accommodate with the incremental volume of data. This approach usually involves single instance of an operating system.

Horizontal scaling, however, is a divide-and-conquer approach where the workload is distributed and processed in parallel across multiple independent computing machines. More machines can be added as much as needed to improve the overall system performance. This approach involves multiple instances of operating systems running on independent machines.

Of course, each approach has its advantages and disadvantages. For example, up or vertical scaling is restricted to the upper ceilings of the system upgrades. Nonetheless, out or vertical scaling shows more elasticity in this regard. In fact, scaling out is more complicated than scaling up since multiple instances of different operating systems have to be managed by a single mastering node. Table 1 shows a summarized comparison between vertical and horizontal scaling.

Table 1. Comparison between vertical and horizontal scaling

	Vertical Scaling	Horizontal Scaling
Scaling	Limited, compelled by technology manufactures.	Unlimited, unrestricted to specific technology
Managemen complexity	Easy, Most software applications can benefit additional resources easily.	Complex, management software has to handle the complexities of parallel processing on distributed data.
Financial investment	Considerable financial investment.	Affordable, added machinery is high-end servers.

In fact, the financial investment and scalability upper ceiling aspects are the major drawbacks of vertical scaling. These two considerable drawbacks come in favor of horizontal scaling when it comes to SCs. It is more reasonable to rely on horizontal scaling rather than vertical scaling in a multi-domain SC projects. This note interprets why most of the researches and designs of BDA frameworks and platforms are built using horizontally scalable platforms.

As for the data analysis, (Chun-Wei Tsai, et al., 2015) provided a thorough survey on the studies on BDA frameworks, platforms, machine learning and data mining algorithms. The survey demonstrated the dominant technologies in the area of BDA, such as parallel processing, cloud computing and Apache Hadoop. Apache Hadoop is a widely known open-source fault-tolerant software framework used for distributed storage and parallel processing of BD (Apache, n.d.).

(Chun-Wei Tsai, et al., 2015) adopted analogues approach using Knowledge Discovery in Databases (KDD) model to study the corresponding bottlenecks arise in the case of BD rather than data. In the KDD model, analytics is divided into three operators: input, analysis and output (Figure 2). In the case of BD, the processes of input operator affect the efficiency of the performance of data analysis execution. Although input operator processes are of high importance, Chun-Wei noted a significant observation that number of research articles and technical reports focusing on data analysis is significantly more than the number focusing on other operators.

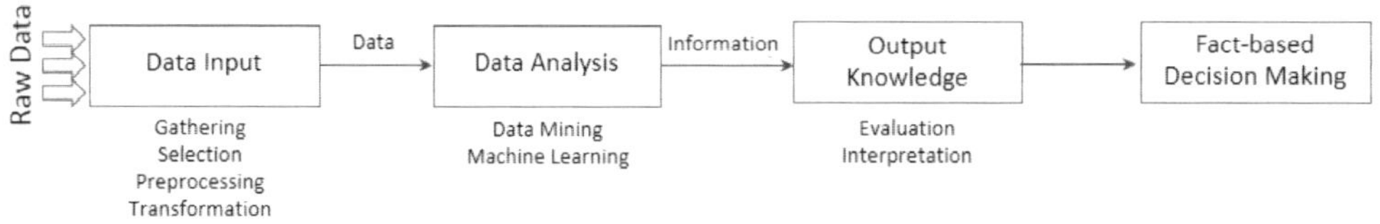

Figure 2. Knowledge Discovery in Databases

2.3 Smart Cities (SCs)

Although the term "Smart City" seems to be simple and intuitively understandable, there is no global agreement on a unified definition of the term. There are various number of definitions in literature. Despite the variations of these definitions, there is a common consent on the centric role of ICT in realizing city smartness (Michael Kehoe, et al., 2011; YIN ChuanTao, et al., 2015). Within the context of SCs, the meaning of "smartness" has different connotations according to which perspective it is regarded; marketing, planning or technology (Nam, 2011). From technology perspective, a SC is composed of smart components such as smart buildings, smart farms and smart hospitals. "Smartness" of these components is realized through intensive use of digital artifacts such as sensors, actuators, mobiles and ICT applications. However, "smartening" of various city domains is not enough for a city to be smart. On the city level, a SC is viewed as a whole body of systems, *i.e. system of systems*, where the interrelationship between the underlying systems and subsystems are taken into account. This integrated vision for a SC implies cross domain sharing of information (Michael Kehoe, et al., 2011) and clarifies the difference between smartening of specific city domain and smartening a city as a whole. Therefore, the process of evaluating and modelling SCs encounters considerable complexities (Leonidas G. Anthopoulos, et al., 2015).

Researches pursue different approaches to establish assessment frameworks for SCs (Giffinger, 2010; Nam, 2011; Hafedh Chourabi, et al., 2012; Lazaroiu, 2012; Lombardi, 2012; Söderström, 2014; Neirotti, 2014; Felix Herrera Priano & Cristina fajardo Guerra, 2014; Lee, 2014). However, the pioneering work of Rudolf Giffinger, et al. is the most common in literature (Giffinger, 2010). Giffinger defined six main traits or domains that characterize the city smartness. These domains are: smart economy, smart people, smart governance, smart mobility, smart environment and smart living. These domains are further divided into factors and evaluate indicators.

2.4 Smart Cities (SCs) and Big Data (BD)

From an ICT perspective, industrialist and scholars adopt the layered (or tiered) approach to model smart cities. For example, IBM adopt a three-layer model for SCs including instrumented layer, interconnected layer, and intelligent layer (Michael Kehoe, et al., 2011). Similarly, YIN ChuanTao proposed a four-layer model for SCs: data acquisition and transmission layer; data vitalization layer; common data and service layer; finally applications layer (YIN ChuanTao, et al., 2015). Despite the number of layers, these models aim at projecting the journey of the data from its birth in raw form until valuable information is extracted benefiting end users, the citizens and decision makers. Recognizing the analogy (or even congruence) between SC models and BD value chain is straightforward. This analogy manifests the intersecting area between BDA and SCs.

In this context, an important question poses itself, what are the characteristics and features of the analytics platforms/frameworks to benefit BDA in SCs? The answer of this question led to the first research question of this article RQ1. In the literature, there are many articles about BD applications in SCs proposing solutions for specific domains such as energy and transportation using BDA frameworks. However, most these articles discuss functional requirements and architecture designs for specific domain. To develop an appropriate domain-independent and resilient analytic framework for SC purposes, there are two driving aspects that should be considered. Firstly, the framework should be capable, at least, of managing the 4V's of BD. Secondly, the design of the framework should consider, at a high level, functional and non-functional requirements pertained to SC's from a holistic perspective.

3. THE SCOPE AND SEARCH PROCESS OF THE REVIEW STUDY

This systematic literature review is based on the taxonomy proposed by (Cooper, 1988) and adapted by (Vom Brocke, 2009). In this literature review the focus is on research outcomes, practices and applications. The goal is to integrate finding about BDA frameworks in the development and evolution of smart cities and analyze the findings in order to identify research gaps. These gaps guide the design of integrated scalable BDA and future research directions and identify both conceptual and methodological structures. The perspective introduced leans to be neutral representation rather espousal of position and the coverage is exhaustive coverage with selected citations. Finally, the target audiences are specialized scholars, practitioners and SCs planners and decision makers. Literature search involves four steps: 1) identifying search databases; 2) search keywords; 3) forward and backward search and 4) evaluation of articles.

Step 1-Identifying search databases: To collect quality scholar articles and conference proceedings, the following internationally recognized online information systems databases were used for the search process: ACM DL, IEEE, SCOPUS, Springer Link, INSPEC and Web of Science.

Step 2-Search- keywords: As this paper comes at the intersection between the two subjects, the search keywords were "big data" and "smart city" and the search parameter was the document title. The search keywords did not include the two words "framework" or "analytics" to widen the scope of the search process as these keywords might not be used explicitly in the article title while they are used within the article contents. The search process was limited to English publications only. The total number of the retrieved publications was 247 distributed as shown in Table 2:

Table 2. Search Databases and number of hits

Database	ACM DL	IEEE	SCOPUS	Springer Link	INSPEC	Web of Science	Total
No of hits	6	26	53	114	40	8	247

Step 3-Forward- and backward search: Returned articles were published between 2012 and 2017, which reflect the relative novelty of subject. Additionally, the 247 articles are considered enough pool for the analysis step, hence the authors decided not to apply forward nor backward search.

Step 4-Evaluation- of articles: Search database, article id, type, title, year, source title, authors, volume, abstract, URL and DOI attributes of the retrieved publications were collected in an Excel sheet. An elimination process was applied to exclude duplicates, work in progress and irrelevant publications from the analysis process, resulting exclusion of (85) articles. The remaining (162) articles are further filtered according to how likely they address the main objective of this review i.e. big data analytics in smart cities. This filtration process was performed by evaluating the abstracts of the remaining (162) articles, resulting exclusion of additional (132) articles do not fit with the objectives of this article. The remaining (30) articles were used for analysis. The sources of the final articles candidate for analysis are listed in Appendix A.

3.1 Literature analysis and synthesis

The final list of the thirty articles subjected to the analysis are classified according to their relevance to the three operators of BDA value chain: input, analysis, and output (Figure 2). Articles classification process involved reviewing each article's abstract and conclusion to decide how likely the article belong to one or more of the three classification operators. In case of article abstract and conclusion does not lead to clear decision for classification, the article full body is reviewed for final decision. Results of the classification process are shown in Appendix B.

To answer research questions RQ1 and RQ2 the contribution(s) of the articles are evaluated to identify the uncovered requirements of the value chain operators/processes and SC domain, if any. Compiling the results of the two research questions will derive the answer for the third research question RQ3. The answer to the last research question will derive the design of the conceptual BDA framework to serve SCs requirements.

3.1.1 Data Input

In (Takuro Yonezawa, et al., 2016) authors introduced a scalable, distributed infrastructure city-wide sensor network for sharing *social big sensor data* in SCs called SOXFire. By social big sensor data authors mean the data which has usefulness and sociality to be shared. Through this access city employees, citizen and WEB developers can contribute through unified APIs. Design of *SOXFire* rely on already matured IoT communication protocols. The essential design goals of *SOXFire* are: coping with heterogeneous types of sensors; securing access, that enable different formats; easing management; and providing Scalability and Federation of multi-community system.

In (Bo Tang, et al., 2015), authors presented a prototype for hierarchical distributed architecture based on Fog Computing to integrate massive number of infrastructure components and services in SCs. Fog computing is a decentralized computing infrastructure in which data, compute, storage and applications are distributed in the most logical, efficient place between the data source and the cloud. The prototype was tested to evaluate event detection performance of the recognition of 12 distinct events. Results demonstrate the feasibility to implement the proposed hierarchical architecture in a city-wide implementation.

Civitas is a distributed object-oriented middleware designed for SCs (Villanueva, et al., 2013). It is used to facilitate the development and deployment of SC applications. Citizens connect to the middleware via a special device called the *Civitas Plug* to ensure privacy and security. To promote software consistency and reusability. The middleware design adopted two principles: Everything is a Software Object and City Layout should be Independence.

In (Kemp, G., et al., 2015) authors presented an approach for developing data storage, cleaning and integration services. Such integration aims at making an efficient decision support system based on cloud computing using a new programming paradigm called Service Oriented Computing. The objective of the presented approach is to manage and aggregate cloud services for managing BD and assist decision making for transport systems. The proposed decision support system relies on the following services: data acquisition service; information extraction and cleaning service; integration and aggregation services; BD analysis service; and decision support service. The proposed approach was applied to the transport industry, which can bring new understanding to town transport infrastructures.

3.1.2 Data Analysis

In (Debopriya Ghosh, et al., 2016) authors presented intelligent solution using machine learning to automate and support crime analysts. The proposed solution enables identifying connected entities and events by collecting, integrating and analyzing diverse data sources. It helps crime analysts identify dead end leads to avoid having the investigators spend time on these leads. A prototype for the proposed solution is built using R package for machine learning classification module and preprocessing with MySQL as a backend database.

A novel system for sentiment analysis using convolutional neural network is introduced in (Tang B, et al., 2015) for visual sentiment prediction. The research focuses on images and fine-tuned convolutional neural network initially trained on a large natural image recognition dataset (Imagenet ILSVRC2012) to learn feature representations for visual sentiment prediction. To evaluate the proposed method, real world dataset has been taken from Twitter. Authors used a benchmark including 603 tweets with photos. Experimental results led to two important conclusions: 1) Logistic regression model has more accuracy compared to J48 and Random Forest; and 2) Domain specific fine-tuning is effective in improving the performance of neural network.

(Ciprian Barbieru & Florin Pop, 2016) addressed important issue regarding scheduling of analysis tasks in a SC environment. In some cases, data must be analyzed on real-time bases while others can be analyzed as a batch process. To handle these cases, authors design a real-time and job scheduler using Hadoop for BD processing. Hadoop processing addresses both the problem of small tasks that need to be executed in real time, and in the same time, adjust long-running jobs. A case study is applied as a support of SC applications. Data gathered, routed, stored via mobile devices, while processed and diffused via cloud. Experimental results showed that the proposed scheduler behaved better than the standard one when fed with the same job distribution. Unfortunately, performance degraded when the distribution is the exact opposite. Authors expect that this can be solved by choosing other schemes of resource limits in real implementation.

Authors of (D. Singh, et al., 2016) proposed a BDA framework for video recorded data, through the analysis of images or videos to find semantic patterns that are useful for interpretation. The research aims at providing a solution for city traffic control for detection of bike-riders without helmet in city traffic. The proposed framework utilizes data recorded by video surveillance cameras for visual data analytics.

In (Tosi D & Marzorati S., 2016) authors describe a novel use of BD coming from the cellular network to extract mobility patterns for SCs. These mobility patterns are able to describe different mobility scenarios of the city, starting from how people move around Point of Interests (PoI) of the city in real-time. These mobility patterns can be exploited by policy makers to improve the mobility in a city or by navigation systems and journey planners to provide users with accurate travel plans. Several BD mining algorithms have been discussed to support the prediction and estimation of vehicular traffic conditions, speed profiles for roads, flows of people moving among subway stations and around PoI of the city.

3.1.3 Output

Few articles address the output operator. In (Rathore MM, et al., 2016) authors addressed the subject as a part of complete proposals for BDA system for SCs based on IoT. Results are displayed to end user in terms of predefined graphs to facilitate decision making process.

3.2 Discussion

From the above literature survey, we can draw the following observations about big data analytics frameworks from infrastructure, platform and functional aspects.

Since SCs rely on sensed data collection, IoT technology provides a viable means for this requirement via large number of data acquisition devices through the Internet. Also, cloud computing technology provides an elastic, robust and high available infrastructure technology capable for accommodation with the dynamic nature of SCs and increasing volumes of data. Marriage between the two technologies, i.e. IoT and cloud computing (sometimes referred to as ClouT),) represents a workable infrastructure platform for BDA. Additionally, Fog computing is an efficient infrastructure for raw data processing on the edge of the network, where raw data can be preprocessed close to data sources before analysis processing.

Hadoop/Spark provides an efficient scalable fault tolerant platform for developing efficient BDA frameworks of SCs.

Surveyed BDA frameworks dealt with both batch analysis of historical data and real-time analysis for stream data. Most of the surveyed articles introduced solutions for specific SC application domains (*e.g. mobility, sentiment analysis*…etc.). However,.) while few articles addressed BDA from the holistic perspective of SCs (Martin Strohbach, et al., 2015; Khan, Z., et al., 2015).

Despite of its importance for decision making processes, few articles addressed the output operator processes (evaluation and interpretation).

The aforementioned observations give an overview of the characteristics of BDA frameworks applied in SCs. They also provide an answer to the first research question RQ1. Furthermore, it indicates the tight relation between BDA and SCs development. However, with the re-emphasis on the holistic perspective of the SC as a multi-domain system of systems, we can identify the following missing features on the surveyed frameworks:

- How extracted knowledge for different city domains can be merged together for more detailed and complicated analytics (*i.e. ensemble modeling*)?
- Considering the computational complexities of BDA, including a repository for extracted knowledge retention, will enable saving extracted data models for future services without additional cost (*i.e. model persistence*).

The above two missing features answers the second research question RQ2 and motivated the proposal of a novel conceptual analytics framework.

4. PROPOSAL FOR NOVEL CONCEPTUAL FRAMEWORK

Based on the knowledge surveyed in the above section, we can summarize the design guidelines of integrated scalable BDA frameworks for SCs in the following points:

- Ability to analyze stream data for online and real time applications (D. Singh, et al., 2016; Debopriya Ghosh, et al., 2016),

• Ability to analyze batch data for applications that afford latency (Ciprian Barbieru & Florin Pop, 2016),
• Ability to retain extracted models for future processing,
• Ability to merge one or more extracted models for higher level of analytics.

Based on these guidelines, we present a novel conceptual framework for developing of BDA frameworks for SCs (Figure 3). The design of the proposed framework is domain independent and satisfies the above-mentioned features. The function of each component is described hereafter:

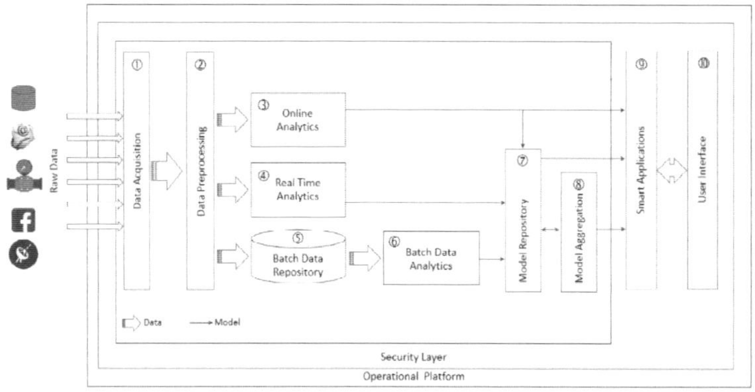

Figure 3. Proposed Big Data Analytics Framework for Smart Cities

① **Data acquisition**: The main characteristics of this layer are scalability, interoperability and location awareness.

② **Data preprocessing**: The ability to clean input data and transform these data transformation into standard output messages.

③ **Online analytics**: The ability of performing stream data processing for applications that involve interactivity with acceptable limited latency.

④ **Real time analytics**: The ability of performing stream data processing for real time applications. Real time applications are applications that functions within time frames that the user senses as immediate or current. The latency must be less than a defined value.

⑤ **Batch data repository**: Data storage management system (e.g. Hadoop HDFS, NoSQL database management systems).

⑥ **Batch data analytics**: Batch data analytics for applications that have latency tolerance.

⑦ **Model repository**: Model storage management system, where resultant data analysis models can be persisted with relevant metadata for current and future inquiries.

⑧ **Model aggregation**: Ability to ensemble persisted resultant data analysis models for higher level and more complicated inquiries.

⑨ **Smart application**: SC applications built on resultant data analysis models.

⑩ **User interface**: End user interface that provides with efficient flexible tools allowing access, reporting and ad hoc inquiries for persisted and/or aggregated models.

Although a complete vision for the functionality of the security layer will be clearer during physical implementation, the following security measures should be adhered to on physical design especially for critical analytics:

• Restricted sign on access to the framework should be granted for critical and sensitive data;
• Multi levels user authentication;
• A complete audit log should be kept for important operations.

Apache Hadoop and Spark are viable platform options to realize the proposed framework. Hadoop has robust ecosystem that is well suited to meet the analytical needs of developers. Hadoop Ecosystem comes with a suite of tools and technologies making it a very much suitable to deliver to a variety of data processing needs.

The distributed parallel processing feature of Hadoop platform enables handling massive volumes of unstructured and structured data efficiently. Also, as an open source software and horizontally scalable using commodity hardware, the initial cost saving is considerable while it can continue to grow as needed.

Technology companies provided various distributions of Hadoop bundled with other software tools to simplify Hadoop usage and extend its functionality e.g. Cloudera, Hortonworks, MapR, IBM InfoSphere, Amazon Elastic MapReduce and Windows Azure HDinsight.

5. FUTURE RESEARCH DIRECTIONS

Future research directions involve the following points:

- Realize the proposed conceptual framework using Hadoop/Spark ecosystems.
- Develop efficient model persistence and ensemble algorithms.
- Enable analytical model export/import functionality to/from other analytical frameworks.
- Develop efficient, powerful and friendly end-used interfaces. This involves multi model visualization.
- Test the framework in real case SC application.

Since the ultimate goal behind SCs is improving citizens' quality of life, elevation of the moral and cultural aspects of citizens' lives represents a significant challenge. Yet, it has been observed that this aspect is not given the necessary attention. More research dedicated to studying human privacy, behaviors, education, innovations, emotions and sentiments is required.

6. CONCLUSIONS

This paper is a literature survey on BDA frameworks in SCs. The paper aimed at answering the three research questions. RQ1: What are the big data analytics frameworks applied in smart cities? RQ2: What are the gap(s) in the current available frameworks? RQ3: What are the conceptual guidelines of designing integrated scalable big data analytics frameworks for smart cities purposes? To answer these questions, 30 articles have been reviewed and analyzed. The analysis process indicated that available proposed frameworks lack two important features, namely model persistence and ensemble. To fill in this gap, a novel conceptual framework is proposed to provide the ability to persist and ensemble extracted models. The proposed framework enables the ability to retain the extracted models, enabling future studies on these models without the need to re-analyze the data. This feature saves the considerable time for data re-analysis. Additionally, extracted model ensemble will enable the ability for more complicated cross-domain analytics.

REFERENCES

Anthopoulos, L. G., et al, 2015. Comparing Smart Cities with different modeling approaches. 24th International Conference on World Wide Web. Florence, Italy,pp. 525-528.

Apache, H., n.d. Hadoop Apache. [Online] Available at: http://hadoop.apache.org/

Barbieru, C. and Pop, F., 2016. Soft Real-Time Hadoop Scheduler for Big Data Processing in Smart City. IEEE 30th International Conference on Advanced Information Networking and Applications. Crans-Montana, Switzerland, , pp. 863-870.

Brocke, V. J. e. a., 2009. Reconstructing the giant: On the importance of rigour in documenting the literature search process. Verona, Italy, s.n., pp. 2206-2217.

Cheng, B. et al., 2015. Building a Big Data Platform for Smart Cities: Experience and Lessons from Santander. IEEE International Congress on Big Data. New York, USA, pp. 592-599.

Chourabi, H. et al, 2012. Understanding Smart Cities: An integrative framework. Hawaii, 45th Hawaii International Conference on System Sciences (HICSS), pp. 2298-2297.

Chun-Wei Tsai, et al, 2015. Big data analytics: a survey. Journal of Big Data, 2(1), p. 20.

Cooper, H. M., 1988. Organizing knowledge syntheses: A taxonomy of literature reviews. Knowledge in Society, 1(1), pp. 104-126.

Corradi, A. et al., 2015. Automatic extraction of POIs in smart cities: Big data processing in ParticipAct. IFIP/IEEE International Symposium on Integrated Network Management (IM). Ottawa, Canda, pp. 1059-1064.

Costa, C. and Santos, M.Y., 2016. BASIS: A big data architecture for smart cities. In SAI Computing Conference (SAI). London, United Kingdom, pp. 1247-1256.

Curry, E., 2016. The Big Data Value Chain: Definitions, Concepts, and Theoretical Approaches. In: New Horizons for a Data-Driven Economy. Gewerbestrasse: Springer International Publishing, pp. 29-37.

Deng, L. and Zhou, C., 2015. Protype Framework of Smart City Base on Big Data and Smart Grid. 2015 International Conference on Computer Science and Mechanical Automation. Hangzhou, Zhejiang, China,pp. 102-107.

Felix Herrera Priano, F. H. and Guerra,C.F., 2014. A Framework for measuring smart cities. Proceedings of the 15th Annual International Conference on Digital Government Research. Aguascalientes, Mexico, pp. 44-54.

Ghosh, D.; Chun. S.A.; and Shafiq, B., 2016. Big Data-based Smart City Platform: Real-Time Crime Analysis. 17th International Digital Government Research Conference on Digital Government Research. Shanghai, China, pp. 58-66.

Giffinger, R. a. H. G., 2010. Smart cities ranking: an effective instrument for the positioning of the cities?. ACE: Architecture, City and Environment, 4(12), pp. 7-25.

Gilbert, M.H. and Mork, P., 2013. From Data to Decisions: A Value Chain for Big Data. IT Professional, 15(1), pp. 57-59.

Girtelschmid, S. et al, 2014. On the application of big data in future large-scale intelligent smart city installations. International Journal of Pervasive Computing and Communications, 10(2), pp. 168-182.

Hashem, I.A.T., et al, 2016. The role of big data in smart city. International Journal of Information Management, 36(5). pp. 748-758.

Horban, V., 2016. A Multifaceted Approach to Smart Energy City Concept through Using Big Data Analytics. IEEE First International Conference on Data Stream Mining & Processing. Lviv, Ukraine, pp. 23-27.

Huanan, Z.; Shijun, L. and Hong, J., 2015. Guangzhou smart city construction and big data research. International Conference on Behavioral, Economic and Socio-cultural Computing (BESC). Nanjing, China, pp. 143-149.

Iancu, V., et al, 2016. A Smart City Fighting Pollution, by Efficiently Managing and Processing Big Data from Sensor Networks. In: Resource Management for Big Data Platforms. Springer International Publishing AG., pp. 489-513.

Jara, A.J., et al, 2015. Big data for smart cities with KNIME a real experience in the SmartSantander testbed. Software - Practice and Experience, 45(18), pp. 1145-1160.

Jara, A. J.; Genoud, D.; and Bocchi,Y., 2014. Big Data in Smart Cities: From Poisson to Human Dynamics. 28th International Conference on Advanced Information Networking and Applications Workshops. Victoria, Canada, pp. 785-790.

Kemp, G., et al., 2015. Aggregating and managing realtime big data in the cloud: Application to intelligent transport for smart cities. 1st International Conference on Vehicle Technology and Intelligent Transport Systems, VEHITS 2015. Lisbon, Portugal, pp. 107-112.

Khan, Z. et al, 2015. Towards cloud based big data analytics for smart future cities. Journal of Cloud Computing, 4(1), p. 11.

Lazaroiu, G. C. a. M. R., 2012. Definition methodology for the smart cities mode. Energy - ElSevier, 47(1), pp. 326-332.

Lee, J. H. M. G. H. a. M.-C. H., 2014. Towards an effective framework for building smart cities: Lessons from Seoul and San Francisco. Technological Forecasting and Social Change, pp. 80-99.

Lombardi, P. E. A., 2012. Modelling the smart city performance. Innovation: The European Journal of Social Science Research 25.2, 25(2), pp. 137-149.

Kehoe, M., et al., 2011. Smart Cities Series: A Foundation for Understanding IBM Smarter Cities. s.l.:IBM Redbooks.

Moreno-Cano, V. et al, 2015. Big Data for IoT Services in Smart Cities. 2015 IEEE 2nd World Forum on Internet of Things (WF-IoT). Milan, Italy, pp. 418-423.

Nam, T. a. T. A. P., 2011. Conceptualizing smart city with dimensions of technology, people, and institutions. 12th Annual International Digital Government Research Conference: Digital Government Innovation in Challenging Time. Maryland, USA, pp. 282-291.

Nandury, S.V. and Begum, B.A. , 2016. Strategies to handle big data for traffic management in smart cities. 2016 International Conference on Advances in Computing, Communications and Informatics (ICACCI). Jaipur, India, pp. 356-364.

Neirotti, P. E. A., 2014. Current trends in Smart City initiatives: Some stylised facts. Cities, Volume 38, pp. 25-36.

Psomakelis, E., et al, 2016. Big IoT and Social Networking Data for Smart Cities Algorithmic Improvements on Big Data Analysis in the Context of RADICAL City Applications. s.l., s.n.

Rathore, M. M.; Ahmad, A.; and Paul A., 2016. IoT-based smart city development using big data analytical approach. IEEE International Conference on In Automatica (ICA-ACCA). Curicó, Chile,pp. 1-8.

Schatzinger, S. and Lim, C.Y.R., 2017. Taxi of the future: Big data analysis as a framework for future urban fleets in smart cities. In: Smart and Sustainable Planning for Cities and Regions. Switzerland: Springer International Publishing, pp. 83-98.

Singh, D. and Reddy, C.K. 2014. A survey on platforms for big data analytics. Journal of Big Data, 2(1), p. 8.

Singh, D.; Vishnu, C.; and Mohan, C. K., 2016. Visual Big Data Analytics for Traffic Monitoring in Smart City. 15th IEEE International Conference on Machine Learning and Applications (ICMLA). Los Angeles, California, USA, pp. 886-891.

Shuangmei Ma and Liang , Z., 2015. Design and Implementation of Smart City Big Data Processing Platform Based on Distributed Architecture. 2015 International Conference on Intelligent Systems and Knowledge Engineering, Taipei, Taiwan, pp. 428-433.

Söderström, O. T. P. a. F. K., 2014. Smart cities as corporate storytelling. City: Analysis of urban trends, culture, theory, policy, action., 18(3), pp. 307-320..

Souza, A., et al., 2016. Using Big Data and Real-Time Analytics to Support Smart City Initiatives. IFAC-PapersOnLine, 49(30), pp. 257-263.

Strohbach, M., et al, 2015. Towards a Big Data Analytics Framework for IoT and Smart City Applications. In: Modeling and Processing for Next-Generation Big-Data Technologies. Gewerbestrasse, Switzerland: Springer International Publishing, pp. 257-282.

Tang, B. et al., 2015a. A Hierarchical Distributed Fog Computing Architecture for Big Data Analysis in Smart Cities. ASE BigData & Social Informatics. Kaohsiung, Taiwan, p. 28.

Tang, B., et al., 2015b. A hierarchical distributed fog computing architecture for big data analysis in smart cities. Proceedings of the ASE BigData & SocialInformatics. Kaohsiung, Taiwan, p. 28.

Tosi, D. and Marzorati, S., 2016. Big Data from Cellular Networks: Real Mobility Scenarios for Future Smart Cities. IEEE Second International Conference on Big Data Computing Service and Applications. Oxford, UK, pp. 131-141.

UN - Department of Economic and Social Affairs, 2014. World Urbanization Prospects - The 2014 Revision, New York: United Nations.

Villanueva, F. J., et al, 2013. Civitas: The Smart City Middleware, from Sensors. 2013 Seventh International Conference on Innovative Mobile and Internet Services in Ubiquitous Computing. Taichung, Taiwan, pp. 445-450.

Wang, X., 2015. Calibration of Big Traffic Data for a Transport Smart City. 15th COTA International Conference of Transportation Professionals: Efficient, Safe, and Green Multimodal Transportation, CICTP 2015. Beijing, China, pp. 387-397.

Xiong, L., et al, 2015. Multi-source macro data process based on the idea of sample=overall in big data: An Applicability Study on Influence Factors to Smart City. 2015 International Conference on Logistics, Informatics and Service Sciences (LISS). Barcelona, Spain,

YIN ChuanTao, et al., 2015. A literature survey on smart cities. Science China Information Sciences, 58(10), pp. 1-18.

Appendix A - Sources of Analysed Articles

Springer Book Chapter
Modeling and Processing for Next-Generation Big-Data Technologies 2015
Resource Management for Big Data Platforms 2016
Conference Proceedings
Database: ACM DL
2015 Proceedings of the 17th International Digital Government Research Conference on Digital Government Research
2015 Proceedings of the ASE Big Data & Social Informatics
2016 Proceedings of the 2Nd International Workshop on Smart
Database: IEEE
2013 Seventh International Conference on Innovative Mobile and Internet Services in Ubiquitous Computing
2014 28th International Conference on Advanced Information Networking and Applications Workshops
2015 10th International Conference on Intelligent Systems and Knowledge Engineering (ISKE)
2015 IEEE 2nd World Forum on Internet of Things (WF-IoT)
2015 IEEE International Congress on Big Data
2015 IFIP/IEEE International Symposium on Integrated Network Management (IM)
2015 International Conference on Behavioral, Economic and Socio-cultural Computing (BESC)
2015 International Conference on Computer Science and Mechanical Automation (CSMA)
2016 15th IEEE International Conference on Machine Learning and Applications (ICMLA)
2016 4th IEEE International Colloquium on Information Science and Technology (CiSt)
2016 IEEE 30th International Conference on Advanced Information Networking and Applications (AINA)
2016 IEEE First International Conference on Data Stream Mining & Processing (DSMP)
2016 IEEE International Conference on Automatica (ICA-ACCA)
2016 IEEE Second International Conference on Big Data Computing Service and Applications (BigDataService)
2016 International Conference on Advances in Computing, Communications and Informatics (ICACCI)
2016 SAI Computing Conference (SAI)
Database: INSPEC
CLOSER 2016. 6th International Conference on Cloud Computing and Services Science Proceedings
Database: SCOPUS
2015 International Conference on Logistics, Informatics and Service Science, LISS 2015
CICTP 2015 - Proceedings of the 15th COTA International Conference of Transportation Professionals
VEHITS 2015 - Proceedings of the 1st International Conference on Vehicle Technology and Intelligent Transport Systems
Journal Article
Database: SCOPUS
Green Energy and Technology
International Federation of Automatic Control (IFAC) Papers Online
International Journal of Pervasive Computing and Communications
Journal of Cloud Computing
Software - Practice and Experience
Total = 30

Appendix B - Value Chain Classification

Operator	Reference
Data Input	
Gathering	(Takuro Yonezawa, et al., 2016), (Bo Tang, et al., 2015), (Villanueva, et al., 2013), (Cheng, et al., 2015), (Costa C & Santos MY., 2016), (Rathore MM, et al., 2016), (Kemp, G., et al., 2015), (Girtelschmid, S. , et al., 2014)
Selection	(Rathore MM, et al., 2016), (Kemp, G., et al., 2015), (Girtelschmid, S. , et al., 2014)
Processing	(Rathore MM, et al., 2016), (Kemp, G., et al., 2015), (Li Xiong, et al., 2015), (Girtelschmid, S. , et al., 2014)
Transformation	(Rathore MM, et al., 2016), (Kemp, G., et al., 2015), (Girtelschmid, S. , et al., 2014)
Analysis	(Debopriya Ghosh, et al., 2016), (Tang B, et al., 2015), (Vasylyna Horban, 2016), (Ciprian Barbieru & Florin Pop, 2016), (Jara, et al., 2014), (D. Singh, et al., 2016), (Cheng, et al., 2015), (Shuangmei Ma & Zhengli Liang , 2015), (Costa C & Santos MY., 2016), (Rathore MM, et al., 2016), (Psomakelis E, et al., 2016), (Souza A, et al., 2016), (Voichita Iancu, et al., 2016), (Huanan Z, et al., 2015), (Tosi D & Marzorati S., 2016).
Output	(D. Singh, et al., 2016), (Rathore MM, et al., 2016)

THE IMPORTANCE OF CITIZEN ENGAGEMENT IN REALIZING SMART CITY BENEFITS

Guochao Peng, Miguel Nunes, Ning Zhang, Meng Wang and Fei Xing
School of Information Management, Sun Yat-sen University
No 132, Waihuan Dong Road, Guangzhou, China

ABSTRACT

There is an increasing trend for deploying and using smart technologies and services to resolve critical challenges (e.g. climate change, pollution, the ageing population, and energy shortage) faced by modern cities, and creating so-called "smart cities". Nevertheless, although smart cities are driven by advanced information technologies, their success is highly dependent on user/citizen engagement. The study reported in this paper seeks to provide empirical evidence to demonstrate that lack of citizen engagement can significantly affect the realization of the benefits promised by smart cities. The research team selected and used London's smart parking service as a case study, in which a questionnaire was distributed to local car owners and a total of 212 responses was collected. The results showed that London's smart parking service can potentially help: 1) individual drivers to save an average of £68 on petrol annually and reduce CO2 emissions by 238.14 kg per car per year; and 2) the whole city to save £183.6 million worth of petrol per year and reduce its annual CO2 emissions by 642,978 tons. However, public engagement (in terms of citizen awareness and usage) in this smart service was found to be extremely low, and so presented substantial barriers to realize these potential economic and environmental benefits.

KEYWORDS

Smart Services, Smart City, Smart Parking, Citizen Engagement, Economic Benefits, Environmental Benefits

1. INTRODUCTION

Smart cities are built by utilizing a set of advanced information and communication technologies (ICT), including smart hardware devices (e.g. wireless sensors, smart phones), mobile networks (e.g. Wi-Fi, 3G/4G/5G network), data storage technologies (e.g. data warehouse, cloud platform), and software applications (e.g. back-office control systems, mobile apps, big data analytical tools). Since the concept emerged in early 2010s, smart city has attracted increasing attention from government leaders, industrial practitioners and academics, and is now widely perceived as one of the essential means of resolving critical and global challenges like climate change, resource crises and ageing population (Nam and Pardo, 2011; Neirotti et al., 2014).

Nonetheless, although smart cities are driven by advanced information technologies, their success is highly dependent on the engagement of citizens as potential service users (Peng, 2015). Specifically, prospective users need to be fully aware of the existence and usefulness of the smart services available in the city, as well as to be able and willing to use these services. The daily usage of smart services can then lead to the economic and environmental benefits proposed by local authorities and service providers, such as cutting resources usage, saving on bills, and eventually reducing CO2 emissions.

Historically, gaining user engagement has been a difficult task, especially considering individual differences in terms of age, education, skills, income levels, and family composition. Lack of user participation and engagement has been frequently reported in information systems (IS) literature as a major cause of ICT failure (Ferneley and Sobreperez, 2006; Lanzaronea and Zanzia, 2010; Claussen et al., 2013). However, since smart city is still a relatively new concept, there is currently very limited research and evidence to a) demonstrate the importance of user engagement in smart city, and more importantly to b) explore how poor citizen engagement may affect the realization of smart city benefits. The study reported in this paper therefore aimed to fill this knowledge gap.

In order to generate more in-depth and meaningful findings, the research team specifically selected the first (and by far) the largest smart parking project in the UK as a case study. A questionnaire survey was used as the main method of data collection in this case study, and aimed to achieve three research objectives: first, the study attempts to examine current levels of user engagement (in terms of citizen awareness and usage) of London's smart parking service; second, it aims to quantify the economic and environmental benefits that may be delivered by this smart service at both individual and city levels; and finally, the study intends to explore how user engagement may affect the realization of the economic and environmental benefits of smart parking. The rest of this paper is structured as follows: the next section presents the research methodology including an introduction of the case study in details. Subsequently, the findings derived from the study are presented and discussed, with conclusions drawn.

2. METHODOLOGY

2.1 The case of London's smart parking system

Smart city covers a wide range of applications and services in the areas of transportation, healthcare, energy, public safety, to name a few. This paper particularly focuses on one of the essential smart services included in the smart city umbrella, namely smart parking. Results of a large number of studies showed that parking problems are ubiquitous in most major cities across the world, and are long-lasting causes of traffic congestion and air pollution within metropolitan areas (Allen, 1993; Rodier et al., 2004; Shoup, 2006).

In light of this discussion, as one of the most developed economies in the world, the number of cars used in Great Britain has been constantly high. According to government statistics, there were over 35 million vehicles licensed for use on the road in the UK in 2012 (Department for Transport, 2014). Although the usage of vehicles makes people's traveling more convenient and effective, it also caused many problems in UK cities, most notably traffic congestion, air pollution and noise. Specifically, the City of Westminster, which is well located in central London, is one of the most traffic congested areas in the UK and even the world. In order to improve the status quo, the Westminster City Council invested around £890,000 to implement a smart parking solution in the West End area. Over 3000 wireless sensors were mined into the on-street parking spaces located in West End by July 2014 (Westminster City Council, 2014). These sensors are used to collect real-time data on occupancy status of related parking bays. An associated mobile app called 'ParkRight' was built to allow citizens (especially drivers alike) to see parking availability and find empty spaces in real-time, as well as to pay for parking and manage their parking sessions (https://www.westminster.gov.uk/parkright). It is worth mentioning that this ParkRight app was given the Parking Technology Award at the 2014 British Parking Awards and the Innovation Award at the 2013 Tech Success Awards. Since this award-wining smart parking system had been implemented and used for nearly 3 years by the time of this research, it is a timely moment to explore the level of citizen awareness and engagement in this case study.

2.2 Questionnaire survey in the case study

Questionnaire survey was selected as the main data collection method in the case study to capture a snapshot of local citizens' perceptions and views towards London's smart parking service. In order to achieve the research objectives presented above, the designed questionnaire was structured into three main sections:

- The first section covered a set of 5-point Likert scale questions to find out local drivers' awareness of the existence and usefulness of the smart parking service.
- The second section used another set of 5-point Likert scale questions to explore the frequency of smart parking usage and user satisfaction rates.
- The third part of the questionnaire involved questions to explore local drivers' demand of using parking facilities, as well as to measure potential saving on parking search time as a result of using the smart parking service. Such data were then used in a specially designed formula (as further discussed in section 3.3) to quantify economic and environment benefits delivered by the usage of smart parking.

In addition, demographic data were also collected at the end of the questionnaire in order for the research team to further compare the views of respondents with different backgrounds (i.e. different gender, age, education level, and monthly income). During the survey administration process, the research team particularly targeted on local drivers who would visit the West End area on a regular basis (and so would be prospective users of the smart parking services) rather than general citizens or occasional visitors in London. Three research assistants of the project stayed near the parking meters installed in different on-street parking areas in West End. After drivers came and paid their fees by using the parking meters, the researchers immediately approached them and introduce the study. Consequently, the researchers approached 1044 London drivers, and received a total of 212 responses, representing an overall response rate of 20.3%. Table 1 gives a summary of the demographic features of these respondents.

Table 1. Sample demographics (N = 212)

Measure	*Items*	*Count*	*%*
Gender	Male	120	56.6
	Female	92	43.4
Age	18-24	54	25.5
	25-34	52	24.5
	35-44	60	28.3
	45-59	34	16.0
	60 or above	12	5.7
Education level	Less than high school	12	5.7
	High school diploma	58	27.3
	Bachelor degree	90	42.5
	Master degree	41	19.3
	PhD degree	11	5.2
Monthly income	£1499 or less	62	29.2
	£1500-£2499	50	23.6
	£2500-£3499	50	23.6
	£3500-£4499	36	17.0
	£4500 or more	14	6.6

3. DATA ANALYSIS AND RESULTS

The questionnaire data collected was carefully handled and analyzed by using a range of statistical methods, including means, frequencies, pie charts, histograms, and spearman's correlation. A uniquely designed formula was also used to calculate and estimate potential economic and environmental benefits generated by the usage of the smart parking service. The results and findings derived from the data analysis are presented and discussed in the following sections.

3.1 Level of citizen engagement in smart parking

The questionnaire results indicated that the majority of the 212 respondents were regular drivers (rather than occasional visitors) in the West End area (i.e. 76% of them stated that they visited and drove in the area very often or often). In other words, these respondents should have a strong need to use the smart parking service being deployed in the area since 2012. Surprisingly, and despite the very substantial investment being made, the survey results showed that current level of citizen engagement in London's smart parking service (in terms of both awareness and usage) was extremely low.

In particular, 74% (156 out of 212) of the respondents stated that they never or just occasionally heard about the service (Figure 1). In addition, when being asked whether they know what the smart parking app can do for them (e.g. show parking availability and empty spaces in real-time, allow drivers to pay for parking, and manage/extend their parking sessions on the phone), around 70% of the respondents stated that they did not know any (or know very little) of these functions. Similarly, a substantial number (i.e. over 47%) of the respondents did not have any (or had very little) knowledge about the benefits that could potentially be delivered by the smart parking service (e.g. saving time in seeking parking space, easing traffic pressure, saving petrol usage and cost, and reducing CO2 emission).

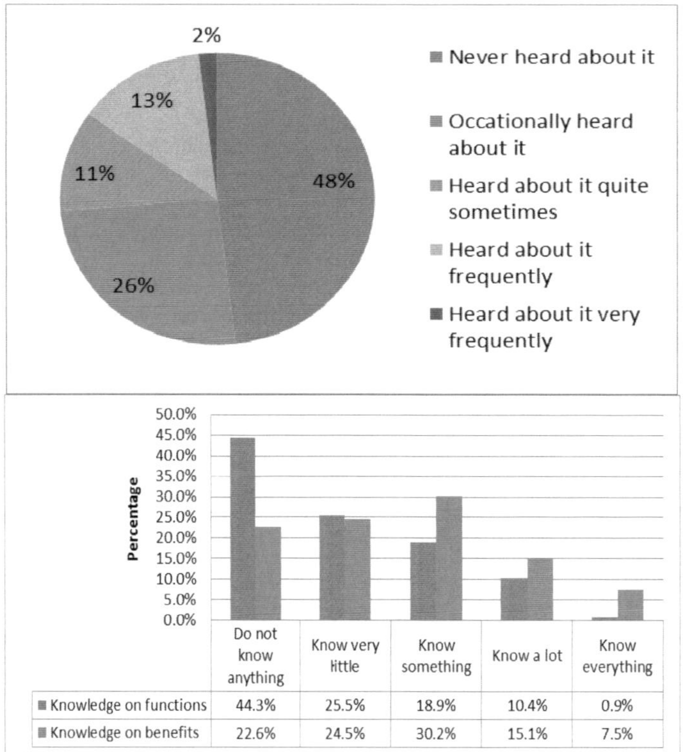

	Do not know anything	Know very little	Know something	Know a lot	Know everything
Knowledge on functions	44.3%	25.5%	18.9%	10.4%	0.9%
Knowledge on benefits	22.6%	24.5%	30.2%	15.1%	7.5%

Figure 1. Citizen awareness in London's smart parking service

Further to the lack of awareness of smart parking, the questionnaire results indicated that current usage of this service was also very low - 78% (165 out of 212) of the respondents stated that they never or rarely use the service (Figure 2). In contrast, only 17% of the respondents indicated that they would use the smart parking service often or very often. It can be argued that the fact that such low usage rate could be the result of a lack of awareness of the existence and usefulness of the service. This hypothesis was proved by a further Spearman's correlation test, which showed that these two variables are positively correlated with a coefficient of $r = .749$ ($p < .001$).

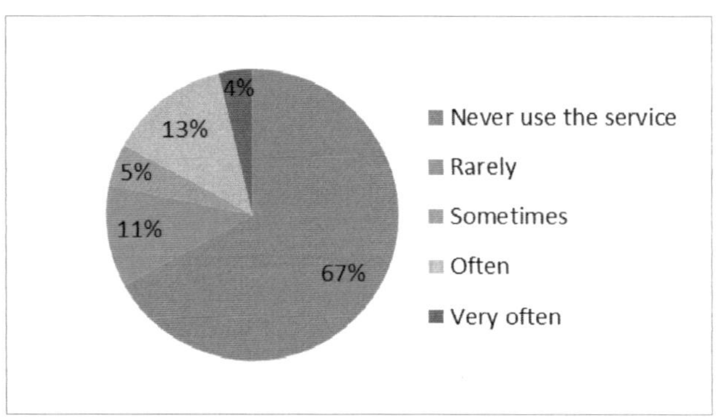

Figure 2. Citizen usage of London's smart parking service

In sum, the study found that current usage of London's smart parking service was generally low, and this was directly caused by people's low awareness of the service. These findings provided very strong evidence to demonstrate the imperative need for the London city council to make more essential efforts to raise citizen awareness and usage towards smart parking, if they want to maximize the return of their investment in this smart service and transform the city into a more liveable place.

3.2 Quantification of economic and environmental benefits of smart parking

Economic and environmental benefits generated by the usage of smart services may not always be apparent to users and often cannot be measured directly. This study developed and applied a unique approach that consisted of a set of formulas to quantify the economic and environmental benefits of smart parking, and so provided an exemplification to show how smart city benefits could be measured systematically. The questionnaire contained a set of four questions/measures to collect the necessary data to be used in the benefit quantification process. The results of these questions are summarized in Table 2.

Table 2. Time and frequency for looking at parking spaces in West End

Measures used in questionnaire	*Average*	*N*
Minutes to search for parking spaces without smart parking	17.65 minutes per time	212
Minutes to search for parking spaces with smart parking	10.17 minutes per time	70
Sample's frequency of searching for parking spaces	12.3 times per week per car	212
Sample's frequency of searching for parking spaces by using smart parking	2.2 times per week per car	212

The questionnaire results in Table 2 showed that originally, the respondents needed to spend 17.65 minutes in average to search for an on-street parking space in the West End area. For those who used the smart parking service (33% of the total sample, N = 70 out of 212), their average parking search time could be reduced to 10.17 minutes. In order words, smart parking could help London drivers to save an average of 7.48 minutes (i.e. 17.65 – 10.17 = 7.48) per time for parking search. On the other hand, the respondents indicated that they averagely needed to search for on-street parking facilities in West End for about 12.3 times per week per car. However, due to a significant lack of awareness, the frequency for the respondents to use the smart parking service in helping them to find empty spaces was only around 2.2 times per week per car in average. In other words, the actual usage rate of smart parking currently was only at 17.9% (i.e. 2.2 / 12.3 = 17.9%).

These measurement results derived from the questionnaire, together with other existing secondary indicators/data supplied by authorised sources (as discussed below), provided the fundamental inputs for the researchers to calculate the economic and environmental benefits of smart parking by using the following designed formulas and steps.

Step 1: Average travel distance saved each time by using smart parking

According to official data provided by Transport for London (2012), the average vehicle travel speed for the 12 hours between 07:00 to 19:00 across Central London was about 8.98 mph (or 14.452 km/h). Since this time band covers the active traffic period of the day, which has stronger demand of parking facilities than the rest of the day, this travel speed was considered as a good indicator to be used in the calculation of the travel distance that could be saved as a result of using the smart parking service. Specifically, the average travel distance that drivers could save each time by using the smart parking service was calculated as follows:

Average Distance Saved per Time (ADST) = Average Travel Speed * Average Time Saved by Smart Parking = 14.452 km/h * 7.48 minutes / 60 minutes per hour = 1.8 km per time

Step 2: Potential travel distance saved per car per year by using smart parking

As mentioned above, the respondents needed to search for parking facilities in West End for about 12.3 times per week per car in average. If drivers always use the smart parking app to search for empty spaces, the weekly and yearly travel distance that each car could potentially save can be calculated as:

Average Distance Potentially Saved per Week (ADPSW) = ADST * Average Times for Parking Search per Week = 1.8 km per time * 12.3 times = 22.14 km per week

Average Distance Potentially Saved per Year (ADPSY) = ADPSW * Number of Weeks per Year = 22.14 km per weeks * 52 weeks per year = 1151.28 km per year

Step 3: Potential petrol saving per car per year by using smart parking

The comprehensive report provided by the International Energy Agency (2013) made very thorough comparison of vehicle fuel consumption levels across 26 different countries of the world. This report indicated that UK vehicle's average fuel consumption rate was 5.4 litres per 100 km in 2013 (i.e. cars in the UK would consume an average of 5.4 litres of petrol for every 100 km). This piece of data was then used to calculate the amount of petrol that could be potentially saved by using smart parking per car per year:

Individual's Potential Petrol Usage Saving per Year (IPPUSY) = ADPSY * UK Vehicle Fuel Consumption Rate = 1151.28 km * 5.4 litres per 100 km = 62.2 litres per year

It is obvious that local petrol prices can be influenced by many market factors (e.g. international oil price) and so can be changed over time. Nevertheless, the most recent Fuel Price Report provided by the Automobile Association (AA) in the UK showed that the country's national average petrol price was £1.09 per litre in Oct 2015 (Automobile Association, 2015). The potential economic saving that could be made by each car as a result of using smart parking was thus calculated as:

Individual's Potential Petrol Cost Saving per Year (IPPCSY) = IPPUSY * Petrol cost per litre = 62.2 litres * £1.09 per litres = £68 per year

Step 4: Potential CO2 reduction per car per year by using smart parking

A jointed report published by the Department of Energy and Climate Change and the Department for Environment, Food and Rural Affairs in the UK provided very useful indicators to covert fuel consumption into kilograms of carbon dioxide equivalent (CO2e), and so allow individuals and companies to generate a clear view of CO2 emissions related to their energy usage (AEA, 2012). It was estimated in this official report that the direct CO2 emission for a medium petrol car with 1.4-1.6 litres engine is 0.20685 kg CO2e per km. The environmental impact (in terms of CO2 reduction) that each car can potentially make by using smart parking can thus be calculated as:

Individual's Potential Reduction in CO2 Emissions per Year (IPRCOEY) = ADPSY * CO2 emission per km = 1151.28 km * 0.20685 kgCO2e per km = 238.14 kg per year

Step 5: Potential economic and environmental benefits per year at city level

By far, the authors had shown how economic and environmental benefits of smart parking could be calculated at an individual level. This final step aimed to estimate such benefits at the city level. According to the official open dataset provided by the Department for Transport in London, there were about 2.7 million licenced private and light-good vehicles in the city by the end of 2014 (Department for Transport, 2015). This total number of registered private vehicles was thus used to calculate and estimate the economic and environmental benefits, which the smart parking service could potentially bring to the city (note: London has a large number of commuters who drive daily into the city from surrounding areas, but due to a lack of official number of these daily commuters, the researchers did not include this group of potential users in the calculation):

City's Potential Petrol Usage Saving per Year (CPPUSY) = IPPUSY * Total Number of Registered Private Vehicles = 62.2 litres * 2.7 million = 167.9 million litres per year

City's Potential Petrol Cost Saving per Year (CPPCSY) = IPPCSY * Total Number of Registered Private Vehicles = £68 * 2.7 million = £183.6 million per year

City's Potential Reduction in CO2 Emissions per Year (CPRCOEY) = IPRCOEY * Total Number of Registered Private Vehicles = 238.14 kg * 2.7 million = 643 million kg per year = 642,978 tons per year

Overall, our calculations and estimations showed that London's smart parking service can potentially generate very substantial benefits to both individuals and the city. At individual level, the service could potentially help each driver to save an average of £68 (62.2 litres) on petrol annually and reduce CO2 emissions by 238.14 kg per car per year. At city level, the smart parking system could help London save £183.6 million worth of petrol per year and reduce its annual CO2 emissions by 642,978 tons. However, the prerequisite for making these benefits come true is that each London driver shall use the smart parking service every time when they need to search for an empty space in the city centre. Unfortunately, and as discussed above, due to the current lack of awareness and usage of the service, the sample respondents only used the smart parking service for about 2.2 times (rather than 12.3 times) per week per car in average, representing an actual service usage rate of 17.9%. When repeating steps 2-5 above by using the actual service usage rate, it became clear that the benefits that London's smart parking service could deliver at the moment would be much lower than its potential expectations (as shown in Table 3).

Table 3. Potential VS current estimation of benefits delivered by London's smart parking

	Potential	***Current***
Sample's average smart parking usage	12.3 times per car per week	2.2 times per car per week
Average travel distance saved by individuals	1151.28 km per year	206 km per year
Average petrol usage saved by individuals	62.2 litres per year	11 litres per year
Average petrol cost saved by individuals	£68 per year	£12 per year
Average CO_2 reduction by individuals	238.14 kg per year	42.6 kg per year
Petrol usage saved by the city	167.9 million litres per year	30 million litres per year
Petrol cost saved by the city	£183.6 million per year	£32.9 million per year
CO_2 reduction by the city	642,978 tons per year	115,093 tons per year
Overall percentage	100%	17.9%

It is important to note that the researchers in this study aimed at providing only approximate estimations (rather than absolutely accurate calculations) of benefits of London's smart parking service. In fact, the accuracy of quantification of such benefits would inevitably be influenced by a range of factors (e.g. the size of the sample, the currency of secondary data provided by other sources, changes of petrol prices, and even changes of vehicle technologies over time). Nonetheless, in this paper the researchers attempted to offer a quantifiable view of potential benefits that might by delivered by smart parking, and more importantly to show local authorities, service providers and fellow researchers how the realisation of such benefits might be significantly affected by low citizen awareness and usage of smart services.

4. CONCLUSION

This paper reported on a research that adopted London's smart parking service as a case study. The main conclusion that we reached in this study is that successful deployment of a smart service would neither naturally lead to a high level of citizen engagement nor guarantee the realisation of the full potentials and benefits of the service. In the case of London's smart parking system, despite the very substantial investment made by the local city council, less than 18% of the possible economic and environmental benefits might be delivered owing to a lack of public awareness and insufficient service usage. It is apparent that such failures occurred in smart city development do not just lead to waste of investments and efforts, but may also damage the reputation and image of the local authority and service provider. Therefore, when much current attention and efforts were given to the technological development and deployment of smart solutions, there is a clear need for local authorities and service providers to make a stronger endeavour to enhance public engagement towards smart services, in order to realise the promises of such solutions.

REFERENCES

AEA, 2012. *2012 Guidelines to Defra/DECC's GHG conversion factors for company reporting*. Available at https://www.gov.uk/government/uploads/system/uploads/attachment_data/file/69554/pb13773-ghg-conversion-factors-2012.pdf. [Accessed 15 July 2015]

Allen, P A , 1993. Driver response to parking guidance and information systems. *Traffic Engineering and Control*, Vol. 34, pp. 302–307.

Automobile Association , 2015. *Fuel price report*. Available at http://www.theaa.com/motoring_advice/fuel/. [Accessed 05 Nov 2015]

Claussen, J. et al., 2013. The effects of rewarding user engagement: the case of Facebook apps. *Information Systems Research*, Vol. 24, No. 1, PP. 186-200. http://dx.doi.org/10.1287/isre.1120.0467

Department for Transport , 2014. *Vehicle licensing statistics: 2013*. Offical government report. Available at https://www.gov.uk/government/uploads/system/uploads/attachment_data/file/302409/vls-2013.pdf. [Accessed 15 July 2015]

Department for Transport , 2015. *Licenced vehicles – numbers, borough*. Open Dataset provided by local authority. Available at http://data.london.gov.uk/dataset/licensed-vehicles-numbers-borough. [Accessed 10 Nov 2015].

Ferneley, E.H. and Sobreperez, R. , 2006. Resist, comply or workaround? An examination of different facets of user engagement with information systems. *European Journal of Information Systems*, Vol. 15, pp. 345–356. doi:10.1057/palgrave.ejis.3000629

International Energy Agency, 2013. International comparison of light-duty vehiclefuel economy: evolution over 8 years from 2005 to 2013. *IEA working paper 11*. Available at http://www.fiafoundation.org/media/45112/wp11-iea-report-update-2014.pdf. [Accessed 05 Nov 2015].

Lanzaronea, G.A. and Zanzia, A., 2010. Monitoring gas and water consumption through ICTs for improved user awareness. *Information, Communication & Society*, Vol. 13, No. 1, pp. 121-135. doi:10.1080/13691180902992962

Nam, T. and Pardo, T.A. , 2011. Conceptualizing smart city with dimensions of technology, people, and institutions. *In Proceedings of the 12th Annual International Conference on Digital Government Research*, 12-15 June 2011, College Park, MD, USA, doi: 10.1145/2037556.2037602

Neirotti, P. et al., 2014. Current trends in Smart City initiatives: some stylised facts. *Cities*, Vol. 38, pp. 25-36. doi: 10.1016/j.cities.2013.12.010

Peng, G.C. , 2015. Smart cities are built by smart citizens. *Expert article in Financial Express*. http://www.financialexpress.com/article/fe-columnist/smart-cities-are-built-by-smart-citizens/136353/. [Accessed 16 Sep 2015].

Rodier, C.J. et al., 2004. Transit-based smart parking in the San Francisco bay area: an assessment of user demand and behavioral effects. *Research report submitted to Transportation Research Board (TRB)*. http://citeseerx.ist.psu.edu/viewdoc/download? doi=10.1.1.514.7121&rep=rep1&type=pdf. [Accessed 10 Oct 2015].

Shoup, D. C., 2006. Cruising for parking. *Transport Policy*, Vol.13, No.6, pp. 479–486. doi: 10.1016/j.tranpol.2006.05.005

Transport for London , 2012. *London Street: Performance Report Quarter 1 2012/13*. Official government report. http://www.tfl.gov.uk/cdn/static/cms/documents/london-streets-performance-report-q1-2012-13.pdf.[Accessed 15 July 2015].

Westminster City Council, 2014. *Parking technology and systems*. http://www.local.gov.uk/documents/10180/6360115/Westminster+Parking+case+study+-+FINAL.pdf/2a56ddb9-bf77-416c-abff-83893a680521. [Accessed 15 July 2015].

TAMING THE FLOOD: INTELLIGENT INCIDENT REPORT MANAGEMENT IN SMART CITIES

Pouyan Fotouhi Tehrani, Stefan Pfennigschmidt, Ulrich Kriegel,
Andreas Billig, Frank Fuchs-Kittowski and Ulrich Meissen
Fraunhofer-Institut für Offene Kommunikationssysteme
ESPRI – Electronic Safety and Security Systems for the Public and Industries, Germany

ABSTRACT

Confronting disasters or crises, be it natural or human-caused, require adequate access to information and a high degree of cooperation between involved organizations, authorities and citizens. This paper addresses the problem of information integration and manageability by proposing an approach resilient to high data influx and partial system failures which uses semantic technologies to make sense of the information flood emerged during the crises, allows citizens to provide real-time information about ongoing incidents, and finally warns people of acute dangers in their vicinity. This approach integrates people in the information feedback loop and allows authorities to manage the situation more efficiently and effectively.

KEYWORDS

Smart city, urban safety, crowdsourcing, decision support, expert system, incident management

1. INTRODUCTION

Natural and human-caused crises, emergencies and catastrophes are and have been an inevitable part of human societies and as such an integral subject of public discourse. Technological advances in software, hardware, and telecommunications, specifically in ubiquitous computing, sensor networks, and broadband wireless transmission have continuously provided new means of predicting, analyzing, communicating, and managing such events. In smart cities where sensors (real or virtual) are deployed to harness information and organizations as well as government institutions are interconnected, data is evaluated "to achieve new efficiencies" (Harrison et al. 2010) in various spheres of *city administration*, *safety*, *transport* etc. (Washburn & Sindhu 2009). Broad access to versatile information in cities and communities has brought new opportunities to address crises and incident management.

The circuit of information in smart cities, however, gives rise to the question of data manageability. The mere abundance of information can only be of use if the relevant and the irrelevant are separated, related data is bundled together, and raw input is contextualized. In other words, it is not only the access to data that makes a city smart, but also the capability of creating intelligible information out of collected (or crowdsourced) data. It cannot be expected, nonetheless, for this task is to be carried out in a centralized manner by a single entity; and also means for information dissemination among multiple actors has to be arranged. In this sense and despite the fact that smartness of a city can be qualified by different factors of "economy, people, governance, mobility, environment and living" (Giffinger & Gudrun 2010) or other philosophical, sociological, etc. perspectives (see Nam & Pardo, 2011), from a technical point of view, being smart reduces to an iteration of *data*, *develop*, and *dispatch* (the *DDD model*), whereas *data* refers to information collection, develop to data processing, enrichment, and filtering, and dispatch to data exchange with other parties. Take the 2016 Munich shooting for example, where 9 people were shot dead and many were left injured. Citizens, as well as authorities, used social media to publish (at times paradoxical) information, images, and videos about the ongoing incident. The high influx of information rendered these channels as rather disruptive than constructive in managing the situation and it was an overwhelming situation not only for the authorities but also for the citizens in how to cope with information of such magnitude. If the required infrastructure and procedures were established and the imperatives of the DDD model were fulfilled, the cooperation between citizens and authorities in facing the massacre would have surely been more effective.

This paper introduces an incident management system which uses real-time crowdsourced data using smartphones, leverages semantic technologies to filter, classify, and correlate them, and provides the result to authorities, organizations, and citizens. The system is distributed among loosely coupled components which allow seamless horizontal scaling to handle massive data throughput and timely processing. Adhering to the DDD model, the main goal is on the one hand to avoid the common "information overload" integral to crises (Turoff et al. 2004) for authorities (e.g. operation centers) by automating data analysis, and to close the feedback loop with citizens on the other hand.

The structure of this work is as follows: section 2 gives an overview of related works. Section 3 provides functional and technical requirements, section 4 introduces the proposed concept, section 5 discusses its implementation, and section 6 concludes the paper and provides an outlook.

2. RELATED WORK

Managing crises and large-scale incidents is a multifaceted enterprise involving different fields of study: harness useful real-time data, turning data into information, relate information in context of previous knowledge, coordinate all parties and provide them with relevant information, and finally improve the information cycle by closing the feedback loop. Adam et al. propose *SMART-C* as blueprint of a system that covers all aspects of the DDD model and focuses on multimodal "data collection", "data enrichment", and "customized alerting" (Adam et al. 2012). Data heterogeneity in terms of form and content in context of multimodal information harvesting as well as uniform data models between system components are, however, not addressed and considered as given. Another relevant project is EARS (Earthquake Alert and Report System) which uses Twitter API as its main data source, filters and enhances data using a custom trained module, and acts as an early warning system over a web interface (Avvenuti et al. 2014). However, it does not create targeted warnings with regard to recipient's location and/or other features. Other less holistic concepts and approaches relevant for incident and disaster management, which are of relevance to our work and amount to our motivation, are categorized in terms of the DDD model and are enumerated in the following.

With regard to data collection, it has been striven to achieve scalable and reliable wireless networks to collect environment information since the early days of wireless microsensors (see Bult, Burstein, Chang, & Dong, 1996). It didn't take long until smartphones were considered as mobile wireless sensors and the Internet as de facto the communication infrastructure (Turner & White 2011). Zambonelli contemplates on the idea of "pervasive urban crowdsourcing" where collaboration of "humans as devices" leads to an improvement of "the way we live, work, move, and play in our towns" (Zambonelli 2011). Similarly, the idea of *people as sensors* suggests enhancing sensors with "contextual intelligence and comprehensive knowledge" through humans (Resch 2013). An intuitive example of how people as sensors can be deployed in urban safety scenarios is to make a picture of an incident, geo-tag it, and send it to responsible organizations (Goncalves et al. 2014). Blom et al. introduce and evaluate a mobile communication system focusing on urban safety where participants share their location and own safety perception of that location with other users to provide a sense of comfort by showing presence and also to warn others of possibly unsafe areas (Blom et al. 2010). The idea of people as sensors/devices raises the question of how to integrate human perception/knowledge with raw sensor measurements to produce structured data suitable for computer processing. Moreover, the most important overlooked aspect in nearly all aforementioned approaches is scalability and fault tolerance during data collection which cannot be neglected throughout urban crisis or incidents. Using smartphones as sources of information is rather an intuitive enterprise, but providing infrastructure that can handle high amounts of data influx and inevitable server failures required comprehensive considerations.

Collecting data on a large scale is interleaved with challenges of manageability and requires methods of contextualizing data and coping with information overload. The potential of public social media and web content is taken advantage of in a "crowd sensing based burst computation algorithm" to dynamically detect notable events of real life as projected in the internet (Xu et al. 2017). Many researches focus on employing semantic technologies to harvest information from social media (Zavarella et al. 2014; Ghahremanlou et al.

2015; Purohit et al. 2014). Han & Kim review how expert systems, GIS, decision support systems, databases, and AI in general can be used to build *intelligent* urban information systems to "provide more intelligent and effective solutions to urban problems" (Han & Kim 1989) and *FRED* (Freeway Real-Time Expert System Demonstration), a practical example of an expert system, shows how its deployment can prevent human operators from being overwhelmed by high amounts of real-time information in context of incident management on urban highways (Ritchie & Prosser 1991). The work at hand uses semantic ontologies to develop structured data for automatic data processing and uses a special urban incident ontology to isolate relevant reports from irrelevant ones and to bundle related reports together to logical incidents to provide a better overview of ongoing happenings.

After adaptation, data must be provided or even automatically disseminated to involved parties. Hale pinpoints the lack of "communication needed to access to relevant data or expertise" as the "key obstacle to effective crisis response" (Hale 1997). "Information validity" and "free exchange of information" has also been identified as two of design premises for the *Dynamic Emergency Response Management Information System (DERMIS)* (Turoff et al. 2004). The need for a standardized, "interoperable communication process" which goes beyond the borders of agencies and jurisdictions is also well recognized by *the National Interagency Incident Management System model* (Annelli 2006). Yates & Paquette investigate intra-organizational knowledge transfer and the positive impact of social media technologies (e.g. Wikis) by studying their application in disaster management and response of 2010 Haiti earthquake (Yates & Paquette 2011) and Babitski et al. introduce an ontology to integrate heterogeneous information among organizations (Babitski et al. 2009) which can be used to enable inter-organization information exchange. In this paper, semantic technologies are used to normalize data to enable information integration among authorities and organizations, and citizens are also brought into the information cycle by providing proactive targeted messages.

3. REQUIREMENTS

As part of a larger European project, *CityRisks* (http://project.cityrisks.eu), during a research and discussion period with regard to related works and literature, an abstract reference use case (without loss of generality) was crafted and a number of corresponding requirements and performance indicators were determined.

The conceptualized use case assumes an urban incident with citizens and authorities as actors. Citizens at site can report the ongoing incident and provide authorities with information which is processed and digested automatically, and can be verified manually by operators. Eventually citizens in the vicinity of incident are also warned about the situation. The use case was analyzed by project partners in context of a number of real-life scenarios and the following functional requirements for an incident management system were crystallized:

1. **Means of information exchange**: send reports / receive updates and warnings
2. **Data normalization**: transform data to a common format and/or language
3. **Content analysis**: extract keywords from textual content / tag visual content
4. **Semantic processing**: measure similarity / classify content / filter
5. **Spatiotemporal reasoning**: assign reports to (logical) incidents / dispatch targeted alerts
6. **Automatic task coordination**: designate tasks to components without human interception

To fulfill functional requirement 1, mobile devices (i.e. smartphones) were selected due to their ubiquity and their capability of acting as a duplex communication channel, i.e. capable of sending and receiving data at the same time (e.g. over the Internet). For requirements 2 to 6 an intelligent system, referred to as *Risk Management and Response service* (RMRS), was conceptualized. In addition to functional requirements, various technical requirements are also defined for both RMRS and mobile applications:

- **Risk Management and Response Service:**
  - Distributed
  - Fault tolerant
  - Highly available
  - Extendable and expandable
  - Capable of real-time data flow
- **Mobile Application**:

- o Intuitive interface with short learning curve
- o Functions both actively and proactively
- o Enables real-time communication
- o Supports secure and anonymous communication
- o Capable of receiving live warnings

Such incident management ecosystem aims to rectify the shortcomings of existing incident management systems on data gathering level by enhancing mobile sensor data with human perception (i.e. *people as sensors*), on data development level by transforming information to knowledge using semantic technologies to avoid information overload, and finally on communication level by providing updates and alerts to citizens to close the information feedback loop.

4. CONCEPT

This paper proposes an incident management system which gathers crowdsourced information using mobile devices and does the processing and analysis through a number of services in a distributed manner. This section investigates the concepts and next section the implementation of the system.

4.1 Mobile Application

Throughout this work an emphasis has been put on involving people as viable sources of critical information and their role in the information feedback loop. In contrast to common media (e.g. radio, television, etc.) used for communication during crises and urban safety related matters, smartphones allow a two-way data exchange. Complying with functional and technical requirements of section 3, a smartphone application has been designed to provide means for individuals to fetch a list of registered incidents, submit new incident reports or enhance incidents with new reports, and receive warnings about ongoing incidents and acute dangerous situations in the vicinity. To ensure users' privacy, the communication is to be encrypted and no personal data or any kind of metadata, that could reveal users' real identity, is required. The only absolutely necessary piece of information is a user's latest timestamped known location so that RMRS can decide if they are affected by any incident or not. In terms of the DDD model, the mobile application fulfills the *data* task.

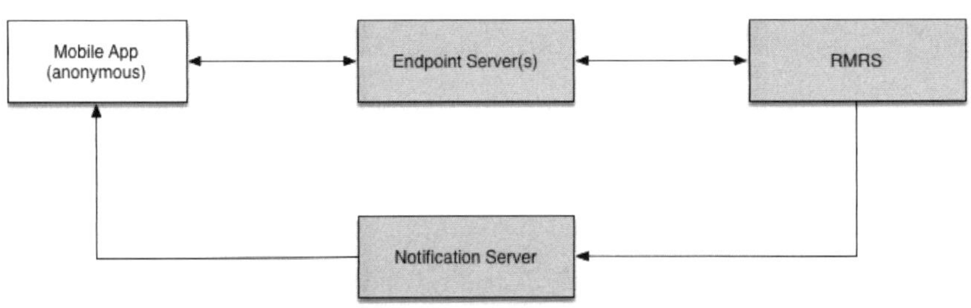

Figure 1. Mobile application communication overview

Figure 1 depicts the information flow between the mobile application and RMRS. A number of task-specific servers, called *endpoints*, are designated as part of the RMRS to allow sending and receiving of data in a predefined format in a common server/client approach. To assure fault tolerance and scalability severs are designed to be replicable and independent of each other. The communication with endpoints is always initiated through the mobile app. In contrast, alerts, warnings, and messages of high priority are proactively sent by RMRS over a notification server.

4.2 Risk Management and Response Service

To process data and dispatch warnings, a number of loosely coupled (Kaye 2003) components, collectively called the Risk Management and Response Service, has been designed. In terms of the DDD model, the task of RMRS is to *develop* and *dispatch*: to filter, classify, correlate reports and generate logical incidents (a collection of reports about same event) on the one hand, and to provide authorities (e.g. an operation center) and mobile app users with this useful information on the other hand.

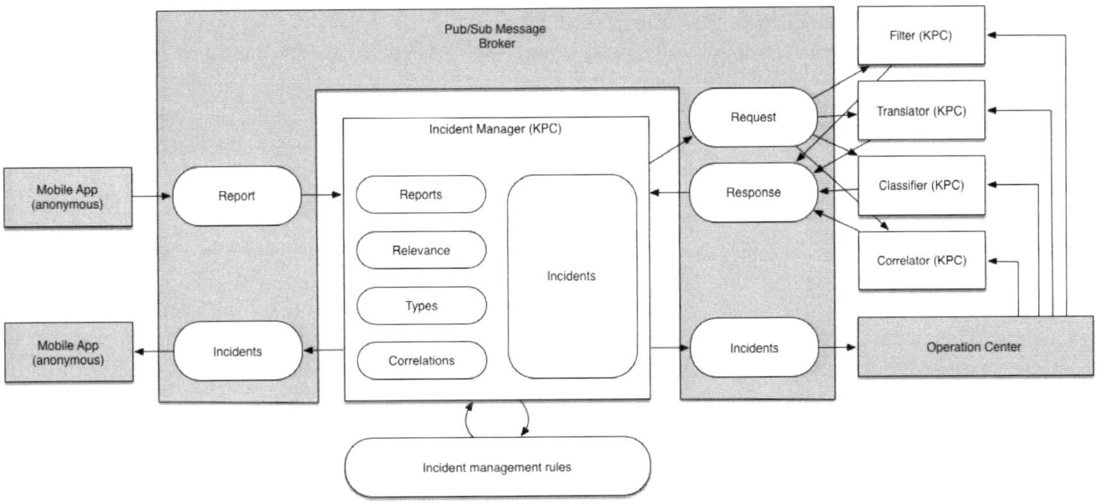

Figure 2. RMRS architecture overview

An overview of RMRS is given in Figure 2. From an architectural point of view, the system is considered to be a distributed one, i.e. of independent components communicating and coordinating only by means of message passing (Coulouris et al. 2005). The building blocks of RMRS are *Knowledge Processing Components* (KPC) corresponding asynchronously over a publish/subscribe (Tarkoma 2012) message broker. The advantage of such approach is twofold: first, there is no software/hardware constraints on components (as long as they are attached to the message broker), and second, the asynchronous communication allows parallel computing. Moreover, each component may maintain its own state, but a global state is neither given nor required.

Within RMRS, the smallest processable piece of data is called a *report*, which is initiated through a mobile device. A report contains information such as location, timestamp, description of an incident and can have a complimentary image or video attached. A collection of related reports is called an *incident*. A list of logical KPCs, acting on reports and incidents, is as follows:

- **Incident Manager**: is the gateway between mobile devices and RMRS (through endpoint servers), orchestrates KPCs using predefined rules, and dispatches alerts (requirement 5 and 6)
- **Translator**: translates text content (i.e. description) of a report and tags its attached media (requirement 2 and 3).
- **Filter**: approves or discards a report as respectively relevant or irrelevant with regard to its spatiotemporal information or its classification (requirement 4).
- **Classifier**: classifies a report using a predefined ontology (requirement 3 and 4).
- **Correlator**: correlates incoming reports with existing incidents (requirement 4 and 5).

Following extendibility requirement, it is noteworthy that the system is conceptualized to manage different instances of the same logical KPC at the same time. The idea is to employ an asynchronous *one-request/multiple-response* communication scheme, where a single request, e.g. for classification, from the Incident Manager may be processed by several Classifier components that independently produce their results, which in a following step are combined by the Incident Manager based on confidence ratings. Also, a human, such as an operator in the operation center, may respond to such a request, for instance, to have a final say. This allows a rapid and more efficient data processing, where, for example, while a human operator verifies textual content, the rest of the system can proceed with automatic machine translated content for classification, etc. until data of better quality is provided.

A typical workflow is initiated by receiving a report from a mobile device. First stop for a new report is the Incident Manager. Users can either send *orphan reports*, i.e. belonging to no previously known incident, or enhance existing incidents with a new report. In either case, the Incident Manager sends reports' contents (textual and visual) first to the Translator where textual content is translated into the base language of used ontology and visual content is tagged with keywords. The Translator sends the results back to the Incident Manager, where they are added to the corresponding report, and the report is then sent to the Filter to check for relevance. Reports, for example, with visual content not safe for work (as tagged by the Translator) are marked as irrelevant by the Filter and are not further processed. At this stage, if necessary, the Incident Manager wraps an orphan report inside a new incident. New or updated incidents are then sent to the Classifier. At the core of the Classifier lies an ontology used to assign predefined incident types to incidents by analyzing translated and tagged content. In the next step, the Correlator uses common approaches known from information retrieval and semantic technologies (e.g. calculating textual and semantic distances), and also spatiotemporal features of incidents to measure similarities among them. The result, again, is provided to the Incident Manager. If the similarity value between any pair of incidents reaches a threshold, Incident Manager merges them together and the resulting incident is again fed through the pipeline of classification, correlation, etc. Finally, the Incident Manager publishes the results on the message bus for everyone (e.g. local operation center) to access. Moreover, using the latest known location of mobile users, those who may be exposed to the incident are selected and are proactively provided with updated incident information. All other users may access respective information actively by querying the endpoints.

5. SYSTEM DEVELOPMENT

Within the framework of the CityRisks project, the proposed concept has been realized using a smartphone application (for Android OS) and a collection of RMRS components.

5.1 Mobile Application

The mobile application enables users to compose text and attach images to generate reports and get updates about incidents on the one hand and receive warnings through push notifications on the other hand. Each new report is automatically enhanced by the application with geolocation information from the GPS sensor and is marked with a creation timestamp. The communication with RMRS is done through HTTPS endpoints and the default message format is JSON. Visual content is transferred as binary data and the corresponding URI is embedded in the report JSON.

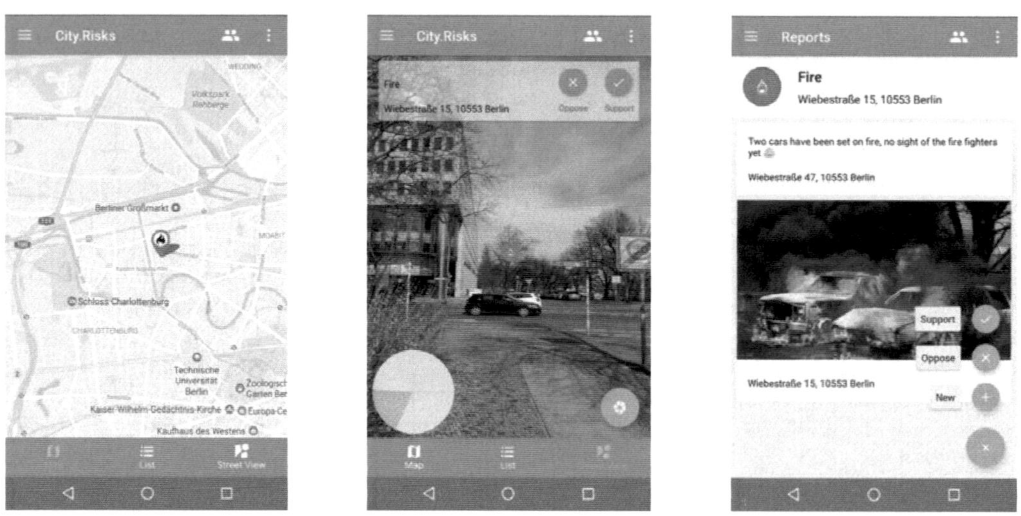

(a) Map view (b) Virtual reality view (c) List view

Figure 3. Incident report and view

Figure 3 depicts different views of how users can interact with the application to (a) view active incidents on the map, (b) view active incidents through a virtual reality view, and (c) create new reports or review and add supplemental reports to existing incidents.

5.2 Risk Management and Response Service

The implementation of RMRS follows the imperatives of microservices architecture, i.e. composed of a number of “small application[s] that can be deployed independently, scaled independently, and tested independently” (Thönes 2015). The system has been realized with high scalability and component independence in mind. Components can logically be divided into endpoint servers providing REST APIs (communication gateway to mobile applications) realized in JavaScript using *restify* framework, and KPCs realized in Java using *Vert.x* framework. A persistence layer has been created using two NoSQL database types: a document-oriented database (specifically *MongoDB*) for longtime persistence and a key-value store (namely *redis*) for short-time caching. Moreover, all components are isolated in Docker containers which guarantees effortless scaling, migration, and orchestration.

Incident Manager uses *JBoss* Drools as its business rule engine to coordinate tasks among KPCs. Translator makes use of *Clarifai Image and Video Recognition API* to tag visual content of reports, and *Yandex Translation API* to translate their textual content in English. The remaining KPCs, i.e. Filter, Classifier, and Correlator, all depend (in different ways and with regard to different features) on *Apache Lucene* as base engine for information retrieval tasks and *Apache Jena* for ontology related semantic tasks.

6. CONCLUSION AND OUTLOOK

This paper introduces an approach to manage incident reports in urban settings using semantic technologies. It tackles the information overflow inherent to urban emergency events by filtering, classifying, correlating, and bundling reports in manageable units which provide a better overview of the situation. Using smartphones, it brings citizens into the information cycle of incident management both as sources and targets of information while protecting their anonymity and providing privacy. The necessity of fault-tolerance and availability has been fulfilled through the distributed, microservice architecture of the framework which foresees potential bottlenecks of a monolithic system and counters them with seamless horizontal scaling and redundancy. Within the framework, the one-request/multiple-response paradigm, where multiple components process the same request and provide multiple responses, enables preliminary data processing with responses of lower quality until responses of higher quality are provided so that soft real-time constraints are enforced and retrospective data correction is achievable. With respect to requirements of expandability and extendibility, it is also possible to imagine data sources other than smartphones (e.g. traffic cameras) attached to ecosystem of this framework to improve information quality. Access to real-time data can be provided to authorities and organizations through the pub/sub message bus without further requirements or impairment of the system.

Challenges such as infrastructure failures (e.g. network blackouts) and heterogeneous data from multimodal data sources (e.g. SMS, voice messages) as well as tradeoffs between timeliness and accuracy, anonymity and liability, etc. are to be investigated in future works. Moreover, simulation results and pilot projects are to be evaluated in a separate work. For now, we know that the future smart city will a be safe one.

ACKNOWLEDGEMENT

This research has received funding from the European Union's *Horizon 2020 Research and Innovation Program* under grant agreement № **653747** as part of the project *CityRisks* (http://project.cityrisks.eu/).

REFERENCES

Adam, N. et al., 2012. Social Media Alert and Response to Threats to Citizens. In *Proceedings of the 8th IEEE International Conference on Collaborative Computing: Networking, Applications and Worksharing*. IEEE, pp. 181–189.

Annelli, J.F., 2006. The national incident management system: A multi-agency approach to emergency response in the United States of America. *Revue scientifique et technique (International Office of Epizootics)*, 25(1), pp.223–231.

Avvenuti, M. et al., 2014. EARS (earthquake alert and report system). In *Proceedings of the 20th ACM SIGKDD international conference on Knowledge discovery and data mining - KDD '14*. New York, New York, USA: ACM Press, pp. 1749–1758.

Babitski, G. et al., 2009. Ontology Design for Information Integration in Disaster Management. *Informatik 2009.*, pp.3120–3134.

Blom, J. et al., 2010. Fear and the City: Role of Mobile Services in Harnessing Safety and Security in Urban Use Contexts. *Chi'10*, pp.1841–1850.

Bult, K. et al., 1996. Low power systems for wireless microsensors. *Low Power*, pp.17–21.

Coulouris, G.F., Dollimore, J. & Kindberg, T., 2005. *Distributed Systems: Concepts and Design*, Pearson Education.

Ghahremanlou, L., Sherchan, W. & Thom, J.A., 2015. Geotagging Twitter Messages in Crisis Management. *Computer Journal*, 58(9), pp.1937–1954.

Giffinger, R. & Gudrun, H., 2010. Smart cities ranking: an effective instrument for the positioning of the cities? *ACE: Architecture, City and Environment*, 4(12), pp.7–26.

Goncalves, A. et al., 2014. Crowdsourcing for public safety. *8th Annual IEEE International Systems Conference, SysCon 2014 - Proceedings*, pp.50–56.

Hale, J., 1997. A Layered Communication Architecture for the Support of Crisis Response. *Journal of Management Information Systems*, 14(1), pp.235–255.

Han, S.-Y. & Kim, T.J., 1989. Can expert systems help with planning? *Journal of the American Planning Association*, 55(3), pp.296–308.

Harrison, C. et al., 2010. Foundations for Smarter Cities. *IBM Journal of Research and Development*, 54(4), pp.1–16.

Kaye, D., 2003. *Loosely coupled : the missing pieces of Web services*, RDS Press.

Nam, T. & Pardo, T. a., 2011. Conceptualizing smart city with dimensions of technology, people, and institutions. *Proceedings of the 12th Annual International Digital Government Research Conference on Digital Government Innovation in Challenging Times - dg.o '11*, p.282.

Purohit, H. et al., 2014. Identifying Seekers and Suppliers in Social Media Communities to Support Crisis Coordination. *Computer Supported Cooperative Work (CSCW)*, 23(4–6), pp.513–545.

Resch, B., 2013. People as Sensors and Collective Sensing- Contextual Observations Complementing Geo-Sensor Network Measurements. In *Progress in Location-Based Services*. pp. 391–406.

Ritchie, S.G. & Prosser, N.A., 1991. Real-Time Expert System Approach to Freeway Incident Management. *Transportation Research Record*, No. 1320(1320), pp.7–16.

Tarkoma, S., 2012. *Publish/subscribe systems: design and principles*, John Wiley & Sons.

Thönes, J., 2015. Microservices. *IEEE Software*, 32(1), pp.113–116.

Turner, H. & White, J., 2011. Building Mobile Sensor Networks Using Smartphones and Web Services: Ramifications and Development Challenges Abstract. *Handbook of Research on Mobility and Computing: Evolving Technologies and Ubiquitous Impacts*, 1, pp.502–521.

Turoff, M. et al., 2004. The Design of a Dynamic Emergency Response Management Information System (DERMIS). *Journal of Information Technology Theory and Application (JITTA)*, 5(4).

Washburn, D. & Sindhu, U., 2009. Helping CIOs Understand "Smart City" Initiatives. *Growth*, 17(2), pp.1–17.

Xu, Z. et al., 2017. Crowdsourcing based social media data analysis of urban emergency events. *Multimedia Tools and Applications*, 76(9), pp.11567–11584.

Yates, D. & Paquette, S., 2011. Emergency knowledge management and social media technologies: A case study of the 2010 Haitian earthquake. *International Journal of Information Management*, 31(1), pp.6–13.

Zambonelli, F., 2011. Pervasive urban crowdsourcing: Visions and challenges. In *2011 IEEE International Conference on Pervasive Computing and Communications Workshops (PERCOM Workshops)*. IEEE, pp. 578–583.

Zavarella, V. et al., 2014. An Ontology-Based Approach to Social Media Mining for Crisis Management. *SMILE. Workshop on Social Media and Linked Data for Emergency Response*.

Short Papers

AN EARLY ALERT FEEDBACK SYSTEM IN LEARNING

Annette van der Merwe, Hennie Kruger and Tiny du Toit
North-West University, School of Computer-, Mathematical-, and Statistical Sciences
11 Hoffman Street ,Potchefstroom 2531, South Africa

ABSTRACT

The fields of teaching and learning are evolving as a result of new techniques like blended-, online-, and exploratory learning being implemented. Lecturers need to ensure successful teaching and also create an environment in which students can learn effectively. Two important factors that a lecturer can control to enhance learning are instruction and feedback. A learning analytics system was developed for the latter, utilizing mathematical programming models, which enables a lecturer to provide real-time progress feedback to students at regular intervals during the course of a program. This paper highlights flaws identified in some existing feedback scenarios, discusses the development of an electronic feedback system, and explains how its implementation can keep students informed on their progress from an early stage of instruction and present them with actionable targets for reaching their ultimate goal.

KEYWORDS

Data envelopment analysis; early alert feedback system; mathematical modelling; student ranking

1. INTRODUCTION

The parties involved in a teaching and learning environment are the lecturers, who must establish an optimal learning setting, and the students who must participate and learn. Although the common perception among students is that their main responsibility is partaking in lectures, they still feel that lecturers have to provide guidance and motivation for them to achieve success (Geçer, 2013). In order to enhance learning, lecturers must adopt effective instruction- and subsequent feedback methods that jointly creates an ideal environment for learning. They supplement their teaching regimes with examples, topical case studies relating to new work, and in-depth class discussions. The pace at which technology is advancing enables lecturers to adapt their teaching and assessment techniques (Landau, et al., 2014) by augmenting them with the use of learning management systems (LMSs) (Sin & Muthu, 2015). Different forms of LMSs are used to aid the learning process and are readily accepted by students. Most LMSs have analytic capabilities which can provide useful feedback statistics regarding students' use of certain fields in the LMS (Siemens, 2011). Together with effective teaching, feedback plays an equally important role in enhancing the learning environment (Hattie, 2005).

With all the challenges lecturers face (Brühwiler, 2011), the role of the lecturer has indeed shifted from explicit teaching to facilitating and trying to create an environment in which students accept responsibility for their own learning progress (Ozel, 2015). Additionally, with the incorporation of novel teaching methods like blended learning and online facilitation, many new systems are being implemented to aid in the teaching and learning processes (Reyes, 2015) but methods in student feedback are still lacking. Feedback can be defined as information that is provided about a person's progress in his/her efforts towards reaching a specific goal (Wiggins, 2012). Analytical methods used to process student data need to adapt so as to ensure effective-, learning enhancing feedback. The use of a hierarchy structure to provide feedback can assist students in understanding improvable factors which determine their academic success (Barker & Garvin-Doxas, 2004). For feedback to be helpful to students, it needs to be target/goal-referenced, demonstrable and obvious, actionable, user-friendly or manageable, timely, dynamic, and consistent (Wiggins, 2012).

The changing face of education has highlighted flaws in existing teaching and learning environments relating to feedback, which can be addressed by the development and implementation of novel learning analytics systems. Section 2 will outline some of the shortcomings identified in previous research. In section

3, the development of a learning analytics system in the form of an early alert feedback system as solution to the identified shortfalls, will be discussed. This is followed by section 4, which will evaluate the developed system according to the criteria for effective feedback. The paper will conclude with some closing statements and plans for future work.

2. LEARNING INHIBITING SHORTFALLS IDENTIFIED IN FEEDBACK

Studies by Bond, et al. (2000) have shown that while feedback is hard to record, feedback frequency is mostly low. Although lecturers realize the value that feedback provides, the associated administrative tasks can be so time consuming that even if they wanted to provide early or frequent feedback, it can be an almost impossible task. Hattie and Timperley (2007) found in their research, that there are three important issues that should be addressed by a feedback model. It must provide a student with information on completed tasks that helps him/her understand what the goal is, how to progress to that goal, and which activities to perform to reach the goal. Students need to understand how they are progressing toward their end-goal, and to get directions on how to attain that goal (Wiggins, 2012). Lecturers use different ways to provide students with information on their progress, many of them unofficial.

Du Toit (2015) developed a computer program, benchMark, which assisted lecturers in calculating the participation levels of students, taking into consideration the activities in which they were required to participate. The program calculates average marks for each class activity (class attendance, practical assignments, etc.) that a lecturer in a specific module expects the students to participate in. An overall participation mark is then calculated as the sum of these averages, each multiplied by a weight representing that activity's importance. If, for example, the averages of two activities were 35% and 45%, then the participation can be calculated as $50\% \times 35 + 50\% \times 45$, meaning they are equally important, or $40\% \times 35 + 60\% \times 45$, meaning the ratio of importance is 40:60 for activity_1:activity_2, with a total of 100%. To write the equation in a general form for an example of 4 activities, let w_1 denote the weight level of activity 1, likewise $w_2, w_3,$ and w_4 the weights for activities 2, 3, and 4 respectively. Subsequently, let s_1 denote the average (of all marks achieved) for activity 1, and $s_2,\ s_3,$ and s_4 the averages for activities 2, 3, and 4 respectively. The overall participation mark, p, is then calculated according to the following equation:

$$p = s_1w_1 + s_2w_2 + s_3w_3 + s_4w_4 \qquad (1)$$

The program orders the activities according to importance and constrains the weights to be in multiples of 5. It empirically calculates a set of participation marks for each student, using all of the different weight combinations allowed by the model. Feedback is provided in the form of spreadsheets wherein students are identified by means of their student numbers. It shows their activity averages, the minimum participation mark, and their ranking in relation to the rest of the class. The program has the unique capability of performing these calculations as frequently as required by the lecturer, who will have access to the maximum-, minimum-, and average participation marks as well as other useful statistical information. The benchMark system enables lecturers to present students with regular updates on their progress in the form of participation marks (Du Toit, 2015).

In a pilot study, it was found that the students were very satisfied with the feedback frequency and most of them wanted the system to be implemented in all of their programs. Table 1 presents a short summary on some statistical insights gained from this study.

Table 1. Summarizing statistics of student responses on the benchMark system

Question	% of 25 students agree
The frequency of feedback is acceptable.	96%
The marks system should be implemented in all of my modules.	88%

The benchMark system presented timely, goal-referenced, and dynamic feedback to students. Issues that were however identified included concerns regarding privacy (personalization), ease of use of the system (user-friendliness), and the lack of actionable goals that will help in creating a future perspective (demonstrable).

Section 2 summarized the operation of an existing feedback system that has been implemented in actual teaching/learning environments and identified areas in which improvement is required. Section 3 will discuss the development of the early alert feedback system which uses the optimizing attributes of mathematical models to perform its calculations.

3. DEVELOPMENT OF AN EARLY ALERT FEEDBACK SYSTEM

The positive response elicited by benchMark (Du Toit, 2015), justifies its use as a steady foundation for development of a two stage early alert feedback system. In the first stage, an NLP model was formulated and solved for each student in order to eliminate the repetitive nature of benchMark:

$$\begin{aligned} &maximize/minimize && p_\alpha = \textstyle\sum_{j=1}^{n} s_{\alpha j} w_j && (2)\\ &subject\ to && \textstyle\sum_{j=1}^{n} w_j = 1 && (3)\\ & && w_j \bmod k = 0 && (4)\\ & && l < w_j \leq u && (5)\\ & && w_j \geq w_{j+1}, \quad j < n && (6)\\ & && 0 \leq s_{\alpha j} \leq 1 && (7)\\ & && l, u \geq 0 && (8) \end{aligned}$$

where p is the participation mark, s_i is the student average for activity i, w_i is the weight assigned to activity i, (4) ensures that w_i is a multiple of k, l is the lower limit for all the weights, u is the upper limit for all the weights, n is the number of activities used, and $i = 1, \dots, n$. Minimizing the model yields a minimum participation mark and its corresponding weights, and maximizing the model yields a maximum participation mark and its corresponding weights. An average participation mark is determined from the results, according to which a student ranking is created. The model is therefore solved twice per student before the average participation marks are calculated. Applying an existing student data set, the student ranking obtained by solving the NLP model was compared to that resulting from benchMark, by calculating the Spearman's rank order correlation coefficient (Puth, 2015). This coefficient was calculated for the two sets of rank values and resulted in a value of ρ=0.99, which shows that there is a very strong positive association between the rankings resulting from benchMark and the NLP. This model represents an adaptation of the benchMark program but is optimized in terms of the number of calculations, and follows a consistent process.

A feedback system should provide students with information on personalized (user-friendly) actions towards reaching a goal (actionable). In the second stage of the feedback system, the activity averages for each student are used to perform an output oriented data envelopment analysis (DEA) which determines an efficiency score for each student based on performance (Kao & Lin, 2008), and divides them into classes of equal efficiency:

$$\begin{aligned} E_k = &\quad Maximize \textstyle\sum_{j=1}^{n} s_{kj} w_j && (9)\\ subject\ to &\quad \textstyle\sum_{j=1}^{n} s_{ij} w_j \leq 1,\ i = 1, \dots, m && (10)\\ &\quad w_j \geq \varepsilon > 0, \qquad j = 1, \dots, n && (11) \end{aligned}$$

where E_k represents the efficiency score for student k, s_{ij} is the average of student i in activity j, w_j is the weight for activity j, n is the number of students to be considered, m is the number of activities, and ε is a small number. This class-ranking is used for solving the dual formulation of the outputs-only DEA (in (12) to (14)) to present each student with personalized targets to reach in each of the activities to improve his/her position on the class-ranking.

$$\begin{aligned} E_k = &\quad Minimize \textstyle\sum_{i=1}^{m} \lambda_i - \varepsilon \sum_{j=1}^{n} q_j && (12)\\ subject\ to &\quad \textstyle\sum_{i=1}^{m} s_{ij} \lambda_i - q_j = s_{kj},\ j = 1, \dots, n && (13)\\ &\quad \lambda_{ji}, q_j \geq 0, \qquad i = 1, \dots, m;\ j = 1, \dots, n && (14) \end{aligned}$$

where E_k represents the composite index for student k, s_{ij} is the average of student i in activity j, w_j is the weight for activity j, n is the number of students to be evaluated, m is the number of activities, ε is a small positive number, q_j is the change in activity j, let $\theta = \sum_{i=1}^{n} \lambda_i$, then $(s_{kj} + q_j)/\theta$ is the target for activity j, and $j = 1, \ldots, m$. The model successfully calculates personalized improvement targets for each activity, indicating how much each student needs to improve in each activity, to progress to a level of higher efficiency.

The two-stage early alert feedback system successfully addresses most of the concerns lacking from existing feedback systems. It consistently incorporates an optimized method for calculating participation marks and provides personalized, actionable improvement targets that demonstrate to students how they can improve.

4. RESULTS

Wiggins (2012) presented seven criteria for effective feedback according to which the success of the developed system will be evaluated (Table 2).

Table 2. Criteria and evaluation of the developed system

Criteria	Evaluation
Target/goal-referenced	The system provides students with feedback directly related to activities needed to reach their goal.
Demonstrable, obvious	Students are presented with tangible results related to each sub goal (activity).
Actionable	The DEA model provides targets that show students how to improve in each activity.
User-friendly	A certain amount of explanation from the lecturer is needed for students to effectively understand the feedback.
Timely	The system can calculate feedback information as often as required by the lecturer.
Dynamic	Every time feedback is provided in real-time, all previous sets of marks are included. This means that students can see how they are progressing by comparing their latest results with all those previously calculated.
Consistent	The marks are consistently calculated by solving the same optimized models for all students.

One of the most important advantages the developed system presents to lecturers, is that the mathematical models are consistent. This means that whenever an activity has been completed, the marks can be imported into the database and a new set of feedback statistics can be calculated automatically.

5. CONCLUSIONS

This paper discussed the need and development of an early alert feedback system that regularly provides students with information on their ultimate goal, how the goal can be achieved, which activities to perform to reach that goal, and which is easy to use. A two-stage early alert feedback system was developed that implements an NLP to consistently calculate an average participation mark for each student and that uses a class-ranking method to calculate personalized improvement targets for each student in each activity. The system was evaluated according to the seven attributes of successful feedback presented by Wiggins (2012).

To efficiently address remaining concerns regarding student privacy as well as user-friendliness, the system is to be implemented in an electronic dashboard that will allow individual students private access to solely their own marks and statistics. Also, for very large student numbers, a specialized solver is required to implement the dual formulation of the outputs-only DEA because of an exponential increase in decision variables. Therefore an improved model for activity target calculation is currently being developed.

ACKNOWLEDGEMENT

The financial assistance of the National Research Foundation (NRF) towards this research is hereby acknowledged. The author initiated the research and opinions expressed and conclusions arrived at, are those of the author and are not necessarily to be attributed to the NRF.

REFERENCES

Barker, L. J., and Garvin-Doxas, K., 2004. Making visible the behaviors that influence learning environment: A qualitative exploration of Computer Science classrooms. *Computer Science Education,* Vol. 14, No. 2, pp. 119-145.

Bond, L. et al., 2000. *Certification system of the National Board for Professional Teaching Standards: A construct and consequenctial study.* National Board for Professional Teaching Standards, Washington, DC.

Brühwiler, C. and Blatchford, P., 2011. Effects of class size and adaptive teaching competency on classroom processes and academic outcome. *Learning and Instruction,* Vol. 21, No. 1, pp. 95-108.

Du Toit, J. V., 2015. Using participation marks to manage, motivate and inform on academic progress. *Conference for Outstanding Teaching/Learning and Innovative Technology Use*, Potchefstroom, South Africa.

Geçer, A., 2013. Lecturer-student communication in blended learning. *Educational Sciences: Theory & Practice,* Vol. 13, No. 1, pp. 362-367.

Hattie, J. and Timperley, H., 2007. The power of feedback. *Review of Educational Research,* Vol. 77, No. 1, pp. 81-112.

Kao, C. and Lin, P.-H., 2008. Class ranking of the managament colleges in Taiwan. *Lecture Notes in Management Science,* Vol. 1, pp. 129-140.

Landau, R. et al., 2014. Instances: incorporating computational scientific thinking advances into education and science courses. *Concurrency and Computation: Practice and Experience,* Vol. 26, pp. 2316-2328.

Ozel, E., 2015. The effect of students' undisciplined behaviors upon Social Studies teachers' instructional performance. *European Journal of Educational Studies,* Vol. 7, No. 1, pp. 59-65.

Puth, M.-T., et al., 2015. Effective use of Spearman's and Kendall's correlation coefficients for association between two measured traits. *Animal Behaviour,* Vol. 102, No. 1, pp. 77-84.

Reyes, J. A., 2015. The skinny on big data in education: Learning analytics simplified. *TechTrends: Linking Research & Practice to Improve Learning*, Vol. 59, No. 2, pp. 75-79.

Siemens, G. and Long, P., 2011. Penetrating the Fog: Analytics in Learning and Education. *Educause Review,* Vol. 46, No. 5, pp. 30-32.

Sin, K. and Muthu, L., 2015. Application of big data in education data mining and learning analytics - A literature review. *ICTACT Journal on Soft Computing: Special Issue on Soft Computing Models for Big Data,* Vol. 5, No. 4, pp. 1035-1049.

Wiggins, G., 2012. Seven keys to effective feedback. *Educational Leadership,* Vol. 70, No. 1, pp. 10-16.

FROM LEARNING OUTCOMES TO THE OPEN CONTENT DEVELOPMENT (OCD) IN ICT ENVIRONMENT

András Benedek and György Molnár
Budapest University of Technology and Economics, Department of Technical Education
Magyar Tudósok boulevard 2. Q. building., Budapest 1117, Hungary

ABSTRACT

The content of education and training is constantly changing in the case of Vocational Education and Training (VET) where the rapid technological and fast labor market shifts accelerate the process. Therefore educators must offer new insights regarding modern learning outcomes, especially in the ICT environment. Our new model entitled Open Content Development (OCD) focuses on a collaborative technique that allows the participants to create and use their own materials within the framework of a cloud service supported by e-learning and web technologies. Open online contents are innovative in a sense that they guarantee the essential openness, visualization, and eliminate the restrictions of traditional technologies. Our post-graduate students have contributed to our OCD research as evidenced in SysBook.

KEYWORDS

Learning Outcomes; Micro-content; Open Content; ICT

1. PROPOSAL INFORMATION

One of the constant changing element is the content of the education and training. Especially that is true in the case of Vocational Education and Training (VET) where the rapid technological and accelerated labor market changes give a special acceleration for the imperative change (Grenfield, 2009; Allen, 2014). This topic strongly linked to the VET didactical features (Gessler & Herrera, 2015), and is partly connected to the endeavours which strive to shape the alternatives of the traditional VET curricula in a learning environment determined by modern ICT and which require interactivity not only in the learning process but during the construction of the curriculum as well (Colons & Halverson, 2009; Benedek & Molnár, 2015). Previous research as our project „E-teaching Culture and Digital Content Development at BME" was implemented between 2013 and 2015. This project aimed at developing contents, methodologies and services related to the competitiveness of higher education.

For community curriculum development, teacher training might provide especially good conditions which we exemplify by presenting our research data. Developing Open Educational Resources (OER) with students' participation means a potential of content and methodology and the applied ICT solutions (open source and ICT supported Learning Management System (LMS), memory independent management of complex visual elements and the flexible management of micro-contents) is capable of surpassing traditional, school- and notebook based teaching (Bell, 2011). Only two decades having passed since the introduction of the Open Access principle and its adoption in a wider context of practice put pedagogical thinking – open up education (Kumar 2008, 2012; Santos, Punie & Muñoz, 2016) - in motion, as well. We concentrated to the current methodological renewal and we wish to introduce the construction process in the course of which we moved from our theoretical presumption through the first empiric surveys to the creation of our Open Content Development (OCD) model.

Our hypothesis may be summarized as open learning and open content development may provide opportunities to use parables that are able to improve the efficiency of human learning in ICT environment (Molnár, 2016).

Today the descriptions of the Learning Outcomes became the important input factors in the formal education (Mészáros & Baróti, 2017). The new kind of these descriptions connects to the requirements of the European Framework for Qualifications and it is easy to achieve their operationalization at the itemization level. The "input" competencies and motivations of the learners/students attending the given course are also of great importance and must be treated with the necessary diversification; these factors can have a considerable impact on the successfulness of education. For that reason our researches are focused at secondary level VET. The innovation skills of the teachers involved in the training can also be considered as input factors since their active and proactive participation is a decisive component of successful development the OCD model.

Especially in the era of the dominance of the constructivist learning theories, the Learning Outcomes were built on the well-constructed curricula and the determination of the adequate duration of teaching – this was well indicated by the terms seat-time learning and time-based teaching. The main component of this model (Figure 1) was assessment closing the studies in the form of examinations and with the connecting certification. The model of competency-based learning has created a new order: the description of competencies, which more and more includes the detailed description of the Learning Outcomes, has become the main component.

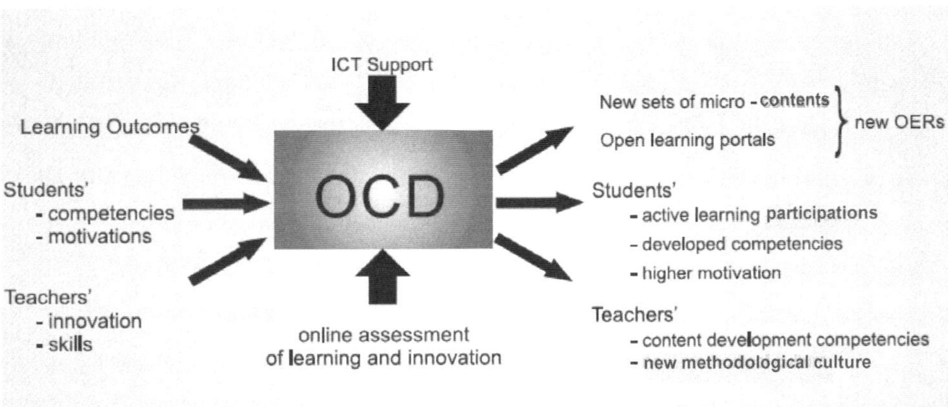

Figure 1. Inputs and outputs of the OCD

According to these inputs and outputs our network concept, as the feature of active student's contribution, encouraged the new educational content development. The result of these activities integrated an original model of OCD to formulate a real open environment where information exchange is organized into an informal network. Our hypothesis states that knowledge elements interlinked at the level of micro-contents could form a complex curriculum. The creation of open curricula with rich visual contents has become an important direction for the international development of contents. This process is typically characterized by the constructive contribution by learners.

2. METHODOLOGY

In 2015-2016 we undertook to elaborate a new complex curriculum which on one hand offered a framework for a general course on the analysis of system theory and on the other hand it allowed students to prepare case studies by which they could participate in the development of the curriculum of the course. We followed the general rules of OER development, and in the autumn of 2015 we started teaching the "System theory" course to a major group of exactly the students questioned in our survey; an e-learning resource was also made for the course, and this material, together with the solutions of the exercises, was administered in the Moodle system.

Our research on didactics essentially focused on the content development work done by vocational teachers and students by the application of new educational methods and processes. According to this approach, a new e-learning textbook was created in the fall semester in 2016 by the curriculum developers (subject: Systems in Vocational Education) with the SysBook platform (Figure 2) assisting those who were interested. We asked the students to make "case studies" as micro-contents, with the compulsory inclusion of visual elements. These case studies had to be optimized for a screen (laptop, smartphone, etc.) according to the rules applying to micro-contents, include visual content that described the operation of the system and, if possible, also include a mathematical formula for the same purpose.

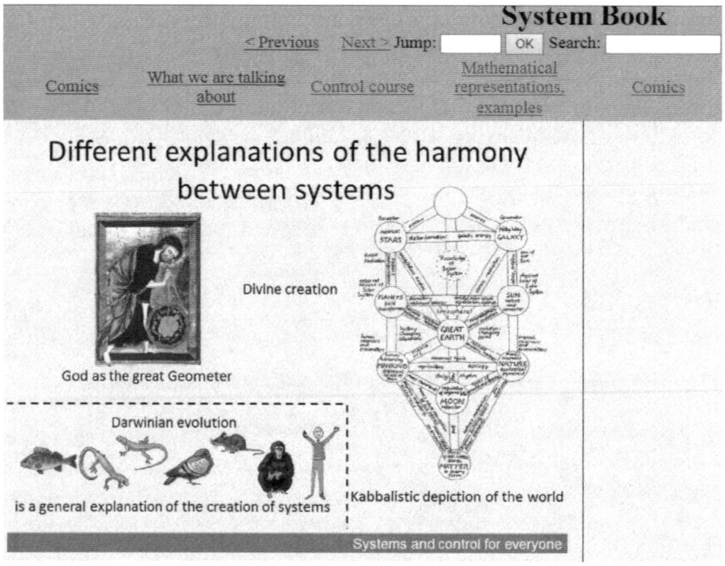

Figure 2. Illustration from SysBook – Different explanations of the harmony

The post-graduate students proved to be extremely creative when completing this task. For illustration, we selected the picture explaining four-stroke Otto engine operation (Figure 3), a perfect example of how well such a relatively complex phenomenon can be illustrated, explained and understood this way.

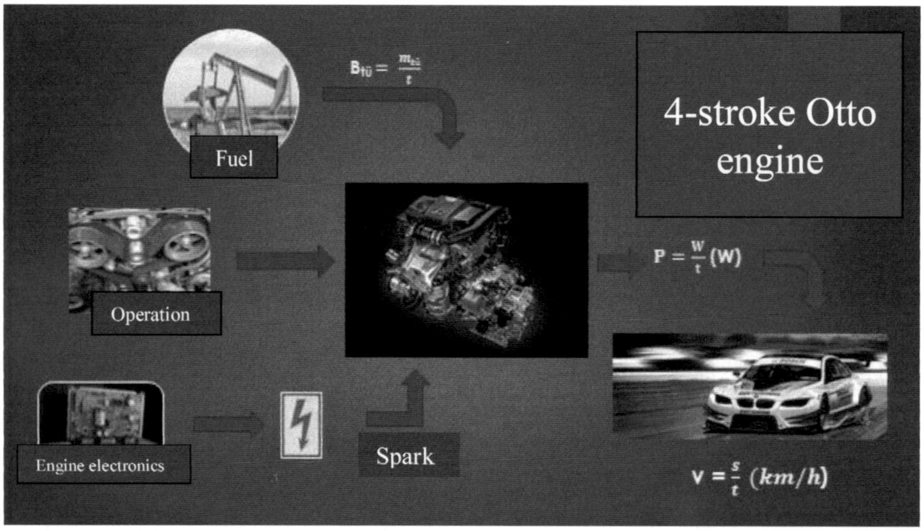

Figure 3. Example for a student work: four-stroke Otto engine operation where photos are edited with a mathematics formulas to illustrate the effects

Diversifying the generation of micro-contents in a new ICT environment (broadband, mobile, increasingly memory-independent cloud services) positions educational contents in a new media. Generating interactive image outputs for micro-contents also carries a new didactic innovation potential. The educational function of image contents (icons) is illustrated by student case studies. This presentation describes the main elements of our development work thus far. Our results demonstrate the use of Web 2.0 under the conditions of new networks and the physical and virtual transformation of the teaching environment.

3. CONCLUSION OUTCOMES

The OCD model that created the real operational space for both online teaching and learning and the collaborative methods. According to certain opinions, it is the e-Learning 3.0 and Web 3.0 technologies that make the solutions (personalization, knowledge construction, mobility, visualization, and interoperability) offering the future learning environment and the opportunity of applying a new methodology possible. Our research regarding vocational didactics is the use of cloud-based services i.e. storing the complex open access didactics material that is being expanded continuously regarding both the number of elements and their connections.

Within the vocational education of the Hungarian education system, the structures of traditional learning resources were reduced, and the possibility of switching over to a relatively developed ICT technology strengthened. One of the reasons for this was that the importance of practice-orientation increased in this field of education which urged the methodological developments to break with the traditions in the new learning material constructions and to utilize the technical possibilities offered by the digital environment. Focusing on key aspects, the conscious strengthening of the role of visual learning may yield the following results:

A chance for collaborative development where the construction of micro-contents by students and teachers facilitates a strong and efficient horizontal communication to replace the conventional vertical communication and thinking outside the box of formal education which is limited both in space and time.

Open on-line contents that can be considered key results of the innovation. The new ICT environment and the applied technical tools guarantee the essential openness of these contents. This method helps to extend the flipped classroom method in ICT environment.

The most important result here is that the restrictions forced by traditional technologies (allowed number of characters, pages, etc. in the curricula) can be now eliminated; hence images will cease to be the "necessary evil". Cloud services make it possible. They clearly indicate advantages, limitations and possible applications.

REFERENCES

Allen, I.E.; Seaman, J., 2014. *Grade change: Tracking online education in the United States*. Babson Survey Research Group and Quahog Research Group, LLC.

Beetham, H.; Sharpe, R. (ed.) 2013. *Rethinking Pedagogy for a Digital Age: Designing for 21st century learning* (2nd edition). Abingdon: Routledge.

Bell, F., 2011. Connectivism: Its place in theory-informed research and innovation in technology-enabled learning. *In The International Review of Research in Open and Distance Learning*, 12(3), 98-118.

Benedek, A.; Molnár, Gy., 2011. The empirical analysis of a Web 2.0-based learning platform. *In: ConstantinPaleologu, Constandinos Mavromoustakis, Marius Minea (ed.): ICCGI 2011*, The Sixth International Multi-Conference on Computing in the Global Information Technology, Luxembourg, Luxembourg, 56-62.

Benedek, A.; Molnár, Gy., 2015. E-teaching and Digitalization at BME. New Technologies and Innovation in Education for Global Business*: 19th International Conference on Engineering Education - PROCEEDINGS. Zagreb, 2015.07.20-2015.07.24.* (University of Zagreb, Faculty of Economics & Business) Zagreb: Zagreb School of Economics and Management, 349-356.

Benedek, A.; Molnár, Gy., 2014. ICT in Education: A New paradigm and old obstacle. *In: The Ninth International Multi-Conference on Computing in the Global Information Technology*. Arno Leist, Tadeusz Pankowski (ed.)Sevilla: IARIA, 2014. 54-60.

Breslow, L. et.al, 2013. Studying learning in the worldwide classroom: Research into edX's first MOOC. *Research & Practice in Assessment*, 8. 13-25.

Colons, A.; Halverson, R., 2009. *Rethinking Education in the Age of Technology*. Teacher College Press, New York.

Grenfield, P., 2009. Technology and informal education. What is taught, what is learned. *Science*. 323, 68-71.

Kumar D., A., 2008. *Open Access to Knowledge and Information: Scholarly Literature and Digital Library Initiatives & the South Asian Scenario*. New Delhi:UNESCO

Mészáros A., Baróti E., The culture assessment of the Széchenyi István University and the structural training of professors and leaders in 2010-2012 built on the assessment In: Satef Brdarevic, Sabahudin Jasarevic (szerk.) 8th Research/Expert Conference with International Participation. 636 p. Konferencia helye, ideje: Neum, Bosznia-Hercegovina, 2013.06.06-2013.06.08. Zenica: University of Zenica Faculty of Mechanical Engineering, pp. 373-378. (Quality Proceedings; 2013.)

Molnár, Gy., 2016. The Impact of Modern ICT-based Teaching and Learning Methods in Social Media and Networked Environment : *Milan Turčáni, Zoltán Balogh, Michal Munk, Ľubomír Benko (ed.) 11th International Scientific Conference on Distance Learning in Applied Informatics: Štúrovo, Slovakia, 2016.05.02-2016.05.04*. Nitra: Wolters Kluwer, 341-351.

Santos, I., Punie, A., Cstaño Y.,Muñoz, J., 2016. *Opening up Education: A Support Framework for Higher Education Institutions. JRC Science for Policy Report*, EUR 27938 EN; doi:10.2791/293408

Siemens, G., 2005. *Connectivism: A learning theory for the digital age: International Jornal of Instructional Technology and Distance Learning*. Available online at http://www.elearnspace.org/Articles/connectivism.htm

A PRELIMINARY STUDY OF A DIGITAL AND WEB LITERACY PROJECT FOR YOUNG SOUTH AFRICAN WOMEN

Mmaki Jantjies
Department of Information Systems, University of the Western Cape, South Africa

ABSTRACT

Digital literacies have an effect on the participation of a population in the digital economy. In this research we evaluate how technology clubs in schools using open educational resources can impact the digital skills growth in a country. The University of the Western Cape (UWC) Information Systems Department, Mozilla foundation web literacy and a local South African NGO Peo Ya Phetogo (PYP), recently embarked on a partnership to start digital literacy clubs that empower young girls in South African schools. The project began in March 2016 where the UWC Department of Information Systems graduate female students would go into schools and teach digital literacy skills to young girls aged between 13-16 years of age. The pilot phase involved 5 clubs with 5 graduate students running clubs consisting of 10-15 clubs in each high school. Using the Mozilla framework, graduate female Information Systems students, used their educational knowledge, open educational resources as well as the Mozilla framework to prepare for club sessions. In this study we explore the role of the clubs in providing basic digital skills to young children and how such initiatives can improve the uptake of STEM related careers amongst young South Africans.

KEYWORDS

Web Literacy, Women in Technology, Digital literacies, STEM, Women in STEM, South Africa

1. INTRODUCTION

The theme of the 4th industrial revolution dominated the agenda of the 2017 World Economic Forum (Schwab, 2017). While this discussion is exciting for innovators and makes way for the advancement of artificial intelligence and further research into the use of big data to advance nations, the dynamic of existing digital divides across the world as a result of a variation of factors, affects the impact of digitization on economies and the participating labour force.

In this paper, we explore the role of digitization and preparing for the digital revolution and its impact on South African women. The South African report on the status of women in the economy by the Ministry of Women and Girls, recently reported that while there was a high ratio of women and girls enrolled for high school education, the throughput rate was low in both high school and higher learning education (DWSA, 2015). High schools and higher learning institutions continue to be the mainline source of digital skills or exposure to advance digital skills in South Africa and many other countries. The enrolment and completion of higher education thus becomes vital in these environments.

With the advent of Massive Open Online Courses (MOOCS) advance digital skills can be easily obtained. However access to MOOCs continues to be hindered by the lack of access to the Internet with high data rates, and lack of basic literacy to enable access to online resources, lack of contextual MOOC's and many other challenges (Castillo et al., 2015). Other measures of obtaining basic digital literacy skills are various NGO programmes such as Girl Hype and Geek culture in South Africa aimed at specifically upskilling women with digital literacy skills.

Without access to basic digital literacy skills, many South Africans and particularly women cannot become contributors and participants of the digital revolution. In this paper we report on a programme focused on skilling young girls with basic digital literacy targeted to girls in schools with the aim of upskilling them and motivating them into careers in Science Technology Engineering and Mathematics (STEM) related fields. South Africa has one of the best legislation provisions which cater for the empowerment of women in many sectors, creating an opportunity for diverse representation of the labour force in key areas of STEM which can be a catalyst for the advancement of these areas. While South Africa has significant policies which position the role of ICT as a fundamental aspect of education and entrepreneurship, there is a need for programmes which are targeted at fostering innovation in the informal learning environment to motivate and enable an environment for young children to explore STEM fields as an early age of development.

2. THE DIGITAL REVOLUTION AND WIDENING DIVIDE

The digital revolution has introduced efficient ways of contributing and participating in the digital economy. While digitization has brought on significant benefits to countries across the world, it has also introduced widening digital gaps as many societies hope to catch up with the latest innovations. There have been significant research publications that outline how digital divides have affected many developing and developed countries. Digital divides have often been characterized by the lack of certain sectors of the population access or ability to afford access to digital skills as well as digital infrastructure and resources (West, 2015; Rogers, 2016; Philip et al., 2017).

In a world where essential digital economy resources require access in the form of physical and educational access, digital skills become an imperative need of the digital age. Antonio and Tuffely (2014) conducted a study that reflected on how women are often deeply affected by digital divides due to their lack of access to education and technology platforms. The study further reflected on the lack of women skilled in ICT and programming skills and thus the subsequent lack of women also producing gender relevant content which could motivate the uptake of programming amongst women. Another fundamental finding of their study was the lack of multilingual online content which excluded women who don't speak English from participating on the internet.

South African has been ranked in the 17th position from 145 countries on countries sampled on their Gender Gap by the World Economic Forum (WEF, 2015). The attributes of the ranking included economic participation and opportunity, educational attainment, health and survival and political empowerment. While the South African legislation enables opportunities for women to participate in the digital economy, there is a need for programmes targeted at fostering innovative learning environments which will foster an interest for technology and STEM by young women.

2.1 Technology clubs

The Mozilla Foundation which is a Non-Governmental Organization (NGO) partnered with the United Nations Women to improve access of digital skills and resources to women. The programme was established in various countries working with local partners in those countries to access members of the public. In South Africa, in partnership with the University of the Western Cape as well as a local NGO, PYP which is focused on upskilling teachers with technology skills, the programme focused on imparting digital skills to young girls in grade 9 mainly aged between 13-16 years of age. Grade 9 is the level at which learners in high school have to choose their final high school years subject areas of choice. The aim of targeting this level of learners was to try and spark their interest into a possible career choice of technology.

In this study we present a preliminary review of an extra- curricular programme dedicated to increasing the pipeline of young females in technology. A total of five technology clubs were initiated in five different schools in Cape Town, South Africa. The clubs have since grown to other South African provinces which include Gauteng and the North West province. Each participating school was based in a township location in South Africa. The clubs objective was to teach basic digital literacy skills through traditional and digital teaching and learning approaches. Graduate technology female students lead technology clubs in these schools, playing the role of club leaders. The club leaders facilitate the process of learning in the various clubs. Each club has twenty members and one cub leader. Each leader has to prepare an activity for each club session. The club leaders use the Mozilla web literacy framework to guide their preparation of the clubs sessions and also use open resources such as Google drive to place any learning material, video and related resources which other club members and leaders can access. Supporting these clubs, the university of the Western Cape also conducts additional programming lessons teaching learners fundamentals of programming using scratch for members of the clubs.

2.2 Co-creating learning content

The learning clubs are structured to enable a co-creation of knowledge guided by curriculum frameworks. The technology clubs aim to attain the Mozilla web-literacy framework as well as the University of the Western Cape first year student's ICT competencies. In imparting digital literacy skills' the clubs are designed to ensure that members of the club have basic computer interaction skills and are able to access and use digital tools for their own benefit. Guided by these frameworks, the content is co-created with graduate students who have an undergraduate degree in Information Systems. Furthermore, the curriculum is reviewed to obtain feedback from club members. The clubs have a yearly cycle and clubs meet at intervals of a fortnight or monthly, where their objectives are guided by the Mozilla framework objectives. In preparation for club sessions the club captains sit to reflect on current issues which affect young women in the South African context. Considering these issues, each club captain links an activity for the day surrounding the agreed theme with the aim of achieving the framework objectives. An example of this was when young girls in South African high schools fought for policies surrounding their hair in school to be changed as the young girls felt that these policies infringe on the rights of girls with African hair (Pather, 2016). In writing the web (one of the objectives of the Mozilla framework explained below), the girls were expected to express their views of the topic through a website which they were taught how to create. The following summary provides an overview of the Mozilla web-literacy framework (Mozilla, 2016).

2.2.1 Read

Club members are expected to understand the basics of network and the World Wide Web. Members are then taught to be able to curate and use information from across the web for a specific objective such as completing an assignment or doing research.

2.2.2 Write

Club members are trained to understand the fundamentals of programming using the basic Hyper Text Markup Language (HTML). Members are then able to use these basic skills to create their own sites.

2.2.3 Participate

Clubs members are taught about digital identities and what it means to have online presence. Clubs also discuss online bulling and handing online bulling. Members further discuss the benefits and challenges on being able to participate online.

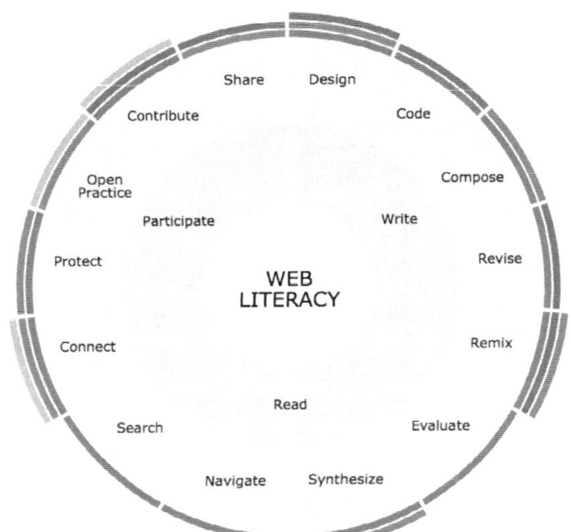

Figure 1. Web literacy map (MozillaFoundation, 2016)

2.3 Supporting initiatives

In ensuring that the project continuously expose the members of the clubs to STEM related fields, UWC also ensured other parallel events. Every year South Africa celebrates women's month. As part of the celebration UWC Information Systems academic department hosts a "take a girl child ICT work" day where club members are invited to the university campus along with other girls from the local community. A range of activities which includes motivational talks from women in the field of technology, programming and gaming sessions and competitions, the club members are further supported to ensure continuous engagement in this field.

2.4 Challenges of the project

The project began with a visit to schools to engage school principals as well as teachers on the importance of a digital literacy programme. Obtaining buy in from schools was not always easy as some schools did not want programmes which were only dedicated to females and in such schools we initiated a co-educational programme. At the beginning of the programme, club leaders were meant to transfer the leadership to the club members who are part of the participating school community. We found that clubs still required more support in the second year of instating clubs before the sustenance of the clubs could be left to the schools. This was mainly due to the fact that club leaders from UWC had easier access to various learning resources, the Internet as well as financial resources related to sourcing educational material.

3. CONCLUSION

This study presented a technology initiatives dedicated to increasing the number of young women skilled with basic digital and web literacy skills. Guided by the Mozilla framework which focused on participants ability to read, write and participate on the web, the club weaved in topical women related issues which required members of the programme to address while learning how to use technology. While the study aims to foster an interest of technology while imparting skills to young women, there is a need for more sustainable initiatives which motivate and cultivate innovation amongst young women. This can decrease the lack of women taking up careers in the technology space and increase web content and tools which are inclusive. The study also found that club leaders gained more mentorship and leadership skills as they were responsible for mentoring and learning young leaners into a career specialty. Mentors thus always sought various resources and ideas to enhance their various clubs.

While the South African legislation and ICT white paper make provision for ICT in schools, the challenge of resources such as limited number of teachers skilled in ICT skills, high costs associated with the use of the internet as well as lack of computers in some schools, hinders the possibility of ICT skills gains in schools. In our next study we aim to present findings on the skills and knowledge discovery process which participants have obtained since the commencement of the programme, to evaluate the impact of the learning content, structure and teaching and learning approach.

ACKNOWLEDGEMENT

I would like to acknowledge Mozilla Foundation, UN Women, school teachers as well as schools which support the clubs, the technology club leaders, Peo Ya Phetogo as well as the South African National Research Foundation for supporting the study.

REFERENCES

Antonio, A. and Tuffley, D., 2014. The gender digital divide in developing countries. *Future Internet*, *6*(4), pp. 673-687.

DWSA, 2017. The department of women South Africa. The status of women in the South African economy. 1-176. Online: http://www.gov.za/sites/www.gov.za/files/Status_of_women_in_SA_economy.pdf

Castillo, N.M., Lee, J., Zahra, F.T. and Wagner, D.A., 2015. MOOCS for development: Trends, challenges, and opportunities. *Information Technologies & International Development*, *11*(2), pp.pp-35.

Hilbert, M., 2011, December. Digital gender divide or technologically empowered women in developing countries? A typical case of lies, damned lies, and statistics. In *Women's Studies International Forum* (Vol. 34, No. 6, pp. 479-489). Pergamon.

Mozilla Foundation, 2016. Web Literacy. https://learning.mozilla.org/en-US/web-literacy

Pather, R., 2016. Mail and Guardian: Pretoria Girls High School pupil: I was instructed to fix myself as if I was broken. Online at: https://mg.co.za/article/2016-08-29-pretoria-girls-high-school-pupil-i-was-instructed-to-fix-myself-as-if-i-was-broken

Rogers, S.E., 2016. Bridging the 21st Century Digital Divide. *TechTrends*, *60*(3), p.197.

West, D.M., 2015. Digital divide: Improving Internet access in the developing world through affordable services and diverse content. *Center for Technology Innovation at Brookings*.

World Economic Forum (WEF)., 2015. Global gender gap 2015 – South Africa. Online at http://reports.weforum.org/global-gender-gap-report-2015/economies/#economy=ZAF

STAKEHOLDER INFLUENCES ON THE GRENADA IXP DEPLOYMENT – PRELIMINARY FINDINGS

Claire C. Craig
PhD Candidate – Sir Arthur Lewis Institute of Social and Economic Studies, The University of the West Indies, St. Augustine Campus, Trinidad & Tobago

ABSTRACT

This paper seeks to investigate the Grenada Internet Exchange Point (IXP) as a catalyst for promoting the Internet EcoSystem in Grenada and the value creation of stakeholders in its development and deployment. As the Internet continues to expand globally questions arise about its actual value and usefulness for social transformation and economic development especially for developing nations. IXPs have been implemented in developing countries to address these concerns. This paper is a subset of a wider study that employs Case Study methodology based on Stakeholder Theory and uses a qualitative approach for data collection to investigate this challenge.

KEYWORDS

Internet Exchange Points, IXP, Caribbean Development, Internet infrastructure, Caribbean Internet ecosystem, stakeholder theory, Grenada

1. INTRODUCTION

Internet infrastructure is considered to be a foundational ICT pillar for social development, and Internet Exchange Points (IXPs) are just one component within the domain of critical Internet infrastructure. "An IXP interconnects Internet service providers (ISPs) in a region or country, allowing them to exchange domestic Internet traffic locally without having to send those messages across multiple international hops to reach their destination" (Mc Laughlin 2004, 1). Because the Internet is not a single entity, but is made up of thousands of independent networks that communicate with each other, the key task is to ensure that its users are cost-effectively, rapidly, and securely interconnected (ISOC 2014). An increasing number of ICT based programs have been introduced by Governments of CARICOM Member States within the last decade which support the fact that "they have identified ICT as a key component for social development and a catalyst for improving education, increasing innovation, reducing unemployment, and improving human capacity building" (CARICOM-Secretariat 2008). This paper is a follow-up of an exploratory study of the Grenada IXP which was examined to understand and identify its usefulness as well as the power or control of various stakeholders. The United Nations (UN) has been using a multi-stakeholder approach by working with governments, civil society and other partners to build on the momentum generated by the Millennium Development Goals (MDG) (UN 2016) established in 2000 and the Sustainable Development Goals post 2015 when the MDG expired.. It is within the context of Social Policy and Stakeholder Theory that this study is located. According to the UN (ITU 2012) there is a need for statistical indicators on ICT developments and, particularly in developing countries, there are major gaps in the collection of official ICT statistics. It is expected that this study could be instrumental in helping to reduce the dearth of information on Internet connectivity in the Caribbean region by contributing to the emergence of a broader body of empirically based knowledge on this topic.

The objectives of this paper is to present the preliminary finding of the responses to interviews conducted with stakeholders in an attempt to assess the Grenada IXP as a catalyst for the social development of that country. This paper in divided into a further five sections as follows:

- Literature on IXPs
- Research design;
- Limitation of the study;
- Study findings; and
- Conclusions.

2. LITERATURE ON IXPS

Several studies support the adoption of local IXPs in both developed and developing nations and confirm their implementation is a strategy widely adopted globally to reduce costs and improve quality of service (QoS) as well as develop the local Internet ecosystem (Bruegge et al. 2011, 32, Chatzis, Smaragdakis, and Feldmann 2013, 9, Edelman and Woodcock 2012, 1, 7, Galperin 2013, 14, Gerson and Ryan 2012, 21, IGF 2011, 114, 261, ISOC 2014, 33, Jensen 2012, 13, Silvius 2011, 11, Weller and Woodcock 2013, 8). Nonetheless, IXes are understudied and have received little attention in the literature (Sowell 2012, 13), in spite of their growing deployment globally. In the studies undertaken, the Caribbean remains underrepresented.

Some studies on connectivity in Latin America and the Caribbean (LAC) (Galperin 2013, 2014, 2015, Galperin and Ruzzier 2013, Garcia-Zaballos and Lopez-Revas 2012) focus on the traffic routing, peering and pricing. It is important to note that in some of these studies which focus on the LAC region, the Caribbean Data is inconspicuous. Therefore, this research builds on the findings of the Galperin (2013) study which concluded that there are several enabling factors for IXPs. In his study, Galperin (2013), identified a competitive telecommunications market, governments providing political support, and active cooperation by incumbent operators as key enabling factors. This study continues the discourse by examining the role of the stakeholders as another enabling factor. The focus of this study is a change in the way IXP research has been conducted, where in this studies, the emphasis is placed on the social engineering issues and not the technical and operations issues. Moreover, this is in line with literature on Internet governance which speaks to the issue of the multi-stakeholder model and stakeholder participation. "The multi-stakeholder approach can be conceptualized as a mode of governance that involves actors of different types, expressing different interests, in a political process characterized by interaction among actors and interconnection among levels of authority" (Padovani 2005, 147).

3. RESEARCH DESIGN

This evaluative study uses a qualitative approach based on case study method applying Stakeholder Theory. The case is the Grenada IXP, and the interests and contributions of various stakeholders who were part of the implementation are taken into account. Data collected primarily through interviews with various stakeholders such as the Government of Grenada, the Telecom Regulator, Telecom Operators/ISPs and other stakeholders who may have contributed to the deployment of this IXP, are included in this study as well as observations and data from online documents and databases. Purposive sampling was used to ensure that a broad spectrum of relevant participants was included in the study. One of the main objectives of the study is to assess the role of stakeholders in deploying the Grenada IXP and identify any social impact they may have had. The study presents the answers to the following research questions:

1. What was the role of each stakeholder in facilitating the establishment of the Grenada IXP?
2. Has the Grenada IXP delivered improved traffic flow, latency and reduced cost?
3. How has the Grenada IXP contributed to the social development and the Internet economy of Grenada?

4. LIMITATION OF THE STUDY

There are two provocative limitations to this research. Firstly, it is not a study of the economic impact of the Grenada IXP as no economic evaluation was not conducted. Neither is it a cost benefit analysis of the IXP. It attempts to deduce conclusions based on the value of stakeholders in planning and implementing the Grenada IXP as a creativity strategy for social transformation of Small Island Developing Nations (SIDS). Thus the focus is kept on people and organizations (stakeholders) rather than costs. Secondly, the single case study may not be generalizable to other territories because of case study method employed. Recognising the varying geo-political conditions of Grenada, the country selected as the case investigated, it may not be representative of other countries in the region, or other IXPs deployed but may be anecdotal. Nonetheless the findings may still be useful in understanding characteristics about the case and may lead to some general social policy guidelines.

5. STUDY FINDINGS

The Grenada IXP implementation was a very informal process. Even though both the Memorandum of Understanding (MOU) and peering agreement were signed by the two telecom operators (ISPs), the association to incorporate the Grenada Internet Exchange (GREX) was not completed. This was also a low cost implementation so all costs were kept to a minimum, with all start-up costs being borne by the regulator. Two preliminary findings are discussed: the role of the stakeholders to answer research question one (1), and the benefits delivered to answer research questions two (2) and three (3).

5.1 The role of the stakeholders

The analysis is based on the responses to the interview questions by the study participants as they reflected on the role of the stakeholders as well as the perceived benefits.

5.1.1 The government

Some participants felt that "The government was the initiator of the IXP"; and that the government's interest was more about "bragging rights...the Prime Minister being the head of CARICOM ICT...for Grenada having the first IXP in the English speaking Caribbean" was very important because "the IXP was launched during the Texpo Event, a "big" government sponsored ICT event in Grenada". They felt that the Government supported the IXP and their views were "channelled through the regulator". There was the view that the government as a shareholder in the incumbent ISP (LIME) was also perceived as putting "a lot of pressure on them to conform" and take their place on the IXP as a peering partner. Other opinions expressed suggested that the Government should be "its own ISP" and bring content to the IXP, but this did not happen because the government buys Internet services from the ISP and its "IP infrastructure is provider assigned" making them dependent on the ISPs services. The stakeholders felt that the government was a strong advocate for the IXP and demonstrated the political will need for its implementation.

5.1.2 The regulator

The National Telecommunications Regulatory Commission (NTRC) in Grenada is the agency responsible for telecommunications regulations at the national level. It is responsible for the processing of applications and advising the Minister on the award of licences (ECTEL 2016). The respondents saw the regulator as a facilitator. One participant said that within their role of regulating the telecom sector, the regulator was required to "bring the peering partners together and get them to agree on the establishment of a peering agreement" and this is part of their role as an advisor to the government. Another respondent saw the NTRC "as a facilitator of getting the knowledge about the IXP into the minds of both providers...they acted as the mediator".

"The NTRC regulator was the one actually playing the lead part in developing the IXP". Another participant defined them as "conciliator, working along with both parties to get them to the table to discuss, to look at the long term benefits and the greater good; and the wider necessity of it". "They would independently interact with the players to try to bring us to a point where we could come to an agreement. They played a coaching role and it was a positive role." It can be said that the NTRC was perceived as playing the role of the Chief Technical Liaison, "bring them into to the room...get them to have a common understanding...lead to the development of the IX". The NTRC also financed the project, and provided an area at their headquarters to host the IXP, moving it from its original location which was not considered to be provider neutral. The regulator was seen as instrumental in the implementation of the Grenada IXP.

5.1.3 The Isps

There were two main ISPs in Grenada at the start of the project. Columbus Communications (FLOW) and Cable and Wireless (LIME). FLOW was in full support of the IXP and went as far as donating space (although this is not recommended) a "meet me room" for the facility and "a few megs of Internet access for the purpose of updating the L-root server" because "there are certain services that need Internet access". LIME "had reservations about having the IXP in a location that was not provider neutral". One interviewee expressed the view that "The main role of the ISPs was to be peering parties". One service provider "didn't believe that the service providers had a lot of interest in expanding or developing the IXP". The other expressed a dissenting view: "we have an agreement in place; the IXP is functioning, it has a purpose but we are the partners to the agreement and the onus is on us to make it work". They both saw their role as supportive because they are commercial entities, but they are in business to make money, so their role was "providing technical assistance where they can and providing a network that is strong enough to support it and enable creativity".

5.1.4 Other stakeholders

One participants expressed the view that promoting the IXP "this should be the responsibility of local organisations and ICT groups" like the Caribbean Telecommunication Union (CTU) who jointly facilitated the Grenada IXP workshop working with the Grenada NTRC and brought together the local ISPs and other stakeholders. These meetings were designed to arrive at agreements among the stakeholders on the way forward. The Grenada IXP is not located in a commercial data centre, so organisations like the Internet Society (ISOC), and Packet Clearing House (PCH) provided technical assistance and worked along with the IXP volunteers and donated devices to assist with the day to day operations. ISOC donated a modern gigabit switch which was used as a back-up switch and provided some redundancy. They also donated a tool for managing the IXP known as the IXP Manager. The Regional Internet Registry for Europe (RIPE) Atlas probes were also donated and used by the IXP volunteers to measure latency and to perform comparative worldwide statistical measurements. Volunteers played an important role in managing the IXP.

5.2 Benefits Delivered

All internal and external respondents were of the view that the Grenada IXP delivered technical benefits as expected. One respondent indicated that the process of getting the IXP up and running "has completely and significantly changed the conversation around local, digital economic development". From inception, there was evidence that local traffic was exchanged and the promise of reduced latency was achieved. These benefits include observable reduction in latency as a result of the immediate increase in the exchange of local traffic; therefore, there was a reduction in the use of transit traffic for local messages. The latter was expected to produce reduced costs to the telecom operations, but this was not immediately evident. There were however some unique circumstances that impacted the operations of the Grenada IXP including the merger of the two telecom operators peering at the exchange which had implications for the value of the exchange at that point. It therefore became necessary to seek new participants to join the exchange. Because of the merger and a number of other operational issues, it is difficult to quantify the social or developmental benefits that may have been achieved. All of the respondents indicated that there was work to be done in this area. These responses presented only partly answered research questions two (2) and three (3) so more in-depth analysis of these responses is required to arrive a conclusive finding.

6. CONCLUSIONS

A preliminary assessment of the responses show that the Grenada IXP provided some technical benefits while the expected social and developmental benefits were not as easily identifiable. More in-depth analysis of the responses is required to accurately answer that question. At the same time, there is very little doubt that the government and the regulator were very supportive of the IXP and were strong advocates, which supports the findings of the study by Galperin (2013). The political will to successfully deploy the IXP was the strategic driving force behind the implementation. One telecom operator willingly participated but not the incumbent. It took government's interventions to encourage that organization to eventually peer.

The informal structure was not a hindrance to the IXP from becoming operational. This was a 'low' budget implementation so there was greater reliance on the 'other stakeholders' to provide not only technical expertise, but also equipment for the day to day operations of the IXP which included the DNS and L-root servers to augment the IXP peering infrastructure. Even the management functions of the Grenada IXP were performed by volunteers.

The respondents all felt that the IXP was beneficial to the country after its implementation because local traffic was exchanged immediately and latency was reduced. Nevertheless, an in-depth investigation is required to answer the question on the IXP's contributed to the social development and the Internet economy of Grenada. One benefit that was clear is that the process of planning and deploying the IXP has successfully employed the multi-stakeholders approach in not only having the discourse about the digital economy, but also working together to engender activity for the development of the Internet economy in Grenada.

REFERENCES

Bruegge, Chris, Kayoko Ido, Taylor Reynolds, Cristina Serra-Vallejo, Piotr Stryszowski, and Rudolf Van Der Berg. 2011. The Relationship between Local Content, Internet Developmnet and Access Prices.

CARICOM (Caribbean Community)-Secretariat. 2008. "About Ict4d." CARICOM Secretariat, Last Modified September Accessed July 7, 2011. http://www.caricomict4d.org/about-ict4d-left-side-menu-217.html.

Chatzis, Nickolaos, Georgios Smaragdakis, and Anja Feldmann. 2013. "On the Importance of Internet Exchange Points for Today's Internet Ecosysem." Last Modified July 19 Accessed April 23, 2014. http://arxiv.org/abs/1307.5264.

ECTEL (Eastern Caribbean Telecommunications Authority). 2016. "About Ectel." Eastern Caribbean Telecommunications Authority Accessed June 1, 2016. http://ectel.int/index.php/background/about-ectel.

Edelman, Benjamin, and Bill Woodcock. 2012. "Towards Efficiencies in Canadian Internet Traffic Exchange." Canadian Internet Registration Authority Accessed 11 January, 2015. http://www.cira.ca/assets/Uploads/Toward-Efficiencies-in-Canadian-Internet-Traffic-Exchange2.pdf;.

Galperin, Hernan. 2013. "Connectivity in Latin America and the Caribbean: The Role of Internet Exchange Points." Last Modified November Accessed January 14, 2014. http://www.internetsociety.org/doc/connectivity-latin-america-and-caribbean-role-internet-exchange-points.

Galperin, Hernan. 2014. "Do Internet Exchange Points Really Matter? Evidence from Bolivia." 42nd Telecommunications Policy Research Conference, Arlington, VA.

Galperin, Hernan. 2015. "Localizing Internet Infrastructure: Coorperative Peering in Latin America."

Galperin, Hernan, and Christian A. Ruzzier. 2013. "Price Elasticity of Demand for Broadband: Evidence from Latin America and the Caribbean." *Telecommunications Policy* 37 (6-7):429 - 438.

Garcia-Zaballos, Antonio , and Ruben Lopez-Revas. 2012. Socioeconomic Impact of Broadband in Latin American and Caribbean Countries. In *Technical Note No. IDB-TN-471*. Washington, DC: Inter-Ameircan Development Bank.

Gerson, Jason, and Patrick S. Ryan. 2012. "A Primer on Internet Exchange Points for Policymakers and Non-Engineers." Last Modified August 11 Accessed August 27, 2012. http://ssrn.com/abstract=2128103.

IGF. 2011. *Igf 2011 - 'Internet as a Catalyst for Change: Access, Development, Freedoms and Innovation'*. Edited by Brian Gutterman. Nairobi: United Nations.

ISOC (Internet Society). 2014. "Internet Exchange Point Toolkit & Best Practices Guide." Accessed 11 January, 2015. http://www.internetsociety.org/ixptoolkitguide;.

ITU (International Telecommunications Union). 2012. "Partnership on Measuring Information and Communications Technology for Development." [E/CN.3/2012/12]. United Nations Economic and Social Council Accessed January 15, 2013.

Jensen, Mike. 2012. Promoting the Use of Internet Exchange Points(Ixp): A Guide to Policy Management, and Technical Issues. Internet Society.

Mc Laughlin, Andrew. 2004. Internet Exchange Points: Their Importance to Development of the Internet and Strategies for Their Deployment - the African Example. Washington: Center for Democracy and Technology.

Padovani, Claudia. 2005. "Wsis and Multi-Stakeholderism." *D. Stauffacher und W. Kleinwächter (Hg.): The World Summit on the Information Society, New York*:147-155.

Silvius, Stephanie. 2011. Internet Exchange Points - a Closer Look at the Differences between Continental Europe and the Rest of the World.

Sowell, Jesse Horton. 2012. "Empirical Studies of Bottom-up Internet Governance." Proc. TPRC.

UN (United Nations). 2016. "We Can End Poverty - Millennium Development Goals and Beyond 2015."Accessed February 22, 2016. http://www.un.org/millenniumgoals/.

Weller, Dennis, and Bill Woodcock. 2013. Internet Traffic Exchange: Market Developments and Policy Challenges. OECD Publishing.

MOBILE DEVICE SECURITY: USER AWARENESS AND RESPONSE

Christopher Wallenreiter, Jean-Pierre Kuilboer, Noushin Ashrafi and Daniel Lee
University of Massachusetts Boston, 100 Morrissey Blvd., Boston, MA 02125, USA

ABSTRACT

This study aims to explore and model mobile users' perception of security threats and their consequent behavior to take actions in an attempt to minimize vulnerability. While there have been a number of attempts in the literature to illustrate users' reaction to positive and negative aspects of mobile technology, a paradigm to define a clear path from perception to action taking into consideration both the external and internal motivating factors has not been introduced. Reflecting on various models in other areas of research such as healthcare and psychology, we have been building a model to show the impact of both external and internal stimuli on taking action against exponentially increasing mobile security threats. Our research will benefit both academicians and IT industry interested in users' response to both positive and negative impacts of technology in their daily lives.

KEYWORDS

Security threats, mobile device, protective action, user awareness, user response

1. INTRODUCTION

The concept of proactive behavior to secure sensitive information by mobile users is a fairly new phenomenon and a needed area of research. As the use of mobile devices in many aspects of daily life is exponentially increasing so does the possibility of a security breach and privacy violation of personal information. A model of cause-and-effect could help better understand the relationship between factors leading to certain human behavior to assert protective measures in the context of mobile devices.

Three emerging behavioral areas are related to our research; the increasing use of mobile devices for critical transactions, consumer perception of mobile security, and the protective action against breaches of security and privacy. Prior studies in these areas imply that people try to balance the convenience of using mobile devices and attempts for protection such as installing security applications, comparing platforms for best security measures, and the overall efforts to be aware of the threats and cope with them as new forms of threats introduced. At this stage, we mainly focus on examining existing models in various areas of research to find a connection between human awareness of vulnerabilities and consequent behavior to best avoid them. This would be the first step to answering the question of what needs to be done to protect mobile users, as the mobile devices are becoming the favorite mode of communication, transactions, and exchange of information.

The next section looks into overall work conducted in recent years addressing security perception and awareness of individuals and their actual security behavior. We conclude with our plan for future research.

2. LITERATURE REVIEW& CONCEPTUAL DEVELOPMENT

Because violations of mobile security and privacy have become ubiquitous in both personal and work environments, academic attention to mobile security and privacy has taken on paramount importance. Consequently, a key focus of mobile security research has been around discovering perceptions of mobile security and finding ways to motivate individuals to engage in more secure behaviors. For our research, three areas of research emphasizing perception and awareness leading to actual actions are highlighted.

2.1 Security Perception and Awareness

A lot of research has been conducted with regard to individuals' perception and awareness of security threats. The main question researchers try to answer – mostly by conducting surveys and interviews – is; 'what are the factors that influence user perceptions of smartphone security?' Research finds that IT-knowledge as well as the impact, severity, and possibility of threats have a significant effect on the perceived overall danger of security threats (Mylonas et al. 2013; Huang et al. 2010). Thus, changing user's perceived knowledge, controllability and awareness can enhance people's adoption intention and compliance, e.g. their intention to adopt e-banking, or their intention to set strong passwords for IT systems (Huang et al. 2011).

Another topic that is often discussed is that of fear appeals. Research has found that fear appeals do affect end users' behavioral intentions to comply with recommended acts of security. It is determined in part by user perceptions of self-efficacy, response efficacy, threat severity, and social influence (Johnston & Warkentin 2010). Other studies focus more on user's internal feelings. Kraus et al. (2015) find that user's security behavior is guided by feelings of autonomy, competence, relatedness, and self-esteem, which prevent users from adopting security technologies. Therefore, they propose to establish a feeling of achievement if end-users adopt or execute a security mechanism. A few studies have been conducted regarding operating systems concluding that Android users are more privacy aware than iOS users (Benenson et al. 2013).

Overall, some researchers draw a dark picture of information security awareness (Mylonas et al. 2013), while others are more optimistic (Parker et al. 2015). The former perspective finds an ongoing complacency towards security, as the majority of users trust the app repositories, neglect security controls, and disregard security during application selection and installation. The majority of smartphone users believe that downloading applications from the app repository is risk-free. The latter presents positive evidence for more security awareness amongst younger smartphone users. Respondents report knowledge of malware and security software, as well as the adoption of various authentication and (to a lesser extent) anti-theft controls. However, both studies agree that there are several risks connected to user complacency, risky behavior, or lack of security control adoption.

2.2 Actual Security Behavior

While security perception and awareness seem to be important areas of information security research, researchers also search for more signs of the relationship between people's perception of information security and their actual behaviors regarding IT devices and security methods (Huang et al. 2010). Chin et al. (2012) find out that users are apprehensive about running privacy and financially sensitive tasks on their phones as a consequence of four main factors: fear of theft and data loss, misconceptions about the security of their network communications, worries about accidentally touching/clicking, and mistrust of smartphone applications. They also find out that users are more concerned with privacy on their phones than on their laptops. However, results show that security measures that are relatively easy to adopt are being ignored. Unlock patterns, for example, are often perceived as unnecessary (Harbach et al. 2014). The reasons for using or not using protection mechanisms are highly diverse. Often, they are neither objective nor valid from a technical perspective (Harbach et al. 2014). Self-efficacy, vulnerability awareness, threat awareness, and risk awareness about mobile information security are often mentioned when it comes to determining smartphone user's security practices and behaviors (Simpson 2016). At the same time, the protection motivation theory (Ifinedo 2012) and the health belief model (Williams et al. 2014) suggest similar determinants of security behavior with additional considerations of individuals' coping appraisal, perceived benefits of security actions, and social influences, which also should be examined with regard to mobile security behaviors.

2.3 Cultural Influence

Many researchers complain that only very few studies look at how context and culture change information security behavior (Simpson 2016). One of the few culture-related studies uses a contextualization of the protection motivation theory (PMT) to online security behavior and a polycontextual lens for a cross-national comparison of users' security behaviors in the United States and China (Chen & Zahedi 2016). It finds that cultural differences play a significant role in security behavior. When it comes to coping behaviors, users in the two nations are far apart in seeking help and avoidance. Chinese users are significantly more disposed to seek help in the face of a threat and inclined to adopt avoidance as a coping behavior. In contrast, U.S. users are less inclined to adopt avoidance as a coping strategy. So, it will be required to consider such cultural influences in our model on mobile security behaviors.

3. CONCLUSION AND FUTURE RESEARCH

In conclusion, researchers agree that information security threats are changing rapidly, often times faster than detection and prevention methods (He et al. 2015). They suggest that, in order to keep pace with evolving threats, collective security intelligence must be leveraged by finding a systematic way to collect and share security threat data. In line with this, some important directions have been proposed for future research. First, researchers suggest investigating particular social and technical contexts which play a significant role in information security, e.g., the influence of security news (Harris et al. 2014), specific threat sources such as viruses, malware, botnets, and spyware (Arachchilage et al. 2016). Second, several researchers suggest that information security research should expand to emerging technological trends of mobile devices (Harris et al. 2014) by distinguishing laptop security behavior and mobile device security behavior (Chin et al. 2012). Finally, there is a consensus in literature that future research should investigate how cross-culture differences (Chen & Zahedi 2016; Ifinedo 2012; Huang et al. 2010) and factors like language, ethnicity, gender, and demographic variations (Parker et al. 2015; Chin et al. 2012) affect information security awareness and behavior.

To respond to these calls for future research, we propose to adopt various theoretical lenses such as the protection motivation theory and the health belief model that can augment extant information security studies. Based on these theoretical perspectives, our research, currently as work in progress, investigates how the external stimuli as a social influence and the intrinsic factors of an individual lead to the internal appraisal processes of security cognition and the decisions about her/his security actions. Moreover, our research is conducted through global collaboration efforts for data gathering in multiple cultural contexts, including U.S., Europe, and Asia. Comparison results among these regions will be interpreted from their different cultural backgrounds.

REFERENCES

Arachchilage, N. A. G., Love, S., and Beznosov, K. 2016. Phishing Threat Avoidance Behaviour: An Empirical Investigation. *In Computers in Human Behavior*, Vol. *60*, pp. 185-197.

Benenson, Z., Gassmann, F., and Reinfelder, L. 2013. Android and iOS users' differences concerning security and privacy. In *CHI'13 Extended Abstracts on Human Factors in Computing Systems* (pp. 817-822). ACM.

Chen, Y., and Zahedi, F. M. 2016. Individuals' Internet Security Perceptions and Behaviors: Polycontextual contrasts between the United States and China. In *MIS quarterly*, vol. 40, No. 1, pp. 205-222.

Chin, E. et al. 2012. Measuring User Confidence in Smartphone Security and Privacy. In *Proceedings of the Eighth Symposium on Usable Privacy and Security*, ACM, Washington DC USA, p. 1.

Harbach, M et al. 2014. It's a hard lock life: A Field Study of Smartphone (Un) Locking Behavior And Risk Perception. In *Symposium on Usable Privacy and Security (SOUPS 2014)*, Menlo Park, California, USA, pp. 213-230.

Harris, M. A., Furnell, S., and Patten, K. 2014. Comparing the Mobile Device Security Behavior of College Students and Information Technology Professionals. In *Journal of Information Privacy and Security*, Vol. *10, No.* 4, pp.186-202.

He, D., Chan, S., and Guizani, M. 2015. Mobile Application Security: Malware Threats and Defenses. *In IEEE Wireless Communications*, Vol. *22, No.* 1, pp.138-144.

Huang, D. L., Rau, P. L. P., and Salvendy, G. 2010. Perception of Information Security. In *Behaviour & Information Technology*, Vol. *29, No.* 3, pp. 221-232.

Ifinedo, P. 2012. Understanding Information Systems Security Policy Compliance: An Integration of the Theory of Planned Behavior and the Protection Motivation Theory. In *Computers & Security*, Vol. 3, No. 1, pp. 83-95.

Johnston, A. C., and Warkentin, M. 2010. Fear Appeals and Information Security Behaviors: An Empirical Study. In *MIS quarterly*, Vol. 34, No. 3, pp. 549-566.

Kraus, L., at al. 2015. Analyzing End-Users' Knowledge and Feelings Surrounding Smartphone Security and Privacy. *In Proceedings IEEE Security & Privacy Workshops - Mobile Security Technologies (MoST).*

Mylonas, A., Kastania, A., and Gritzalis, D. 2013. Delegate the Smartphone User? Security Awareness in Smartphone Platforms. In *Computers & Security*, Vol. *34*, pp. 47-66.

Parker, F. et al. 2015. Security Awareness and Adoption of Security Controls by Smartphone Users. In *2015 Second International Conference on Information Security and Cyber Forensics (InfoSec)*. Cape Town, South Africa, pp. 99-104.

Simpson, J. P. 2016. Empirical Analysis of Socio-Cognitive Factors Affecting Security Behaviors and Practices of Smartphone Users. Doctoral Dissertation, Nova Southeastern University.

Williams, C. K. et al. 2014. Explaining Users' Security Behaviors with the Security Belief Model. In *Journal of Organizational and End User Computing (JOEUC)*, Vol. *26, No.* 3, pp. 23-46.

CITIZENS' ACCEPTANCE OF THE ELECTRONIC HEALTH RECORD

Filomena Papa, Enrico Nicolò and Bartolomeo Sapio
Fondazione Ugo Bordoni - Viale del Policlinico 147, 00161 Roma, Italy

ABSTRACT

The present paper proposes a reference framework to investigate acceptance by the users (e.g. citizens and medical personnel) of the Electronic Health Record (EHR). This framework refers to the Human Centered Design discipline and specifically to the Unified Theory of Acceptance and Use of Technology (UTAUT) model. Qualitative and quantitative investigations in progress about the TreC EHR system, implemented in an Italian province, are described.

KEYWORDS

Electronic Health Record, technology acceptance, UTAUT

1. INTRODUCTION

The Electronic Health Record (EHR) is the set of health and socio-health digital data and documents generated by present and past clinical events concerning patients. Critical aspects in the implementation of the EHR are connected to its acceptance by users: citizens, health workers, health facilities (hospitals, clinics, pharmacies, etc.) and Public Administrations (regions, autonomous provinces, etc.).

Acceptance models are powerful tools to explain individual acceptance and usage of a technological system: they allow the identification of the most relevant factors facilitating/hampering usage. The Unified Theory of Acceptance and Use of Technology (UTAUT) (Venkatesh et al., 2003) is one of the most recognized acceptance models. This model, comprising different aspects of usage behavior, has been extensively used to explain the adoption and use of various innovative ICT products and services. Using the UTAUT model, the present paper proposes a reference framework to investigate acceptance of an EHR by citizens and medical personnel.

In Sections 2 and 3 the current state of EHR development in Italy is introduced, analyzing the results obtained in significant experiences and surveys. In Section 4 the proposed reference framework is described. Section 5 summarizes investigations in progress, using the proposed approach to evaluate the EHR system implemented by the Trento Autonomous Province in Italy. In Section 6 conclusions are drawn and future developments are introduced.

2. ELECTRONIC HEALTH RECORD IN ITALY

The Electronic Health Record (EHR) or Electronic Medical Record (EMR) is the set of health and socio-health digital data and documents generated by present and past clinical events concerning the patient. Its main objectives, as declined in Italy, are to facilitate patient care, to facilitate the integration of different professional skills and to provide a consistent information base.

As provided by national regulation, the EHR is set up by the Regions and the Autonomous Provinces, in compliance with current legislation on the protection of personal data, and is integrated into a broad spectrum of activities related to the provision of health services, from prevention to quality control of care. Specifically, the initiative is aimed at improving the overall quality of services regarding prevention, diagnosis, care and rehabilitation; study and scientific research in medical, biomedical and epidemiologic fields; health planning, quality assurance and health care assessment.

From the point of view of the content and documentation made available, the Electronic Health Record includes a minimum set of documents that must be made available by the system plus supplementary documents allowing expanding its scope of use in support of different care paths to ensure continuity of care. The minimum nucleus consists of patient's identification and administrative data, medical reports, First Aid records, discharge letters, synthetic health profile, pharmaceutical dossier, consensus or denial of organ and tissue donation.

3. USER REQUIREMENTS OF THE TREC SYSTEM

The user of e-health services and the EHR can be an end user (e.g. citizen, healthcare provider), an organization (e.g. healthcare facility) or as an institution (e.g. region). EHR users in this sense include citizens, health workers, health facilities (hospitals, clinics, pharmacies, etc.) and Public Administrations (regions, autonomous provinces, etc.). This section identifies specific user requirements (for citizens and healthcare providers) of e-health and EHR services, analyzing the results obtained in the experiences with the TreC system of the Autonomous Province of Trento.

In 2014 Azienda Provinciale dei Servizi Sanitari, Fondazione Bruno Kessler and Università di Trento (Dipartimento di Sociologia e Ricerca Sociale) carried out a research oriented to investigate the opinions of citizens about the TreC service, one of the most advanced implementations of an EHR in Italy. The TreC system provides citizens with different health services: access to a series of online services, such as management of medical reports, online payment of health services, management of digital doctor's prescriptions, access to health reservations; recording of information on personal clinic history and on the clinic history of relatives; personal health register containing observations about health status; transmission of information to citizens; possibility to gather data from patients through mobile technology and sensors.

The research study (Bonato and Zanutto, 2014) was carried out using CAWI (Computer-Assisted Web Interviewing) techniques. The survey campaign was conducted in the period December 2013 - January 2014. Initially, a sample of 6,836 users was involved, who accessed the system at least three times in 2013. 4,269 users out of 6,836 users filled the online questionnaire completely. A great deal of information derives from the analysis of the results of the study. This is relevant to user (citizen) requirements as to services and contents (available on TreC), new functionalities required by citizens (not available on TreC), interaction with the system, new ways of interaction (not available on TreC) and information on the system.

4. REFERENCE FRAMEWORK

The reference discipline proposed for the analysis of user requirement of the Electronic Health Record (EHR) and e-health services is the set design methodologies centered on end users, Human-Centered Design (HCD), developed as part of Human-Computer Interaction (HCI). These methods consider the user as the recipient of the design process and as the only expert about himself and about his way of living, working and learning.

At the center of the HCD approach there are two key concepts: system usability and user experience. System usability is mainly related to pragmatic aspects of the interaction between technology and user: the achievement of a given objective and the execution of a given task with the technology (Scapin and Berns, 1997; ISO, 2002). User experience is a very broad concept dealing with all the aspects of the user's interaction with the product/service: how it is perceived, learned, and used (Norman, 2013). Behind the user experience concept, there is a holistic approach aiming for a balance between pragmatic aspects mainly related to the execution of the task and "non-task-related" aspects (Hassenzahl et al, 2010).

The evaluation of different user experience aspects can be utilized as input for user acceptance models. These models are powerful tools to explain individual acceptance and usage of a technological system: they allow the identification of most relevant factors facilitating/hampering usage (see, for instance, Sapio et al, 2010). The Unified Theory of Acceptance and Use of Technology (UTAUT) (Venkatesh et al., 2003) is one of the most recognized acceptance models. This model, comprising different aspects of usage behavior, has been extensively used to explain the adoption and use of various innovative ICT products and services (see for instance Williams et al, 2015; Papa et al, 2017).

The UTAUT allows explaining use behavior of an innovative technology or service starting from the central role of behavioral intention. The key dependent variable in the UTAUT model is the intention and/or the use of technology; hence the final purpose of the model is that of understanding and providing an explanation of the phenomenon 'use of information technology', taken as a dependent variable. In the formulation of the UTAUT model four constructs are identified, which may play a significant role as direct determinants of user acceptance and usage behavior: *Performance Expectancy* is the degree to which an individual believes that using the system will help him/her to attain gains in job performance; *Effort Expectancy* is the degree of ease associated with the use of the system, which is strongly connected to the degree to which a person believes that using the system would be free of effort; *Facilitating Conditions* are related to the degree to which an individual believes that an organization or technical infrastructure exists to support the use of the system; *Social Influence* is the degree to which an individual perceives that important others believe he/she should use the new system.

In specific case of e-health and EHR it is possible to measure the above-mentioned constructs using the following indicators.

Performance expectancy: Degree of interest of the user towards provided services and contents; Update of provided contents; Service interaction and fruition modalities; Service capability to attract and to entertain the user, avoiding banality and tediousness in the interaction; Satisfaction in use in comparison to the same kind of service delivered through other channels (for instance by telephone or traditional offices).

Effort expectancy: Ease of access to the e-health service; Ease of e-heath system use; Ease of navigation; Perception by the users of possible system dysfunctions (difficulties in establishing the internet connection, excessive waiting times, unclear costs, etc).

Social influence: Behavior in e-health services fruition of the persons considered important by the user (e.g. affective and charismatic leaders); Behavior in e-health services fruition of own reference groups (e.g. friends, associations).

Facilitating conditions: User manuals; Call center or contact center.

Variables age, gender, experience and voluntariness of use are important moderators included in the UTAUT model. Income and education have been proposed as moderators to be validated in future studies (Sapio et al, 2010). More recently the UTAUT2 model was proposed as an extension of the UTAUT model. UTAUT2 can be utilized in larger contexts and includes new constructs connected to use habits, price value and hedonic motivation in use (Venkatesh et al, 2012). Furthermore, in the particular case of e-health and electronic health records, it is necessary to consider an additional construct concerning security perception (Papa et al, 2010), privacy protection and personal data confidentiality.

5. INVESTIGATIONS IN PROGRESS

A new investigation about the TreC EHR users started in 2016 and adopted the HCD. User experience and user acceptance models were proposed to identify the most relevant factors facilitating/hampering usage. Qualitative and quantitative investigations are in progress in cooperation with the University of Trento.

The items summarized in Table 1 to measure the constructs of the UTAUT2 were added to the CAWI questionnaire administered to citizens using the TreC system in October 2016.

Table 1. Questions to measure the UTAUT2 constructs

Construct	Item
Performance Expectancy	• The TreC system is useful in my every day life
	• The TreC system helps me to manage my health
	• The TreC system allows me to save time
Effort expectancy	• Learning how to use TreC is easy for me
	• After the first accesses, TreC is easy to use
Perceived security	• TreC protects confidentiality of my personal data
Social influence	• My relatives/friends think that it is useful for me to use TreC
Hedonic motivation	• Using TreC is enjoyable
Facilitating conditions	• I have the technological resources to use TreC
	• I have the knowledge necessary to use TreC
	• I can get the necessary help when I have difficulties using TreC
Behavioral intention	• I intend to continue using TreC in the future
	• I would like to continue using TreC more and more

From the statistical processing of collected data, quantitative user experience and acceptance evaluations with the TreC services are being evaluated, together with useful input for user requirements of the EHR.

User experience and acceptance qualitative investigations are in progress considering TreC frequent users. Investigations about acceptance of medical operators and citizens not using the EHR are foreseen in the framework of the next filed studies about the TReC system.

6. CONCLUSIONS

The HCD methodology proved extremely efficient in dealing with the introduction of Electronic Health Records. This methodology is based on the involvement of end users from the early stages of the development process, investigating needs and requirements, and evaluating prototypes in intermediate and final stages. As a reference framework, user experience and user acceptance models were proposed and adopted to identify the most relevant factors facilitating/hampering the usage of the EHR.

Future studies will include: "ad hoc" qualitative investigations to deepen requirements of particular classes of citizens, for instance elderly people and adults non-internet users, and investigations considering the e-health and the EHR impact on the health structures/institutions (e.g. hospitals).

ACKNOWLEDGEMENT

The authors wish to thank Rosamaria Barrese, Stefano van der Byl, Francesca Ivana Iozzi and the entire work team on the Electronic Health Record at AgID (Agenzia per l'Italia Digitale); Diego Conforti (Provincia Autonoma di Trento), Stefano Forti (Fondazione Bruno Kessler), Alberto Zanutto (Università di Trento).

REFERENCES

Bonato, M. and Zanutto, A., 2014. *TreC La cartella clinica del cittadino, Report indagine qualitativa CAWI*. Dipartimento di Sociologia e Ricerca Sociale Università di Trento, Marzo 2014.

Hassenzahl, M., Diefenbach, S., and Goritz, A., 2010. Needs, affect, and interactive products - Facets of user experience. *Interacting with Computers*, Vol. 22, No. 5, pp. 353–362.

ISO 14915-1:2002, 2002. Software ergonomics for multimedia user interfaces - Part 1: design principles and framework.

Norman, D.A., 2013. *Design of everyday things: revised and expanded.* MIT Press (UK edition), London.

Papa, F., Cornacchia, M., Sapio, B., Nicolò, E., 2017. Engaging technology-resistant elderly people: Empirical evidence from an ICT-enabled social environment. *Informatics for Health and Social Care,* Vol. 42 ,No. 1, pp. 43-60

Papa, F., Nicolò, E., Livi, S., Sapio, B., Cornacchia, M., 2010. Factors Affecting the Usage of Payment Services through Digital Television in Italy. *Proceedings of European Interactive TV and Video (EuroITV 2010) Conference*, Tampere, Finland.

Sapio B, Turk T, Cornacchia M, Papa F, Nicolò E, Livi S., 2010. Building scenarios of digital television adoption: a pilot study. *Technology Analysis & Strategic Management,* Vol. 22, No.1, pp. 43–63.

Scapin, D.L., Berns, T. (eds.), 1997. Usability and evaluations methods. *Special Issue of Behaviour & Information Technology,* Vol. 16, No 4/5.

Venkatesh, V., Morris, M. G., Davis, G. B., Davis, F. D., 2003. User Acceptance of Information Technology: Toward a Unified View. *MIS Quarterly*, Vol. 27, No. 3, pp. 425-478.

Venkatesh, V., Thong, J., Xu, X., 2012. Consumer Acceptance and Use of Information Technology: Extending the Unified Theory of Acceptance and Use of Technology. *MIS Quarterly*, Vol. 36, No. 1, pp. 157-178.

Williams, M. D., Rana, N. P., and Dwivedi, Y. K., 2015.The Unified Theory of Acceptance and use of Technology (UTAUT): A literature review. *Journal of Entreprise Information Management*, Vol. 28, No. 3, pp. 443–488.

EMOTION RECOGNITION USING MUSICAL MNEMOTHERAPY WITH THREE PHYSIOLOGICAL SENSORS

Chaka Koné[1], Cécile Belleudy[1], Jean Claude Broutart[2] and Nhan Le-Thanh[3]
[1]*University cote d'azur, University of Nice Sophia Antipolis, LEAT Laboratory CNRS, UMR 7248, France*
Campus SophiaTech - Bâtiment Forum, 930 route des Colles, BP 145, 06903 Sophia Antipolis cedex, France
[2]*Igam Faculty of medicine of NICE, GSF JL Noisiez foundation Address, France, 55 Allée Charles Victor Naudin, 06410 Biot, France*
[3]*University cote d'azur, University of Nice Sophia Antipolis, I3S Laboratory CNRS, UMR 7271, France*
Euclide B, Les Algorithmes, 2000 Route des Lucioles, 06900 Sophia Antipolis, France

ABSTRACT

It exists some non-drug therapy relaying emotions to take care Alzheimer patients. This paper presents a new application for emotions detection. Indeed, a subject listen music to stimulate his emotional state and 3 physiological sensors are used to acquire his bio-signals for emotions detection. After constructing an emotion data base during the learning phase, we apply the recognition algorithm on each modality separately. Then, these decisions are merged separately by applying a decision level fusion. The experiments show the strength of our methodology to detect efficaciously these 3 emotional states when a subject is listening to music, indeed, we get a recognition rate of 84.245%

KEYWORDS

Mnemotherapy, automatic playlist, multimodal emotions detection, physiological signals, BITalino

1. INTRODUCTION

Historically, emotions had a great impact on our behavior, our feelings and we are constantly trying to manage our emotions as well as the people that surround us, to live together in harmony. Indeed, emotions enable us to communicate with our environment but also to adapt, to innovate, to succeed, and to flourish. On the other hand, our current life is subject to science, technologies then came the idea of affective computing by Rosalind Picard in 1995. It is a field studying the interactions between technologies and emotions to give to machines the ability to understand, to synthesize our emotions and even to express emotions. It offers many advantages such as the fight against depression, interactive games, e-learning...

A lot of research based on facial, vocal expressions and physiological signals (Picard et al., 2001), (Haag et al., 2004), (Busso et al., 2009) have emerged to analyze emotions, with the aim, amongst other, to provide a real-time, aggregate view of user's feelings and in general to identify customer dissatisfaction. Up to now emotion recognition systems are not yet usable in realistic applications. Fewer studies have been focused on emotion detection using physiological signals. Physiological signals have considerable advantages. We can continuously gather information about the users' emotional changes while they are connected to physiological sensors. Moreover, physiological reactions should be more robust against possible artefacts of human social masking since they are directly controlled by the human autonomous nervous system which is a part of the nervous system responsible for functions, not under voluntary control (Wagner et al., 2005).

Many works have demonstrated that physiological signals measurements can be used to detect efficaciously fundamental emotions (sadness, anger, joy, disgust, fear and surprise) (Koné et al., 2015). These six basic emotions "Big Six" are respectively link to six behaviors: *"the reintegration, the destruction, the reproduction, the rejection, the protection and the attention"*. The fundamental emotions can be defined like the basis of development of other emotions called secondary emotions that develop throughout the life by interaction with the environment in which we are living. These primary emotions are innate, automatic, unconscious and are generally expressed to protect themselves facing an emergency.

There are many physiological signals used for emotion detection, the signals commonly used are:

a) *Galvanic skin response (GSR)*: This data reflects the electrical skin conductivity level. In situations involving emotions, this electrical activity varies very sensibly and can provide an indirect measurement of emotional intensity. It gives a good information about *stress, anxiety*, and this response increases linearly with a person's level of overall arousal (Nakasone et al., 2005).

b) *Electromyographic activity (EMG)*: The EMG measures muscle activity and has been shown to correlate with negatively valanced emotions.

c) *Rhythm Electroencephalographic (EEG)*: It measures the brain electrical activity and is used to detect mental states.

d) *Heart Rate (ECG)*: This sensor measures the electrical changes that accompany the heartbeat. The ECG works mostly by detecting and amplifying the tiny electrical changes on the skin that are caused during the heart muscle cycle during each heartbeat.

Below figures show some typical phycological signals. The abscissa axis of the first three figures (GSR, ECG, EMG) is expressed in seconds and their ordinate axis in volts, and the abscissa and ordinate axis for the last figure are respectively expressed in millisecond and micro-volts.

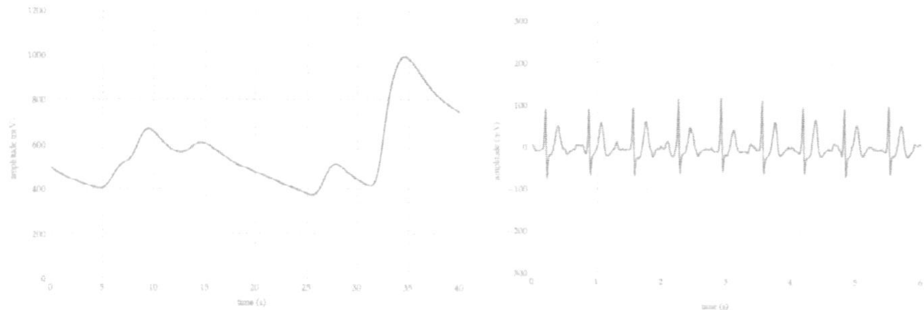

Figure 1. GSR and ECG signal

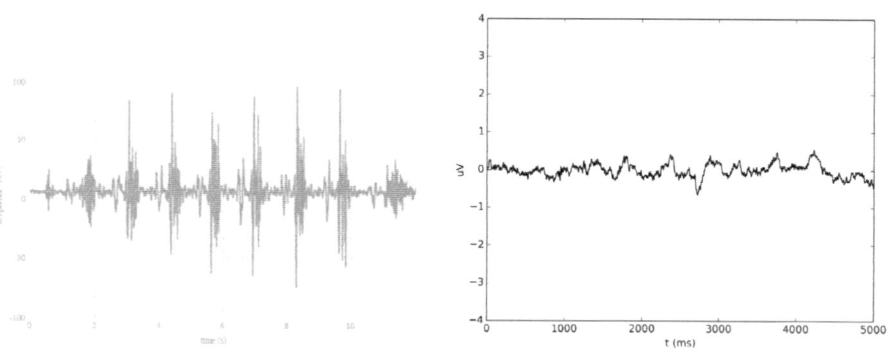

Figure 2. EMG and EEG signal

Our goal is to collect the physiological signals of a person under different conditions of real life to detect emotions automatically. In this paper, we propose to detect emotions of a person using physiological signals when he is listening to music. In our methodology, we use an acquisition platform including three sensors (EMG, GSR, ECG) and we merge these data for the goal of multimodal emotion recognition. The paper is structured as follows. In Section 2, a brief state of the art on the multimodal recognition of emotions. In Section 3, the experimental protocol and the methodology of emotions detection are briefly explained; in Section 4, a comparison is made between our results and those obtained in the state of the art; finally, conclusion and future work are reported in Section 5.

2. STATE OF THE ART

Emotions detection systems are based on three fundamental steps: acquisition of the signals, features extraction of these signals and the emotions detection. Recently some works are focused on emotions detection using physiological signals but fewer studies are based on the multimodal approach of emotions recognition (Sebe et al., 2005). The use of a multimodal approach allows not only enhancing the recognition rate but it gives more strength to the system when one of these modalities is acquired in a noisy environment (Pantic et al, 2003). In theory, there are three methods (Kim et al., 2004) to merge the signals from various sensors: fusion at the signal level (fusion of physiological signals), feature level fusion (fusion of features) and decision level fusion (fusion of decisions) (Hamdi, 2012), (Sharma et al, 1998). These different methods to merge data for the multimodal purpose are well explained in (Koné et al, 2015). In our study, the decisions level fusion is chosen because it is simple and intuitive to implement this algorithm.

2.1 Fusion of Decisions

After having classified separately from each sensor signals, this is a way to merge these different decisions to obtain a global vision of the emotion. Unlike features level fusion, this fusion technique is independent of the nature of the low-level features used for decision making [5]. The most used and most intuitive technique is to consider for the vote all modalities (each sensor: Electromyogram (EMG), Electrocardiogram (ECG), Galvanic Skin Response (GSR) and to choose the decision expressed by the maximum of modalities.

3. METHODOLOGY

In this section, we present the bio signals acquisition process and briefly the method of emotions recognition based decision level fusion. Our method is divided into two major phases, namely: The Learning phase and the detection phase.

3.1 Learning Phase

This phase consists of four steps (signal splitting, filtering, feature extraction, creation of the basis for learning) to provide a learning base which will then be used in the detection phase for the automatic detection of emotions. Figure 3 shows the synoptic of the learning phase.

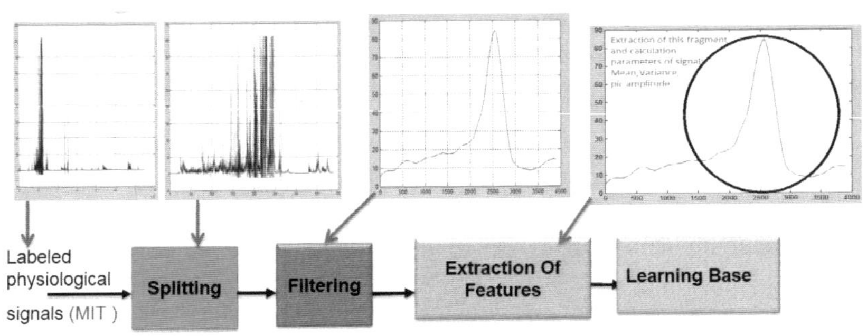

Figure 3. Synoptic of the learning phase

3.1.1 Signal Splitting

In this step, after having acquired the physiological signal, we isolate the part of the signal corresponding to a given emotion because we have information on the period in which each of the 3 emotions is expressed. Therefore, this step divides the input signal into 3 portions of signal corresponding to 3 emotions.

3.1.2 Filtering

After having isolated the signal, we filter it to remove the noise of the useful signal, which will facilitate the extraction of the features. We have opted for the convolution method for filtering, which consists in convoluting the signal in the spatial domain with different filters (for which we chose the Hanning filter, Koné et al, 2015). This method is less computationally expensive in calculations.

3.1.3 Extraction of Features

For each isolated and filtered signal, we proceed to the detection of peaks, which is done by calculating the gradient of the signal and then, finding the sign changes in the gradient, because it is rare to find points in discrete signals where the gradient is zero. A maximum is shown by the passage of a positive gradient to a negative gradient, a minimum by the passage of a negative gradient to a positive gradient. To detect and isolate a peak, our method should detect a minimum followed by a maximum followed by a minimum. Once a peak is isolated, we calculate a feature vector composed of five features that are: the mean, the variance, the mean of the filtered signal, the variance of the filtered signal, and the amplitude of the peak.

3.1.4 Creation of the Learning Phase

After extraction of the features vectors, we create a learning base for each modality. Thus, at the end of this step, we get 3 (corresponding to the number of sensors available on our used platform) learning bases. 35% of the signals available for each modality were used for the creation of the learning base and the remaining 65% were used for detection (test). The cross-validation method has been used to validate the classification parameters.

3.2 Detection Phase

This phase consists of two steps. The first step consists in the extraction of features, requiring the same steps as in the learning phase, without going through the splitting step since in this phase, there is no information beforehand on the period at which every emotion is expressed. The remainder of our process will be based on this features extraction step. It is necessary to detect a peak (an emotional activity) before pass to classification step. Indeed, thanks to this condition on the necessity of detecting an emotional activity, our method allows an instantaneous recognition of emotions. The second step is classification, the purpose of which is to predict the emotional class of the features vector extracted using our learning base, which was developed in the learning phase. We opted for the classification using the K-Nearest Neighbors (KNN) algorithm, which is based on the calculation of the Euclidean distance between the extracted feature vector, the emotional class of which is to be predicted, and features vectors which are in our learning base. This allows determining the K nearest emotions in our database of extracted feature vector. the studies conducted have allowed to find the optimal value of $K = 10$ and the size of the Hanning window $n = 230$ enable a best detection. Our objective being thereafter to put these algorithms in mobile devices which do not have a great memory size, it is thus necessary to set up simple algorithms. That is the reason why we chose this fusion approach on the decisions level. It is simpler and more intuitive than the two others.

3.3 Experimental Protocol

In this experience, we use BITalino platform which is a sensor kit to support the medical devices development and health monitoring applications because it brings all the advantages of a sophisticated bio-signal acquisition while remaining cheap. On this platform, we have 3 sensors of bio-signals *EMG, ECG, GSR*.

Throughout each experimental session, the subject keeps his eyes closed and listening the musical playlist using headphones, try to submerge himself in emotion that the music produces to him. Indeed, before the experimental session, the subject provides 3 playlists susceptible to help him to express the 3 emotional states Neuter state (No emotion state) - Pleasure state (pleasure by listening music) and - Joy state (when the music makes him happy). Data was collected during 15 days in an office on four subjects (2 women and 2 men). Approximately 21 minutes of data was recorded at each experimental session. The sampling frequency of EMG, ECG and GSR sensor was set at 10 samples per second. We have done this first study on just these

3-emotional states because the valences of these emotions are not so far, they all have a positive valence and if our algorithm can distinguish each other; that will proof the strength (efficiency and robustness to discern one emotion from others) of our methodology. This application could be a playlist generator from a very quick calibration because we plan to make up a general database which could be used by the most people. Henceforward, one can face that according to the emotional state of a person in a smart home, the system can automatically put a good music.

4. RESULTS

For these results, we use as data base the signals acquired on the 4 subjects. 35% of the acquired signals were used for the creation of the learning base and the remaining 65% were used for detection.

Table 1. Result of multimodal approach

Emotion	*Accuracy in % (ECG, EMG, GSR)*
No emotion	**68.33**
Pleasure	**93.175**
Joy	**91.23**

The results grouped in the Table 1 show a good average recognition rate. Furthermore, we note that our method allows to detect each of the 3-emotional state with a good recognition rate, where the minimum of 68.33% is obtained for the "Neuter" emotional state and the maximum is obtained for the " Pleasure" emotional state with a good classification rate of 93.175%. The low and high recognition rate respectively for neutral and pleasure states can be explained by the fact that these two emotional states have relatively the same value of excitement. Therefore, sometimes the system detects pleasure instead no emotion for this reason. However, the system is pretty good, because we found a recognition rate of 84.245%.

Table 2 allows doing a comparison between our results and the different results obtained in the state of the art methods that allow an instantaneous detection of emotions. This application is focused on emotion detection by listening to music using physiological signals, there is not much study in the same area but the above table is just to give an idea on the recognition rate of emotions using physiological signals and the multimodal approach.

Table 2. Comparison of results

Methods	Emotions	Rate in %
Method of Kim (Koné et al, 2015)	**8 emotions**	61.2
HHT features Fusion (Koné et al, 2015)	**8 emotions**	62
Baseline (Koné et al, 2015)	**8 emotions**	71
DLF fusion with KNN (Koné et al, 2015)	**8 emotions**	81.69
Fuzzy-Adaptive (Monajati et al., 2012)	**Negative & positive**	87

Therefore, a rigorous comparison of our result is difficult because of the lack of study in this area but, analyzing the recognition rate noted in the above table, one can mention that the recognition rate found with our methodology is very good. Most of the state of the art studies have been done on 8 emotions divided on 3 groups. Each group has a different valence from other (negative valence, neutral valence and positive valence). Most errors in the emotions detection algorithms comes from the difficulty to distinguish emotions which have the same valences. In this case, when we augment the emotions number which have same valences, emotion recognition rate will decrease. Considering these 3 emotions which have relatively same valences, we show the efficiency of our algorithms to distinguish one emotional activity from others.

The work presented in this paper is the primary step of a great project. Indeed, our project is in wellbeing area. We are essentially in improving of Alzheimer patient's daily life. It exists some non-drug approaches to take care of Alzheimer patients like Memorial stimulation. The musical Mnemotherapy is to arouse and to grow reproducibly reliving of the retrograde memories by indexed sensory stimulation. Apathy, very present in several patients of Alzheimer is the lack of self-presence and through the music Alzheimer patients can find their self-presence. We will focus our study on musical Mnemotherapy to provide a system which could give some advantages like:

• Thanks to anteretrograde, one can be able to give even at home an hour (or more) of joy each day to an Alzheimer patient.

• Cognitive stimulation and the brain plasticity reeducation which mean by listening to the music to Alzheimer patients to stimulate their old memories that it can still fetch and express.

5. CONCLUSIONS AND PERSPECTIVES

We have presented in this paper a multimodal recognition of emotions method based on the processing of physiological signals when a subject is listening to music. The physiological signals of 3 modalities were used for the recognition of 3 emotional states. The method for multimodal recognition based on the fusion decision level has been used. The different results show a marked improvement in the recognition rate of emotions.

In our future work, on one hand, we will generate a bigger database where physiological signals will be acquired on many subjects and on the other hand set up a complete system from the acquisition of physiological signals to the detection of emotions of the Alzheimer patients. Moreover, this system will allow creating a more appropriate recognition base for a wide range of people.

REFERENCES

Busso, C., Lee, S., & Narayanan, S. (2009). Analysis of emotionally salient aspects of fundamental frequency for emotion detection. *IEEE Transactions on audio, speech, and language processing*, *17*(4), 582-596.

Haag, A., Goronzy, S., Schaich, P., & Williams, J. (2004, June). Emotion recognition using bio-sensors: First steps towards an automatic system. In *Tutorial and research workshop on affective dialogue systems* (pp. 36-48). Springer, Berlin, Heidelberg.

Hamdi, H. (2012). *Plate-forme multimodale pour la reconnaissance d'émotions via l'analyse de signaux physiologiques : application à la simulation d'entretiens d'embauche* (Doctoral dissertation, Université d'Angers).

Kim, K. H., Bang, S. W., & Kim, S. R. (2004). Emotion recognition system using short-term monitoring of physiological signals. *Medical and biological engineering and computing*, *42*(3), 419-427.

Koné, C., Meftah, I. T., Le Thanh, N., & Belleudy, C. (2015, July). Detecting and Classification of the Basic Emotions Using a Multimodal Approach for Emotions Detection. In *the Fourth International Conference on Global Health Challenges, GLOBAL HEALTH 2015.*

Monajati, M., Abbasi, S. H., Shabaninia, F., & Shamekhi, S. (2012). Emotions States Recognition Based on Physiological Parameters by Employing of Fuzzy-Adaptive Resonance Theory. *International Journal of Intelligence Science*, *2*(04), 166.

Nakasone, A., Prendinger, H., & Ishizuka, M. (2005, September). Emotion recognition from electromyography and skin conductance. In *Proc. of the 5th International Workshop on Biosignal Interpretation* (pp. 219-222).

Pantic, M., & Rothkrantz, L. J. (2003). Toward an affect-sensitive multimodal human-computer interaction. *Proceedings of the IEEE*, *91*(9), 1370-1390.

Picard, R. W., Vyzas, E., & Healey, J. (2001). Toward machine emotional intelligence: Analysis of affective physiological state. *IEEE transactions on pattern analysis and machine intelligence*, *23*(10), 1175-1191.

Sebe, N., Bakker, E., Cohen, I., Gevers, T., & Huang, T. S. (2005, August). Bimodal emotion recognition. In *Proceedings of the 5th International Conference on Methods and Techniques in Behavioral Research*.

Sharma, R., Pavlovic, V. I., & Huang, T. S. (1998). Toward multimodal human-computer interface. *Proceedings of the IEEE*, *86*(5), 853-869.

Wagner, J., Kim, J., & André, E. (2005, July). From physiological signals to emotions: Implementing and comparing selected methods for feature extraction and classification. In *Multimedia and Expo, 2005. ICME 2005. IEEE International Conference on* (pp. 940-943). IEEE.

CITY DATA 3.0 - A GENERIC INITIATIVE TO PROMOTE AND ASSESS THE REUSE OF GEOGRAPHIC INFORMATION IN CITIES - EARLY STEPS

Fernando Benitez, Sergi Trilles and Joaquín Huerta
Universitat Jaume I
Av Vicente Sos Baynat, S/N, Castellon - Spain

ABSTRACT

Nowadays, authorities around the world discuss on the way to engage their data users and involve to being part of open data initiatives in cities. Thereby, assess the re-use level of available information through those portals is a significant challenge to achieving the real potential of open data in cities. This article presents the early steps of an initiative called CityData 3,0 which is a generic strategy to improve and assess the re-use and discovery level of available open geographic data in cities. This initiative has been developed in three phases, to analyze, define and test a group of recommendations for both data consumers and data authorities. Using an on-line survey to know the current status of cities' open data portals and a set of participatory workshops in cities in Colombia (Bogotá, Medellín, Cali) and Spain (Valencia, Castellon). The project aim is to understand which barriers can affect the data selection process of data re-users and attend data producers authorities to assess the re-use level of open data initiatives in cities.

KEYWORDS

Open Data, Open Cities, Data Re-use, Open Government, Data Discoverability

1. INTRODUCTION

For a long time, one of the main authorities' concern was to set up and populate open data portals with high data quality services (Attard et al. 2015), so that they were enriched by extensive data catalogs that follow most of the current standards.

However, the current challenge is not only downloading data or publishing web services; it is about data consumer requirements, their needs, engagement and about finding the way to involve them to be a part of the data selection process. What data selection process means, is the group of activities, that data users should face when they are looking for data.

The amount of data and comprehensive metadata could make challenging the data selection process (Janssen et al. 2012). Some official open data portals provided no more than simple data downloads and limited functionalities (Alexopoulos et al. 2013; Attard et al. 2015). Thereby, the availability of data has created a strain of barriers (Janssen et al. 2012) that data consumers must consider before using and transforming in new information; in many cases, they must download the data and after they can use it in their projects.

According to, The Belmont Forum's Open Data Survey (Schmidt et al. 2016) understand how to interpret and re-use data, how to access data and, varying degrees of quality in different datasets, and varying data formats, are the most significant aspects to take into account in open data portals.

Data consumers are demanding different and new ways to use and identify the relevant data for supporting applications to societal problems according to (Schmidt et al. 2016).

City Data 3.0 is a user-center initiative that can be beneficial for two city stakeholders, initially for authorities (Data producer or compilers) who need to assess and improve the re-use and impact level of available open data in cities, and data users who need to find the data for their projects.

Re-usability and discoverability are most frequent topics of discussion in events on open data and geographic standards. Several talks presented about data user's engagement mechanisms, tools to improve available information.

The main contributions of this work are: (1) Understand from perspective's data user the current barriers that avoid (developers and analysts) taking full advantage of available open data in cities, especially open geographic data. (2) Study the current status of cities open data portals. (3) Validate the responses gathered from on-line survey against data user suggestions in the hands-on activity. Once the analysis phase finished, the second aspect of this initiative is creating a generic strategy with indicators to assess the reuse level of available open data, which is a constant concern of the selected authorities.

2. METHOD DEFINED

This section describes the methodology employed, including three phases to cover the requirements and analysis steps, the definition of strategy and a final stage to testing. Whereby we started to develop the initial analysis stage for a better understanding of the real needs and barriers of data consumers might have once they are looking for open data in cities.

Phase No1. Contains two sub-phases, Discovery which was an on-line survey to assess the current status of open data portals in cities, it was public and share to everyone. The second sub-phase was a set of participatory workshops that allowed to interact with data users especially in places where we got more survey online responses, to prove what people say and what people do, not matter which role they have.

Phase No2. Which is the current stage, also contains two sub-phases, Strategy design and Proof-of-concept this stage is focused on the strategy and the indicators to assess the reuse level creating a guideline for selected cities.

Moreover, Phase No.3 Test and Evaluate is about testing the strategy and usefulness of the created guidelines with targeted cities stakeholders to have feedback.

3. INITIAL RESULTS PHASE 1

The aim of this stage was studying the current barriers present among data consumer and cities' open data portals. For better understanding about how data consumers find available data in cities and which could be the barriers to re-use the official open data portals. The first step was the developing an on-line survey.

On-line Survey. We have used Google Forms to create a survey, and we shared to open data users such as, researchers, developers, analysts, managers and overall people who are actively involved with data especially open geographic data in cities.

To learn about the knowledge level of open data portals in cities, backgrounds of the data consumer, barriers to reusing open data, feedback from data user perspective and still rooms where open data portals can be improved. The survey was shared in several countries, but most of the responses were from Colombia and Spain.

Participatory Workshops. To contrast the perception' data users (on-line survey) and issues mentioned by data users, we created Open Data for Open Cities workshop which had two parts, finding the available open data and discussion related to re-use level in cities.

During the first part, we observed activities made by data users, and we attempt to identify how data consumers are looking for data. Then, the second part of this workshop was an open discussion over the reuse importance, impact of use available data in cities, which barriers they have to overcome and which issues they found in the first part of the workshop.

3.1 On-line survey results

From 9 August 2016 to 16 March 2017, 195 responses were gathered from the on-line survey that was publicly shared. The survey had 22 questions some of them were non-mandatory, i.e. could be skipped by respondents.

However, this article presents the most significant results. The survey had several sections as follows.

General information. Overall data gathered from 16 countries and several cities based on the information of 195 responses. Bogota, Cali, Medellin and Spanish cities were the most frequent chosen cities in this survey (Cities with 1 or 2 replies were clustered).

Your Work. For the section related to respondent's role, 25 % of roles are geographical data analysts, and the next categories are researchers (19%), project managers (18%) and developers with 17% (n = 195 responses). It means most of the respondents have a critical role to improve the re-use level; they are data consumers by definition, they have knowledge to create analysis processes, to develop applications, and to lead projects where the geographic data is considered.

City open data. In this section, the respondents were consulted about their knowledge over cities' open data portals and the reasons to use this geographic information. Using three categories, the respondents had to choose among "very important," "neutral" and "not important." Those who provided a response (n=195), only 37,4% consider "very important" use city open data for economic benefits. However, 95.38 % consider very importantly the accessibility of geographic information and 92,2% recognize data quality as important feature as we expected. From our point of view is relevant that 69.23% of respondents mentioned academic and research improvement as "very important" category when open data is reused.

Barriers and features. Overall, the most important barriers to use cities' open data portals were a lack of update published data, low integration of data sources, and low relevance of URL to access published data (see Figure 1). Over 90 % of respondents (n=194 valid responses) considered the time spent searching open data was likewise marked a major and moderate barrier. Barriers such as technology used for publishing data and understanding about how to re-use the data were least marked up as a major barrier.

In contrast to barriers, the respondents provided information related to the most used functionalities available in cities' open data portals (n=186 valid responses). Filters for advanced search (61,29%), Data categories (59,14%) and access data URL (54,30%) were marked up as every time. Nevertheless, feedback from other data users (25.27%), terms of re-use were less pronounced (22.58%).

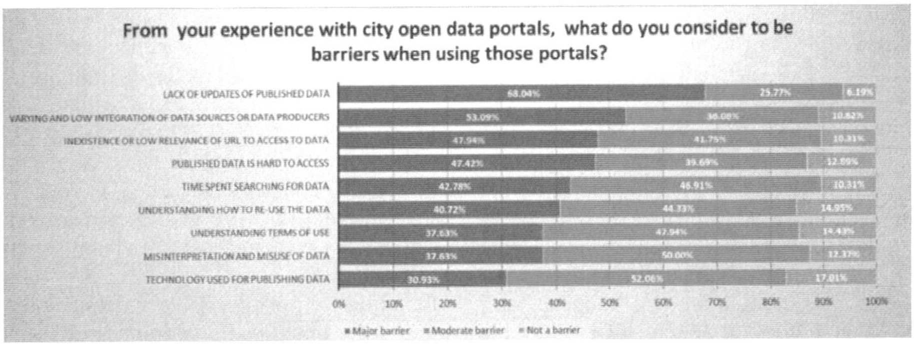

Figure 1. Barriers to use open data portals, n= 194 valid responses

Searching for geographic data. Related to which features are considered when data users are choosing available open data in cities. With 184 valid responses, the creation/ publication date (77.17%) and data quality (73.91%) are main features marked up by respondents.

Although, the term of use and re-use which is currently a major discussion topic only considered by 35.87% of responses. Note that 65,22% of answers determined author as the main feature to choose available open data, even though the geometry (64.67%) of available data is highly considered. The survey also asked about output formats or web services more suitable where data consumers are choosing open data in the city.

Overall respondents (80.11%) still want to have access to shapefiles format and downloadable files (64.52%) in another way around of the new capabilities of open data portals with functionalities to create API to serve direct connection between data and users.

Surprisingly, one of the recent formats to access open data RDF only has 16.67%, and formats as JSON and REST services are seen least useful (44.62%, 30,11%). KML and OGC standards (WMS, WFS, WMTS) have 50% and 54.30 % of 186 valid responses.

3.2 Open Data for Open Cities - participatory workshops results

The second sub-phase after on-line survey was a set of participatory workshops; those activities were prepared to collect information related to barriers and suggestions to compare the first data user's perception with the real actions when users are looking for data in specific challenge.

Taking into account only cities where we got more responses, Bogotá, Medellín, Cali (Colombia), Castellón and Valencia (Spain) those workshops had more than 140 attendants and cooperation of local authorities (IDECA[1] which is the Spatial Data Infrastructure of Bogota and Medellin[2], Cali[3], and Valencia[4] City Hall).

The aim was to discuss and evaluate suggestions to improve the re-use level of open geographic data. Using the open data categories, we request to data users find open data and explain to data authorities why they are facing issues to access and reuse open data in their city. Collecting suggestions, and observing how data users find open data, those participatory workshops were an interesting opportunity to engage more data consumers with the current cities' open data initiatives and enrich the open data reuse discussion.

During these hands-on activities, the initiative collected several different sorts of barriers that were not mentioned during the on-line survey for instance in Valencia the main concerns of data users was the integration and cooperation among the data producer departments, especially in mobility sector. In Bogota, re-users such as entrepreneurs do not have enough knowledge about available services, although IDECA has integrated city geographic data. Medellin is in the middle of open data initiative; however, data users expect to know more over the process about, with concerns like, how city open data project will be release? What technology will be used? Moreover, how data user communities are involved?

4. DISCUSSION

Currently, most of cities have their open data initiatives, through those projects accessibility, discoverability, and reusability of open data have been promoted. As Andrus Ansip, Vice-President for the Digital Single Market said "If we want our data economy to produce growth and jobs, data needs to be used. However, to be used, it also needs to be available and analyzed."[5]

Notwithstanding, cities have different ways to promote their open data. Through a local SDI in Bogota and Cali web services of mobility, environment, cadastral, security and more are accessible. In Medellin and Valencia, is the open data projects the way to release data from several categories.

These initiatives also include geographic data which are not the core of those initiatives. The way to display data can affect the re-use level and engagement level of new data consumers, likely the data communities in both situations are different.

Regarding barriers faced by data consumers, we found that terms to use and understanding about how to re-use the data were the options least marked in contrast with the argue by workshop attendants mentioned where terms of use are not clear in current cities' open data portals. Despite most of the open data portals have the terms of use available, probably the language used is not natural, these terms come from legal perspectives which are not a common skill and language for data re-users.

The on-line survey and workshop results also have some mutual points. Access to URL and advanced filters to search data were common requirements present in both methods. It means that data users expect to have the enough accessibility to find and re-use the available data in external applications. Data quality criterion was likewise an important fact mentioned by data consumers.

Criteria such as date of publication, how data was produced and which authority has created the data are important when users are looking for data. The authorities should put more relevance in those features to engage more users and most importantly, not lose data user confidence.

Another interesting finding of the survey was the persistence to have access to downloadable data. Re-users want to have easy and quick access to download the data and process it by themselves. The question

[1]https://www.ideca.gov.co
[2]https://www.medellin.gov.co
[3]http://idesc.cali.gov.co
[4]https://www.valencia.es
[5]http://europa.eu/rapid/press-release_IP-17-5_en.htm

is, that option promote the re-use level of available data, considering all barriers that data producers should overcome. How authorities can assess the impact of available data if data consumers download data. This one is an important discussion point that this strategy wants to involve and present some recommendation for both data consumers and data producers as a future work.

However, there is a limitation regarding last point of discussion which is the sample group in the on-line survey, is likely that respondents that prefer local access and downloadable formats belong to the Geoscience community, where those formats and processes in local environments are common. Nevertheless, participatory workshops were critical comparison tool, promoted by the local administration and with more 140 participants with different roles, to contrast if this finding is correct or not. We observed that when data users mentioned the accessibility barrier was when they could not download the data, not for lack of web services and during the discussion the most requirement by data consumers was more efficient ways to download data.

5. CONCLUSION

Data consumers who need an easy tool to find the right way available open data around the city, filtering gaps of data, creation/publication date, geographic properties, the term of use without spending much time to understand how data should be utilized.

In this article, we present the preliminary results of phase 1 of this initiative. We identified the important barriers and features requirements of cities' open data portals based on 195 data re-users responses, and finally, we tested with other data users with different roles through a set of participatory workshops called *Open data for Open Cities* to discuss the economic and socials benefits and real impact in targeted cities.

We plan to integrate those results and conclusions of an on-line survey and set of workshops to analyze the barriers to re-use available open data in the selected cities, through MCA (Multiple Correspondence Analysis) we will determine which barriers are most statistical significance for the current requirements of open data consumers.

This initiative attends authorities to have a generic strategy to engage and assess the reuse of the open data. For better understanding of cities' behavior, the next step is to integrate the project with other research themes such as a participatory framework to understand which information the authority should consider and focus on improving their upcoming decisions.

ACKNOWLEDGEMENT

The European Commission has funded this work through the GEO-C project (H2020-MSCA-ITN-2014, Grant Agreement number 642332, http://www.geo-c.eu/).

REFERENCES

Alexopoulos, C., Spiliotopoulou, L. & Charalabidis, Y., 2013. Open data movement in Greece: A Case Study on Open Government Data Sources. *Proceedings of the 17th Panhellenic Conference on Informatics - PCI '13*, p.279. Available at: http://dl.acm.org/citation.cfm?doid=2491845.2491876.

Attard, J. et al., 2015. A systematic review of open government data initiatives. *Government Information Quarterly*, 32(4), pp.399–418. Available at: http://www.sciencedirect.com/science/article/pii/S0740624X1500091X [Accessed December 14, 2015].

Janssen, M., Charalabidis, Y. & Zuiderwijk, A., 2012. Benefits, Adoption Barriers and Myths of Open Data and Open Government. *Information Systems Management*, 29(4), pp.258–268.

Schmidt, B. et al., 2016. Open Data in Global Environmental Research: The Belmont Forum's Open Data Survey R. Guralnick, ed. *PLOS ONE*, 11(1), p.e0146695. Available at: http://dx.plos.org/10.1371/journal.pone.0146695 [Accessed July 11, 2016].

WORK-RELATED IMAGE SHARING ON INSTAGRAM: IMPLICATIONS FOR THE UNDERSTANDING OF SOCIAL MEDIA AFFORDANCE OF VISIBILITY

Claudine Bonneau and Viviane Sergi
ESG-UQAM, Case Postale 8888, Succursale Centre-ville, Montreal, Quebec, H3C 3P8, Canada

ABSTRACT

In this paper, we show how workers from various professional domains adopt a personal mode of 'visual discourse' to communicate informally about their work on public social media. The analysis of a corpus of 85 public Instagram posts revealed the sensorial, emotional, material and temporal dimensions of work that are made visible in a visual form. We propose that the extra-organizational reach of public social media and the use of the evocative power of photos should be taken into consideration when conceptualizing social media affordance of visibility and its implications for organizational practices.

KEYWORDS

Social media, Instagram, work, visibility, visuality, organization

1. INTRODUCTION

As communication technologies such as email, chat, instant messaging, and short message service (SMS) have become embedded in the work practices of many occupations, formal and informal interactions rely extensively on such tools. Social media are another form of communication technology increasingly used in work organizations. These technologies comprise 'Internet-based applications that build on the ideological and technological foundations of Web 2.0, and that allow the creation and exchange of User Generated Content' (Kaplan & Haenlein, 2010, p. 62). The term 'social media' thus refers to different types of online platforms such as social networking sites (SNS), wikis, and blogging platforms. When considering social media uses in organizational contexts, it is important to distinguish 'public social media' like Facebook, LinkedIn, Twitter and Instagram from 'enterprise social media' (ESM), which are corporate versions of these platforms, aimed at an internal audience to encourage information sharing and collaboration within the organization (Oostervink et al, 2016). As employees' professional and personal networks increasingly become interconnected online (Ollier-Malaterre et al, 2013), many workers frequently transition between formal online workspaces (such as ESM) and extra-organizational tools such as public social media. However, most organizational researchers who have examined social media in work context have focused on ESM intended for communication within the enterprise (Leonardi & Vaast, 2016). Therefore, little is said on how workers are using the same social media tools that are already integrated in their personal life (e.g. Facebook, Twitter and Instagram) to make their work visible outside their organization. It is in this larger context that our ongoing empirical study is located. We have started in 2015 an inquiry into work-related sharing practices on public social media. This inquiry has led us to document a new practice, labelled 'working out loud' (hereafter WOL; Bonneau, 2013; Williams, 2010), that we define as a communicative and sociomaterial practice where individuals voluntarily turn to public social media platforms to share what is part of their daily process of work (Sergi & Bonneau, 2016). Our studies of WOL have already shown that some workers in a variety of professional settings turn to public SNS that are not controlled by their employers to share elements that are usually left in the shadows of formal discussions of work. We started our investigation on Twitter where we identified the various forms the WOL practice can take. We have argued that in spite of their shortness, these tweets not only make visible elements that tend to remain hidden (such as work-in-progress, informal processes and reflection 'in action'), but help in materializing work and professional experiences through their being textualized. While this previous work focused on the textual side of tweets, we noticed that many of these publications also included pictures and videos. To explore in greater detail the visual aspect of working out loud and what is made visible through this practice, we now turn to Instagram, a visual social media platform, as the site of this study. Our inquiry is articulated around the following questions: if workers turn to public social media to visually share elements related to their work, what do these visual elements make visible, and how should we conceptualize the visibility afforded by public social media at work?

2. CONCEPTUAL APPROACH

We adopted a perspective that focuses on the relational affordances that public social media provides for enabling visibility. In this view, affordances are not exclusively properties of people or of artifacts: they are constituted in relationships between human agency (people's goals) and the material agency of the things with which they come in contact (the things a technology's materiality allow or do not) (Leonardi, 2011; Bucher & Helmond, 2017). Treem & Leonardi (2012) relied on such perspective to distinguish four affordances of SNS: visibility, persistence, editability, and association. Flyverbom et al (2016) recognized that the affordance of visibility supersedes the others. Leonardi (2014; 2015) proposed a "Theory of Communication Visibility" based on the study of ESM uses inside an organization where employees can see the communications occurring amongst others. His findings showed that such awareness of ambient communications can be an important antecedent for knowledge acquisition and can lead to significant increases in employees' ability to innovate and learn. For the purpose of this paper, we build on this idea to suggest that Instagram affords visibility in particular ways, when used informally in organizational contexts. Like in the case of the ESM studied by Leonardi, Instagram allows for greater message transparency than other tools such as email. Indeed, the broadcasting capability of Instagram opens visibility and communication to non-targeted users since there is no need to indicate an intended addressee in the publications. This facilitates the serendipitous discovery of users and publications through the "passive diffusion" (by the author) and "passive access" (by the audience) (Zhang et al, 2010). After presenting our preliminary findings, we will discuss their implications for the conceptualization of the aforementioned affordance of visibility.

3. METHODS

The visual nature of Instagram is not naturally suited for big data approaches to social media (Highfield & Leaver, 2016). Hence, we adopted a 'small/thick data' approach (Latzko-Toth, Bonneau, & Millette, 2017), in order 'to illuminate specific patterns of use that would have been difficult, if not impossible, to ascertain with a more automated method' (Marwick, 2014, p. 118). Our data collection rest on a qualitative approach, inspired by digital ethnography (Hine, 2015), and is based on the manual collection of a small corpus of 85 naturally occurring public Instagram posts (data collection is still ongoing). Since Instagram's users create meaning by connecting contextual hashtags to images, hashtags should represent an initial point of departure for studying activity on such platform (Highfield & Leaver, 2014). Therefore, we began the collection process by using the site search engine to find posts using work-related hashtags (e.g.: #work, #working, #showyourwork, #shareyourwork). Using a snowball sampling approach on the posts we already collected, we were able to find new users through their comments and to find other hashtags describing work contexts (e.g., #workingforaliving, #behindthework). Since our primary objective was to identify the various forms of working out loud on Instagram, we were also looking for atypical cases and thus selected posts based on their 'potential for learning' (Stake, 2008) rather than to facilitate generalizations to all Instagram users. Hence, the 'diversity criterion' was preferred over representativeness. In order to collect posts in various professional areas, we also performed queries on Instagram's internal search engine after asking ourselves, 'Who would share his or her work and what would he or she say about it?' For example, we searched for domain-related hashtags such as 'nurse', 'firefighter', 'accountant', etc. All posts collected were documented in a log, along with their date of publication, URL, and details about how we found them. Qualitative content analysis was used to proceed to a manual thematic coding of each post in an open and inductive manner.

Images were analyzed in conjunction with captions, comments and hashtags to avoid a significant loss of context (Leastadius, 2017). For example, the hashtags #workingonsunday and #deadline add temporal information to consider in addition to the descriptive features of images. Then, we grouped posts based on commonalities.

4. PRELIMINARY RESULTS

Our emergent analysis allowed us to identify the various forms that these posts can adopt, by revealing aspects that are part of the daily accomplishment of work and to mundane side of organizational life. Table 1 presents the experiential dimensions exposed by individuals on Instagram, which are then described.

Table 1. Emerging repertoire of categories of Instagram posts related to the experience of work

Category	Sub-category
1. Embodied experience	1.1 Sensorial
	1.2 Physical
2. Intensity of work	2.1 Difficulties and challenges
	2.2 Emotions and feelings
3. Materiality	3.1 Setup and environment
	3.2 Tools
4. Backstage	4.1 Context that is rarely seen
	4.2 Mundane aspects of work
5. Temporality	5.1 Working at unexpected time
	5.2 Temporal ordering
6. Presence	6.1 Work-life boundaries
	6.2 Giving presence to women
	6.3 Unexpected presence
7. Atmosphere	7.1 Life at work
	7.2 Fun and informal

1. Embodied experience. These posts share the sensorial experience of work, either by describing odors (for example, a firefighter describes the smell of a burning garbage truck), sights or sounds which characterize a specific work setting. It also regroups posts related to physical aspects of work, such as tiredness from working long hours or working while being sick.

2. Intensity of work. These posts show the difficulties and challenges involved in the daily work. In the example shown in Figure 1, a worker shares the painful side of his work, by posting a picture of the scratches on his hand. We also found a great number of expressive posts in which workers verbalize and exteriorize their emotions and feelings, whether positive (e.g., happy moments) or negative (e.g., boredom or anger).

3. Materiality. The posts belonging to this category describe and/or show the setup and environment in which work unfolds and give details about its spatial and material setup, such as the tools used.

4. Backstage. Such posts give visibility to backstage work (Star & Strauss, 1999) that is usually inaccessible to people who are not in the situation, by showing the context and side of work that is rarely seen. Workers also expose their ways of doing things, including the ordinary and mundane aspects of their work.

5. Temporality. This form of posts shows the temporal conditions in which work happens, such as working at unexpected time. We also found instances showing the temporal ordering of work, in which users share the milestones accomplished and articulate the planning and continuation of actions.

6. Presence. The posts belonging to this form reflect on the work-life boundaries, like in the example shown in Figure 2 in which a mother working from home shows the presence of her baby in her 'work setting'. There are also a number of instances giving presence to women and making them visible in non-traditional roles. Some of these posts also reveal unexpected presence, showing empty or vacant workspaces, or revealing the presence of a worker in a place where other coworkers would not expect him to be.

7. Atmosphere. These posts document life at work, in various professional domain, as exemplified by the hashtags #officelife, #bankinglife and #accountantlife, for instance. They also expose fun and informal aspects of work.

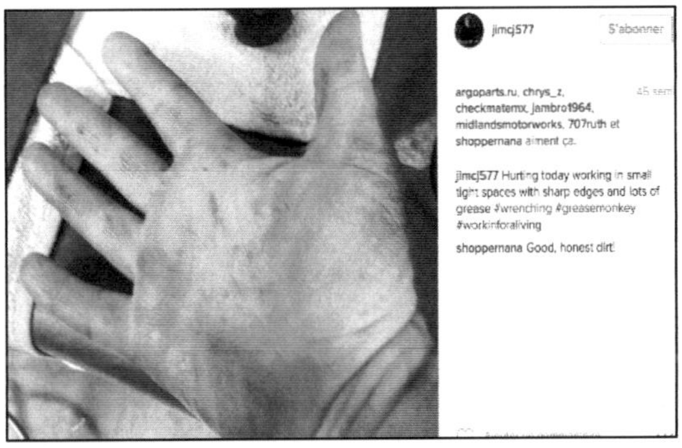

Figure 1. Intensity of work / difficulties and challenges

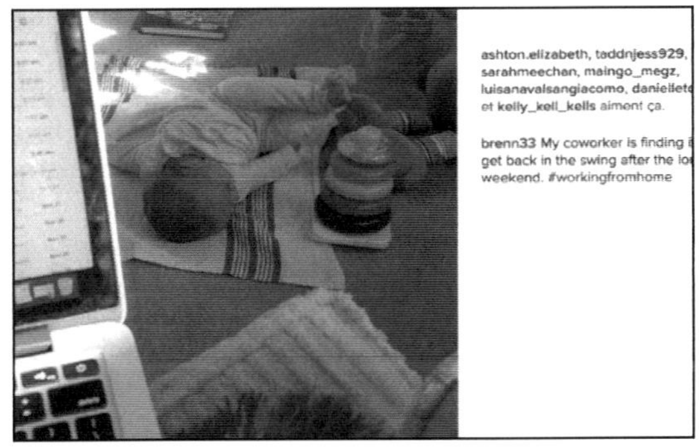

Figure 2. Presence / work-life boundaries

5. DISCUSSION AND CONCLUSION

Leonardi's Theory of Communication Visibility (2014) was developed following the study of workers who shifted their communication activity from private channels (e.g., phone, email, instant messaging, etc.) to an ESM where their written communications were visible to others in the same organization. Our case highlight different elements that should also be considered in such theorization of communication visibility: 1) the extended reach of public social media and 2) the visual mediation involved in communication practices.

Given the increased usage of personal smartphones by employees (Archambault & Grudin, 2012) and the growing popularity of "Bring your Own Devices" (BYOD) policies (Willis, 2013), employees can use external public SNS such as Instagram during work hours, even when enterprises prohibit access to them from workplace computers (Zhang et al, 2014). The fact that public SNS are not controlled by their employers means that workers can adopt their own mode of visual discourse to share mundane details of work and organizational life outside the boundaries of their organizations. Therefore, public SNS represent a rich site to explore the unexpected learning and collaboration opportunities enabled by such "extended" and "globally networked" visibility. As we have shown, what is shared on Instagram is more closely related to the personal experience of work rather than to its content or process. The sensorial, emotional, material and temporal dimensions made visible by this particular type of visual communication changes what can be known about work, and might differ from other textual ways of knowing (Hand, 2012). We believe that the evocative power of photos should be taken into consideration when trying to conceptualize social media's affordance of visibility and its implications for organizations. Since this "visual expression of the ordinary" is extended and intensified by the sharing functionalities on public social media (Hand, 2017), we propose that SNS affordance of visibility can be better described by taking into account the visual mediation capabilities of image-sharing platforms. Interestingly, such "visual turn" brings us back to the original concept of affordance, which was first developed in a theory of visual perception (Gibson, 2015). Of course, more empirical work should be done in order to provide the insights needed to formulate such theoretical contributions.

REFERENCES

Archambault, A., & Grudin, J. 2012. A longitudinal study of Facebook, Linkedln, & Twitter use. *Proceedings of the 2012 ACM annual conference on Human Factors in Computing Systems - CHI '12* (pp. 2741–2750). New York, USA: ACM Press.

Bonneau, C. 2013. Travailler à haute voix sur Twitter : quand la collaboration informelle emprunte un réseau public [Working out loud on Twitter: Informal collaboration on a public network]. *TIC & Société*, Vol. 6, No. 2, pp 1-19.

Bucher, T., & Helmond, A. 2017. The affordances of social media platforms. *SAGE handbook of social media. London: Sage.*

Flyverbom, M., Leonardi, P. M., Stohl, C., & Stohl, M. 2016. The Management of Visibilities in the Digital Age Introduction. *International Journal of Communication*, No. 10, pp 98–109.

Gibson, J.J. 2015. *The Ecological Approach to Visual Perception*. Classic Editions. New York: Psychology Press.

Hand, M. 2012. *Ubiquitous photography*. Polity.

Hand, M. 2017. Visuality in social media: Researching images, circulations and practices. *The SAGE Handbook of Social Media Research Methods*, in Quan-Haase, A and L. Sloan (eds), Sage, pp 215-231.

Highfield, T., Leaver, T. 2014. A methodology for mapping Instagram hashtags. *First Monday*, Vol. 20, No. 1.

Highfield, T., Leaver, T. 2016. Instagrammatics and digital methods: Studying visual social media, from selfies and GIFs to memes and emoji. *Communication Research and Practice*, Vol. 2, No. 1, pp. 47-62.

Hine, C. 2015. *Ethnography for the Internet: Embedded, embodied and everyday*. London, UK: Bloomsbury Publishing.

Kaplan, A. M., & Haenlein, M. 2010. Users of the world, unite! The challenges and opportunities of social media. *Business Horizons*, 53, pp 59-68.

Latzko-Toth, G., Bonneau, C., Millette, M. 2017. Small Data, Thick Data: Thickening Strategies for Trace-Based Social Media Research. In Quan-Haase, A. and Sloan, L. (eds), *The SAGE Handbook of Social Media Research Methods*, chapter 13, pp 199-214.

Laestadius, L. (2017). Instagram. In Quan-Haase, A. and Sloan, L. (eds), *The SAGE Handbook of Social Media Research Methods*, chapter 34, pp 573-592.

Leonardi, P. M. 2011. When flexible routines meet flexible technologies: affordances, constraints, and imbrication of human and material agencies. *MIS Quarterly*, Vol. 35, No. 1, pp 147–167.

Leonardi, P. M. 2014. Social Media, Knowledge Sharing and Innovation : Toward a Theory of Communication Visibility. *Information Systems Research*, Vol. 25, No 4, pp 796-816.

Leonardi, P. M. 2015. Ambient Awareness and Knowledge Acquisition: Using Social Media to Learn"Who Knows What" and" Who Knows Whom". *MIS Quarterly*, Vol. 39, No 4, pp 747-762.

Leonardi, P. M., E. Vaast. 2016. Social Media and Their Affordances for Organizing : A Review and Agenda for Research. *The Academy of Management Annals*.

Marwick, A. E. 2014. Ethnographic and qualitative research on Twitter. In K. Weller, A. Bruns, J. Burgess, M. Mahrt, & C. Puschmann (Eds.), *Twitter and society* (pp. 109–122). Bern, Switzerland: Peter Lang.

Ollier-Malaterre, A. et al, 2013. When worlds collide in cyberspace: How boundary work in online social networks impacts professional relationships. *Academy of Management Review*, Vol. 38, No. 4, pp 645-669.

Oostervink, N., Agterberg, M., & Huysman, M. 2016. Enterprise social media: Practices to cope with institutional complexity. *Journal of Computed-Mediated Communication*, Vol. 21, No. 2, pp 156-176.

Sergi, V., Bonneau, C. 2016. Making Mundane Work Visible on Social Media : a CCO Investigation of Working out Loud on Twitter. *Communication Research and Practice*, Vol. 2, No. 3, 378–406

Stake, R. E. 2008. Qualitative case studies. In N. K. Denzin & Y. S. Lincoln (Eds.*), Strategies of qualitative inquiry* (pp. 119-150). London, UK: SAGE.

Star, S. L., & Strauss, A. 1999. Layers of Silence, Arenas of Voice : The Ecology of Visible and Invisible Work. *Computer Supported Cooperative Work*, (1995), pp 9–30.

Treem, J. W., & Leonardi, P. M. 2012. Social Media Use in Organizations: Exploring the Affordances of Visibility, Editability, Persistence, and Association. *Communication Yearbook*, No. 36, pp. 143-189.

Williams, B. 2010. When will we Work Out Loud? Soon! *TheBrycesWrite*. Retrieved from http://thebryceswrite.wordpress.com/2010/11/29/when-will-we-work-out-loud-soon/

Willis, D. A. 2013. *Bring Your Own Device: The Facts and the Future*. Gartner.

Zhang, H., De Choudhury, M., & Grudin, J. 2014. Creepy but Inevitable? The Evolution of Social Networking. *CSCW'14*, February 15–19, 2014, Baltimore, Maryland, USA.Zhang, J., Qu, Y., Cody, J., & Wu, Y. 2010. A case study of micro-blogging in the enterprise: use, value, and related issues. *Proceedings of the 28th international conference on Human factors in computing systems* (pp. 123–132). Atlanta, Georgia, USA: ACM.

PUSH OR PULL? USING SOCIAL MEDIA TO INTERACT WITH CITIZENS

Daniel Skog
Umeå University, 90187 Umeå, Sweden

ABSTRACT

This paper reports from an ongoing study of how municipalities and local government agencies in Sweden and Norway, use social media to interact with citizens. The empirical material comprises interviews with representatives from seven different local authorities. The findings display how the social media strategies among the local authorities included in the study mostly involves push tactics, not really contributing to citizen engagement. Recommendations based on the obtained findings are provided for local government agencies striving for a higher level of interaction with citizens.

KEYWORDS

Social media strategies, local government, citizens

1. INTRODUCTION

For local government agencies, eager to engage with local residents, social media offer new possibilities for interaction and dialogue with citizens. Accordingly, Lev-On and Steinfeld (2015) state that social media sites now are becoming essential channels for communication between municipalities and citizens throughout Europe and the US. The Scandinavian countries are no exception. In Sweden, for example, almost all municipalities are present on Facebook (Stockenstrand, 2015) and in Norway, Johnsen, et al (2014) report that many municipalities are advanced users of social media.

This paper reports from an ongoing study of how municipalities and local government agencies in Sweden and Norway use social media to interact with citizens. The purpose of the study is to explore different social media strategies within the public sector, and to gain an understanding of the variety of approaches towards social media on local government level.

2. SOCIAL MEDIA STRATEGIES FOR LOCAL GOVERNMENT

Unlike traditional media, social media is characterized by its interactivity. In that way, social media is an umbrella for different online technologies designed for interaction (Bertot, et al, 2012), encompassing social network sites, blogs, chat and file sharing tools, and more. These technologies are social as they are situated in a social context, where everyday users interact with each other and create content (Feeney & Welch, 2016).

From a local government perspective, social media platforms create new arenas for interaction, where it's easy to reach residents with information, offer guidance, initiate dialogue, and identify citizen needs. However, even though the value of social media activities is widely acknowledged, the maturity level in relation to social media varies a lot among municipalities and local governments. Having studied the adoption of social media strategies in government agencies, Mergel (2013a) presents a framework for categorizing different social media strategies. The different strategies are labelled representation of the agency, engagement of citizens, and networking with the public, with its corresponding tactics push, pull and networking.

Mergel (2013a) argues that the different strategies also can be seen as different levels of maturity - the first level being representation. At this level, the main focus is to be present in the same social media channels as the citizens, to build identity and good reputation. The easiest and most straight-forward way to achieve this would be through a push tactic, considering all social media channels to be more or less similar to each other, using the same message everywhere with small or no effort of tailoring channel specific content. Thus, the push tactic is based on a broadcasting one-way communication, with no great interest in bidirectional conversations with citizens.

The next strategy and maturity level is characterized by engagement and dialogue. Instead of just pushing out news messages, this strategy involves a pull tactic where citizens are invited to respond and co-produce content (Mergel, 2013a). This approach is very much aligned with the characteristics of social media technology, and it's perhaps not until reaching this level that the agency can gain new insights from their social media activities. However, as the level of social media engagement rises, so does the demands for resources, and lack of financial or human resources can be an obstacle for government agencies trying to reach above the initial levels of broadcasting towards engagement with the public (Lee & Kwak, 2012).

The third and final strategy could be labelled as networking or collaboration (Mergel 2013a; 2013b). Moving beyond the notion of local authorities having conversations with citizens, this level is more about facilitating conversations among citizens and stakeholders, being a curator rather than playing the main role. In this way, local governments can gain valuable insight about current issues and important local topics being discussed online.

This framework elaborated by Mergel (2013a; 2013b) can be a basis for reviewing local government social media strategies, and will serve as a backdrop for the current study.

3. METHOD AND MATERIAL

The empirical material in this study, comprises interviews with representatives from seven different local government agencies. The seven agencies are situated at six different locations and vary in size and resources, as they represent different geographical areas and populations. In addition, five of them are in fact municipalities, while the remaining two are national government agencies. Being situated in the northern parts of Sweden and Norway, they do however share some common conditions. They are all being brought together as partners in an ongoing transnational research and development project, aiming for sustained innovation capacity and effectiveness within the public sector. Hence, this pilot study, that will be followed by further studies in the years to come.

Face to face interviews were conducted at local visits, during November 2016 – March 2017. Informants included web editors, communication personnel and information mangers. At some of the local agencies, an additional interview was conducted in order to get a more comprehensive understanding of the diverse use of social media, resulting in ten interviews in total. The interviews were semi-structured (Galletta, 2013), guided by thematic, open-ended questions, concerning their use of social media, existing social media strategies, and views on citizen engagement. The recorded interviews lasted for 45-70 minutes, and were transcribed before analysis. Being an exploratory pilot study, the analysis has been mostly descriptive, identifying common themes and strategies, and trying to pinpoint key activities concerning social media usage.

4. FINDINGS

This section summarizes some of the common themes emerging from the empirical data, highlighting key aspects of how the local government agencies use social media. Annotation A-E will be used when quoting some of the informants. It should also be noted that all quotes are translated from Swedish or Norwegian by the author.

4.1 Social Media Presence with Unclear Purpose

All government agencies included in the study share an awareness of how social media can facilitate a dialogue with local residents. This is considered positive, and consequently they all want to extend their social media activities. Nevertheless, one of the smaller municipalities made a decision a couple of years ago, not to engage with social media at all, mainly due to lack of personnel resources; *"There is a few years old decision [...] that the municipality should not be using social media, but we still do"* (A). Gradually they even so had begun entering Facebook, now having a couple of accounts representing different operational areas.

Among the seven participating organizations, their presence in social media corresponds quite well with their relative size, with the largest agency being most active in various social media channels followed by the second largest agency and so on. However, since the main web site presenting the organization and available services is considered the main priority for all participants, their social media activities are not typically prioritized. Furthermore, the purpose of using social media is generally quite unclear; *"We have no communication strategy. [...] Why are we on Facebook? What are the consequences of not being there?"* (B), *"We need to be on Facebook. Why? Because everybody is there!"* (C).

Since citizens use social media, the local government agencies feel a need to have a social media presence as well. Having the notion that it can probably develop into an arena for increased interaction, most of the agencies in the study still are in an early stage of social media maturity, without a comprehensive social media strategy.

4.2 Individual Initiatives Guide Social Media Activities

Without a thorough and anchored social media strategy, the floor is open for individual initiatives. Especially among some of the municipalities, social media activities are not always centrally organized but rather the outcome of initiatives from individuals who want to promote a specific operational area; *"Now, those that are the most interested, publish things on their own [on Instagram]"* (D). Some of these initiatives are quite successful, others not so much. Typically, someone decides to create another Facebook account, presenting news related to a specific area without considering how this new account should relate to other existing accounts belonging to the agency, and without regards to the laws and regulations guiding local governments online presence.

4.3 Social Media as News Channel

While some of the participating organizations have tried using Instagram, YouTube and Twitter, Facebook is the predominant social media platform. It is however mainly used for pushing news, often already posted earlier to the main web site. Some of the participants describe how they actually prefer not to have conversations on Facebook, but rather want to forward any comments or questions to their ordinary support channels available via their main web sites. They do not want to have extensive discussions on Facebook, being afraid of losing control and not being able to monitor all postings; *"We never engage in discussions on Facebook. [...] We do not have resources to participate in dialogues."* (B).

There are indeed some examples of extended dialogue, as well as attempts on asking citizens for their opinions related to specific municipal decisions; *"I wrote a question on Facebook, asking our citizens for their opinions. [...] I think the politicians thought it was a bit of fun."* (E). But in relation to the framework presented by Mergel (2013a) all organizations in this study are still mainly using push tactics, focusing on being present in social media, rather than having dialogues or curating networking activities.

5. CONCLUSIONS

There is indeed a variation among the local government agencies included in this study, when it comes to their social media maturity level. There are agencies with only very basic social media presence, but also examples of more multifaceted social media use aiming for dialogue with local residents, guided by an actual social media strategy. Nevertheless, it is evident that they all mainly use push tactics when entering the social media arena. Recognizing the potential benefits of having more interaction with citizens, most local government agencies still have not invested in advancing their social media presence.

The findings are quite surprising considering the general Internet saturation and heavy social media usage in both Sweden and Norway. Why do we find the public sector still lingering on the entry levels of social media maturity? And what are the steps needed to advance forward?

This present study suggests that lack of resources, capability, or a thoughtful social media strategy, can be some of the reasons to why the local government agencies under study have not been able to engage more with citizens through social media. Thus, it could be argued that there is a need for education, to increase the knowledge and awareness among local governments when it comes to social media strategies and functionality (Kietzmann, et al, 2011). In addition, it needs to be recognized that this will not happen without additional resources. If local agencies want to engage with the public they need to appoint staff and focus on making it happen. Finally, every local government needs to decide if, and why, they should use social media, and then establish a strategy that guides all online activities. Only then can they advance and mature in their use of social media.

This study is a first attempt on analyzing the use of social media among seven local government agencies in the northern part of Sweden and Norway. Further research will include evaluating the coming steps, unique for each and every agency, towards more advanced social media usage and increased interaction with citizens.

ACKNOWLEDGEMENT

This research is funded by the EU-programme Botnia-Atlantica 2014-2020, as a part of European Territorial Cooperation (Interreg).

REFERENCES

Bertot et al., 2012. The impact of policies on government social media usage: Issues, challenges, and recommendations. *Govenrment Information Quarterly*, Vol 29, pp. 30–40.

Feeney, M. K., and Welch, E. W., 2016. Technology–task coupling: Exploring social media use and managerial perceptions of e-government. *The American Review of Public Administration*, Vol 46, No. 2, pp. 162-179.

Galletta, A., 2013. *Mastering the semi-structured interview and beyond: from research design to analysis and publication.* New York University Press, New York, USA.

Johnsen, O. E. et al, 2014. Hvordan lykkes kommunesektoren i sosiale medier? [In Norwegian. English title: How successful is the municipal sector in social media?], The Norwegian Association of Local and Regional Authorities, accessed 5 April 2017, <http://www.ks.no/contentassets/40a67437a2b3485d9e995fe061fee0f0/kommunesektorens-bruk-av-sosiale-medier.pdf>.

Kietzmann, J. H. et al., 2011. Social media? Get serious! Understanding the functional building blocks of social media. *Business horizons*, Vol 54, No. 3, pp. 241-251.

Lee, G. and Kwak, Y. H., 2012. An open government maturity model for social media-based public engagement. *Government Information Quarterly*, Vol 29, No. 4, pp. 492-503.

Lev-On, A. and Steinfeld, N., 2015. Local engagement online: Municipal Facebook pages as hubs of interaction. *Government Information Quarterly*, Vol 32, No. 3, pp. 299-307.

Mergel, I., 2013a. Social media adoption and resulting tactics in the US federal government. *Government Information Quarterly*, Vol 30, No. 2, pp. 123-130.

Mergel, I., 2013b. A framework for interpreting social media interactions in the public sector. *Government Information Quarterly*, Vol 30, No. 4, pp. 327-334.

Stockenstrand, M., 2015. Nästan alla kommuner använder Facebook, [In Swedish. English title: Almost all municipalities use Facebook], The Swedish Association of Local Authorities and Regions, accessed 5 April 2017, <https://skl.se/tjanster/press/nyheter/arkiveradenyheter/nastanallakommuneranvanderfacebook.5731.html>.

Posters

DESIGN OF A MULTI-SENSOR BASED EXERCISE MOTION RECOGNITION SYSTEM

Seung-Taek Oh[1] , Heon-Tag Kong[2] and Jae-Hyun Lim[2]

[1]*Dept. Smart Natural Space Research Center - Kongju National University, Republic of Korea*

[2]*Dept. of Computer Science & Engineering - Kongju National University, Republic of Korea*

ABSTRACT

As the importance of health management is emphasized recently, the number of people utilizing smart devices for their personal exercise management is increasing. Most smart devices only provide information about the number of simple motions and the amount of exercise and do not provide services related to exercise motions. This study proposes a design of a multi-sensor based exercise motion recognition system that combines a smart-band, a motion sensor device, and a smartphone. The proposed system uses a motion sensor device in addition to existing Smart Band to acquire Motion Raw data of X, Y, and Z axes for each exercise motions. After that, it is to support the effective personal exercise management of users by recognizing the exercise motion through filtering for noise removal, selection of each motions range, DTW (Dynamic Time Warping) algorithm process and providing information to the exercise motion through the smartphone.

KEYWORDS

Multi-Sensor, Exercise Motion, Recognition System, health management, DTW

1. INTRODUCTION

As interests in health management increased recently, various technologies combining smart-device and smartphones have been introduced to promote health. Particularly, smart-bands acquire motion data by means of an embedded accelerometer and provide statistical data on momentum and activity records (Lee et al, 2002). However, most accelerometer-based services provide information merely on momentum and simple motions such as walking, and they are unable to recognize specific exercise motions (Coleman et al, 1999). Some studies have compared the algorithms that classify the exercise types such as cycling, running, and squatting by using a wrist-wearing accelerometer but did not present the judgment as to whether each exercise is performed accurately or not (Margarito et al, 2016).

In this paper, we propose a multi-sensor based motion recognition system that recognizes the user's motion and informs the number of motions in the correct posture. The proposed system acquires acceleration data for x, y and z axes through motion device using wrist wearing type smart band and 9-axis motion sensor and analyzes it to support the calculation of accurate exercise statistics and user's personal exercise management by recognizing a exercise posture and informing if the motion is successful.

2. EXERCISE MOTION RECOGNITION SYSTEM

Figure 1 shows the general overview of the proposed exercise motion recognition system. A user wears a smart-band on one wrist and additional motion devices in other body parts that are used for exercise. When the user takes a certain motion, motion data is acquired in the x, y, and z axes and transmitted to a smartphone through Bluetooth. The smartphone application then removes noise from the received data and recognize motions by means of the recognition algorithm.

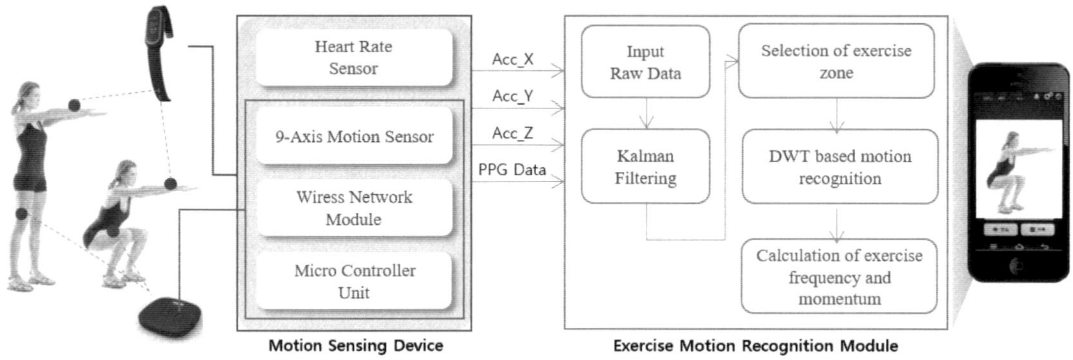

Figure 1. Exercise Motion Recognition System

The motion sensing device consists of the smart-band and motion device. It also includes the 9-axis motion sensor, wireless communication module, and MCU. The smart-band adopts an optical heart rate sensor in order to provide services related to heart rates. For motion recognition, Kalman filtering is applied to remove noise from motion data, and then the motion section is determined on the basis of the threshold. Motions were recognized in comparison of pre-defined standard motion templates with motion data of each section. Since there might be some time difference among motions, the DTW(Dynamic Time Warping) algorithm was used for dynamic pattern matching. Figure 2 shows an example of motion sensing data. While the squat motion was being taken with a smart-band and a motion device worn on the left wrist and left thigh respectively, the acceleration data in the x, y, and z axes were acquired. The data of relatively regular motion (b) on the left thigh was used for selection of motion sections while the data of motion on (a) the left arm was used for precise recognition of specific motions.

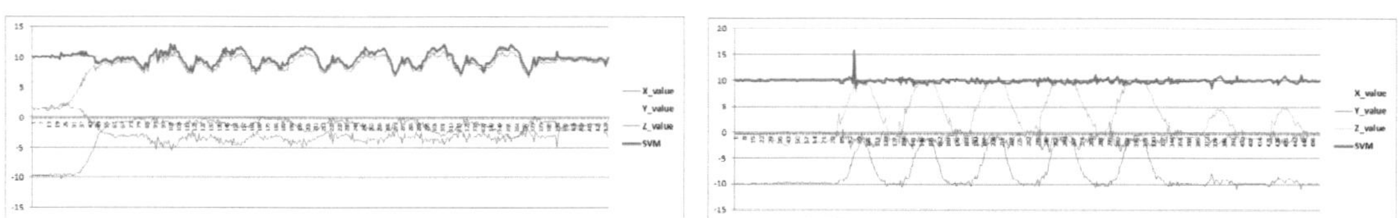

(a) Raw Data collected by Means of a Smartband (left arm)

(b) Raw Data Collected by Means of a Motion Device (left foot)

Figure 2. An Example of Motion (squat) Data Acquisition

In Figure 3, the blue waveform indicates the raw data, and the red waveform indicates the result of applying the Kalman filter. The Kalman filter functions to remove noise and smooth the wave pattern of raw data. Motion sections are indicated in a green box.

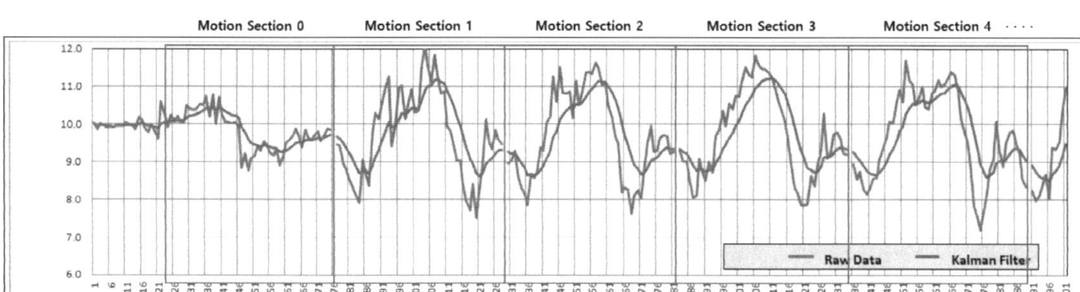

Figure 3. An Example of Kalman Filter Application and Section Identification

The DTW(Dynamic Time Warping) algorithm was utilized to determine the similarity of each motion pattern, and then the similarity of motions was compared with the threshold determined in the previous experiment. Table 1 shows an example of experiment to judge if there was a squat motion. In each section, the DTW algorithm was performed. When the similarity was under the threshold, it was 'TRUE.' Otherwise, it was 'FALSE'.

Table 1. Application of the DTW Algorithm for Judgment

Motion section	DTW Result (Similarity)	Judgment
section 0	0.286	FALSE
section 1	0(standard template)	TRUE
section 2	0.986	TRUE
section 3	0.084	TRUE
section 4	0.068	TRUE
section 5	0.131	TRUE

3. CONCLUSION

This study proposes a multi-sensor based exercise motion recognition system for support the effective personal exercise management of users. The proposed system acquires raw data of motions in the x, y, and z axes by means of a smart-band and a motion sensing device. The smartphone application removes noise through Kalman filtering, and the motion sections are decided on the basis of the threshold. The DTW algorithm was performed in each section, and then it was determined if the specific motion was taken based on the threshold similarity (0.2). The future study needs to define a standard template for accurate exercise motions and to develop a smartphone application through which the motion information can be delivered to the user.

ACKNOWLEDGEMENT

This work was supported by Institute for Information & communications Technology Promotion (IITP) grant funded by the Korea government(MSIP) No. R7118161016000203, Development of Interlocked Multi Wearable Sensor Smart Device and Service Platform for Effective Personal Training

REFERENCES

Kim L. Coleman. et al, 1999. Step activity monitor: long-term, continuous recording of ambulatory function. *Journal of Rehabilitation Research and Development*, Vol.36, No.1, pp.8-18.

Margarito, Jenny. et al, 2016. User-independent recognition of sports activities from a single wrist-worn accelerometer: A template-matching-based approach. *IEEE Transactions on Biomedical Engineering*, Vol 63, No. 4, pp.788-796.

S. H. Lee. et al, 2002. Design of a Portable Activity Monitoring System, *The Korean Institute of Electrical Engineer*, Vol.51, pp.32-38.

DESIGNING OF SLEEP SUPPORT LIGHTING BASED ON SHORT WAVELENGTH RATIO OF NATURAL LIGHT

Young-Won Kim[1] and Jae-Hyun Lim[2]
[1]*Dept. Smart Natural Space Research Center - Kongju National University, Republic of Korea*
[2]*Dept. of Computer Science & Engineering - Kongju National University, Republic of Korea*

ABSTRACT

Modern people, who spend most of their time indoors, are always living in a fixed lighting environment, which causes imbalance of the circadian rhythm, or adversely effects on the physiological function of the body such as the quality of sleep. In this paper, four channels were fabricated to control each light sources by using four types of light sources to reproduce seasonal characteristics of natural light such as ratio of short wavelength and color temperature matching to circadian rhythm of natural light. Analysis results showed that among 15 control ratios, 12 types of controls fell under "comfortable" and four types of light fell "relaxing" with the ratio of short wavelength at 11%~18% and color temperature at around 3000K, and illuminance at around 300lux which are suitable to support sleep.

KEYWORDS

Illuminance to support sleep, ratio of short wavelength, natural light, illumination control index, situation illumination

1. INTRODUCTION

Natural light has various colors and energies according to its wavelength, and function and role of the light become different depending on the specific wavelength band [1-3]. The sleep - arousal and deep body temperature of the human biorhythm are controlled by the distribution of melatonin in the body according to the change of the spectral distribution of the natural light. Therefore, a constant pattern is maintained. Melatonin is a hormone that regulates sleep rhythm of humans, which is secreted less during the day so that awakening is maintained. While, it is secreted more in the night, thus constant pattern that maintains sleeping condition is exhibited. The melatonin is sensitively responds the wavelength of 446nm~477nm among short wavelength band of the light. It is necessary to develop a situation illumination which reproduces natural light that can make lighting environment similar to natural light which is being changed by time in order to provide a suitable lighting service suiting to comfort, health improvement, and situation (sleep, study, and rest) to the users.

In this study, four-channels LED lighting that reflects characteristic of the light such as ratio of short wavelength and color temperature was fabricated to match with circadian rhythm of the natural light. The quality of the lighting was evaluated using ratio of short wavelength, color temperature, and Kruithof's curve according to the control ratio of LED lighting. The lighting control ratio effective for sleep was then drawn.

2. DESIGNING OF LIGHTING THAT SUPPORTS SLEEP BASED ON THE CHARACTERSTICS OF NATURAL LIGHT

2.1 Designing of Lighting to Support Sleep

The data obtained at weekly interval starting from 1st of Jan. 2015 until 1st of Aug. 2016 were used to design a lighting that supports sleep based on the characteristics of the natural light. Spring season (March ~May), summer (June~ August), autumn (Sept.~ Nov.), and winters (Dec. ~ Feb.) were categorized to analyze characteristics of the light by the season. Ratio of short wavelength and color temperature were analyzed accordingly. Analysis results showed that the color temperature by season was around 3200K~5800K during spring, around 3400K~5600K during summer, around 3100~5600K during autumn, and around 3300K~5500K during winters. Whereas, the ratio of the short wavelength was around 7%~ 24% in spring, around 7% ~ 23% in summer, around 6% ~ 23% in autumn, and 8% ~ 22% in winter. Therefore, four types of light sources were selected so that all the seasonal characteristics could be included. Besides, lightings for supporting sleep were fabricated as four channels to regulate each of the light source. Figure 1 shows the four types of light sources and color coordinates that express all the seasonal characteristics.

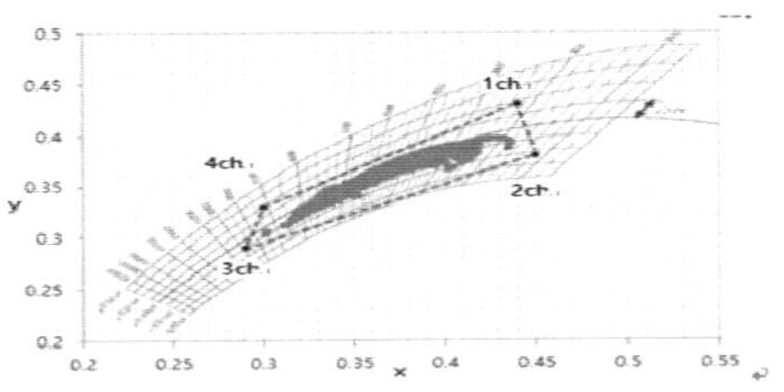

	1 ch	2 ch	3 ch	4ch
X	0.42	0.43	0.30	0.30
Y	0.40	0.37	0.31	0.33
CRI	83	84	88	85

Figure 1. types of light sources, color coordinates and CRI

2.2 Analysis Results

In order to analyze characteristics of the light for sleep support, a LED lighting was installed and it was controlled at 16 different rates. The distance between the light and the light-receiving part was maintained at 170 cm and measured by CAS 140CT. Table 1 shows the evaluation results for the short wavelength, color temperature, and lighting quality according to lighting control ratio.

Table 1. Short wavelength, color temperature, and lighting quality according to lighting control ratio

	lighting control ratio				Analysis of lighting Characteristic							
No	1ch	2ch	3ch	4ch	cct	lux	SWR	MWR	LWR	446to477	MSP	evaluation of lighting
0	0	0	0	0	0	0	0	0	0	0	-	
1	255				3,312	278	11%	25%	63%	9%	70.5	Relaxing
2		255			2,792	255	12%	19%	68%	9%	70.1	Uncomfortable
3			255		7,553	275	31%	31%	39%	23%	72.6	Uncomfortable
4				255	6,944	289	26%	33%	41%	19%	72.4	Uncomfortable
5	128	128			3,046	282	12%	22%	66%	9%	70.5	Relaxing
6	128		128		4,705	295	21%	28%	51%	17%	71.5	Comfortable
7	128			128	4,682	300	19%	29%	52%	15%	71.3	Comfortable
8		128	128		4,394	284	22%	25%	53%	17%	71.52	Comfortable
9		128		128	4,390	285	19%	27%	54%	15%	71.2	Gathering
10			128	128	7,201	296	28%	32%	40%	22%	72.6	Gathering
11	85	85	85		3,925	290	18%	25%	56%	15%	70.9	Relaxing
12	85	85		85	3,952	294	17%	26%	57%	13%	70.6	Relaxing
13	85		85	85	5,363	302	23%	30%	47%	18%	70.64	Gathering
14		85	85	85	5,177	291	23%	28%	49%	19%	71.95	Gathering
15	64	64	64	64	4,543	296	20%	27%	52%	17%	71.5	Comfortable

The ratio of short wavelength was at 11%~28%, color temperature range was at an around 2790K~7500K, and illuminance was around 250lux~300lux. Of the 15 types of control ratio, 12 were classified as 'comfortable', while four other types of control ratios corresponded to 'relaxing'. In a conclusion, #1 lighting having the smallest short wavelength ratio was found as the most suitable lighting characteristics among the lightings corresponded to 'relaxing' for sleeping support.

3. CONCLUSION

In this study, four channel natural light reproduction lighting was designed based on the seasonal characteristics of the natural light such as short wavelength ratio and color temperature of the natural light to match with the circadian rhythm of the natural light. Firstly, four different light sources were used to reproduce all the seasonal characteristics of natural light, and four channels were used to control each light source. The evaluation results for the light using the short wavelength ratio, color temperature, and Kruithof's curve according to the control ratio of each light channel showed that 12 types corresponded 'comfortable' and four types corresponded to 'relaxing' among 15 different lightings. The ratio of the short wavelength was 11%~ 18% and color temperature was about 300lux, confirming that these lightings were suitable for sleep support.

In the future, we will build a lighting control index database according to the situation by experimenting with a more diverse combination of light sources in order to provide lighting suitable for user's situation (bedroom, living room, study room, etc.) based on the characteristics of natural light.

ACKNOWLEDGEMENT

This work was supported by the National Research Foundation of Korea (NRF) grant funded by the Korea government (MSIP) (No. 2014R1A2A1A11054509). The research was supported by the International Science and Business Belt Program through the Ministry of Science, ICT, and Future Planning (2016K000298).

REFERENCES

E. J. Jo, K. M. Lee, C. H. Lin, 2015, Effective of Led Context Lighting Control System, *Conference of The Institute of Electronics and Information Engineer*, Korea, pp.235-238.

J. S. Yang, M. Y. Lee, 2012, A Study on direction of LED Lighting Color development through analysis of the Daylighting, *Journal of the Korean Institute of Illuminating and Electrical Installation Engineers*, Korea, pp.9-19.

K. S. Kim, A. S. Choi, 2011, Study of Relationship between Light and Melatonin, *The Korean Institute of Illuminating and lectrical Installation Engineers*, Korea, pp.7-8.

Ruzena Kralikova, Miriama Piňosová, Beata Hricová, 2016, Lighting Quality and Its Effects on Productivity and Human Health, *International Journal of Interdisciplinarity in Theory and Practice*, ISSN 2344-2409.

Y. J. Park, J. H. Choi, M. G. Jang, 2009, Optimization of Light Source Combination through the Illuminance and Color Temperature Simulation of Circadian Lighting Apparatus, *Journal of The Korea Contents Association*, Korea, pp.248-254.

HOME AUTOMATION SYSTEM FOR ELDERLY HOUSING

Sung-Hoon Mah[1], Dong-Hak Kim[2], Byung-Seo Kim[2], Jong Kim[3] and Jae Hee Chung[4]
[1]*Dept. of Electronics and Computer Eng., Hongik University, 2639, Sejongro, Jochiwon, Sejong-City, Republic of Korea*
[2]*Dept. of Computer and Information Communications Eng., Hongik University, Republic of Korea*
[3]*Seon Architects and Engineering Group, Cheongju-City, Chungbuk-Do, Republic of Korea*
[4]*Department of Architecture, Hongik University, Republic of Korea*

ABSTRACT

As the number of the elderly increases, the various IT-based home automation systems for the elderly housing are actively studied and implemented. However, while most systems for the elderly housing focus on detecting emergency cases, systems considering energy reduction in the elderly housing are rarely found. In this paper, an emergency monitoring system including energy reduction capability is proposed and implemented.

KEYWORDS

Elderly, Home Automation, Energy, Emergency

1. INTRODUCTION

According to estimates by Korean Statistical Information Service, the proportion of elderly citizens, which has been increasing from 1970, is expected to reach 37.4 percent in 2050.(KOSTAT, 2013) and 39.8% of the elderly people is suffering from financial difficulties and health problems.(Ko, 2014) As a result, the housing technologies are actively engaged with Internet of Things (IoT) health care services such as emergency alerts and remote patient monitoring systems.(Jeong 2016) While most of housing technologies focuses on emergency monitoring, few system deals with reducing wasted energy due to the elderly's physical limitness. Therefore, this paper proposes and implements an automation system for the elderly housing mainly focusing on not only emergency monitoring function, but also reducing the consumed energy.

2. PROPOSED SYSTEM

The proposed system includes energy reduction functions as well as emergency monitoring functions for the elderly housing. The key features of the proposed system are as follows:

- Automatic window closing when heaters and air-conditioner is operating to reduce unnecessary energy wastes due to the elderly's physical limit and forgetfulness.
- Operating surveillance cameras just-in-case of an emergency to minimize cameras' energy consumption.
- Using low-cost LED sensors instead of expensive high-cost Passive Infrared Sensor (PIR).
- Automatic stand-by power off according to the absent of the elderly in the house
- Ability to detect the abnormal behavior and heart rate of the elderly in the home.

The proposed system's operational algorithm is shown in Fig. 1(a) and described as follows:

- Step 1: Initially the number of the elderly in a house is set to 0. When a sensor at the door detects an elderly people coming into the house, it transmits the sensed data to the central control board (CCB). Then, the CCB increase the current number of people in the house by one and remotely initiates a motion sensing sensor to monitor behavior of the elderly people in order to the emergency situations.
- Step 2: When a heater or air-conditioner is turned on by the elderly, the CCB checks out if any window is opened by using ultrasonic sensors equipped on the windows. If any window is opened, the CCB activates the motors installed the window to close the window. By doing this, the elderly can save energy.

In many cases of the elderly housing, the elderly turns on heaters or air-conditioners while opening window due to amnestic, so that unnecessarily energy is wasted.(http://news.khan.co.kr)

• Step 3: If a motion sensing sensor does not sense any movement for more than 10 seconds, the CCB checks out the heart rate from the information sent by a heart rate sensor that the elderly wears.

• Step 4: If the CCB decides the heart rate obtained from the heart rate sensor of the elderly is abnormal, it imitates a monitoring camera so that it makes administrator in the control room watch the situation and do appropriate action. Furthermore, even though the heart rate is normal, if an emergency button worn by the elderly is pushed, a monitoring camera is instantly operated.

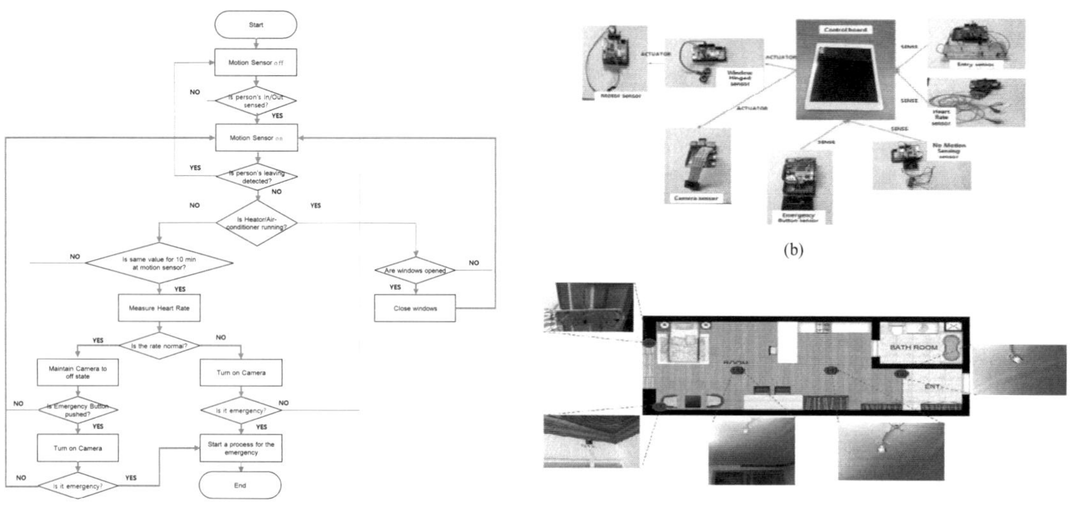

(a) (c)

Figure 1. (a) Process flow of the proposed system, (b) implemented system components, and (c) Installed test-bed

As shown in Fig. 1(b), all the sensors are equipped with Arduino board with Wi-Fi shield, so that all sensors are able to wirelessly communicate with CCB (notepad). To verify the system functionalities, the proposed system is installed in one-room as shown in Fig. 1(c) and we verified the proper operations of the system as designed.

3. CONCLUSION AND FUTURE WORKS

In this study, a home automation system for the elderly housing is proposed. Unlike conventional systems, the proposed system targets on not only reducing unnecessary energy consumption, but also monitoring emergency situation. The system is implemented and its functionalities are verified through one-room test bed. For the future works, the system needs to be fine-tuned for the more complicated scenarios for the elderly housing.

ACKNOWLEDGEMENT

This research was financially supported by the Ministry of Education (MOE) and National Research Foundation of Korea (NRF) through the Human Resource Training Project for Regional Innovation (No. 2014H1C1A1066943).

REFERENCES

http://news.khan.co.kr/kh_news/khan_art_view.h tml?artid==201508171717411&code=620106

Jeong, Y.-S., 2016. An Efficient IoT Healthcare Service Management Model of Location Tracking Sensor. *In Journal of Digital Convergence*, pp.261-267.

Ko, J.-Y. and Kim, H.-K., 2014. A Study on the Monitoring System for Emergency Recognition of Elderly People Living Alone. *In Journal of KIIT*. Vol.12, No. 3, pp. 61-68.

Korean Statistical Information Service (KOSTAT) (2013). Available at: (http://sgis.kostat.go.kr/publicsmodel/

"TUE GUTES" – UTILIZING SOCIAL NETWORK MECHANISMS, CROWDSOURCING AND GAMIFICATION TO FACILITATE SOCIAL AWARENESS AND PROMOTE SELFLESS HELP

Daniel Kadenbach, Nick Nolting and Carsten Kleiner
University of Applied Sciences and Arts, Hannover, Germany

ABSTRACT

Described is the implementation of social system named "Tue Gutes" (German for "doing something good") which is aimed to advertise good deeds to directly help other nearby located users in the real world utilizing mechanisms of social networks, crowdsourcing and gamification aiming to build intrinsic motivation and foster social cohesion among its users.

KEYWORDS

Social network, common good, crowdsourcing, gamification, trust

1. INTRODUCTION

Software applications utilizing the mechanisms of social networks and crowdsourcing have become quite popular in recent years. Several of the most frequently accessed and used websites of the world are from this category. In popular systems like Facebook, YouTube, Wikipedia, Twitter or Instagram the users themselves are generating most of the content which creates the value of these systems. The success of these systems is strongly based on their usage of social mechanisms through which users are motivated to create and provision content and are intrinsically rewarded for their efforts (e.g. with reputation, visibility, self-presentation, feedback, interest, connecting with others). Many of these underlying social mechanisms and rewarding systems of social networks have already been analyzed in recent research.

The question which drives us is: Can these obviously very powerful mechanisms not be used with the primary goal to make this world a better place (where more people directly help each other)? To connect people in the real world and let them take responsibility for each other and their environment and even – by doing this – be intrinsically rewarded for their efforts and gain more happiness?

We were not able to find an accepted system like this in our region. Therefore, a project was started in October 2016 with faculty members and students to try to answer these questions by creating a prototypical system of a social network where small, direct good deeds can be advertised, assigned and accomplished (or rather their accomplishment can be tracked and made visible). Small in this context means they can be accomplished in under a few hours (e.g. taking a walk with or read sth. to elder people), direct means in person from human to human or human to environment.

2. RELATED WORK

We greatly benefited from the work of Shneiderman on how to build trusted social media communities (Shneiderman 2015), as trust is a fundamental aspect of our system. He analyzes mechanisms to build trust, describes potential risks and a framework for credible communities, which we tried to follow. Anik et al. inspired us to build a system which is based on selfless giving (Anik et al. 2009).

3. RESEARCH QUESTIONS

With our prototypical implementation of such a system we want to analyze:

1. If users of such a system can intrinsically be rewarded for accomplishing good deeds (like helping others or caring for the environment) and if these rewards (the aforementioned plus the directly sensed gratitude of helped people) can be enough motivation for the users to engage themselves in such a system and actually apply for good deeds and carry them out,
2. if users are willing to advertise help requests. Even though we plan to work together with organizations which are in need of help and are able to offer a high number of good deeds, normal users are also be able to advertise new deeds,
3. which social mechanisms have to be implemented to generate the best user experience and motivation. We also plan to include elements of gamification to further motivate users to adhere to a high quality level for their contributions (Ziesemer 2013) and
4. how to start a social system. We want to analyze the beginning of a social system, the factors of its success or the causes for its failure.

The aims of the system itself are the promotion of selfless help, the extension of social contacts of its users (through helping each other and helping together), the promotion of social cohesion and a positive influence on the well-being of its users. The prototype of a web based system has already been implemented and we are conducting first tests, but we are highly interested in the input, opinions and experiences from other researchers not only to refine our research but also regarding the further evolution of the system.

There are also a number of big challenges for such a system: How to filter and control the advertisements of good deeds, how to rate them, how to reliably measure and establish trust in the system (since there are deeds which need less or more trustworthy applicants), how to prevent misuse and fraud, how to optimally motivate the users, and how to generate the critical user mass when the system is introduced (there is a „chicken or the egg" causality dilemma with the advertised deeds and the registered users).

4. METHODOLOGY

The project was started with a study if similar systems already exist. We found multiple social web pages and mobile apps which have similar aims. There are multiple neighborhood networks, social initiatives looking for help and favor apps where users can help other users, gain points, and exchange them for help by others. But all these systems differ in essential aspects from our endeavor. We are focused on selfless, direct, small good deeds from human to human or human to environment and on a system which can be easily used by everyone without long–term obligations. Additionally, none of these systems reached a high acceptance rate, none of them was known to any of the project participants or has a huge user base right now. So, either the idea does not have the potential to reach a huge audience or the current solutions could be improved and changed to do so. We want to find an answer to this question with our research.

Following this analysis and demarcation, we specified our first requirements on this basis and implemented a prototypical web based social system for offering and realization of good deeds, called "Tue Gutes" (which is German for "do something good"). The students soon realized that they can greatly benefit from current research on social networks. Especially, in such crucial aspects of the system as how to motivate the users to participate and create valuable content, how to foster trust in the system and other users and how to prevent misuse. Therefore, our requirements analysis and implementation were backed up by multiple phases of research into different aspects. Special attention was given to an easy to use user interface, the safety of the users' personal data and the security of the system.

After finishing the first version of the prototypical system we invited persons from the social sector and students (as target group representatives) and presented the system to gather feedback and their thoughts about the potential of the idea and its implementation. The feedback was throughout positive and we were able to gather more requirements from this discussion. On this basis we reworked our web based system and also implemented an accompanying mobile app for Android to further extend and ease the use of the system.

Before starting a two phase real rollout, we also want to gather feedback from scientists on the system and the ideas it is based on. Therefore, we are going to present it at the WBC 2017 conference. We are also currently working on releasing the project to open source.

After working in the feedback we want to start with a controlled rollout in a limited, "controllable" environment. We chose the social system of our university for this, mainly with its student members to test the system and its acceptance in a manageable environment. This also has some drawbacks, because probably students may not need that much help from others as possible other target groups would. But we nevertheless hope to gather valuable data from this step.

Finally, we want to rollout the system for a whole city. This step will be critical. Since the rollout will be accompanied by some sort of promotion of the system, there will probably only be one chance to reach a critical mass of users. Since the attractiveness of the system mainly depends on its user base and the good deeds it offers, we want to gather good deeds from social facilities before releasing the system to the public, so that it already has content. It will be most important to rapidly react to user feedback in this phase, to instantly remedy errors, implement improvements and steadily gather user input and usage data which can be used to improve the system based on its scientific evaluation.

5. OVERVIEW OF THE PROTOTYPICAL IMPLEMENTATION

"Tue Gutes" provides some common base functionality of social systems: New users can create new accounts, create a profile, select their privacy settings and view profiles of other users.

The core of the system is the management of good deeds. These deeds can be created by the users themselves. Roughly a deed is characterized by a description, a person who is responsible for it, a location where it will be carried out, the number of needed persons and their trust level.

After a good deed has been created by a user it has to be validated by a moderator of the system to prevent misuse. A moderator can be an administrator or a user who gained special reputation and trust in the community. In this validation process the moderator can contact the creator of the deed and will eventually release it, so that other users can see it.

The overview of offered good deeds has a list and a map view of deeds, so that users can see the distance to the them from their own location. Users can apply for a good deed they want to carry out by which the creator of the deed will automatically be informed. The creator can check the profiles of the candidates consult them and finally accept or reject them. After the deed is carried out by a user or a group of users, the creator can rate the participants, so they will gain reputation and trustworthiness.

6. CONCLUSION

From our point of view, the project is an ideal base to analyze many different aspects of social networks which – due to the complexity of these systems – can only be investigated in live systems. In the worst case the project will be able to research the factors leading to the failure of such a system, which is also valuable.

But we hope to gain some momentum in the rollout and have a chance to further analyze aspects like motivation, trust, cooperativeness and may also have the chance to make its users happier by enabling them to help each other. Enabling them to take over social responsibility, but just as much, as they can handle. We also really hope to start some discussion how social networks can actually be used to improve the cohesion of a society especially in big cities, where anonymity increases and where therefore there is often a lack of social cohesion.

REFERENCES

Anik, Lanin, et al., 2009, Feeling Good about Giving: The Benefits (and Costs) of Self-Interested Charitable Behavior. Working Paper. Harvard Business School.

Shneiderman, Ben, 2015, Roles, Trust, and Reputation in Social Media Knowledge Markets – Chapter 2 – Building Trusted Social Media Communities: A Research Roadmap for Promoting Credible Content. Springer International Publishing, Switzerland.

Ziesemer, Angelina, et al., 2013, Gamification Aware: Users Perception About Game Elements on Non-game Context. Proceedings of the 12th Brazilian Symposium on Human Factors in Computing Systems. Manaus, Brazil, 276-279.

AUTHOR INDEX

International Association for Development of the Information Society (IADIS)
Rua Sao Sebastiao Da Pedreira
No. 100, 30, 1050-209
Lisbon, Portugal

ISBN 978-1-5108-6531-0
9 781510 865310

CURRAN ASSOCIATES INC.
proceedings.com